IN AID OF THE UNEMPLOYED

IN AID OF THE UNEMPLOYED

Edited by

JOSEPH M. BECKER, S.J.

THE JOHNS HOPKINS PRESS, BALTIMORE, MARYLAND

Contents

TABLES

FIGURES

Acknowledgments

This symposium was made financially possible by the Institute for Social Science Research and the W. E. Upjohn Institute for Employment Research. The Institute of Social Order at Saint Louis University made its facilities available during the considerable period that the essays were in preparation. None of the sponsoring institutes is responsible for views expressed in any of the essays.

A special panel, convened in Washington early in 1964, reviewed the first thirteen chapters and discussed the possible content of the final chapter. The panel consisted of Wilbur J. Cohen (U.S. Department of Health, Education, and Welfare), Ernest J. Eberling (Vanderbilt University), Eli Ginzberg (Columbia University), Clarence D. Long (United States Congress), and Arnold R. Weber (The University of Chicago). Although the panel members are not to be held responsible for the positions adopted in any of the chapters, the entire symposium, and the final chapter particularly, profited from the work of the panel.

The editor gratefully acknowledges the valuable assistance rendered by the numerous readers of the essays in the various stages of composition. Thanks are due to the officials in the Department of Labor, especially in the Bureau of Labor Statistics and the Bureau of Employment Security, who supplied materials and reviewed parts of the symposium.

Thanks are due also to Frances Bittner and Elizabeth Rogers, who contributed substantially to the readability of the volume by their unusually thorough and constructive editing, and to Elizabeth Sposato, who maintained impeccable order within and among what seemed at times a blizzard of successive drafts of text, tables, and figures.

PART I

Preliminary Overview

Introduction
by the Editor

IN HIS LAST major public address the late President Kennedy spoke of unemployment as the number one domestic problem in the United States. It is with this problem, or more exactly with an essential aspect of it, that this symposium is concerned.

The essays that make up this symposium are concerned with programs of aid for the unemployed. The scope of the symposium, therefore, does not extend to the more complex and intractable problem of the prevention of unemployment—for example, through the use of fiscal and monetary measures or through the improvement of the nation's educational system. Proceeding on the assumption that some unemployment is inevitable in modern industrial society, the essays discuss a limited problem: the alleviation and cure of unemployment after it has occurred. Programs of alleviation seek to provide the unemployed person with the means of subsistence until he can find a job. Programs of cure seek to improve the employment prospects of the unemployed person by changing him or his environment in order to restore him to employment.

The assumption of some inevitable unemployment is realistic because American industrial society is complex, continuously changing, and free. The forces which determine the level of employment involve not only the entire economy but also the educational and political structures of society. The difficulty of controlling these enormously complex forces is heightened by the rate of change which marks most features of our society, especially its productive techniques. Because our understanding of these complex and changing forces is far from perfect and because our control over the forces we do understand is far from complete, we shall always have some unemployment.

Some of this inevitable unemployment is the direct result of the degree of freedom that marks both the demand for and the supply of labor. The demand for labor is continually changing, not only because of a changing technology, but even more because of the freedom exercised by consumers to vary the pattern of their purchases. On the side of supply, workers are free to leave their jobs and to refuse alternative jobs that they consider unsuitable. The result of freedom in both cases is likely to be more unemployment, at least in the short run, than if there had been less freedom.

In recent years our society has experienced an unsatisfactorily high level of unemployment, and more than a decade has passed since full employment was last achieved in the American economy. Whether unemployment is higher now than it has been during previous periods of our history is debated among economists but is not particularly relevant here. Today more abundant and refined statistics enable us to measure unemployment more exactly than could be done previously, and greater wealth enables us to move more effectively to aid the unemployed. These are the relevant factors in the current situation. Whatever the outcome of the debate on previous unemployment experience, these two factors make the present situation different from the past.

A confluence of forces have contributed to

3

the uncomfortably high level of unemployment in recent years. Changes in defense technology have caused economic dislocations in many communities. For example, Michigan's share of defense procurement, almost a tenth of the total during the Korean war, dropped to less than 3 per cent in recent years, while California's share increased from 14 per cent to 24 per cent. In private industry new techniques of production and new applications of computer technology have effected a rapid increase in the rate of product obsolescence and generated a demand for new occupational skills. As skills become obsolete, the owners of the skills become unemployed. It has been estimated that changes in technology displace about half a million workers per year.

The changing demand for skills has accentuated older problems within the labor force. There is considerable evidence that the number of job opportunities for the unskilled and the poorly educated is declining. One result of this decline is that unemployment among Negroes, who are represented disproportionately in these groups, has remained consistently more than double the rate of white workers.

Changes that have been taking place in the labor force will continue to make the attainment of full employment a difficult task. Improved technology in the home has made it possible for an increasing number of married women to enter the labor force and to seek employment. Between 1940 and 1962 the proportion of married women in the labor force increased from 7.7 per cent to 18.9 per cent. We can expect, also, in the immediate years ahead an increased influx of young workers, among whom unemployment rates are always double or triple the average rate. The sharp rise in the birth rate following World War II is just beginning to affect the labor market. The number of sixteen-year-olds in the labor market increased by one million in 1963. Since compulsory education stops at age sixteen in most states, an increase of teen-agers in the labor force will continue for several years. Youth unemployment has become and will remain a pressing problem.

The problem of caring for the unemployed is not a new one in our society, but we have developed new attitudes toward the problem and new techniques for solving it. In earlier years, especially before the great depression of the nineteen-thirties, society tended to regard the unemployed with suspicion and to blame unemployment on the unemployed themselves. Gradually we came to understand that, of its very nature, an industrial system produces unemployment—without any necessary fault on the part of the unemployed—and that most of the cost of caring for the unemployed can properly be assessed against the system as an integral part of the cost of doing business.

In the past, income maintenance programs have played the major role in caring for the unemployed and are likely to do so in the future. But in recent years increased attention has been devoted to the curative programs. The late President Kennedy's slogan, "Rehabilitation, not relief," exemplifies the new approach. Emphasis on curative programs is understandable in the light of modern economic conditions, especially the growing need for higher skills. Currently, along with high unemployment there exist many occupational shortages in the newly expanding industries because there do not exist enough workers with the required skills.

The programs of aid for the unemployed serve the interests of both the individual and society. For the individual they provide sorely needed help in a situation that always poses a serious threat to security in industrial society, the lack of a job. Without programs of aid, the cost of economic progress would weigh disproportionately on a few individuals.

In the current war against poverty, the role of programs of aid for the unemployed is twofold. To an extent, these programs attack poverty directly, for some of the poor are technically unemployed (they are not working but are able and willing to work) and some of the unemployed are technically poor (they are individuals with an income of less than $1,000 per year or are in families with an income of less than $3,000 per year). But the great majority of the poor are not technically unemployed (they are employed at low wages, or are underemployed, or are out of the labor force entirely). By definition these are outside the scope of programs in aid of the unemployed. An even larger majority of the unemployed are not technically among the poor. For these, the programs of aid function chiefly to prevent poverty. The programs bring aid during that perilous period between jobs when, if no special assistance were available, the unemployed might easily sink into the mass of the poor.

Quite apart from the satisfaction it may find in doing its duty, society can expect to gain substantial economic and political advantages from aiding the unemployed. The programs of aid promote social peace by decreasing the tensions that otherwise exist between the more fortunate and the less fortunate members of society. The programs also facilitate economic progress. Because there are programs of aid available, it becomes easier to introduce the technological innovations that our society needs if it is to continue to raise its standard of living. Without the availability of such programs of aid, the resistance of labor to technological change understandably would be much greater.

Insofar as the programs of aid are themselves economic forces, a relationship exists between them and the level of employment, and the relationship is relevant to decisions concerning these programs: the extent to which the programs increase employment is an additional reason for their expansion, and the extent to which they decrease employment is a reason for limiting them. But the net long-run effect (sometimes even the gross short-run effect) of the programs of aid on the level of employment is subject to endless debate. Hence this effect is rarely the determining factor in the decisions made about the programs. What is clear and supported by a broad consensus—and therefore usually decisive—is that unemployed persons need help and that programs can be devised to supply the help. The symposium focuses chiefly on this fairly definite, manageable, and urgent problem of how to help persons who become unemployed.

The symposium begins with three preparatory essays: a historical survey of our society's past efforts at aiding the unemployed (Chapter 1) is followed by two statistical surveys of the characteristics of the unemployed persons to be aided (Chapters 2 and 3). These two chapters —and the symposium generally—adopt the definitions of "unemployed" that are used in the official government statistics. The unemployed, thus defined, do not include two shadowy groups on the periphery of the unemployed: the "underemployed" and the "potential" members of the labor force. However, to the extent that society wishes to concern itself with these two groups, it will find useful the same curative programs that are available to aid the unemployed.

The programs of aid are described and analyzed in nine chapters (4 through 12). Some of the programs are primarily alleviative in nature, others primarily curative. Programs which are primarily alleviative include unemployment insurance, supplementary unemployment benefits, severance pay, early pensions, and certain welfare operations. Programs which are primarily curative include the United States Employment Service, various training and area redevelopment programs, public works, and some welfare operations.

A final section of two chapters discusses the major lines of action open to our society. Chapter 13 sets out the principal alternative choices that face us and the logical determinants of each choice. Chapter 14 ventures to evaluate our past choices and to make some concrete recommendations which represent not so much final ideals as realistic goals for the near future.

CHAPTER 1

Early History of Aid to the Unemployed in the United States

*Frank R. Breul**

I. INTRODUCTION

IN THE HISTORY of the United States, all levels of government and many private associations have contributed at some time to the development of programs to aid the unemployed. In the early days of our nation, separate provisions were not available for those considered able to work and those deemed unemployable. All were cared for under the locally financed and administered poor law, which changed little after it was brought to this continent from England during the seventeenth century. As a result of increasing industrialization and the economic and social theories that supported it, this situation was altered during the nineteenth century in that specialized treatment was attempted for specific groups of the poor and greater reliance was placed upon private charity to deal with poverty that was presumably due to unemployment. Apparently, there was agreement among those in a position to influence public policy that not all who were in economic need were worthy of public support but that some differentiation must be made between those unable to work because of age or physical disability and those who were merely unable to find a job.

From about 1870 to well into the present century, most social welfare authorities thought that only private charity could administer relief in a way that would both preserve the

* Professor, The School of Social Service Administration, The University of Chicago.

motivation and self-respect of those seeking work and separate the deserving from the undeserving among those applying for aid. It was not until the great depression of the nineteen-thirties that the private agencies were forced to admit that they were unable to cope adequately with the demands of widespread unemployment. During that same period, it became apparent that the local level of government was not the most appropriate level to administer and finance aid to the unemployed; so first the states and then the federal government assumed some responsibility.

The problem of what to do about the unemployed has always been troublesome. Whenever proposals have been made for providing them with adequate financial assistance, two insistent questions have been raised: does not the very availability of relief encourage indolence? And does not the provision of adequate maintenance to those out of work tend to distort the level of wages in the community? For many nineteenth-century Americans, the answers to these questions were obviously in the affirmative. Even without the support of laissez faire economic theories and Social Darwinism, the experience of England under the Speenhamland plan,[1] during the

---

[1] The plan provided that wages, where inadequate, were to be supplemented by relief based on the size of family and the cost of bread. In time, relief came to be relied upon by employers as a wage supplement and wages fell; then more and more of those who had first received partial relief went on total relief.

forty years prior to the reforms of 1834, was sufficient warning for many that unwise relief results in a less productive and generally demoralized labor force. The unemployed, therefore, were early considered a special group among the poor, but not in the same sense as were the very young, the aged, and the physically disabled; and it was felt that relief to those able to work should be provided with care and in small amounts to avoid affecting adversely the economy of the nation.

By the nineteen-sixties tremendous steps had been taken in making social services and financial aid available to the unemployed on the assumption that their plight was due to general economic and social conditions rather than to any inclination on their part to avoid working for a living. The systems of unemployment insurance set up in all the states after the passage of the Social Security Act of 1935 are perhaps the most convincing evidence of this change in attitude. In 1961 the program of Aid to Dependent Children, a part of the Social Security Act, was amended on a temporary basis to include the children of parents who are unemployed.[2] Other indications of sympathetic concern for the problems of the unemployed have been the Employment Act of 1946, the Area Redevelopment Act of 1961, the Manpower Development and Training Act of 1962, the Public Works Acceleration Act of 1962, the increased appropriations made available by the federal government to expand the state employment services, and the numerous private provisions for protection against unemployment that are becoming a notable part of collectively bargained contracts.

We would be better able to account for the strengths and weaknesses of our present-day programs for aid to the unemployed if we could neatly trace from the first days of this nation's industrial revolution the development of the ideas and the succession of events from which these programs evolved. However, it is not possible to accomplish this with any clarity and consistency for the early years of our history; it

is only after 1930, when the federal government began to assume responsibility, that we can begin to follow the line of development. Before 1930 each state and in many instances single localities developed their own programs at their own pace. Even if there were space to describe the separate experience of each jurisdiction, it would not be possible because, for the most part, the necessary data are lacking, especially for the pre-Civil War period.

For this period, it seemed best to select one leading state and describe its experience as thoroughly as possible. The discussion of the period prior to the Civil War is limited, therefore, to events which occurred in New York State. New York was chosen because its early development of social welfare services is well documented and because, as a leading state, its influence was probably widespread. For the period following the Civil War up to the nineteen-thirties, material is drawn from a wider variety of sources. For both periods information is available chiefly for times of economic stress, so that the chronology of the narrative is dictated largely by the occurrence of depressions. For the period beginning with the nineteen-thirties, the course of events can be traced more fully, since unemployment was attacked on a national basis and detailed information concerning the activities undertaken is available.

II. THE EXPERIENCE IN NEW YORK PRIOR TO THE CIVIL WAR

The first recorded investigation of the unemployment relief situation in New York was conducted by the Humane Society, in 1809. In spite of a severe economic depression existing at the time, its report makes no reference to economic factors as a possible cause of pauperism but concludes that "by a just and inflexible law of Providence misery is ordained to be the companion and punishment of vice."[3] Nine years later, the Society for the Prevention

---

[2] This provision, enacted by Public Law 87-31, was due to expire on June 30, 1962, but was extended by Public Law 87-543.

[3] David M. Schneider, *The History of Public Welfare in New York State, 1609–1866* (Chicago: The University of Chicago Press, 1938), p. 212.

of Pauperism also attempted to determine the causes of poverty. Again, no mention was made of the lack of employment opportunities. Instead, the principal causes were listed as ignorance, idleness, intemperance, want of economy, imprudent and hasty marriages, lotteries, pawnbrokers, houses of ill fame, the numerous charitable institutions in the city, and war.[4] In that same year, Governor De Witt Clinton, in his message to the legislature, declared that "our statutes relating to the poor are borrowed from the English system, and the experience of that country, as well as our own, shows that pauperism increases with the augmentation of funds applied to its relief."[5] A year later, a joint committee of the legislature concluded that the whole problem of poor relief could be solved by discriminating between the "deserving" and "undeserving," that relief should be available only to the "virtuous" poor whose dependent condition could be traced to infirmity, disease, or other disabling causes, and that there was no room in poor law administration for those we would today call the employables.[6]

The first really comprehensive survey of poor relief in the United States was undertaken by New York's Secretary of State, J. V. N. Yates, in 1823.[7] His report not only caused a profound modification of the poor relief system in New York but influenced legislation and administration throughout the country; but the results of his investigation were not of much help to the "unemployed," as he recommended specifically that "no male person in health, with the use of all his faculties, and being between the ages of eighteen and fifty years shall be placed upon the pauper list, or be maintained at public expense." Nevertheless, the report was important in the history of aid to the unemployed, since it formally introduced three controversies which have continuously

plagued the development of suitable aid programs. The first concerned whether poor relief should be provided under public or private auspices. The second concerned the proper form of relief. The third concerned the level of government most appropriate for the administration of assistance.

Yates approached the first problem directly by asking whether the whole system of poor relief should be abolished and the support of the poor left to voluntary contributions, or whether the system was susceptible to improvement. He recognized that there were "many powerful advocates" for the proposition that public relief should be abolished. He wrote: "Men of great literary acquirements and profound political research have insisted that distress and poverty multiply in proportion to the funds created to relieve them, and that the establishment of any poor rates is not only unnecessary but hurtful."[8] Yates, unlike investigators during the latter half of the nineteenth century, concluded that poor relief was a necessary and proper function of government. He insisted that abandonment of public responsibility would not be consistent with a humane, liberal, and enlightened policy. He felt that the individual cases of abuse should not place the total system in disrepute.

In his examination of the way in which the poor law was being administered, Yates found much suffering by those forced to accept aid outside publicly supported almshouses. He found that "outdoor relief" did not mean provision of subsistence to the destitute in their own homes; it meant, rather, that most paupers were either "farmed out" to contractors for stipulated prices or auctioned to those who would support them at the lowest cost to the community. He found this system to be not only cruel to the recipients but also wasteful of tax revenues. He proposed, therefore, that an almshouse be established in each county of the state and that all outdoor relief be discontinued. Although this recommendation was similar to that of the English Poor Law Commission of 1834, the motives behind it were not those of

---

[4] *Ibid.*, p. 213.

[5] *Ibid.*, p. 216.

[6] *Ibid.*, p. 217.

[7] The text of the Yates report, entitled "Report and Other Papers on the Subject of Laws for the Relief and Settlement of the Poor," will be found in Sophinisba P. Breckinridge, *Public Welfare Administration in the United States* (Chicago: The University of Chicago Press, 1927), pp. 39ff.

[8] *Ibid.*, p. 44.

the English commission, which believed that the poor should be punished for their inadequacies. Yates believed that in an almshouse the poor would be better cared for, the children would receive some education, and the adults would be set to useful work. But the manner in which his recommendation was carried out in New York and in other parts of the nation made almshouses places which the poor wished to avoid at all costs.

Yates recognized the evils of local responsibility for the poor and explained how high costs of administration, stringent laws on settlement, residence, and removal, and inhuman treatment of paupers resulted from reliance upon local property-tax revenues. In 1823 federal aid—or even state aid—was, of course, unimaginable. Realizing, however, that some unit of government larger than the township must assume responsibility, he recommended that it be the county and that only one year's residence be necessary to achieve eligibility for relief.

Between the Yates Report and the Civil War, the nation experienced three economic depressions. During the depression period which began in 1837, the nation, in general, was unprepared to meet the emergency. This was particularly true of New York City, where, according to the estimate of Horace Greeley, at least one-third of all workers were unemployed during the first winter.[9] As a result, those in need were maintained by *ad hoc* relief committees (organized on a ward basis), which attempted to furnish subsistence through the collection and disbursement of public and private funds. In addition, there were over thirty relief-giving societies organized on a city-wide basis that provided for specific groups of indigents.

Toward the end of the depression, a group of influential citizens under the leadership of Robert M. Hartley, formerly secretary of the Temperance Society, established the New York Association for Improving the Conditions of the Poor. Disturbed by what they considered indiscriminate relief giving, this society supported the theory that the provision of poor

relief merely intensified the total problem faced by the community, since it encouraged idleness and destroyed character. The society insisted that moral regeneration rather than material aid should be emphasized. As this doctrine was preached by the Charity Organization Societies forty years later, the poor required "not alms but a friend." The cause of poverty must be eliminated and only private charity could accomplish this. Although the association recognized the need for better housing and improvement in other social conditions, its primary emphasis was upon the reformation of the individual. As stated in an early publication, its aim was to end indiscriminate almsgiving and "to visit the poor at their habitations; to aid them, when practicable, in obtaining employment; to inspire them with self-reliance and self-respect; to inculcate habits of economy, industry and temperance; and whenever it shall be absolutely necessary, to provide such relief as shall be suited to their wants."[10] A private agency must take responsibility for the unemployed, since it alone can discriminate between "deserving" and "undeserving" applicants and provide the restorative services necessary to return worthy individuals to self-support. Aid to the "undeserving" could only further their degeneration. The association saw the role of tax-supported relief as being limited to the aged or disabled.

During the depression of 1854–55, citizen relief committees were again organized on a ward basis. This time, however, they came in conflict with the Association for Improving the Conditions of the Poor (AICP), which once again complained that they were entirely too generous in granting relief and were teaching the unemployed that relief was due to them "as a right and not as a favor." The city made grants-in-aid both to ward committees and to the AICP, as well as to other private agencies.

---

[9] Schneider, *Public Welfare in New York State* (*n.* 3), p. 212.

[10] *Ibid.*, p. 267. Discussions of the various associations for improving the condition of the poor will be found in Robert H. Bremner, *From the Depths: The Discovery of Poverty in America* (New York: New York University Press, 1956), pp. 35–38; and in Edward T. Devine, *The Principles of Relief* (New York: The Macmillan Co., 1920), pp. 314–23. (Edward Devine was secretary of the New York Charity Organization Society from 1896 to 1917.)

Despite the activities of these private groups, however, the city government was forced to continue both almshouse care and outdoor relief to the unemployed.[11]

During the severe economic crisis of 1857–58, no citizen emergency relief committees were organized and soup kitchens were very scarce. As a result, the relief load of the AICP increased about 60 per cent and the cost of public outdoor relief rose by about 25 per cent. One aspect of this depression in New York is a signal landmark in the history of unemployment: the unemployed themselves organized in protest against their predicament. There were mass meetings and marches on city hall. Demands for work relief were heard for the first time, the slogan "work or bread" was a popular cry, and petitions to the Common Council insisting on the "right to work" were frequent. For the first time, the unemployed had an important political impact as the council appropriated money for public works projects and passed numerous resolutions expressing concern over the plight of the unemployed. Because of legal technicalities, only a project for the hiring of 1,000 men to make improvements in Central Park could be undertaken, and it did not get under way until the depression was almost over. It was, perhaps, the first public works project in the United States undertaken for the specific purpose of hiring the unemployed.[12]

III. FROM THE CIVIL WAR TO THE NINETEEN-THIRTIES

The Civil War diverted attention from the poor. But even at the end of the war, when the nation again turned its attention to the needs of the poor, there was still no particular concern for the unemployed. Such concern had to wait for the prolonged depression which began in 1873, when the needs of the unemployed could

no longer be ignored. The recurring crises, from the depression of the seventies until the first World War, were to be crucial in shaping the history of aid to the unemployed and also the history of many other social welfare programs.

It must be remembered, as these developments are described, that the ideas expressed and the policies followed reflect their social, economic, and political setting. During the depression of the eighteen-seventies, the public response to unemployment reflected the "gilded age" or, as Parrington called it, "the great barbecue."[13] During the next economic recession, which lasted from 1893 to 1897, the tenets of classical economics and Social Darwinism were being challenged by the Populists, by organized labor, and finally by the Bryan Democrats. By the time of the 1907–8 depression, the reform movement was well under way. The muckrakers had had their effect, the social gospel movement had diluted the severity of Protestantism, and there was general public reaction against the political and commercial excesses of the years immediately following the Civil War. More and more, those believing that free enterprise must be bridled became convinced that only governmental power could accomplish this purpose. Labor legislation, antimonopoly laws, and civil service reform were evidence of this conviction. By the depression of 1914–15, the reform movement led by the Progressives was at its zenith. Among other accomplishments after 1910 were the establishment of a precedent in social insurance through the enactment of workmen's compensation laws by most of the industrial states and the first breakup of the poor laws in the provision of mothers' pensions and aid to the blind by many jurisdictions. But the pace of this program was slow, a laborious push against entrenched opposition; and the approach to something resembling adequate, efficiently administered relief, particularly for the unemployed, was not to be made until well into the twentieth century.

---

[11] Devine, *The Principles of Relief*, (n. 10), p. 271.

[12] Leah H. Feder, *Unemployment Relief in Periods of Depression: A Study of Measures Adopted in Certain American Cities, 1857 through 1922* (New York: Russell Sage Foundation, 1936), p. 32.

[13] Vernon L. Parrington, *Main Currents in American Thought* (New York: Harcourt, Brace & Co., 1927), III, 23.

The first test of social welfare provisions in the United States following the Civil War occurred during the depression of the eighteen-seventies. Although the usual form of public relief prior to that time was almshouse care, as had been recommended in the Yates Report, many urban centers found it necessary, when faced with large numbers of unemployed, to provide relief to families remaining in their own homes. Since this was a new responsibility for these municipalities, it is probably true that the charges against the system—that the responsibility was frequently carried out inefficiently and with political overtones—were not without foundation. Dissatisfied with this system and sharing a suspicion of all governmental activity characteristic of the time, influential citizens in many communities were convinced that public relief was inherently evil and that its very existence was an invitation to idleness. As the decade of the eighteen-seventies progressed, therefore, the principles which had been set forth thirty years before by the New York Association for Improving the Condition of the Poor gained wider and wider acceptance.

The classic example of the movement against public assistance to the unemployed during this period occurred in Brooklyn, New York. As reported by Edward Devine, the cost of public outdoor relief had increased more than 100 per cent between 1872 and 1877, and the cost of administration amounted to 40 per cent of the total expenditure.[14] Seth Low, who was later reform mayor of Brooklyn, recalled the situation as follows:

> The friends of politicians received help whether needy or not, and so the situation was perpetuated. Families with voters were served first. The "outdoor relief" appropriations became a vast political corruption fund. Large numbers of the population were taught to rely on the county help, and sought it for no other reason than that the county gave it. One woman received help under nine different names. Many sold what they received. . . . The poor did not get the chief benefit of increased appropriations. Most of it went to underlings connected with the

work of distribution. In every way, and in every direction, the effect was hopelessly bad.[15]

During 1876 the situation became a matter of general concern. With the consent of the poor law authorities, the State Charities Aid Association recruited a group of volunteers to investigate all recipients during the winter of 1876-77. These investigators reported that many who applied for aid were not in actual need and recommended to the supervisors that all public relief be stopped during the next year. In the meantime, the supervisors consulted their attorneys, who advised that the system of relief to the able-bodied was without statutory sanction. In the middle of the winter of 1878, therefore, outdoor relief was stopped forthwith. According to Devine, this action caused no increased demand upon the private agencies, no overcrowding of the almshouses, and no exceptional suffering. Although he admitted that the improvement in business conditions had something to do with the results, he expressed the opinion of those interested in the private agencies and influential in social welfare policy when he wrote that "the abolition of outdoor relief resulted in a real improvement in the status of the poor."[16] That this opinion persisted and was supported for a long time is evidenced by the fact that almost twenty years later, in 1897, the charter that created Greater New York carried a provision outlawing public outdoor relief.[17]

Throughout the remainder of the nineteenth century, other cities followed the lead of New York by abolishing public relief to the unemployed outside the almshouses. In 1878 the private agencies of Philadelphia charged the public authorities with inefficiency and corruption and proposed a central private organization which would co-ordinate all relief-giving. In response to this suggestion, the city stopped all relief expenditures. Here, as in New York,

[14] Devine, *The Principles of Relief* (n. 10), p. 294.

[15] Amos G. Warner, *American Charities* (Rev. ed.; New York: Thomas Y. Crowell Co., 1922), p. 211.

[16] Devine, *The Principles of Relief* (n. 10), p. 297.

[17] David M. Schneider and Albert Deutsch, *The History of Public Welfare in New York State, 1867–1940* (Chicago: The University of Chicago Press, 1941), p. 47.

exponents of private charity claimed that there was no increased demand upon the voluntary agencies and that no additional burden was placed upon the almshouses. In 1898 the commissioners of the District of Columbia ordered that all allotments for the relief of the poor be distributed through a central private agency. In the same year, the new city charter of Baltimore expressly prohibited all public relief to adults except in the almshouse.[18]

Boston was apparently the only major eastern city which refused to go along with the trend. After investigating the systems in the cities mentioned above, Boston's Board of Overseers concluded that public funds were, in fact, still being used, but in the form of subsidies to private agencies, and that the amount provided families was not sufficient to prevent suffering. In 1888 the secretary of the board stated Boston's arguments in favor of public assistance: (1) it avoids the necessity for breaking up families and substituting institutional care of children; (2) it is more adequate and uniform; and (3) its burdens are fairly distributed, while private relief is spasmodic, rests entirely upon charitably disposed persons, and may fail entirely because of shrinking income at the very time when destitution is greatest and the need for relief most pressing.[19]

Josephine Shaw Lowell, the well-known social work leader of the period, summed up the position of the private agencies in her influential book *Public Relief and Private Charity*, which was published in 1884. First, she said, public relief "fails to provide that no one will starve or suffer, for unless self-restraint and providence be conferred upon those who receive it, all that is bestowed will often be wasted in riotous living, and the innocent and helpless beings dependent upon them will be left to suffer far more than had relief been denied." Second, she claimed, it does the individual and the community moral damage "because human nature is so constituted that no man can receive as a gift what he should earn by his own labor without moral deterioration." Third, public relief

tends to become regular and permanent. Fourth, "the taxpayers are the losers by outdoor relief, because, although the amount given to each individual is, undoubtedly, smaller than would be required for that individual in an institution, yet outdoor relief is so infectious, and once obtained is so easy a way of getting a living, that far larger numbers demand and receive it than could be induced to enter an institution."[20]

These arguments reflect Mrs. Lowell's association with the charity organization movement, which originated in England in 1869 and was initiated in the United States in 1877 as a protest against the unsatisfactory operation of both public and private relief agencies. The aim of this movement was to organize voluntary giving so that only the worthy would receive aid. In this respect, the policy of the Charity Organization Societies was similar to that of the New York Association for Improving the Condition of the Poor and to those of similar agencies throughout the nation. It differed from these other agencies, however, in that it did not itself intend to give any relief but rather set out to organize and integrate all existing relief-giving agencies so that efficiency and selectivity might be achieved. Although the Charity Organization Societies later became a considerable force in the new movement of preventive social work during the Progressive era, it remained opposed to governmental responsibility for financial relief to the unemployed until the nineteen-thirties.[21]

During the depression of 1893–97, emergency conditions provided the impetus for some private agencies to collaborate according to

---

[18] Devine, *The Principles of Relief* (n. 10), pp. 298–303.

[19] *Ibid.*, p. 305.

[20] The book was published in New York by G. P. Putnam's Sons. The extract containing these quotations is reprinted in *Social Service Review*, III, No. 2 (June, 1929), 271–80. Mrs. Lowell was the first woman to be a member of the New York State Board of Charities.

[21] For a brief description of the Charity Organization Societies (COS) in London see C. L. Mowat, "Charity and Casework in Late Victorian London: The Work of the Charity Organization Society," *Social Service Review*, XXXI, No. 3 (September, 1957), 258. The standard work on the COS in the United States is Frank D. Watson, *The Charity Organization Movement in the United States* (New York: The Macmillan Co., 1922).

charity organization principles. In most communities, however, the Charity Organization Societies were not sufficiently influential, and temporary private relief groups were relied upon.[22]

By the time of the economic recession of 1907–8, the established private agencies were clearly in control. During this period, there were no emergency committees or highly publicized fund-raising campaigns. The existing agencies, public and private, took the emergency in their stride, each knowing what its function should be. Private charity, by virtue of wise and energetic leadership, dominated the field of unemployment relief, at least in the thickly populated areas. In those communities where public relief to the able-bodied was still available, the government agency usually assumed a specific and limited area of responsibility—for example, the care of the homeless.[23]

By the beginning of the depression of 1914–15, the reform movement of the previous decade with its reliance upon strong but virtuous government had caused many social workers and community leaders to reconsider their earlier conviction that public aid to the unemployed is inherently evil. This did not mean, however, that they were deserting the principles of the Charity Organization Societies. They now believed rather that those very principles could be applied to the administration of public relief if only there were enlightened leadership and civil servants trained in charity organization methods.

Moreover there was some evidence that such a reformation of public welfare was possible. In 1899 Indiana regulated the administration of relief and required that the township supervisors investigate each case carefully and cooperate with existing agencies.[24] In Denver in 1912, Gertrude Vaile, executive of the Board of Charity and Corrections, was able to demonstrate that the methods found successful by the Charity Organization Societies could be applied

to a municipal public welfare agency.[25] Further evidence that hope for the public agencies had been restored is that in 1915 the National Conference on Charities and Corrections devoted a full session to the potentialities of public relief. The chairman of the section introduced the topic as follows:

We make no apology for presenting this timeworn subject. In the opinion of your committee this matter of public relief has not received the consideration its importance merits. We have been too prone to look upon the evils of outdoor relief, have condemned it as wholly bad, cast it aside with the conviction that it was past redemption and ought to be abolished. We do not seek to minimize the evils in administration, but we think our effort should be directed rather to the improvement of administration than to an abolition of the system.[26]

The rethinking and reassessment of the whole matter of relief and the influence of private agency leadership on municipal action gradually effected the turn to government responsibility. This development was illustrated during the depression of 1914–15 by the many mayor's committees, which replaced the private coordinating groups of earlier emergencies. The trend continued during the postwar depression of 1920–22. During the remaining years of the twenties, as unemployment grew despite the evidences of prosperity, the public agencies assumed increasingly greater responsibility for the unemployed either through the direct administration of relief or the subsidization of private agencies. By 1930, according to a report of the United States Children's Bureau, 70 per cent of all relief in seventy-five cities studied was paid out of public funds.[27] Within the next two years, public expenditures had

---

[22] Feder, *Unemployment Relief in Periods of Depression*, (n. 12), p. 193.

[23] *Ibid.*

[24] Warner, *American Charities* (n. 15), pp. 212–14.

[25] Frank J. Bruno, *Trends in Social Work as Reflected in the Proceedings of the National Conference of Social Work, 1874–1946* (New York: Columbia University Press, 1948), pp. 211–13.

[26] G. S. Wilson, "Introductory Statement," *Proceedings*, National Conference of Charities and Corrections, 1915, p. 436.

[27] Ann E. Geddes, *Trends in Relief Expenditures 1910–1935*, Research Monograph X (Works Progress Administration, Washington, D.C., Government Printing Office, 1937), p. xiv.

increased so much that the amounts provided by private agencies were negligible in comparison.

Controversy during this period between the Civil War and 1930 centered not only on the public-private issue but also on the second of the three issues raised by Yates—the form aid should take. What little information we have on this issue during this period is found in the reports of the large private agencies, in the published proceedings of the National Conference of Charities and Corrections, and in the histories of poor law administration, which have been completed for a relatively few states.

As far as public agencies were concerned, the only relief generally available in most localities was in the almshouse. Those unwilling to enter such an institution could either try their luck with the private agencies or do without. Although as the twentieth century progressed an increasing number of communities provided relief to the unemployed in their own homes, when the depression of the nineteen-thirties arrived, most local jurisdictions were woefully unprepared. Apparently not learning from their experience in previous depressions, the municipalities continued to rely upon bread lines, soup kitchens, and sometimes groceries provided through their police departments.[28] Prior to the Civil War some jurisdictions had attempted to provide work relief, but there was little such activity in the period between the Civil War and the nineteen-thirties.[29]

Throughout their history, the private agencies experimented with all forms of relief. Beginning with commissaries from which food and clothing were issued directly, they moved to providing orders on grocery and other provisions. As the treatment of each family became more individualized, a form of relief was required which would help maintain the self-respect of the family and could be adjusted easily to meet specific needs. By the nineteen-twenties many private agencies were convinced that families in need should receive aid in the form of cash, the amount to be determined in accordance with a carefully formulated budget. The idea of cash relief was not, however, new. As early as 1873, the Chicago Relief and Aid Society reported an experiment with cash relief following the great fire. The society's conclusion was that "the mass of worthy, honest, and economical poor should not be treated as thieves and paupers because a large number of these last classes attempt to defraud us, or because a few of them may possibly succeed in doing so."[30]

Work relief had always played a part in the plans of the large private agencies, although enthusiasm for this form of aid had waned well before the onset of the depression of the nineteen-thirties. During the seventies, the emphasis was upon the use of work relief as a test of the worthiness of the applicant. Most agencies had wood yards and sewing rooms for this purpose. The emergency of the eighteen-nineties was the heyday of large-scale work relief projects. In New York, for example, as many as 887 men were employed at one time cleaning streets under the auspices of the private East Side Relief Committee, work then being considered as a means of giving the "deserving" unemployed a sense of independence and self-respect. Even at that time, however, certain weaknesses of work relief were noted. Among them were the exposure of those out of work to public view, the small amounts of money earned in relation to existing wage rates, and the general availability of only heavy outdoor work, which was unsuitable for many men and of little help in preparing them for future employment. Work relief was again available during the depressions of 1907–8 and 1914–15, but the emphasis was upon small projects rather than on large ones. During 1914–15, the greatest limitation was recognized by many: that it is difficult if not impossible to find work relief undertakings which will not compete in one way or another with private business or which will not displace workers from regular full-time jobs.[31]

[28] Feder, *Unemployment Relief in Periods of Depression* (*n.* 12), p. 347.

[29] Joanna C. Colcord, *Emergency Work Relief* (New York: Russell Sage Foundation, 1932), p. 13.

[30] Joanna C. Colcord, *Cash Relief* (New York: Russell Sage Foundation, 1936), p. 10.

[31] Feder, *Unemployment Relief in Periods of Depression* (*n.* 12), p. 279.

By 1915 there were many who believed that searching for new or improved methods of relieving the unemployed was a waste of time and that more positive actions must be undertaken. Speaking before the 1915 National Conference of Charities and Corrections, John B. Andrews, representing the American Association for Labor Legislation, remarked:

> The time is past when the problem of unemployment could be disposed of either by ignoring it, as was the practice until recent years in America, or by attributing it to mere laziness and inefficiency. We are beginning to recognize that unemployment is not so much due to individual causes and to the shiftlessness of the "won't works," as it is social and inherent in our present method of industrial organization.[32]

He suggested that unemployment insurance, public employment exchanges, public works, and regularization of industry replace unemployment relief. Most of these suggestions had, of course, been tried in the past, but not until the nineteen-thirties were sustained plans for carrying them out developed.

Some insurance benefits for the unemployed had been paid by a few of the better-organized labor unions during the latter part of the nineteenth and the early twentieth centuries, but this was by no means a usual practice. The American Association for Labor Legislation and other organizations agitated for the establishment of government-sponsored unemployment insurance for twenty years or more before it was finally accepted.[33] It was not until the passage of the Social Security Act of 1935 that a nation-wide program of compulsory unemployment insurance was put into effect.

Public employment exchanges, on the other hand, have had a long and checkered career. The first permanent public employment offices in the United States were established in Ohio by state law in 1890. Four years later, Seattle opened the first municipally initiated and managed office. New York State started 2 offices in 1897, and Illinois set up 3 offices in Chicago in 1899. By 1900, there were 15 public offices in operation and by 1912 there were 64. The depression of 1914–15 stimulated the movement to such an extent that there were 109 offices in the latter year, 79 managed by states and 30 by municipalities.

The impetus for a national employment service came with World War I. Prior to that time, the only federal employment offices were the 18 operated by the Bureau of Immigration. In order to improve the allocation of manpower resources during the wartime emergency, the Secretary of Labor in 1918 directed that a separate United States Employment Service be established within his department. New offices were opened rapidly under the direct control of the federal service until there were 850 at the peak of its operations. By February, 1919, however, just three months after the armistice, funds were exhausted. At a national employment conference, it was decided to ask Congress to make grants-in-aid for employment offices to be operated by the states. This request was turned down; instead, Congress appropriated only $400,000 for the maintenance of the federal service. During the nineteen-twenties, therefore, the U.S. Employment Service and the state employment offices were generally dormant, not to be revived until the Wagner-Peyser Act of 1935.[34]

During most depressions, some public works had been undertaken. They were, however, never very effective in meeting the needs of the unemployed. Since there was usually very little or no advance planning, the projects were frequently delayed by legal technicalities and did not get well under way before the end of the depression period. The public works programs that were most effective for the absorption of the unemployed were not new projects but those that hastened the completion of projects that

[32] John B. Andrews, "The Prevention of Unemployment," *Proceedings*, National Conference of Charities and Corrections, 1915, p. 539.

[33] I. M. Rubinow, *The Quest for Security* (New York: Henry Holt and Co., 1934), pp. 428–32.

[34] The history of public employment services in the U.S. is recounted in Paul H. Douglas and Aaron Director, *The Problem of Unemployment* (New York: The Macmillan Co., 1934), pp. 317–42. The Wagner-Peyser Act provided federal grants-in-aid to the states to establish employment services.

were begun before the emergency.[35] Public works were a favorite demand of reformers attempting to influence government to do something about the plight of the unemployed—for example the demands of Coxey and his army in 1894 for road building and other public works.

IV. THE DEPRESSION OF THE NINETEEN-THIRTIES

By the time the depression of the nineteen-thirties was well under way, few would have argued that public funds were not necessary for the relief of the unemployed. The crucial question now was the third question asked by Yates a hundred years earlier: What level of government should assume responsibility? Since the time of the Yates report, the states' responsibility for certain classes of dependent persons—for example, the mentally ill, the deaf, and the blind— had been firmly established throughout the United States; but the responsibility of caring for the poor outside those particular classes remained with the local community. In many states, the boards of charity had some supervisory responsibility; but since all funds for relief came from local property taxes, the influence of the boards was negligible. In some states, commissions were established during periods of emergency to study the problems of unemployment, but no radical changes in poor relief arrangements resulted.[36]

Many social reformers had hoped that the federal government would show some concern for the problems of the unemployed, as it had for other social problems of national scope during the early twentieth century. Apparently, however, all such national action was prohibited by the edict of President Pierce in 1854 that the federal government cannot become "the great almoner of public charity throughout the United States."[37] The only national con-ference on the subject of unemployment called by a government agency was assembled in 1921 at the request of President Harding. Although this conference accomplished little, it did constitute the first official recognition of responsibility by the federal government.[38]

This inactivity on the part of the state and federal governments was due to several factors. The first was the tradition of local responsibility for poor relief, which had been extremely durable since colonial days. The second was the leadership assumed by private charity during times when local governmental responsibility was apparently inadequate and hence vulnerable to criticism. The third factor was to some extent brought about by the first two: the real needs of the unemployed were obscured by the charges of inefficiency and corruption leveled at the local administrations and by the claims of the private agencies that they could handle the problem adequately.

By 1931 the inadequacy of both local relief and private charity was painfully apparent. Conservative estimates indicated that in December, 1930, the number of unemployed had reached about 7 million.[39] Between the first three months of 1929 and the first three months of 1931, the number receiving relief in cities with populations over 30,000 had more than doubled.[40] In order to prevent starvation and suffering in the industrial areas of the nation, it became mandatory that some source of funds be found other than the local property tax and private contributions.

The knell of local responsibility and private agency leadership was sounded in September, 1931, when New York established the first State Temporary Emergency Relief Administration. The need for state participation was set forth clearly by Governor Roosevelt in his message to the legislature. He said:

We must recognize these facts: that the local

---

[35] Feder, *Unemployment Relief in Periods of Depression* (n. 12), p. 347.

[36] *Ibid.*, pp. 233–35.

[37] President Pierce made this statement in his veto message concerning "An Act making a grant of public lands to the several states for the benefit of indigent insane persons," which had been urged upon Congress by social reformer Dorothea L. Dix. The text of the veto message is reprinted in Breckinridge, *Public Welfare Administration* (n. 7), p. 221.

[38] Feder, *Unemployment Relief in Periods of Depression* (n. 12), p. 296.

[39] Edward A. Williams, *Federal Aid for Relief* (New York: Columbia University Press, 1939), p. 15.

[40] U.S. Department of Commerce, Bureau of the Census, *Relief Expenditures by Governmental and Private Organizations 1929 and 1931*, Special Report (Washington, D.C., U.S. Government Printing Office, 1932), p. 6.

subdivisions of government can in most cases not greatly increase their direct employment of labor and that private charity will prove inadequate to meet the added burden of the next few months. By a process of elimination, if by nothing else, the responsibility also rests upon the State.[41]

Within less than a year, New Jersey, Rhode Island, Illinois, Wisconsin, Ohio, and Pennsylvania had assumed similar responsibilities. But state participation was still confined to emergencies, and Roosevelt reflected current public opinion when he put a double limitation into the title of that first program—it was to be "temporary" and "emergency." In his message, he made it plain that he believed the relief of the poor should remain a local function, to be stimulated and supplemented by state funds for a short period. Despite all these qualifications, however, the New York act was a milestone in public welfare administration. From this point on, there would be no turning back to exclusively local responsibility for the unemployed.

Federal responsibility for aid to the unemployed was more difficult to achieve. The administration of President Hoover was generally opposed to such intervention on the basis that large federal expenditures for unemployment relief would unbalance the budget and thus retard recovery and that providing relief would be an improper role for the national government to play in the federal system. In addition, the Hoover Administration had a sincere belief in the methods and values of private charity. But since the situation in 1930 demanded some action, the President appointed an Emergency Committee for Employment. As it had a very small appropriation, this committee initially limited its activities to encouraging and coordinating local efforts. But finally, as a result of its investigations, it realized that some federal action was necessary and recommended greatly increased national expenditures for public works.

Unwilling to accept this recommendation, the President appointed a new committee in August, 1931. This committee, The President's Organization on Unemployment Relief, was headed by business leader Walter S. Gifford, who was also president of the Charity Organization Society of New York. As might be expected, he was unalterably opposed to federal aid for the unemployed and conceived the function of his group as that of helping communities to raise funds and encouraging industry to "spread the work." The autumn campaigns of the Red Cross and the Community Chest raised amounts which, though prodigious, were yet insufficient to meet the needs of the unemployed during the winter. With elections looming the following November, the administration moved toward direct federal participation when the President in March, 1932, approved a joint resolution of the Congress authorizing the Federal Farm Board to give 40 million bushels of wheat to the Red Cross for distribution. A similar resolution in July made cotton and more wheat available. Finally, after much agitation and pressure throughout the nation, the President signed the Emergency Relief and Construction Act on July 22.[42]

Although a compromise measure, the Emergency Relief and Construction Act of 1932 marked the beginning of direct and specific concern by the federal government for the unemployed. It authorized the Reconstruction Finance Corporation to advance $300 million to the states and territories to be used in furnishing direct relief and work relief to destitute persons. Direct grants were not to be made. Instead, the federal government was to make cash advances at an interest rate of 3 per cent per annum; these advances were to be repaid beginning in fiscal year 1935 by means of deductions from the regular federal grants-in-aid for highway construction. In addition, the governor of each state applying for assistance

---

[41] Governor Roosevelt's message is reprinted in Edith Abbott, *Public Assistance, American Principles and Policies* (Chicago: University of Chicago Press, 1940), p. 533.

[42] Discussion of federal activities prior to 1933 may be found in works by Abbott, *Public Assistance (n. 41)*, and Williams, *Federal Aid for Relief (n. 39)* and in Josephine C. Brown, *Public Relief 1929–1939* (New York: Henry Holt and Co., 1940) and in Harry L. Hopkins, *Spending to Save* (New York: W. W. Norton & Co., 1936).

was required to certify that sufficient funds were not available and could not be made available to meet the needs of the unemployed in the state.[43] Despite these difficult requirements and stipulations, all but six states borrowed money under the act; and by the time of the change of administration in March, 1933, almost all the authorized funds were exhausted.

Presidential candidate Roosevelt, although pledging economy and a balanced budget, made one exception to his promises of financial conservatism. In his Pittsburgh speech of October 19, 1932, he said: "If starvation and dire need on the part of any of our citizens make necessary the appropriation of additional funds which will keep the budget out of balance, I shall not hesitate to tell the American people the full truth and ask them to authorize the expenditure of that additional amount."[44] As President, Roosevelt did not wait long before he admitted that such starvation and dire need did indeed exist. During the first month of his administration, he signed the bill establishing the Civilian Conservation Corps, providing temporary employment for unemployed youths in army-like camps.[45] More important, however, was his support of the Federal Emergency Relief Act, which he signed on May 12, 1933.

Under that act, the Federal Emergency Relief Administration (FERA) was created for a period of two years, and all powers were to be exercised by the administrator. The FERA was a positive commitment of the resources of the federal government to the care of the unemployed, as it involved direct grants to the states. The actual disbursement of funds was left to the states and localities, but the federal administrator had power to enforce the rules and regulations promulgated by him and to

assume control in any state where he considered such action necessary.[46]

It was charged that the FERA replaced the activities of the localities and of private charity, but President Roosevelt refused to admit it. The statement which he issued when he signed this act was similar to the speech he made to the New York legislature two years before and read in part as follows:

The bill in effect is a challenge to governors, legislatures and local officials to stimulate their own efforts to provide for their own citizens in need. For these and other good reasons, citizens who are able should voluntarily contribute to the pressing needs of the welfare services.[47]

Nevertheless, in November, 1933, he went even further toward centralized administration when he approved the establishment of the Civil Works Administration.[48]

The CWA came to an end in March, 1934, and the final grants of the FERA were made during the latter part of 1935. The decision to end the FERA was made following the establishment of the Works Progress Administration[49] in May, 1935, and the signing of the Social Security Act in August of the same year. The federal government was now to contribute direct relief to only those unemployed or unemployables who were included in the special categories of the Social Security Act. Nevertheless, it did not abdicate at this time its responsibility for the unemployed: those unemployed for short periods of time would

---

[43] Text of the Emergency Relief and Construction Act of 1932 is reprinted in Abbott, *Public Assistance* (n. 41), p. 728.

[44] Frank Freidel, *Franklin D. Roosevelt: The Triumph* (Boston: Little, Brown & Co., 1956), p. 363.

[45] For a discussion of the beginnings of the Civilian Conservation Corps, see Frances Perkins, *The Roosevelt I Knew* (New York: The Viking Press, 1946), chap. 14.

[46] For a discussion of the beginnings of the FERA, see Robert E. Sherwood, *Roosevelt and Hopkins* (New York: Harper and Brothers, 1948), pp. 44–51. The text of the act is reprinted in Abbott, *Public Assistance* (n. 41). Instances of the assumption of control by the federal government are cited in V. O. Key, *The Administration of Federal Grants to the States* (Chicago: Public Administration Service, 1937), pp. 172–73.

[47] Abbott, *Public Assistance* (n. 41), p. 748.

[48] The CWA is briefly but interestingly described in Arthur M. Schlesinger, Jr., *The Coming of the New Deal* (Boston: Houghton Mifflin Co., 1959), pp. 269–73. For details of program operation, see Williams, *Federal Aid for Relief* (n. 39), pp. 110–24.

[49] The history and operation details of the WPA are presented in Arthur W. MacMahon et al., *The Administration of Federal Work Relief* (Chicago: Public Administration Service, 1941).

receive unemployment compensation benefits as provided in the Social Security Act; those out of work for long periods of time and others not eligible for insurance benefits would be hired by the WPA if they were in need and would work for a living wage on socially useful projects. The federal government relinquished responsibility for the long-term unemployed in 1942, when the WPA was allowed to expire.

In light of the pattern of the programs described above, any controversy about whether relief programs should be carried on by public or by private agencies became necessarily an academic one during the depression of the nineteen-thirties. The statement that placed the controversy in the realm of the academic, for the time being, was made by the Federal Emergency Relief administrator in his now famous Rule Number 1:

> Grants of federal emergency relief funds are to be administered by public agencies after August 1, 1933. This ruling prohibits the turning over of federal emergency relief funds to a private agency. The unemployed must apply to a public relief agency for relief and this relief must be furnished direct to the applicant by a public agent.[50]

This statement was in accord with the principle that "public funds must be administered by public agencies," which was agreed upon by social welfare leaders attending the Conference on the Maintenance of Welfare Standards held in November, 1932.[51] Since the FERA statement, private charitable agencies have given little relief to the unemployed but have, instead, used their influence and experience to help improve the administration of public assistance, social insurance, and auxiliary services.

The public programs for unemployment relief during the depression owed much to their heritage from the private agencies, since the procedures of the Charity Organization Societies were appropriated for use by the public welfare agencies. This adoption of the methods of private charity was due, in no small part, to the professional social work orientation of Harry Hopkins, who was administrator first of the New York State Temporary Emergency Relief Administration and then of the massive federal programs. He was a social worker who had been a supervisor and later an assistant director of the New York Association for Improving the Condition of the Poor. His exposure to the philosophy and methods of that agency account for many of the actions he took and the opinions he expressed. In both the New York and the federal programs, he insisted upon careful and thorough investigation, coordination with other agencies to prevent duplication of relief giving, adequate relief once eligibility had been determined, and the hiring of professionally trained social workers both for their investigative efficiency and for their professional commitment to the welfare of the community and to those they served.

Perhaps most closely related to his previous experience was his fear of the "pauperizing" effects of outdoor relief if continued for any length of time. Testifying before the Senate Committee on Manufactures early in 1933, he said:

> Bear in mind we are dealing with people now who have never had relief before in their whole lives. I saw records recently of a list of 300 families who applied for relief and not one of them had had relief or connection with relief organizations before in their lives. The first time they get a grocery order it is tough, the second time it is tough, and the third time even, but if that man keeps beating a path to a welfare office to get a grocery order, he will gradually learn the way and it will be a pretty hard job to get him off the path.[52]

His solution was work—not work for relief or a work test—but work for wages. As he said later: "To me the only possible solution for those who cannot be absorbed by long-time or

[50] Federal Emergency Relief Administration, *Monthly Report, May 22–June 30, 1933* (Washington D.C.: Government Printing Office, 1933), p. 7.

[51] A summary of the proceedings of the conference will be found in "Chicago Conference on Relief Standards," *Social Service Review*, VI, No. 4 (December, 1932), 592–612.

[52] U.S. Congress, Senate, Subcommittee of the Senate Committee on Manufactures, *Hearings, Federal Aid for Unemployment Relief*, 72nd Cong., 2d Sess., 1933, S. 5125, p. 83.

large-scale public works is a work program." [53]

When the FERA began, it made grants-in-aid to existing programs. The administration, however, emphasized the value of work relief; if work relief was not possible, then it recommended cash payments instead of relief in kind. Cash was considered preferable because it was simple to administer, preserved the normal purchasing arrangements of the family, maintained existing channels of retail trade, and did not mark the family as dependent in the community. Between May and December, 1934, the percentage of direct relief paid in cash increased from less than 10 per cent to 23 per cent.[54] This policy of giving cash was continued in the grants for public assistance under the Social Security Act, which defined such assistance as money payments and prohibited relief in kind.

Rules for work relief were set forth during the first month of the FERA. The rate of wages was to be related to a fair rate of pay for the work performed. If skilled personnel were required, usual wages for such skills were to be paid. These early regulations, however, covered programs that were more "work for relief" than work relief, as total wages were to be based upon the relief need of the worker and his family computed on the basis of a budgetary deficit.[55] The Civil Works Administration (CWA), which began in November, 1933, established a pattern which was to be followed later by the more lasting Works Progress Administration. The CWA was a bold attempt to find real jobs for all the unemployed, whether or not the unemployed persons met the needs requirements of the direct relief programs; only one-half of the 4 million persons employed on projects had been recipients of relief. None was investigated or subjected to a means test. Wage rates were set according to standards developed by the Public Works Administration of the Department of the Interior. Generally, those employed by the CWA worked an eight-hour day and a thirty-hour week.

When the CWA ended, in March, 1934, many of the projects were continued by the FERA, but all the workers had to qualify under a needs test. The Works Progress Administration, which began during the summer of 1935 and continued until 1942, was a compromise. The projects were similar to those developed under the CWA, but it was necessary for most workers to be certified by the local public assistance authorities as being in need before they were accepted for employment. Once employed, they received a monthly "security" wage, which was related to the type of work performed, not to a "budgetary deficit." [56]

The most promising advance in providing aid to the unemployed was embodied in the Social Security Act of 1935, which established a federal-state system of compulsory unemployment insurance supported by designated payroll taxes from which benefits were to be paid in proportion to the claimant's previous wages. Benefits, therefore, were to be paid as a matter of right, not as a gratuity. Although such a scheme had been strenuously advocated at least as early as the 1915 Conference on Charities and Corrections, the idea of insuring workers against unemployment made little headway prior to the Social Security Act.[57] By this legislation, the responsibility of the national government was recognized, since the unemployment compensation program was to be financed by a federal employment tax, which could be offset by a similar state tax if the state law complied with certain standards. By 1939 all states had fully operating unemployment insurance laws and were paying benefits to eligible unemployed workers.[58] This federal-

[53] Hopkins, *Spending to Save* (n. 42), p. 183.
[54] Brown, *Public Relief* (n. 42), p. 243.
[55] Federal Emergency Relief Administration, *Monthly Report, May 22–June 30, 1933* (n. 50), p. 13.

[56] Williams, *Federal Aid for Relief* (n. 39), pp. 247–57.
[57] A small number of private plans for unemployment benefits antedated the Social Security Act by as much as a century. Also, the Metropolitan Life Insurance Company was seriously interested at one time (about 1926) in the possibility of writing unemployment insurance and sponsored a bill which passed the New York legislature to make such insurance legal. By far the most important predecessor of the social security programs was the 1932 Wisconsin unemployment insurance program, which began to pay benefits in 1936.
[58] The story of the enactment of the unemployment insurance section of the Social Security Act is told in Edwin E. Witte, *The Development of the Social Security Act* (Madison: University of Wisconsin Press, 1962).

state system of unemployment insurance was destined to remain the nation's most important instrument for providing aid to the unemployed. During the years following the nineteen-thirties, its expanding coverage and increasing benefits provided a base for building programs of job placement, training, vocational education, and supplemental public assistance.

PART II

Description of the Unemployed To Be Aided

CHAPTER 2

Who Are the Unemployed?

Richard C. Wilcock*

THE TWO CHAPTERS in this part have as their purpose a description of the unemployed in the United States in the early nineteen-sixties. This chapter contains a summary of the available sources of unemployment statistics; a review of the concepts underlying the statistics; a general description of the numbers, characteristics, income, and location of the unemployed; and recommendations for improvements in the existing data and for the collection of new data which would assist in the development of policies to aid the unemployed. Chapter 3 presents in somewhat greater detail descriptions of the long-term unemployed and the geographic distribution of substantial and persistent unemployment.

I. MAJOR SOURCES OF DATA

In the United States there are four major sources of unemployment statistics: (1) the monthly household survey conducted by the Bureau of the Census and interpreted and published by the Bureau of Labor Statistics;[1] (2) statistics, including some on a weekly basis, that are a by-product of the several state and federal unemployment insurance programs;[2] (3) the national population census, which

obtains very detailed data for the entire population and for all geographic areas, but only once in ten years;[3] and (4) estimates of unemployment in states and in local labor-market areas made by the state employment security agencies. This chapter is based primarily on the first two, which are the major sources of current data.

A. THE MONTHLY HOUSEHOLD SURVEY

The most comprehensive unemployment data on a national basis are obtained through the Current Population Survey,[4] which is designed to be representative of the entire population and is based upon an "area probability sample." The representative sample areas include large cities, small towns, rural districts, and farms. Currently there are 357 such areas, with a total sample of 35,000 households, or about 1 household of every 1,500. The basic purpose of the household survey is to provide a comprehensive measure of the labor force; that is, the number and the characteristics of all persons fourteen years of age and over who are employed or unemployed. The labor-force information specifically applies to members of the survey households during the calendar week ending nearest the twelfth day of the month.[5]

Since the data are from a sample of house-

---

* Professor, Institute of Labor and Industrial Relations, University of Illinois. Professor Wilcock died shortly after completing this essay.

[1] For a detailed description, see *Concepts and Methods Used in the Current Employment and Unemployment Statistics Prepared by the Bureau of the Census*, Current Population Reports, Series P-23, No. 5 (Bureau of the Census, Washington, D.C., 1958).

[2] For a detailed description, see "Insured Unemployment, Employment, and Wage Statistics: Their Source, Nature and Limitations," *The Labor Market and Employment Security* (Bureau of Employment Security, Department of Labor, Washington, D.C., March, 1960).

[3] Labor-force data are published in a national summary volume and in separate volumes for each state.

[4] For a brief discussion of the historical development of the household survey, see President's Committee to Appraise Employment and Unemployment Statistics, *Measuring Employment and Unemployment* (Washington, D.C.: Government Printing Office, 1962), pp. 76–86.

[5] The household survey data are published by the U.S. Department of Labor in the *Monthly Report on the Labor Force* and in *Employment and Earnings*. Some of the data are also published each month in other governmental publications.

holds, they are subject to sampling error. The chances are about nineteen out of twenty that any difference between the unemployment estimates and a complete census would be less than 200,000 persons. The main virtue of the household survey is comprehensiveness; its main weakness is lack of geographical detail.

The monthly household survey is used from time to time to obtain additional data relevant to the analysis of unemployment. For example, once a year, in February, data are obtained on work experience in the previous year, including time lost from work because of unemployment or for other reasons. Each March information is obtained on family income for the previous year. Family income is then related to employment and family status.

In April, 1962, an intensive study of unemployment was undertaken by the Bureau of Labor Statistics. Included in the study were some 3,000 persons who were unemployed for five weeks or more in 1961. The results of this study show, among other things, the effect of unemployment on family income, the methods used to maintain living standards, and the extent to which other family members found jobs when the principal breadwinner was out of work.

Special analyses of employment and unemployment are published from time to time in the *Monthly Labor Review* and in reprint form, frequently with many detailed tables. These reports include annual reviews of employment, unemployment, and work experience. In addition, the text material in the *Monthly Report on the Labor Force* often includes special tabulations and analyses. In recent years a number of special reports also have been prepared for congressional committees, often containing tabulations not elsewhere available. Several of these reports are referred to in this and the following chapters.

B. Data from Employment Security Programs

A second major source of unemployment statistics is the federal-state unemployment insurance system and the similar programs for federal civilian employees and railroad workers.

These programs cover roughly four of every five nonfarm wage and salary workers and two of three persons in the civilian labor force. Not included in the statistics are those not covered by the insurance programs, those with no recent work experience (new entrants to the labor force), and those who have exhausted their benefits.[6]

These data supplement the household survey in crucial ways. They provide the geographic detail so necessary for programs of aid. The amount of insured unemployment and the characteristics of the insured unemployed are published by state in *Unemployment Insurance Statistics*, a monthly publication of the Bureau of Employment Security. Data on estimated total unemployment in 150 labor-market areas are gathered by local employment offices and published by the Bureau of Employment Security in *Area Labor Market Trends* and *Unemployment Insurance Claims*. The latter is a weekly publication and thus also provides weekly data on the number of initial claims, a measure of new unemployment.

II. WHO IS COUNTED AS UNEMPLOYED?

Because the determination of who is to be counted as unemployed is important in the development of policies to aid the unemployed, a brief review of the conceptual problems is presented here. The major questions are: (1) When is a person currently not working but who wants work counted as unemployed rather than out of the labor force? (2) When is a person who holds a job counted as unemployed rather than employed? And among those counted as employed, who can be considered partially unemployed because they are employed for short hours or are at work below their occupational and wage-earning capacity?[7]

---

[6] The insured unemployed may include some who are not counted as unemployed in the household survey; for example, some partially employed persons receive benefits.

[7] For more elaborate discussions, see President's Committee, *Measuring Employment* (n. 4), chaps. 1 and 2; also see Albert Rees, "The Measurement of Unemployment," in *Studies in Unemployment*, prepared for the Special Committee on Unemployment Problems (U.S. Senate, 86th Cong., 2nd Sess., 1960), pp. 18–24.

A. Who Is in the Labor Force?

The first and most difficult problem in deciding who should be counted as unemployed is how to determine when a person who "wants" to work or is "available" for work should be counted as in the labor force and therefore unemployed. As used in the household survey, the basic concept of who is "unemployed" puts a good deal of emphasis on current and active search for work. This basic concept and the exceptions to it are shown in the following official description:

Unemployed persons include those who did not work at all during the survey week and were looking for work. Those who had made efforts to find jobs within the preceding 60-day period—such as registering at a public or private employment agency, writing letters of application, canvassing for work, etc.— and who, during the survey week, were awaiting the results of these efforts are also regarded as looking for work. Also included as unemployed are those who did not work at all during the survey week and—
a. Were waiting to be called back to a job from which they had been laid off; or
b. Were waiting to report to a new wage or salary job scheduled to start within the following 30 days (and were not in school during the survey week); or
c. Would have been looking for work except that they were temporarily ill or believed no work was available in their line of work or in the community.[8]

In the household interview the question asked is: "Was ——— looking for work?" If the answer is "Yes," the individual is shown as unemployed, and there is no further probing. The respondent is specifically questioned about his efforts to find jobs within the past sixty days only if he seems uncertain about the meaning of "looking for work." Also a person who did not look for work because of temporary illness or because he believed there were no available jobs is recorded as unemployed only if the information is volunteered by the respondent. These and other ambiguities have created some uncertainty about just who is being counted as unemployed.

[8] Bureau of the Census, *Concepts and Methods* (*n.* 1), p. 2.

Special questions in the household survey of August, 1955, revealed that there were about 1 million persons who did not meet the official definition of unemployment but who had taken one or more job-seeking steps during the two months preceding the survey.[9] Consideration of this problem and the related problem of those who have given up active search for work led the President's Committee to Appraise Employment and Unemployment Statistics to make two recommendations.

First, there should be an intensive investigation of the feasibility of counting as unemployed a jobless person who not only indicates he wants work but who also (1) has taken specific steps to find a job since the beginning of the previous calendar month (about forty-five days prior to the survey) or (2) is waiting to be recalled to a job from which he was laid off since the beginning of the previous month or to report to a new job scheduled to start by the end of the following calendar month.[10]

Second, those who have not actively sought work during the past forty-five days or are not currently registered at the public employment service office would not be counted as unemployed. Because some of these people would be displaced workers who would presumably want work, and because many of the nonactive job seekers would undoubtedly respond to an increase in job opportunities, the committee recommended the compilation of data on persons outside the labor force at least once a year and preferably once a quarter, the data to be based on such questions as these:

1. Given his present personal circumstances (housewife, in school, etc.), does the respondent presently want and would he be able to accept a job if a suitable one were available?
2. Is part-time or full-time work wanted?
3. Under which of a specified set of circum-

[9] President's Committee, *Measuring Employment* (*n.* 4), pp. 50, 282–84.

[10] With respect to the possible discontinuity in the historical series of unemployment rates, the President's committee states: "It is worth a break in the series to get a more objective and reliable measure of unemployment and more detailed information regarding those who are reported as being either unemployed or outside the labor force," *ibid.*, p. 54.

stances would the respondent actually look for a job?

4. What was his previous work experience, including nature of last job held (if any), and when and why was it terminated?

5. What is his educational background, including any vocational or professional training?[11]

Such data could be invaluable in analyzing labor-force withdrawals, particularly if the data show any substantial number of withdrawals resulting from discouragement in job-seeking efforts. Those who have given up the search for work should not be excluded from aid designed for the unemployed without considering the reasons for the cessation of job seeking.

B. Employed or Unemployed?

In the determination of who is unemployed rather than employed, two groups come under consideration: those who have jobs but are not working during the survey week and those who are partially employed—either because they involuntarily work short hours or because they are working below their capacity.

Those with Jobs but Not Working. Because their failure to work is not the result of economic conditions, most of those persons who have jobs but currently are not working are included in the category of the employed. Beginning in January, 1957, however, two groups were shifted from the employed to the unemployed category because they are clearly out of work for economic reasons and therefore are properly considered unemployed: wage and salary workers on temporary layoff who have definite instructions to return to work within thirty days and wage and salary workers waiting to start new jobs.[12] This shift has added from 225,000 to 300,000 persons to the ranks of the unemployed.

Partial Unemployment and Underemployment.

There are two types of the partially unemployed: those working part time but who want full-time jobs, and those without jobs who are seeking only part-time work. Each month the *Monthly Report on the Labor Force* shows the number of persons in nonfarm industries who are working less than thirty-five hours a week for such economic reasons as slack work; it also carries a monthly index of labor-force time lost through unemployment and through part-time work (see Figure 2–1).[13] Beginning with data for January, 1963, the MRLF also shows (by sex, age, and occupation of last job) the proportion of the unemployed looking for part-time work.

Some critics have charged that the data are distorted if those who work only a very few hours during the week are counted as employed. As it turns out, most of the people (particularly those who work less than five hours a week) work such short hours from personal preference. Rather than divide the group between unemployed (those who want more hours) and out of the labor force (those who prefer only a few hours), the President's Committee to Appraise Employment and Unemployment Statistics concluded that the simplest solution is to list all of them as employed but to show them separately in the published tabulations.[14]

A more difficult problem is how to measure the underemployment of those who are working below their highest current level of skill and/or

---

[11] *Ibid.*, p. 56.

[12] For the origin of these changes, see Committee on Labor Supply, Employment, and Unemployment Statistics, "Interim Report of the Review of Concepts Subcommittee," in *Employment and Unemployment Statistics*, prepared for the Subcommittee on Economic Statistics, Joint Economic Committee (84th Cong., 1st Sess., 1955), pp. 10–14.

[13] The labor-force time-lost series shows the number of man-hours lost (on the basis of 37.5 hours per week) because of unemployment and economic part-time employment (the difference between 37.5 hours and the actual number of hours worked) as a per cent of the total number of man-hours potentially available to the civilian labor force. Experiments show that the series varies only slightly if the time lost is based on a standard forty-hour week or on the actual average workweek of the fully employed. See Gertrude Bancroft, "Some Alternate Indexes of Employment and Unemployment," in *Unemployment: Terminology, Measurement, and Analysis*, prepared for the Subcommittee on Economic Statistics, Joint Economic Committee (87th Cong., 1st Sess., 1961), pp. 35–41. For an analysis using aggregate man-hours to show the effect of business cycles on employment, see David J. Farber, *Annual Paid Man-Hours of Employment and Annual Wages, 1946–54* (Social Security Administration, Department of Health, Education, and Welfare, Washington, D.C., 1962).

[14] President's Committee, *Measuring Employment* (*n.* 4), pp. 45–46.

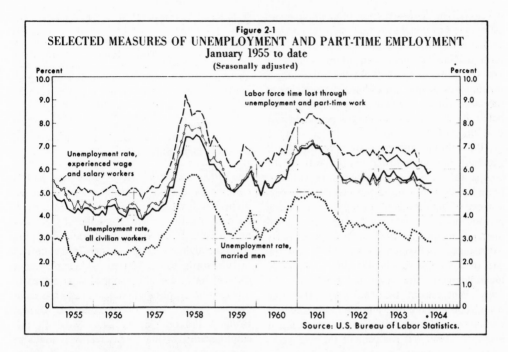

Figure 2-1
SELECTED MEASURES OF UNEMPLOYMENT AND PART-TIME EMPLOYMENT
January 1955 to date
(Seasonally adjusted)

Source: U.S. Bureau of Labor Statistics.

at wages below those normally paid for their skills.[15] Such disguised unemployment is easier to recognize than it is to measure, but numerous case studies testify to its existence.[16] Albert Rees has suggested that only the type of disguised unemployment caused by business-cycle swings should be considered for inclusion in the usual unemployment measures. Such underemployment is comparable to the loss of hours in total or partial unemployment resulting from economic causes.[17] Disguised unemployment from discrimination, on the other hand, cannot be attacked by the usual economic measures; it should be measured separately in order to provide a basis for special attack on labor-market customs and practices.

III. HOW MANY ARE UNEMPLOYED?

In the fourteen years from 1947 through 1960, the unemployment rate averaged 4.2 per cent of the civilian labor force; the estimated average for the eleven years between the end of World War I and 1929 was 4.7 per cent. For the nonfarm labor force, the estimated average rate was 6.7 per cent in the 1900–13 period, 6.8 per cent in the 1919–29 period, and 4.9 per cent between 1947 and 1960.[18] Stanley Lebergott, who

---

[15] Underemployment, as usually defined, does not cover work below the level of skill persons could attain if fully trained. For a discussion of this problem, see *ibid.*, pp. 58–59, and Rees, "The Measurement of Unemployment" (*n.* 7), pp. 23–24; also see Louis J. Ducoff and Margaret J. Hagood, "The Meaning and Measurement of Partial and Disguised Unemployment," in National Bureau of Economic Research, *Measurement and Behavior of Unemployment* (Princeton: Princeton University Press, 1957), pp. 155–66.

[16] See for example Richard C. Wilcock, *Impact on Workers and Community of a Plant Shutdown in a Depressed Area*, Bulletin No. 1264 (Bureau of Labor Statistics, Department of Labor, Washington, D.C.,

1960). In this study 11 per cent of a laid-off work force was classified as underemployed two and one-half years after the plant shutdown.

[17] Rees, "The Measurement of Unemployment" (*n.* 7), p. 24.

[18] James W. Knowles and Edward D. Kalacheck, "Higher Unemployment Rates, 1957–60: Structural Transformation or Inadequate Demand," prepared for the Subcommittee on Economic Statistics, Joint Economic Committee (87th Cong., 1st Sess., 1961), p. 3. The estimates for periods prior to World War II are from Stanley Lebergott, "Annual Estimates of Unemployment in the United States, 1900–54," *Measurement and Behavior of Unemployment* (*n.* 15), pp. 205–16.

developed the historical series of unemployment estimates, has concluded that there is no clear evidence of either a long-term rise or a long-term decline in unemployment rates, and he notes: "It has been 20 years since the annual unemployment rate ran as high as 8 per cent of the labor force . . . unemployment has not run below 8 per cent for so long a period at any time since 1860." [19]

Although unemployment since World War II generally has been lower than it was in the comparable time span after the first World War, there has been mounting concern over the persistence of high levels of unemployment during periods between recessions. The behavior of unemployment since 1957 has been particularly worrisome. Between October, 1957, and the end of 1963 the seasonally adjusted monthly unemployment rate never fell below 5.0 per cent. Whereas in the two years after the troughs of both the 1949 and the 1954 recessions unemployment averaged about 4.7 per cent, it averaged about 6.0 per cent in the two years after the low points of both the 1958 and the 1960 recessions. James Knowles and Edward Kalacheck have pointed out that the over-all trend of unemployment was not clearly upward between 1948 and 1957 but that most of "the deterioration has occurred since 1957." [20] The annual averages shown in Table 2-1 illustrate this conclusion. Almost all of the increase in unemployment rates has come as a result of longer spells of unemployment, on the average, with more of the jobless entering the ranks of the long-term unemployed. [21]

The concern over the substantial upward shift in unemployment rates in the United States has been heightened by the fact that only

TABLE 2-1: UNEMPLOYMENT RATES IN THE UNITED STATES, 1950–1963 (ANNUAL AVERAGES)

Year	Rate	Year	Rate	Year	Rate
1950	5.3	1955	4.4	1960	5.6
1951	3.3	1956	4.2	1961	6.7
1952	3.1	1957	4.3	1962	5.6
1953	2.9	1958	6.8	1963	5.7
1954	5.6	1959	5.5		

SOURCE: U.S. Bureau of Labor Statistics.

one other industrialized country has had a comparable experience: Canada has had even higher levels than the United States since 1957. By contrast, the Federal Republic of Germany has found its unemployment rate dropping from the highest among industrialized countries in 1950 to the lowest in 1961. Unemployment rates in Italy have also dropped since the early nineteen-fifties, although not so drastically as in Germany. In four other countries (Great Britain, France, Japan, and Sweden) unemployment rates have been relatively low and have not had any pronounced upward or downward trend since 1950.

In a study prepared for the President's Committee to Appraise Employment and Unemployment Statistics, the rates of the seven foreign countries cited above were adjusted to United States definitions of unemployment. [22] After this adjustment the seven countries, whose combined labor force is about double that of the United States, had a composite unemployment rate in 1960 of 2.1 per cent, as compared with the 5.6 per cent rate for the United States.

Unemployment during the Year. Although in recent years the number of unemployed persons at any given time has ranged between 3 and 5 million, during the course of any one year more than three times as many people will experience joblessness. For example, in 1962 the number unemployed at any one time averaged 4 million, but in the course of that year 15.3 million different persons experienced some unemployment; of these over 9 million were unemployed for at least five weeks, and more than 5 million were

[19] "Unemployment Statistics for Fiscal and Monetary Policy," *Proceedings of the Fourteenth Annual Meeting* (Madison, Wisconsin: Industrial Relations Research Association, 1962), p. 16.

[20] Knowles and Kalacheck, "Higher Unemployment Rates" (n. 18), p. 5.

[21] Robert L. Stein and Frazier Kellogg, "Unemployment in the Early 1960's," *Unemployment: Terminology, Measurement, and Analysis* (n. 13), p. 96. The annual average rates of very short-term unemployment (unemployment ending within five weeks) fluctuated between 1.4 and 1.8 per cent of the labor force between 1948 and 1961, with very slight upward movements in recessions.

[22] Robert J. Myers and John H. Chandler, "Comparative Levels of Unemployment in Industrial Countries," in *Measuring Employment* (n. 4), pp. 237–39.

unemployed more than once. For the six years of 1957 through 1962 there was an annual average of almost 13.7 million individuals who had some unemployment, as compared with the average unemployment level of approximately 4 million persons.[23]

The special April, 1962, survey of the unemployed conducted by the Bureau of Labor Statistics indicated that of the estimated 9.6 million experienced workers with at least five weeks of unemployment in 1961, 26 per cent were unemployed in April, 1962, while 67 per cent were back at work and 7 per cent had left the labor force. That many workers are prone to unemployment is illustrated by the fact that almost 50 per cent of the total group had had some unemployment in at least three of the five preceding years, and over one-fifth experienced unemployment in all five years.[24]

Extent of Part-Time Unemployment. In the postwar years there has been an upward trend in part-time employment. Although much of this increase is the result of a rapid increase in part-time work by those who do not want full-time jobs, there was nevertheless an average of 2.3 million nonfarm workers in 1963 who were working part time because they were unable to find jobs with full workweeks. Those working part time for economic reasons are really partially unemployed. The behavior of part-time unemployment is similar to that of total unemployment, with higher rates in recession years and with a higher incidence among semiskilled and unskilled workers, teen-agers, older workers, and nonwhites.[25]

[23] *Manpower Report of the President, 1964* and *A Report on Manpower Requirements, Resources, Utilization, and Training*, prepared for the Congress, March, 1964 (U.S. Department of Labor, Washington, D.C., 1964), Tables A–8 and B–19. This report has a large collection of tables and charts drawn from many sources. See also the *Manpower Report of the President, 1963.*

[24] Robert L. Stein, "Work History, Attitudes, and Income of the Unemployed," *Monthly Labor Review* (December, 1963), pp. 1405–13. This study, which reports the results of an interview survey of the states in April, 1962, of about 3,000 persons unemployed for five weeks or more in 1961, will hereafter be referred to as the *BLS 1962 Survey of the Unemployed.*

[25] *Manpower Report of the President, 1963* (n. 23), pp. 50–51, and *Manpower Report of the President, 1964* (n. 23), p. 206.

IV. CHARACTERISTICS OF THE UNEMPLOYED

To develop programs of aid for the unemployed, we must know much more than an over-all unemployment rate. In this chapter a major concern is with those individual characteristics of the unemployed that are related to problems of job search and of matching jobs and workers. These characteristics are of two types: personal characteristics, such as age, sex, and color, which sometimes are not relevant to the ability to perform jobs; and job qualifications, such as educational attainment, training, occupational experience, and industrial experience, which are relevant to formal job requirements.

A. AGE AND SEX

Age and sex are major variables in both the rate and the duration of unemployment. Table 2–2 shows the extent to which the unemployment rates of teen-agers, both boys and girls, exceed those of adults in all phases of the business cycle. Of the millions of teen-agers who have entered the labor force in recent years, usually about one-third have experienced a number of weeks of unemployment before they have found their first jobs. Concern about the unemployment of youth has increased because of the very rapid growth that is anticipated in the number of teen-agers of working age over the next few years, 6 million more young people being expected to enter the labor force in the nineteen-sixties than had entered in the nineteen-fifties. This greater influx is occurring simultaneously with a steady disappearance of the relatively unskilled jobs that have traditionally been a major source of employment for youth.

Unemployment varies much less sharply with sex than with age. Among adults, over-all unemployment rates are somewhat higher for women than for men, and the difference does not vary greatly between periods of prosperity and recession.

When unemployment is rising in the early stages of a recession, however, the most rapid increases in unemployment rates occur among

TABLE 2–2: UNEMPLOYMENT RATES FOR ADULTS, TEEN-AGERS, AND YOUNG MEN, IN FOUR POSTWAR BUSINESS CYCLES (SEASONALLY ADJUSTED QUARTERLY AVERAGES)

Age and sex[a]	1948–1950			1953–1955			1957–1958			1960–1961		
	4th '48	4th '49	2nd '50	3rd '53	3rd '54	1st '55	3rd '57	2nd '58	4th '58	2nd '60	1st '61	3rd '61
Men, age 20 and over	3.3	6.5	5.0	2.2	5.3	4.2	3.6	6.8	5.8	4.3	5.8	5.9
Women, age 20 and over	3.6	5.8	5.3	2.8	5.7	4.5	4.1	6.6	5.7	4.7	6.2	6.4
Men, age 14–19	8.2	14.5	12.4	7.1	12.9	11.3	11.0	15.5	15.2	14.3	15.9	14.8
Women, age 14–19	6.9	12.3	10.9	5.9	11.7	9.7	10.2	13.1	12.6	12.0	15.2	16.4
Men, age 20–24	5.6	10.7	8.1	2.9	10.4	7.7	7.8	13.8	11.2	8.3	10.8	10.9

SOURCE: U.S. Bureau of Labor Statistics. This table, as well as subsequent tables which show unemployment rates in four business cycles, is adapted from Robert L. Stein and Frazier Kellogg, "Unemployment in the Early 1960's," in *Unemployment: Terminology, Measurement, and Analysis*, prepared for Joint Economic Committee (87th Cong., 1st Sess., 1961), *passim*.
[a] Pre-1957 data based on old definitions of unemployment.

men between the ages of twenty and fifty-four. The reasons are that almost all men in these age groups are continuously in the labor force and also are concentrated more heavily in occupations and industries affected by recessions. On the other hand, when employment recovery occurs, unemployment normally declines most rapidly for men in the prime working ages. Older men, particularly those fifty-five years and over, are less affected by recession-caused unemployment; but during recovery periods those who are unemployed are slower to regain jobs than are younger men. In fact, during the early stages of the 1958 and 1961 recoveries, the unemployment rates for older men actually

increased. Table 2–3 shows the trend in unemployment rates for men of different age groups in four postwar business cycles.

Apart from the effect of changes in the business cycle, the relationship between age and unemployment is different for males and for females. Among both sexes unemployment is highest for teen-agers, but for adults the patterns diverge. Among males unemployment rates are usually highest for teen-agers and then drop in each higher age group through the so-called prime working ages of thirty-five to forty-five years. Beyond age forty-five, the rates are higher in each age group, to the age of seventy. Potential unemployment of men sixty-five years

TABLE 2–3: UNEMPLOYMENT RATES FOR MEN, BY AGE, IN FOUR BUSINESS CYCLES (SEASONALLY ADJUSTED QUARTERLY AVERAGES)

Age group[a]	1948–1950			1953–1955			1957–1958			1960–1961		
	4th '48	4th '49	2nd '50	3rd '53	3rd '54	1st '55	3rd '57	2nd '58	4th '58	2nd '60	1st '61	3rd '61
20 and over	3.3	6.5	5.0	2.2	5.3	4.2	3.6	6.8	5.8	4.3	5.8	5.9
25–34	2.6	6.2	4.6	1.7	5.0	3.7	3.5	7.4	6.0	4.4	5.9	5.7
35–44	2.0	4.9	3.7	1.6	4.3	3.4	2.7	5.6	4.7	3.6	4.8	4.7
45–54	2.6	5.1	3.9	1.8	4.4	3.1	3.4	6.1	4.7	3.8	5.1	4.8
55–64	3.4	5.7	5.6	2.6	4.4	4.1	3.6	5.8	5.8	4.4	5.4	6.7
65 and over	3.6	4.9	4.6	1.7	4.8	3.9	3.4	5.0	6.3	4.1	4.8	6.1

SOURCE: U.S. Bureau of Labor Statistics.
[a] Pre-1957 data based on old definitions of unemployment.

and over is reduced substantially by voluntary and "forced" labor-force withdrawal.

Among females unemployment rates, although also highest for teen-agers, drop continuously for each older age group, with no reversal in middle age. The basic explanation is that women much more often than men will withdraw from the labor force when jobs are scarce, even before they reach retirement age. Table 2-4 shows the differing patterns, the data

TABLE 2-4: UNEMPLOYMENT RATES FOR MEN AND WOMEN, BY AGE, 1957-61 (AVER-AGE OF ANNUAL AVERAGES)

Age Groups	Men	Women
All	5.6	6.1
16–17	15.7	15.5
18–19	15.3	12.7
20–24	9.8	8.2
25–29	5.7	6.9
30–34	4.4	6.0
35–39	4.0	5.5
40–44	4.0	4.9
45–49	4.3	4.5
50–54	4.4	4.1
55–59	4.6	4.0
60–64	5.0	3.9
65–69	5.6	3.9

SOURCE: U.S. Bureau of Labor Statistics.

being the averages of unemployment experience over two business-cycle periods. The averages show that women under age twenty-five and over age fifty have had lower unemployment rates than men, but that men between the ages of twenty-five and fifty have had lower rates than women.

B. COLOR

For many years nonwhite workers have been much more subject to unemployment than have white workers. A combination of discriminatory hiring practices and low levels of educational attainment have meant that Negroes and other nonwhites are heavily concentrated in manual and other relatively low-skill jobs, which have a high incidence of unemployment. Even if discrimination were eliminated overnight, it would be many years before Negroes

could attain the same educational, occupational, and employment distributions as whites.

In recent years the unemployment of nonwhites relative to that of whites has actually worsened. This presumably reflects the high over-all levels of unemployment in the economy rather than an increase in discrimination. Nonetheless, it is an important social fact that the differential between white and nonwhite unemployment for both men and women has been greater since the 1954 recession than it was in earlier years. Between 1948 and 1954 the unemployment rate of nonwhite men was about half again as high as that of white men; since 1955 it has been more than twice as high. For women, the change has been less but in the same direction.

C. EDUCATIONAL ATTAINMENT

The occupational level of workers is dictated to a large extent by the amount of formal schooling they have had. A large majority of farm workers, service workers, and nonfarm manual workers below the craftsman level have had less than high-school education. Because unemployment and underemployment among these occupational groups are relatively high, there is also a close relationship between the education of workers and the amount of unemployment they experience. In 1962 the unemployment rate for workers aged eighteen and over was almost 10 per cent for those with less than five years of school, about 7 per cent for those who finished elementary school, 5 per cent for high school graduates, and 1.5 per cent for college graduates.[26]

Failure to complete high school is becoming a more serious handicap in the labor market as the general level of education rises and as employers raise hiring requirements. In October, 1962, youths who had dropped out of high school or grade school during the year had an unemployment rate of 29 per cent, as compared with 14 per cent for the June, 1962, high-school graduates who had entered the labor force.[27]

[26] *Manpower Report of the President, 1964* (n. 23), p. 31.
[27] Jacob Shiffman, "Employment of High School Graduates and Dropouts in 1962," *Monthly Labor Review* (July, 1963), p. 775.

The school dropout is more likely than the graduate to become unemployed, to remain unemployed for a long time, and to obtain a low-level, low-paying job when he does find work.

Since the Current Population Survey does not obtain data regularly on the educational attainment of workers, it is impossible to discover short-run changes in the educational composition of the unemployed; sufficient data do exist, however, to show that educational deficiencies as well as discrimination contribute to the job-seeking difficulties of some groups, particularly older workers and Negroes.

As of early 1962, 39 per cent of the male workers and 49 per cent of the female workers who were forty-five to sixty-four years of age had completed at least four years of high school; but among workers eighteen to thirty-four years old 63 per cent of the men and 72 per cent of the women had completed that much schooling. The tabulations of the 1962 study show, in general, that in each age group unemployment is higher for those with less education than for the better educated. At all educational levels, unemployment rates were lower for older than for younger workers.[28] Nevertheless, the lower average levels of education among older workers is a factor contributing to their unemployment. Larger proportions of the older than of the younger unemployed are likely to have relatively low levels of education.[29] Case-study data, however, suggest that age as such contributes more to continued unemployment for older workers than does their level of formal education; older workers are likely to be handicapped in job search, regardless of education, whereas better-educated workers in the prime age groups are much more successful in job search than those with less schooling.[30]

A similar situation exists with respect to color. Larger proportions of nonwhites than of whites have low levels of educational attainment. As of early 1962, nearly 70 per cent of the white population compared with only 42 per cent of the nonwhite population in the twenty-five to twenty-nine year age group had completed high school. At all educational levels (except for males with less than eight years of school) nonwhites had substantially higher rates of unemployment than whites. Much evidence exists, however, to show that lack of education is only one of the causes of the high unemployment rates among nonwhites. For example, at any given educational level Negroes are much more likely than whites to be in occupations of lower skill and status and with lower pay.[31] If Negroes were in jobs matched to their education to the same degree as whites, their unemployment rates would be substantially lower than they have been though still higher than those of the better-educated white workers.

D. Occupation and Industry of Previous Employment

When an experienced worker becomes unemployed, the immediate "cause" is the temporary or permanent loss of a job in a particular occupation or industry. More often than not, the worker will seek to return to work in the same occupation and/or industry. Unemployment data with these breakdowns therefore show both something about where unemployment is being generated and something about the types of jobs needed to reduce unemployment. Also, since some groups, such as youths, older workers, Negroes, and workers with low levels of education, are concentrated in industries or occupations that have a relatively

---

[28] Denis F. Johnston, "Educational Attainment of Workers, March, 1962," *Monthly Labor Review* (May, 1963), pp. 505–6, 513. For an earlier study see Arnold Katz, "Educational Attainment of Workers, 1959," *Monthly Labor Review* (February, 1960), pp. 114, 117.

[29] *Illinois Job Seekers Survey* (Illinois Department of Labor, Chicago, Illinois, 1962), pp. 28–30.

[30] See Richard C. Wilcock and Walter H. Franke, *Unwanted Workers* (New York: The Free Press of Glencoe, 1963), chap. 3.

[31] Johnston, "Educational Attainment of Workers" (n. 28), pp. 506, 510–15. See also Katz, "Educational Attainment of Workers" (n. 28), pp. 119–20. The labor-market handicap of nonwhites is further illustrated by the fact that the income differential between whites and nonwhites increases with the level of educational attainment; see Herman P. Miller, *Income of the American People* (New York: Wiley, 1955), pp. 42–48.

TABLE 2-5: UNEMPLOYMENT RATES, BY MAJOR OCCUPATION GROUP, SEX, AND COLOR, 1959–1961 (AVERAGE OF ANNUAL AVERAGES)

Major occupation group	Unemployed as per cent of civilian labor force in each category				
	Total	Men	Women	White	Nonwhite
Total, experienced workers	5.3	5.2	5.5	4.7	9.9
Professional, technical, and kindred workers	1.8	1.8	1.9	1.8	3.3
Farmers and farm managers	0.3	0.4	a	0.3	1.0
Managers, officials, and proprietors	1.5	1.4	1.9	1.4	3.7
Clerical and kindred workers	4.0	3.9	4.1	3.8	7.7
Sales workers	4.0	3.1	5.6	3.9	7.7
Craftsmen, foremen, and kindred workers	5.6	5.6	6.4	5.4	10.1
Operatives and kindred workers	8.4	7.4	11.0	7.8	12.2
Private household workers	5.2	4.6	5.2	3.4	7.3
All other service workers	6.6	6.6	6.6	5.6	10.2
Farm laborers and foremen	5.3	6.2	3.7	4.3	8.2
Laborers, except farm and mine	13.1	13.1	15.1	12.0	15.9

SOURCE: U.S. Bureau of Labor Statistics, *Monthly Labor Review* (May, 1960); (April, 1961); and (June, 1962).
a Less than 0.05 per cent.

high incidence of joblessness, trends in unemployment originating in occupations and industries are relevant to the unemployment problems of these groups. Further, continued high unemployment in certain occupations and industries may be an indication that the workers involved are unable to shift to other occupations and industries either because of location or their lack of skills.

Table 2-5 shows unemployment rates for major occupation groups, for men as compared with women, and whites as compared with non-

whites. In recent years manual workers and service workers have had the highest rates of unemployment. Women tend to have higher rates than men in all major occupation groups. Nonwhites have much higher rates than whites, the rates for nonwhites ranging from one-third higher (nonfarm laborers) to more than twice as high (farmers, nonfarm managers, clerks, domestics).

Data on changes during the postwar period show that unskilled workers (both farm and nonfarm) and clerical workers have been the

TABLE 2-6: UNEMPLOYMENT RATES BY SELECTED MAJOR INDUSTRY GROUPS, IN FOUR BUSINESS CYCLES (SEASONALLY ADJUSTED QUARTERLY AVERAGES)

Industry group a	1948–1950			1953–1955			1957–1958			1960–1961		
	4th '48	4th '49	2nd '50	3rd '53	3rd '54	1st '55	3rd '57	2nd '58	4th '58	2nd '60	1st '61	3rd '61
Construction	8.2	13.6	11.6	6.3	11.3	9.7	10.0	14.6	14.0	11.8	14.1	14.3
Durable goods mfg.	3.6	8.5	5.7	1.6	6.9	4.7	4.9	11.5	9.1	5.8	9.7	8.1
Nondurable goods mfg.	3.4	7.6	6.5	2.8	6.4	5.2	5.5	8.2	6.9	5.3	7.1	7.1
Transportation and utilities	3.0	6.6	4.3	1.8	5.2	4.2	3.1	6.7	4.6	3.8	5.1	5.0
Wholesale and retail trade	4.2	6.5	6.4	2.9	5.9	4.7	4.4	7.2	6.6	5.8	6.7	7.5
Government	1.5	3.3	3.3	1.3	2.4	1.9	2.2	3.4	2.6	2.4	2.6	3.1

SOURCE: U.S. Bureau of Labor Statistics.
a Data are for experienced wage and salary workers. Pre-1957 data based on old definitions of unemployment.

most vulnerable to labor-displacing techno-logical change. The increase in unemployment rates between 1948 and 1962 has been greatest for the unskilled in the blue-collar group and for the clerical workers in the white-collar group.

Blue-collar workers have always been much harder hit during a recession than either white-collar or service workers. During recoveries, however, unemployment falls more rapidly among blue-collar workers. In the slow re-covery from the 1960 recession, blue-collar unemployment fell but unemployment for clerical, sales, and service workers continued to rise for many months after the recession's low point.

Industrial patterns of unemployment are of lesser concern than occupational patterns be-cause mobility between industries is more prevalent than between occupations; but the data are useful because they show the industry groups that tend to "create" unemployment and those that are most vulnerable to cyclical fluctuations. Factory workers in durable-goods manufacturing are usually hit first and hardest at the outset of a recession, followed in timing and intensity by mine workers and transportation workers. All industry groups are affected to some degree by recessions, but the finance and service industries and govern-ment and agriculture are influenced the least. In the 1961–63 recovery, reduction in un-employment rates was slow in all industry groups. Table 2–6 shows the patterns for a number of industry groups in four postwar business cycles.

E. Family Status

When one considers the impact of unemploy-ment on the nation's economic health and the utilization of the nation's manpower resources, the unemployment of a breadwinner does not differ from that of a secondary family worker. When, however, the focus is on the relative needs of the unemployed—for financial assist-ance, job retraining, placement—the family or household relationship can be important in the establishment of priorities. In order to provide more information on this aspect of the un-employment problem, the MRLF began, as of January, 1963, to include statistics on the household relationship of the unemployed.

In December, 1963, among the 3.8 million unemployed, 1.7 million (45 per cent) were heads of households. Among the 2.1 million unemployed who were not heads of households, 620,000 were wives of heads and 1.5 million were other relatives of the head (married children, parents, teen-agers living at home, and others). The incidence of unemployment dif-fered markedly according to family status. The unemployment rate was 5.3 per cent for all groups, 11.7 per cent for single men, but only 3.6 per cent for married men.[32]

F. Effect of Labor-Force Changes on Unemployment

Two basic labor-force changes, the shift of farm workers into nonfarm jobs and the in-creased participation of women in the labor force, would lead one to expect higher rates of unemployment. It seems, however, that be-tween 1948 and 1956 these shifts added only an estimated 180,000 to the ranks of the un-employed.[33] The offsetting nature of changes in the age-sex, industrial, and occupational compositions of the labor force led to the conclusion in a 1961 Bureau of Labor Statistics analysis that these shifts have had "no sig-nificant impact on the over-all rate of un-employment or on the average duration of unemployment."[34]

The effect of changes in the age composition of the labor force during the next decade may be significant, however, because of the sub-stantially higher proportions of both older and younger workers who will be in the labor force. If postwar unemployment rates are applied to the projected age composition of the labor

[32] *Monthly Report on the Labor Force* (December, 1963), p. 22, Table A–5.
[33] Bureau of Labor Statistics, "The Extent and Nature of Frictional Unemployment," Study Paper No. 6, prepared for Study on Employment, Growth, and Price Levels, Joint Economic Committee (86th Cong., 1st Sess., 1959), pp. 62–64.
[34] Stein and Kellogg, "Unemployment in the Early 1960's" (*n.* 21), p. 70.

force, the over-all rate of unemployment may increase by at least half of one per cent by 1975 as a result of these factors alone.[35]

V. INCOME OF THE UNEMPLOYED

No current series of data provides information on either the incomes or the income losses of unemployed individuals and their families. We know that, in general, those in lower-paid occupations are more likely to experience unemployment and to be unemployed for longer periods than those in more highly-paid occupations. For many workers, therefore, low incomes are a product of low levels of pay when working and also of the loss of income while not working.

Once a year the Bureau of the Census publishes data from the household survey on the annual incomes of families and individuals. Thus, in February, 1963, a report was issued which relates employment status in March, 1962, to annual incomes for 1961.[36] As an analysis of the income of the unemployed, the report is of limited usefulness because it does not compare unemployment experience in 1961 with income earned in that year.

The *BLS Survey of the Unemployed* measured more directly the impact of unemployment on income and standards of living.[37] The 9.6 million persons unemployed a month or longer in 1961 averaged $2,300 in income from all sources, an amount nearly 40 per cent lower than the $3,700 average income for all other persons with income who had some work experience during the year. Persons employed the entire year primarily at full-time jobs averaged $5,000 in income; only one of every eight of the unemployed reached this income level. Because the unemployed had lower earnings than the year-round worker even when working ($70 as compared with $95 per week),

not all of the difference in yearly income can be attributed to unemployment. Also, about one-fifth of the jobless were out of the labor force during part of the year.

Of income received in 1961 by the unemployed covered in the study, about 80 per cent came from their own wages and salaries, 12 per cent from unemployment insurance, and most of the remaining 8 per cent from welfare and pension programs. Approximately 95 per cent of the unemployed earned some wage income during the year, somewhat over half reported receipt of unemployment insurance payments, and the percentage receiving income from other sources ranged between 8 per cent from supplementary unemployment benefits and 1.5 per cent from private pensions. Income from wages averaged about $1,900 and from all other combined sources about $500 during the year.

About half (55 per cent) of these jobless were family heads financially responsible for other persons.[38] Since the economic consequences of unemployment are likely to be most severe in families in which the head is unemployed, the following discussion focuses on the situation of such persons.

The average income of these families in 1961 was $4,100. This compares with $5,700 for all families and $6,900 for families in which the head was a year-round, full-time worker. The average loss of potential earnings through unemployment was estimated at about $1,100 to $1,300 for the year.[39] About 3.4 million of the 5.3 million unemployed family heads received unemployment compensation; these benefits offset about two-fifths of the earnings lost by those who were beneficiaries. For the 5.3 million families in which the head experienced five or more weeks of unemployment, the head's wage income accounted for nearly three-fifths of total family income; non-wage income, principally unemployment insurance,

[35] Bureau of Labor Statistics, "The Extent and Nature of Frictional Unemployment" (*n.* 33), p. 64.

[36] *Income of Families and Persons in the United States: 1961*, Current Population Reports: Consumer Income, Series P-60, No. 39 (Bureau of the Census, Department of Health, Education, and Welfare, Washington, D.C., Feb. 28, 1963).

[37] Stein, "Work History" (*n.* 24), pp. 1409–13.

[38] An additional 25 per cent were individuals responsible for their own support, and 17 per cent were wives of family heads.

[39] The estimate accounts for difference in wage levels of different groups and the average duration of unemployment of fifteen to sixteen weeks. See Stein, "Work History" (*n.* 24), p. 1412.

and the earnings of other family members accounted for two-fifths. In a high proportion of families, living standards could not be maintained from available current income. Families with an unemployed head supplemented current income primarily with savings (51 per cent), borrowed funds (27 per cent), help from friends and relatives outside the household (20 per cent), and cash assistance from welfare agencies (7 per cent). In only 12 per cent of the families where the head was unemployed did other members of the family enter the labor force as a direct result of the head's unemployment.

A wealth of detail on the relationship between unemployment and the factors of income and educational attainment will be available from the 1960 decennial census data. The Bureau of Labor Statistics has published some of this information for thirty-six cities, including all cities with a 1960 population of a half million or more, plus a few smaller cities.[40] The reports contain statistics both for the cities and for neighborhoods (census tracts) on median family income, median educational attainment, and the unemployment rates for males. The data show, for quartiles, the relationship between each of the variables and the other two.

VI. LOCATION OF THE UNEMPLOYED

Unemployment, whether measured by incidence, duration, or seasonality, differs substantially among regions, states, and communities. These geographical differences are of considerable importance for programs of aid, most of which apply to and are controlled by the states and localities. Both the social philosophy and the economic ability of these political divisions are crucial factors in the development of many programs of aid for the unemployed.

As shown in Table 2–7, the 1958–62 average rate of insured unemployment ranged from

10.0 per cent in Alaska to 2.0 per cent in the District of Columbia; and the average rate of estimated total unemployment for the same years ranged from 11.7 per cent in West Virginia to 3.1 per cent in Iowa. About 20 per cent of covered workers live in states whose average unemployment rate has been 6.5 per cent or higher; 40 per cent live in states whose average rate has been 4.5 per cent or lower.

Even with such sizable geographic differences in the severity of unemployment, a very significant conclusion to be drawn from the data is that the unemployment problem has spread widely throughout the economy. Although there are the so-called pockets of very high levels of unemployment, there are also only relatively scattered pockets of satisfactorily low levels of unemployment. Among the fifty-two political units shown in Table 2–7, only nine had average insured unemployment rates of less than 3.5 per cent from 1958 through 1962, and only four had average total unemployment rates of less than 4.0 per cent during the same years. The widespread dispersion of high levels of unemployment is indicated further by the fact that in December, 1963, after almost three years of recovery from the 1960 recession, there were 17 major labor-market areas, 97 smaller areas, and 460 very small areas with "substantial and persistent unemployment."[41]

Large seasonal swings in unemployment are more localized than are average unemployment rates. The difference between the low and high rates in each state (Table 2–7, col. 5) reflects chiefly seasonal forces. Some industries which are concentrated geographically, such as apparel and automobiles, have substantial seasonal variations in their employment levels. Unemployment in the Detroit area for years has been greatly affected by seasonal layoffs in the automobile and related industries. Both construction and agricultural employment are highly seasonal and may have a relatively great

---

[40] "Income, Education, and Unemployment in Neighborhoods," series of separate reports for 36 cities, 1963. (Bureau of Labor Statistics, Department of Labor, Washington, D.C.)

[41] *Area Labor Market Trends* (December, 1963), p. 2. The term "substantial and persistent unemployment" is used by the Bureau of Employment Security to designate areas that not only have 6.0 per cent or more unemployment but also have been at least 50 per cent above the national average for three of the preceding four years.

TABLE 2–7: INSURED UNEMPLOYMENT RATES, AVERAGE AND RANGE, RANKED FROM HIGHEST TO LOWEST, AND TOTAL UNEMPLOYMENT RATE, FIVE-YEAR AVERAGES, 1958–1962

State or other political division	Per cent of covered employment in each state	Monthly average insured unemployment rate	Rank by monthly average rate	Annual range of monthly average rate	Rank by annual range	Estimated total unemployment rate
(1)	(2)	(3)	(4)	(5)	(6)	(7)
United States	100.0	5.1		4–7		6.0
Alabama	1.3	5.7	16	5–7	43	6.4[a]
Alaska	.1	10.0	1	4–19	1	9.8[a]
Arizona	.6	4.3	33	3–6	47	5.2
Arkansas	.7	6.8	6	4–11	6	6.4
California	9.7	5.5	17	4–8	29	6.0
Colorado	.9	2.8	48	2–5	39	4.1
Connecticut	1.8	4.9	27	4–7	37	6.6[b]
Delaware	.3	3.7	41	2–6	21	5.1
D.C.	.6	2.0	52	1–3	50	n.a.
Florida	2.3	3.9	38	3–5	50	5.2
Georgia	1.9	4.5	32	3–6	44	n.a.
Hawaii	.4	2.8	47	2–4	49	3.7
Idaho	.3	5.1	24	2–10	5	5.6
Illinois	6.5	3.9	39	3–6	39	5.4
Indiana	2.7	4.1	35	2–6	25	6.1
Iowa	1.1	2.6	51	1–5	32	3.1
Kansas	.9	3.3	44	2–6	27	4.1
Kentucky	1.1	7.3	4	5–10	13	n.a.
Louisiana	1.3	5.1	25	4–7	46	6.5[a]
Maine	.5	7.5	3	5–11	11	6.8
Maryland	1.7	5.0	26	4–7	32	5.9
Massachusetts	3.8	5.2	23	4–7	35	5.9
Michigan	4.2	6.6	10	4–11	7	9.1
Minnesota	1.7	4.6	31	2–8	12	5.9
Mississippi	.7	5.9	14	4–9	17	5.6[b]
Missouri	2.4	4.2	34	3–6	37	n.a.
Montana	.3	6.7	7	2–13	3	n.a.
Nebraska	.6	3.0	46	1–5	20	3.1
Nevada	.2	5.4	18	3–9	14	5.8
New Hampshire	.4	4.7	29	3–7	29	4.4
New Jersey	3.9	6.0	12	4–8	23	n.a.
New Mexico	.4	3.9	40	3–6	39	n.a.
New York	12.2	5.4	19	4–7	35	5.7[b]
N. Carolina	2.3	4.8	28	3–7	21	n.a.
North Dakota	.2	5.3	21	1–12	2	4.6
Ohio	5.8	4.7	30	3–7	25	6.0
Oklahoma	.9	5.4	20	4–7	32	5.0
Oregon	.9	5.8	15	3–11	4	5.8
Pennsylvania	7.2	7.3	5	6–10	27	9.0
Puerto Rico	.6	6.7	8	6–8	48	n.a.
Rhode Island	.6	6.0	13	4–9	18	8.1
S. Carolina	1.1	4.0	37	3–6	44	4.8
S. Dakota	.2	2.7	50	1–7	10	2.9
Tennessee	1.6	6.1	11	4–9	19	6.3
Texas	4.4	3.1	45	2–4	50	5.0
Utah	.5	3.5	43	2–6	23	4.7
Vermont	.2	5.2	22	3–8	14	5.8
Virginia	1.8	2.7	49	2–5	39	4.3
Washington	1.5	6.7	9	4–11	7	6.3
West Virginia	.8	8.2	2	6–11	14	11.7[b]
Wisconsin	2.1	3.6	42	2–6	31	4.3
Wyoming	.2	4.1	36	2–8	9	n.a.

SOURCE: U.S. Bureau of Employment Security and state employment security agencies.

[a] Four-year average.

[b] Three-year average.

39

effect where either forms a large component of total employment. Northern states of the Midwest and West Coast, which are for the most part agricultural, experience large seasonal variations in unemployment because of the severity of the winter weather. Alaska, Washington, Oregon, Idaho, Montana, Wyoming, and the Dakotas, all show this pattern. Alaska, with a spread of fifteen points, has the widest annual range of unemployment rates; the District of Columbia, Florida, and Texas, with a spread of only two points, have the narrowest annual range. For the nation as a whole, seasonal unemployment has been estimated at about one-fifth of total unemployment.[42] The extent to which unemployment is seasonal has great relevance for state programs of unemployment insurance and for local programs of relief.

Differences within a state are likely to be at least as great as the differences between states. In Ohio, for example, in 1962 the insured unemployment rates (yearly averages) of the state's eighty-eight counties varied from 2.2 per cent to 27.4 per cent and were distributed as follows:

VII. RECOMMENDATIONS FOR IMPROVED AND ADDITIONAL UNEMPLOYMENT STATISTICS

In its comprehensive report *Measuring Employment and Unemployment* published in September, 1962, the President's Committee to Appraise Employment and Unemployment Statistics made many recommendations for improvement in the labor-force statistics of the United States. The major recommendations on the question of which workers should be considered unemployed have already been discussed above under the heading "Who Is Counted as Unemployed?" The committee further recommended that information be obtained on the number of unemployed who are seeking part-time rather than full-time jobs (this is now being done) and that detailed data be acquired "on the circumstances under which those not in the labor force would look for jobs, on their previous work experience, on their education and training, and so on."[43] Information on the number of hours of work wanted would help in computations of labor-force time lost; and the data on those not in the

Unemployment rate	2.2–3.0	3.1–4.0	4.1–5.0	5.1–6.0	6.1–7.0	7.1–9.0	10.1–14.0	16.1–28.0
Number of Countries	10	20	14	14	8	11	5	6

Intrastate differences are especially relevant to programs of relief and, more recently, to programs of retraining.

Many states, to provide additional guidance for programs to aid the unemployed, have stepped up the collection of data on the number and characteristics of unemployed persons. The establishment of the Area Redevelopment Administration has led to the collection of more data in areas of high unemployment as part of the process of certifying areas for redevelopment assistance and retraining programs.

labor force would provide information about the extent to which workers had withdrawn from active job search because of the scarcity of jobs.

Although data are tabulated on the large flow of individuals in and out of the labor force and in and out of the unemployed category ("gross changes in the labor force"), they are not published because they do not meet a sufficiently high standard of reliability. The committee recommends not only the development of gross-change data sufficiently reliable to be published but also special studies on why these groups enter and leave the labor force. Since many of

[42] *Manpower Report of the President, 1963* (n. 23), p. 53.

[43] President's Committee, *Measuring Employment* (n. 4), p. 15.

those who move in and out of the labor force are secondary earners and have a marginal labor-force attachment, it is recommended that monthly data be published on the income and current employment activity of family members. Such data on family income and on decisions to enter, leave, or stay out of the labor force could help answer such questions as whether there is "hidden unemployment" resulting from perceived scarcity of jobs, whether unemployment of breadwinners and the resulting impact on family incomes bring secondary workers into the labor force, the extent to which workers permanently displaced from jobs are leaving the labor force, and the degree to which changing skill requirements affect movement in and out of the labor force. The committee has commented on the need for these data: "Programs to absorb the unemployed into gainful activity may have to take account of those outside the labor force as an active source of workers competing with the unemployed for new jobs."[44]

The committee has also recommended special surveys "to measure the uneven impact of unemployment on special groups in the population —the aged, the inexperienced, the untrained, and the nonwhite worker."[45] Such information would assist in the evaluation of the effectiveness of special placement and training programs designed to help those most disadvantaged in the labor market.

[44] *Ibid.*, p. 71.
[45] *Ibid.*, p. 83. Rees, "The Measurement of Unemployment" (*n.* 7), p. 35, has recommended regular surveys of the standard of living and sources of financial support among the unemployed.

CHAPTER 3

The Long-Term Unemployed

*Walter H. Franke**

CURRENT CONCERN ABOUT the problem of long-term unemployment and the long-term unemployed arises for a number of reasons. The number of long-term jobless and their proportion among all of the unemployed have been higher in recent years than in the earlier postwar years. The financial impact of lengthy unemployment is likely to be much more severe than that of short-term unemployment. The longer a person is out of work, the harder it becomes to find a new job on his own initiative. Finally, some types of aid that are appropriate for the short-term unemployed are not adequate for the long-term unemployed, who require special programs.

Many of the above factors have caused similar concern about depressed areas, where there is chronic or persistent unemployment. The unemployment in these areas requires some types of aid that are different from those appropriate for unemployment elsewhere.

The major purpose of this chapter is to present data on those characteristics of the long-term jobless which are relevant to a consideration of appropriate policies for aiding the long-term unemployed in the nation as a whole and in areas where unemployment has been high for extended periods of time.

I. THE MEASUREMENT OF LONG-TERM AND PERSISTENT UNEMPLOYMENT

The major source of information on the duration of unemployment is the household

survey data published each month by the Department of Labor in *The Monthly Report on the Labor Force* (MRLF).[1] The *MRLF* designates workers with fifteen or more weeks of continuous unemployment as "long-term" unemployed and those with twenty-seven or more weeks as "very long-term" unemployed.

Although these designations are, to some extent, arbitrary, they are significant. Unemployment of fifteen weeks or more probably signals the onset of a serious unemployment problem. Unemployment of over six months is especially significant because a six-months duration is the usual limit of unemployment insurance benefits, and the situation may require an additional kind of help other than the partial restoration of lost income.

Since August, 1961, the *MRLF* has classified the long-term and very long-term unemployed by various personal and work-history characteristics. For earlier periods, it is necessary to rely on special tabulations and reports, some of which are cited in the text.[2]

A fair amount of data is available on the geographical location of the unemployed (see Chapter 2). A complete count of all the unemployed in state and local areas is provided by

[1] See Chapter 2 for a description of the major sources of data on unemployment generally.

[2] Data on the characteristics of the long-term unemployed who are insured under the regular state unemployment insurance programs are available for each month since January, 1960, in *The Insured Unemployed*, published by the Bureau of Employment Security. While this series of data has certain uses and some advantages over the household survey data, it is not used in this chapter because it applies only to covered workers.

* Associate Professor, Institute of Labor and Industrial Relations, University of Illinois.

the population census every ten years. Data on the insured unemployed are provided by the state employment security agencies, which publish weekly data for states, labor-market areas, and even smaller localities with respect to new claims, claimants drawing benefits, and the insured unemployment rate.

State and local data on the characteristics of the long-term unemployed are not published regularly but are available only in special reports covering occasional periods. To date the most comprehensive report of this nature is the 1961–62 Bureau of Employment Security study of claimants under the temporary extended unemployment compensation (TEUC) program.[3] This and other special studies are cited in the text when used.

The main source of information for identifying the unemployed who are located in areas of persistent unemployment are the monthly unemployment rates published by the Bureau of Employment Security for 150 major labor-market areas (with a work force of 50,000 or more) and a greater number of smaller areas. The rates are estimates prepared by the state employment security agencies under the direction of the Bureau of Employment Security; the estimates are based on records of insured unemployed and other relevant information.[4]

The 150 major labor-market areas, which contain about 70 per cent of the nation's wage and salary workers, are classified each month into six labor-supply groupings. The groupings are designated by letters, from A to F. The rates of unemployment associated with each letter designation are as follows: A, less than 1.5 per cent; B, 1.5–2.9 per cent; C, 3.0–5.9 per cent; D, 6.0–8.9 per cent; E, 9.0–11.9 per cent; F, 12.0 per cent or more.[5] Areas classi- fied as D, E, and F are designated as areas of "substantial" labor surplus. A labor market is designated as an area of "substantial and persistent" labor surplus if the unemployment rate is 6.0 per cent or higher and the average unemployment rate in the area has been above the national average for an extended period of time.[6]

Smaller areas (with work forces as low as 15,000) are listed as "smaller areas of sub- stantial unemployment" whenever they come to the attention of the Bureau of Employment Security, usually by a state or locality requesting a labor-market study. Very small areas are classified if they have both substantial and persistent unemployment and are recommended to the Department of Commerce for considera- tion under the Area Redevelopment Act.[7]

II. EXTENT OF THE PROBLEM OF LONG-TERM UNEMPLOYMENT

A. Trends in Long-Term Unemployment

Although dependable data on the duration of unemployment have been available for only about twenty years, and published data on the characteristics of the long-term unemployed for even fewer years, the phenomenon of long- duration unemployment is not new. In a history of the American worker, Irving Bernstein notes the concern with widespread and pro- longed unemployment during the nineteen- twenties. He cites a 1929 study in Buffalo which "showed 10 per cent of the labor force totally unemployed and an additional 6.5 per cent on part time. Half of the men and almost two-thirds of the women had been out of work more than ten weeks." He also cites an

[3] *Family Characteristics of the Long-Term Un- employed*, BES Nos. U-207-1, January, 1962; U-207-2, April, 1962; U-207-3, September, 1962; U-207-4, January, 1963; U-207-5, March, 1963; U-207-6, June, 1963; and U-207-7, December, 1963 (Bureau of Employment Security, U.S. Department of Labor, Washington, D.C.).

[4] For a description of the estimating procedure, see *Handbook on Estimating Unemployment* (Bureau of Employment Security, U.S. Department of Labor, Washington, D.C., March, 1960).

[5] For a description of other classification criteria used in classifying areas, see any recent issue of *Area Labor Market Trends*, published by the Bureau of Employment Security.

[6] Fifty per cent above for three out of the last four years, or 75 per cent above for two out of the last three years, or 100 per cent above for one out of the last two years.

[7] The classifications are published in *The Labor Market and Employment Security* and in *Area Labor Market Trends*, both publications of the Bureau of Employment Security.

Figure 3-1

Unemployment Rates, by Months, July 1948 to December 1963

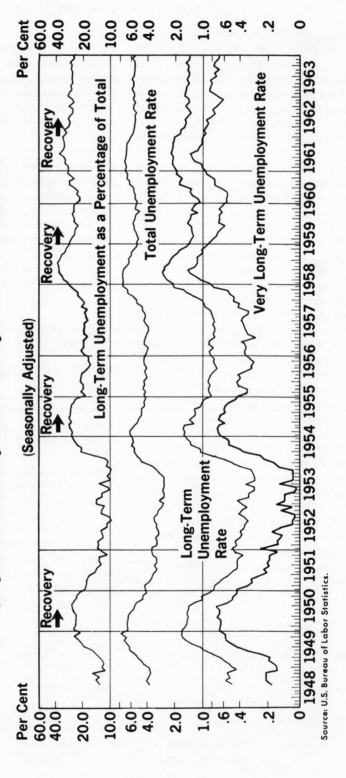

Source: U.S. Bureau of Labor Statistics.

estimate of unemployment due to automation in certain industries: "Between 1920 and 1929 in manufacturing, railways, and coal mining, machines displaced 3,272,000 men, of whom 2,269,000 were reabsorbed and 1,003,000 remained unemployed." Bernstein further points out that during the relatively prosperous nineteen-twenties older workers, Negroes, and other minority groups found it particularly difficult to hold or to find jobs.[8]

Extended joblessness during the nineteen-thirties was, of course, much more prevalent. August C. Bolino, in an analysis of trends in duration of unemployment, cites an estimate made by H. J. Winslow that "the percentage of long-term unemployed for 1932–1934 ranged from 74 to 76 per cent" and an estimate by H. Woll and C. R. Winegarden that as late as 1940 "the percentage [was] approximately 65 per cent." Using composites of periodic federal, state, and local samples of unemployment, Bolino himself estimates long-term unemployment at 44 per cent of total unemployment for the years 1885–1915, 46 per cent for 1921–30, 73 per cent for 1931–39, and 24 per cent for 1950–59. On the basis of these and other limited data available prior to World War II, Bolino concludes that beginning with the year 1885 "the percentage of long-term unemployment was at a consistently high level but declining slightly until the advent of World War II (the great Depression excluded)."[9]

Figure 3–1 shows a number of important aspects of long-term unemployment in the more recent postwar period. First, there has been a pronounced tendency for long-term and very long-term unemployment rates to rise. These rates, like the rates for total unemployment, have been higher in each successive prosperity period.

Second, rates of long-term and very long-term unemployment follow rather closely changes in national output as measured by gross national product (not shown in Figure 3–1). In periods of economic recovery, however, the rates do not drop as fast as national output rises.[10]

Third, the proportion of long-term unemployment to total unemployment has been higher in each successive prosperity period. Also, Bolino has shown that from 1947 through 1962 the average duration of unemployment was 11.6 weeks: duration averaged 10.3 weeks per spell of unemployment from 1947 through 1957 and 13.9 weeks from 1958 through 1962.[11] Stated comparatively, in recent years long-term unemployment has increased faster than has total unemployment. Between 1957 and 1962 total unemployment increased 36 per cent, short-term unemployment (less than 5 weeks) increased only about one-fifth, long-term unemployment doubled, and very long-term unemployment increased nearly two and one-half times. It should be noted, however, that during periods when total unemployment is rising, long-term unemployment can be expected to rise disproportionately.[12]

The tabulation on p. 46 shows the average duration of unemployment and the percentage of the long-term and very long-term unemployed among all the unemployed in selected postwar years.[13]

The increase in the average duration of unemployment in 1963 over the average duration in 1947 was only 4.2 weeks, but the proportion of very long-term unemployed was nearly double.

Finally, the data in Figure 3–1 and in the above tabulation indicate the magnitude of the extended joblessness that can be expected under various economic conditions. Between 1947

[8] *The Lean Years* (Boston: Houghton Mifflin Company, 1960), pp. 57–61.

[9] August C. Bolino, "The Duration of Unemployment: Some Historical Comparisons," unpublished manuscript of a study partially financed by a grant from the Upjohn Institute for Employment Research.

[10] See Richard C. Wilcock and Walter H. Franke, "Will Economic Growth Solve the Problem of Long-Term Unemployment?" *Proceedings of Fourteenth Annual Meeting* (Madison, Wisconsin: Industrial Relations Research Association, 1961), pp. 40–41.

[11] Bolino, "The Duration of Unemployment" (n. 9). The duration figures are based on the household sample survey data.

[12] See Wilcock and Franke, "Will Economic Growth Solve the Problem" (n. 10), for a discussion of the causes of higher rates of long-term unemployment in recent years.

[13] U.S. Department of Labor, *Manpower Report of the President* (Washington, D.C.: Government Printing Office, 1964), pp. 28, 203.

Year	Average duration of un-employment (in weeks)	Per cent of un-employed out of work 15 weeks or more	Per cent of un-employed out of work 27 weeks or more
1947	9.8	16.9	7.0
1948	8.6	13.3	5.0
1950	12.1	23.4	10.7
1952	8.3	12.1	4.4
1953	8.1	11.3	4.2
1954	11.7	22.7	8.9
1955	13.2	24.2	11.6
1956	11.3	18.9	8.2
1957	10.4	19.0	8.1
1958	13.8	31.0	14.2
1959	14.5	27.3	15.0
1960	12.8	24.3	11.5
1961	15.5	31.8	16.7
1962	12.9	27.9	14.6
1963	14.0	26.1	13.3

and 1963 the number of long-term unemployed varied from a yearly low average of 211,000 in 1953 (11.3 per cent of the total unemployed and 0.3 per cent of the civilian labor force) to a high of over 1.5 million in 1961 (31.8 per cent of the total unemployed and 2.1 per cent of the civilian labor force). Very long-term unemployment was also at its lowest and highest postwar levels during those two years: in 1953 an average of 79,000 persons were unemployed more than twenty-six weeks (4.2 per cent of the total unemployed and 0.1 per cent of the civilian labor force), and in 1961 an average of 804,000 persons were among the very long-term unemployed (16.7 per cent of the total unemployed and 1.1 per cent of the civilian labor force).

It can be expected, therefore, that in years of high employment the long-term and very long-term unemployed will constitute a small proportion of the total unemployed and of the labor force, but that in years of high unemployment the long-term and very long-term unemployed will constitute a substantial proportion of the total unemployed and of the labor force.

B. Long-Term Unemployment and the Extent of Financial Hardship

Appropriate policies of aid to the long-term unemployed depend partly on the kind and degree of hardship connected with long-term unemployment. Analysis of the relationship between long-term unemployment and hardship is hampered by the absence of any direct information available on a regular basis about the financial needs and resources of the long-term jobless. For the most part, it is necessary to infer the extent of hardship from the very limited data on the characteristics of the long-term unemployed. The most relevant characteristics are marital status and sex, breadwinner status, number of dependents, and, to a lesser extent, age.

Only since the beginning of 1963 has any regular governmental statistical series on unemployment shown the marital status of the long-term unemployed. Data for 1963 indicate that married men, who account for a little over half of the labor force, constitute only about one-third (33.9 per cent) of those unemployed for fifteen weeks or more. Single and "other" men, who comprise about 15 per cent of the labor force, also make up about a third of the long-term unemployed (31.8 per cent). Married women and all other women each comprise about the same proportion of the long-term unemployed as of the labor force—between 15 and 20 per cent.[14]

The marital status of the very long-term unemployed appears to differ little from that of the long-term jobless. The data for 1963 show that for both the long-term and the very long-term unemployed between 65 and 70 per cent were men and about one-third were married men. Married women comprised 13 per cent of those unemployed twenty-seven weeks or over and 16 per cent of those unemployed for fifteen weeks or more.[15]

[14] U.S. Department of Labor, *Monthly Report on the Labor Force* (January, 1964), p. 46, Table A–8.

[15] For earlier data and related discussions see Jane L. Meredith, "Long-Term Unemployment in the United States," *Monthly Labor Review* (June, 1961), p. 606 (reprinted as *Special Labor Force Report No. 17*, with additional tables). See also Jacob Schiffman, "Marital and Family Characteristics of Workers,

It is sometimes suggested that unemployment among married women, teen-agers, and workers over sixty-five years of age is of secondary importance because these groups have either limited financial responsibilities or sufficient resources to maintain themselves without employment.[16] Many workers in these groups do have irregular attachment to the labor force or are secondary earners, and they constitute substantial proportions of the long-term jobless. Data for 1962 indicate that unmarried teen-agers, married women, and workers age sixty-five and over constitute nearly two-fifths of all workers unemployed fifteen or more weeks. Also, they are nearly a third of the very long-term unemployed.[17] The data are not adequate however, to show the extent of hardship these "secondary earners" experience when they are out of work for extended periods.

Presumably, married men out of work for long periods of time suffer particular hardship because of their primary financial responsibility for the family. Some families, however, obtain help from the income of others in the family. Recent studies indicate that in more than a third of all families where the husband has been out of work fifteen weeks or more the wife is working. In about half of all husband-wife families where the family head is unemployed another member of the family is in the labor force.[18]

Some additional information on the family

status of the long-term jobless is available from the studies that the Bureau of Employment Security made in May and September, 1961, and January and April, 1962, of claimants under the temporary extended unemployment compensation program.[19] A little less than half of the claimants in the surveys were classified as primary earners.[20] If those who were living alone are added to the primary earners, about 60 per cent of all claimants can be designated as the "main" support of a household. In about one-third of the households in which the claimant was a primary earner there were others in the family who were working at the time of the survey. Among all claimants, slightly more than two out of five were either living alone or were members of households in which no other member was in the labor force. Most of the secondary earners and most of the claimants living alone had no dependents. Among the primary earners, nearly all had one or more dependents and 57 per cent had two or more.

Data on marital and breadwinner status provide only indirect clues to the hardship associated with long-term unemployment. It is apparent, however, that there are considerable differences in the economic circumstances of the long-term unemployed. The special April, 1962, survey which the Bureau of Labor Statistics made of the characteristics of the unemployed provides somewhat more direct evidence of the extent of hardship among the long-term jobless. Nearly one-third of the respondents with more than six months of unemployment in 1961 required cash or other forms of assistance from private or public welfare agencies in order to meet living expenses. The proportion increases to more than half if those who received assistance from friends or relatives outside the household are

---

March 1961," *Monthly Labor Review* (January, 1962 [reprinted as *Special Labor Force Report No. 20*]), and the same author and title with March, 1962 data, *Monthly Labor Review* (January, 1963 [reprinted as *Special Labor Force Report No. 26*]), for data on the marital status of the labor force.

[16] For a discussion of this question, see Robert L. Stein and Frazier Kellogg, "Unemployment in the Early 1960's," *Unemployment: Terminology, Measurement, and Analysis*, prepared for the Subcommittee on Economic Statistics, Joint Economic Committee (87th Cong., 1st Sess., 1961), p. 59.

[17] Data for single teen-agers and married women are from the *Monthly Report on the Labor Force* (January, 1964), p. 46. Data for workers age sixty-five and over are in Jane L. Meredith, "Labor Force and Employment, 1960–62," *Special Labor Force Report No. 31*, p. A–39.

[18] See Vera C. Perrella, "Marital and Family Characteristics of Workers, March 1963," *Monthly Labor Review* (February, 1964), pp. 155–56.

[19] *Family Characteristics of the Long-Term Unemployed*, BES No. U-207-4 (*n*. 3). Although the respondents in these surveys differ somewhat from the long-term unemployed generally, they are a major segment of the long-term jobless.

[20] The term primary earner was applied only to multiperson households. A primary earner was defined as the "main" support of the family when he was working. Nearly 90 per cent of the primary earners were men.

added.[21] A report of the TEUC studies, in preparation at this writing, will provide additional information, on a broad geographic basis, on the sources of income and economic adjustments of the long-term jobless.[22]

III. THE NATURE OF THE PROBLEM: WHO ARE THE LONG-TERM UNEMPLOYED?

The long-term unemployed may be described from two points of view. We may view the long-term unemployed as a group and describe their *composition*—that is, describe what proportion of them belong to various labor-force groups, such as young, old, men, women, nonwhite, manual workers, and so forth. Or we may look at the unemployed in various labor-force groups—young, old, men, women, nonwhite, manual workers, and so forth—and describe what proportion of the unemployed in these groups are long-term unemployed. This is to study the *incidence* of long-term unemployment. Both descriptions produce information useful in designing programs of aid for the long-term unemployed. For example, the composition of the long-term unemployed is an indication of their labor-force quality and their ability to fill potential job openings. Likewise, the incidence of long-term unemployment identifies the groups among the unemployed who have a particularly difficult time finding new jobs when they become unemployed. The analysis of the characteristics of the long-term unemployed that follows considers the problem from these two points of view.

A. COMPOSITION OF THE LONG-TERM UNEMPLOYED

The data in Table 3–1 show for the years 1957–63 the proportions of all the long-term

and very long-term jobless by selected characteristics. No general category of workers is immune from long-term unemployment, whatever the economic conditions. Young and old, white and nonwhite, men and women and workers from all major industrial and occupation groups, all are liable to long-term unemployment. This is the case when the level of long-term unemployment is very low, as in 1957, as well as when the level is high.

Some groups, however, carry a disproportionate share of the burden of long-term unemployment. Compared with their proportion in the labor force, long-term unemployment is high among young workers, nonwhite workers, blue-collar workers (particularly semiskilled operatives and unskilled laborers), workers last employed in goods-producing industries (particularly those in durable goods manufacturing, construction, and mining), and new entrants into the labor force (primarily teen-agers looking for their first jobs).

Also, we know from occasional special population surveys that a disproportionate number of the long-term jobless are persons with relatively little education. This results primarily from higher unemployment rates among those with less education. A more educated person is not as likely to become unemployed, but when he does, he remains out of work almost as long as the person with less formal schooling.[23] Nevertheless, in March, 1963, persons with less than a twelfth-grade education comprised about two-thirds of those out of work fifteen or more weeks, although they made up less than half of the labor force.[24]

Particularly high concentrations of long-term unemployment are found among nonwhites, unskilled laborers, and new entrants into the labor force. On the other hand, white-collar workers, farmers, and farm laborers are a relatively small part of the long-term unemployed. Although blue-collar workers and

[21] Robert L. Stein, "Work History, Attitudes, and Income of the Unemployed," *Monthly Labor Review* (December, 1963), p. 1413. Also see Chapter 2 for additional discussion of this study.

[22] This study is being done in thirteen states. See *Family Characteristics of the Long-Term Unemployed*, BES No. U-207-2 (*n.* 3), pp. 3–5, for a brief description of the temporary extended unemployment compensation research program.

[23] Denis F. Johnston, "Educational Attainment of Workers, March, 1962," *Special Labor Force Report No. 30*, p. 513.

[24] *Ibid.*, pp. A–8 and A–15. For data covering an earlier period, see Arnold Katz, "Educational Attainment of Workers, 1959," *Monthly Labor Review* (February, 1960), p. 119.

TABLE 3-1: COMPOSITION OF THE LONG-TERM UNEMPLOYED BY SELECTED CHARAC-
TERISTICS, 1957–1963[a], PER CENT DISTRIBUTION

Selected characteristics	Unemployed 15 weeks or more						Civilian labor force	
	1957	1958	1959	1960	1961	1963	1957	1963
Total Number (000)	560	1,452	1,040	956	1,532	1,088	67,946	72,975
Per cent	100.0	100.0	100.0	100.0	100.0	100.0	100	100
Men	68.9	72.7	71.0	69.5	69.3	65.7	68	66
Women	31.1	27.3	29.0	30.5	30.7	34.3	32	34
Under 25 years	23.0	23.3	24.8	26.3	25.1	27.7	17	19
25–44 years	35.2	41.8	37.5	36.0	37.3	34.4	45	42
45 years and over	41.8	34.8	37.7	37.6	37.5	37.8	38	39
Men	31.4	26.6	27.3	28.2	27.3	26.7	26	26
Women	10.4	8.2	10.4	9.4	10.2	11.1	12	13
White	77.4	78.0	75.7	75.1	77.5	74.0	89	89
Nonwhite	22.6	22.0	24.3	24.9	22.5	26.0	11	11
White-collar workers	17.1	16.1	19.2	18.3	19.0	20.9	40	43
Blue-collar workers	58.3	64.6	56.8	56.4	57.5	51.1	39	37
Craftsmen and foremen	11.0	13.7	12.4	11.7	13.6	11.4	13	13
Operatives	31.8	35.1	28.7	29.0	29.3	26.5	20	18
Nonfarm laborers	15.5	15.8	15.7	15.7	14.6	13.2	6	6
Service workers	13.4	10.5	12.3	12.3	12.2	13.4	12	13
Farm workers	2.7	2.0	2.9	3.0	1.8	2.4	9	7
No previous work experience	8.4	7.0	8.8	10.0	9.2	12.1	1	1
Goods-producing industries	54.6	57.5	51.7	50.0	50.4	45.2	n.a.	n.a.

Selected characteristics	Unemployed 27 weeks or more						Civilian labor force	
	1957	1958	1959	1960	1961	1963	1957	1963
Total Number (000)	239	667	571	454	804	553	67,946	72,975
Per cent	100.0	100.0	100.0	100.0	100.0	100.0	100	100
Men	70.0	73.6	72.6	72.2	70.7	69.3	68	66
Women	29.3	26.4	27.4	27.8	29.3	30.7	32	34
Under 25 years	17.1	21.3	21.5	22.4	21.1	25.1	17	19
25–44 years	34.4	40.4	37.8	35.0	36.8	31.8	45	42
45 years and over	48.5	38.4	40.6	42.6	42.2	43.1	38	39
Men	37.2	29.5	29.5	33.0	31.5	31.9	26	26
Women	11.3	8.9	11.1	9.6	10.7	11.2	12	13
White	75.9	77.0	73.8	74.0	76.4	71.8	89	89
Nonwhite	24.1	23.0	26.2	26.0	23.6	28.2	11	11
White-collar workers	17.7	15.8	18.9	17.4	19.0	20.8	40	43
Blue-collar workers	56.2	55.8	57.6	56.1	58.0	49.7	39	37
Craftsmen and foremen	9.8	12.4	11.7	11.2	12.6	10.7	13	13
Operatives	30.7	36.9	29.9	27.8	29.6	25.7	20	18
Nonfarm laborers	15.7	16.5	16.0	17.1	15.8	13.4	6	6
Service workers	14.6	10.6	11.7	13.2	12.8	14.5	12	13
Farm workers	3.2	1.7	3.2	2.2	1.2	2.0	9	7
No previous work experience	8.3	6.2	8.6	11.1	9.1	13.0	1	1
Goods-producing industries	53.1	58.8	53.2	46.9	50.6	41.0	n.a.	n.a.

SOURCE: U.S. Department of Labor, *Manpower Report of the President* (Washington, D.C.: Government Printing Office, 1964), pp. 203 and 204.   Civilian labor-force figures are from *Monthly Report on the Labor Force*.
    [a] Civilian labor-force figures for sex and age are monthly averages.   Figures for the remaining categories are for July.

49

service workers made up only half of the civilian labor force in 1963, they constituted nearly two-thirds of the very long-term unemployed.

It should be noted that the proportion that any group of workers bears to all of the long-term unemployed is the result of two factors: the incidence of unemployment on the particular group and the duration of unemployment among the unemployed in the group. The proportion may be small, for example, either because relatively few workers in the group experience unemployment at all or because those who do typically are out of work for only short periods. Both factors contribute to the small proportion of white-collar workers among the very long-term unemployed. Among these workers, the incidence of unemployment is low and the duration is short, with the result that in 1962 the chances were only 1 in 244 that a white-collar worker would be among the very long-term unemployed. For nonwhite workers, however, among whom incidence is high and duration long, the chances were 1 in 50. Thus, in 1962 a program of financial aid to the very long-term unemployed would have benefited about 1 out of 50 nonwhite workers and about 1 out of 244 white-collar workers. These ratios would depend, of course, on the nature of the program adopted.

The data have not been compiled often enough for an adequate cyclical analysis, but the indications are that the patterns of long-term unemployment are much the same under all economic conditions. In both good years and bad, older men, nonwhites, blue-collar workers, and new entrants constitute a disproportionate number of the long-term jobless. Older men, however, appear to form a greater proportion of the long-term jobless in times of prosperity than in times of recession. Blue-collar workers, on the other hand, as compared with other groups, tend to be harder hit in poor years than in good. This is particularly the case for workers in durable goods industries. In July, 1961, for example, when only 13 per cent of the employed were working in durable goods industries, 27 per cent of the very long-term unemployed had last worked in durable

goods manufacturing, and the proportion of auto and steel workers among the very long-term unemployed was almost four times their proportion in the labor force.[25] Nevertheless, over the business cycle the major occupational groups tend to maintain their relative positions.

Significant changes have occurred in the composition of the unemployed. Between 1957 and 1963 young workers under twenty-five years of age increased from 17 per cent to 19 per cent of the labor force but increased from 17.1 per cent to 25.1 per cent of those out of work for more than six months. By contrast, workers forty-five years and over are becoming a smaller proportion of the long-term jobless, particularly of those unemployed over six months. In 1963, however, older workers were still a somewhat larger proportion of the very long-term unemployed (43.1 per cent) than of the labor force (38.9 per cent).

In 1963, when only about one of ten in the labor force was nonwhite, nearly three of every ten workers unemployed for over six months were nonwhite; in 1957 about one of four workers unemployed for over six months was nonwhite. Measured by the extent of unemployment experienced, they are the most disadvantaged group in the labor market, and their position seems to be getting worse rather than better.

The proportion of blue-collar workers among both the long-term and the very long-term unemployed was substantially lower in 1963 than in 1957. The decline was limited, however, to the unskilled and the semiskilled; the proportion of skilled workers among those unemployed over six months actually increased. The decline in the proportion of blue-collar workers among the long-term unemployed is associated with the decline in employment in goods-producing industries, where many of the blue-collar workers are employed, and with the decline in the relative number of production workers in manufacturing. Employment in goods-producing industries, which was about 46 per cent of total employment in 1957, had

[25] U.S. Department of Labor, *Monthly Report on the Labor Force* (July, 1961), pp. 7–8.

declined to 40 per cent by 1963.[26] The smaller proportion of blue-collar workers among the long-term unemployed, in other words, is not due to lower unemployment rates or shorter duration of unemployment among them. As the data in Table 3–1 indicate, blue-collar workers are still a disproportionate part of the long-term jobless.

The proportion of service workers among the long-term jobless has changed very little during the six-year period 1957–63 and is only slightly above the proportion of service workers in the labor force. The proportions of white-collar workers and of new entrants among the long-term jobless have been edging upward.

It is difficult to reconcile recent changes in long-term unemployment among nonwhites with those among blue-collar and service workers. Nearly three-fourths of all nonwhite workers are in these two occupational groups, as compared with less than half of all whites. Yet, although the proportion of blue-collar and service workers among the long-term jobless has been declining, the proportion of nonwhites among all the long-term jobless has been increasing. The explanation may be that it has been more difficult for nonwhites than for whites to shift to other occupations when they become unemployed.

One of the difficulties in analyzing the composition of the long-term unemployed is that the long-term unemployed are not described by marital and family characteristics and are not adequately cross-classified by other personal characteristics.[27] Computations based on some rather rough assumptions suggest that the proportion of "disadvantaged" workers (including older, nonwhite, and poorly educated workers) among the long-term jobless changed little between 1957 and 1962. It appears that somewhat over two-thirds of the long-term and very long-term unemployed are either over forty-five years old, are nonwhite, have less than a ninth-grade education, or have some combination of these characteristics.[28]

B. INCIDENCE OF LONG-TERM UNEMPLOYMENT

The preceding section answered one question: How are the long-term unemployed divided among the various labor-force groups? This section is concerned with another question: Among workers in specific labor-force groups who become unemployed, what proportion become long-term unemployed before they find new jobs? The data in Table 3–2 show the incidence of long-term unemployment for 1957, 1960, and 1963 among unemployed workers in selected groups.

In each year and in each age group a larger proportion of unemployed men than of unemployed women experienced lengthy unemployment. The lower rates for women can be partly explained by the greater tendency of women to leave the labor force when they lose their jobs or after short periods of unemployment and by their greater representation in industries and occupations in which long-term unemployment is relatively low.

Among both men and women the older workers who lose their jobs remain unemployed longer than the younger workers. The age differential is particularly great among those unemployed for more than six months. Also, nonwhites among both men and women have longer unemployment than have whites. Since nonwhites also have more spells of unemployment during a year than have whites, nonwhites accumulate more weeks of unemployment in the course of a year.[29]

---

[26] U.S. Department of Labor, *Manpower Report of the President* (*n.* 13), p. 20. Also see *Manpower Report of the President, 1963*, pp. 26–27, for a discussion of changes in the pattern of blue-collar and white-collar employment.

[27] Published data are now cross-classified only by age and sex and color and sex. Examples of other useful cross-classifications would be age and color, color and occupation, and age and occupation. The sample on which the data are based is too small for most of these breakdowns.

[28] Computations were made for the years 1957 and 1960 and for July, 1962. To arrive at the number of older and nonwhite unemployed, computations started with the number of long-term jobless who are forty-five years and over and were based on the assumption that the remainder have the same white-nonwhite composition that the long-term unemployed have as a group. It was further assumed that the remainder of the long-term unemployed are distributed on educational levels like those of the eighteen to sixty-four age groups in the labor force as a whole.

[29] See *Study Paper No. 6* (Bureau of Labor Statistics, U.S. Department of Labor, Washington, D.C.), p. 19. Also see source cited in Table 3–2.

TABLE 3–2: THE INCIDENCE OF LONG-TERM UNEMPLOYMENT AMONG THE
UNEMPLOYED BY SEX, RACE, AND AGE

| | Per cent of total unemployed in each group | | | | | |
| | 1957 | | 1960 | | 1963 | |
Selected characteristics	15 weeks and over	27 weeks and over	15 weeks and over	27 weeks and over	15 weeks and over	27 weeks and over
Total	19.1	8.1	24.3	11.5	26.1	13.3
Males	20.4	8.9	26.1	12.9	28.2	15.1
14–24 years	13.7	4.4	19.4	8.0	20.1	9.7
25–44 years	18.8	8.0	25.4	12.1	27.8	13.6
45 years and over	29.1	14.7	34.4	19.1	39.1	23.8
Females	16.7	6.7	21.0	9.1	22.9	10.4
14–24 years	11.4	3.5	16.4	6.5	16.0	6.8
25–44 years	17.7	7.2	22.3	9.5	25.0	11.0
45 years and over	22.8	10.6	26.1	12.6	31.9	16.4
White	18.6	7.8	23.0	10.8	24.5	12.1
Males	19.7	8.6	24.7	11.9	26.5	13.9
Females	16.5	6.4	19.9	8.7	21.4	9.3
Nonwhite	21.4	9.6	29.7	14.8	32.0	17.6
Males	23.5	10.4	32.1	16.9	35.0	20.0
Females	17.5	8.1	25.2	11.0	27.9	14.4

SOURCE: Jane L. Meredith, "Long-Term Unemployment in the United States," Special Labor Force Report, No. 17 (reprinted from *Monthly Labor Review* [June, 1961]), pp. A-3 and A-4; and Bureau of Labor Statistics, "The Extent and Nature of Frictional Unemployment," Study Paper No. 6, prepared for Study on Employment, Growth, and Price Levels, Joint Economic Committee (86th Cong., 1st Session, 1959), pp. 15, 19. Data for 1963 are from *Monthly Report on the Labor Force* (January, 1964), p. 46.

Part of the longer unemployment of non-whites is attributable to their larger number in unskilled and other occupations in which long-term unemployment is relatively common. However, long-term unemployment is higher for nonwhites than whites in all occupations and industries.[30]

In addition to whatever discrimination older workers and nonwhites may suffer when they attempt to find jobs, many are further handicapped by low levels of education. Recent survey data on the educational level of the unemployed show that older workers and nonwhites have, on the average, less education than younger workers and whites. Among the long-term jobless in March, 1962, for example, about three-fourths of the nonwhites, compared with less than two-thirds of the whites, had less

than twelve years of schooling.[31] Thus, many of the long-term jobless suffer under the combined handicap of discriminatory hiring policies, low levels of education, and low levels of skill.

Long-term unemployment is by no means limited, however, to workers with very low levels of education. Over 25 per cent of the unemployed workers from which the Detroit manpower pilot project selected a sample of very long-term jobless (those with twenty-six weeks or more of continuous unemployment) consisted of workers with at least high-school diplomas.[32] On the average, however, the

[30] Meredith, "Long-Term Unemployment" (*n*. 15), p. 606.

[31] Johnston, "Educational Attainment of Workers" (*n*. 23), pp. 505–6, A-14, and A-15.

[32] "Detroit Area Manpower Development Pilot Project," p. 7. Unpublished manuscript provided by D. Garth Bartley, Project Director of the experimental action program being conducted by the Michigan Employment Security Commission to find solutions to the hard-core unemployment problem.

long-term jobless are at a much lower educational level than the work force generally. In March, 1962, about two-thirds of the long-term unemployed had completed less than twelve years of school; this was true for fewer than half of all members of the labor force age eighteen and over.[33]

Measurement and analysis of the industrial and occupational attachments of the long-term unemployed present problems more difficult than those associated with personal characteristics. Not only do workers often cross industrial and occupational lines rather easily, but data on duration of unemployment are available only for broad industrial and occupational groups. Workers in these groups come from such a wide diversity of jobs that the broad classifications conceal much of the divergent experiences of the unemployed. For these reasons, only the salient industrial and occupational differences can be summarized.[34]

The most notable fact about long-term unemployment among workers attached to different industries in their last job is that the proportion of long-term unemployment differs notably among only a few industries. In 1963, when 26.1 per cent of all the unemployed were unemployed for fifteen consecutive weeks or more, the incidence of long-term unemployment was lowest for unemployed agricultural workers (17.2 per cent) and service workers in private households (22 per cent). Those industry groups in which the incidence was above the all-industry average were transportation and public utilities (30.6 per cent), durable goods manufacturing (33.7 per cent), and public administration (40.2 per cent). The pattern for very long-term unemployment was much the same as for long-term.[35]

Although published data are not available on the incidence of long-term unemployment in detailed industrial classifications, it has been noted that in recent years "long-term unemployment has been especially severe in the metal and metalworking sectors of hard goods manufacturing (mainly steel, autos, and machinery) and in the textiles sector of soft goods manufacturing."[36] Thus a high incidence of long-term unemployment is associated with industries that have declining employment opportunities. In some cases, the unemployment problem has been complicated by the fact that some of these industries are located in areas where employment opportunities in general have been declining.

As in the case of the industrial classifications, the proportions of the long-term unemployed in the broad occupational groupings do not differ greatly from group to group. In 1963, among those occupations in which the proportion of long-term unemployment exceeded the all-industry average of 26.1 per cent, long-term unemployment was highest (32 per cent) among managers and proprietors. The blue-collar group (28.6 per cent) was the only other group that exceeded the average for all workers by as much as one percentage point. Unemployed farm workers had the lowest proportion (18 per cent) of workers unemployed for fifteen weeks or more. As with the industrial groups, the pattern was much the same for those with more than six months unemployment.

The incidence of long-term unemployment does not appear to differ greatly even when blue-collar workers are compared as a group with white-collar workers. In 1963, 28.6 per cent of the unemployed blue-collar workers, and 25.8 per cent of the unemployed white-collar workers had a period of unemployment lasting fifteen or more weeks. If, however, the duration of unemployment is measured over the course of an entire year, rather than during a given spell of unemployment, the length of unemployment is much greater for blue- than

[33] Johnston, "Educational Attainment of Workers" (n. 23), pp. A-8 and A-15.

[34] More detailed data for certain time periods can be found in Meredith, "Long-Term Unemployment" (n. 15), and in Bureau of Labor Statistics, *Study Paper No. 6* (n. 29), pp. 20–27.

[35] U.S. Department of Labor, *Monthly Report on the Labor Force* (January, 1964), p. 45. The pattern apparently differs from one year to the next. In 1957, for example, agricultural workers and wage and salary workers from nondurable goods manufacturing were above average.

[36] Meredith, "Long-Term Unemployment" (n. 15), p. 607.

for white-collar workers. In 1957[37] about 37 per cent of the blue-collar and only 27 per cent of the white-collar workers who experienced any unemployment had a total of fifteen or more weeks of unemployment during the entire year. Since nearly half of the unemployed blue-collar workers (47.8 per cent) and only a third of the unemployed white-collar workers (33.9 per cent) had two or more spells of unemployment, it would appear that the difference in duration is primarily a result of blue-collar workers having less steady jobs.

One other characteristic of the long-term jobless is noteworthy. Turnover among the long-term unemployed is very low. A worker who has been out of a job for a prolonged period of time is much less likely to find a job quickly than is one who has had only a brief period of unemployment. In 1957 about 41 per cent of the jobless who had reported four weeks or less of unemployment in any given month had found jobs by the following month. In contrast, among those who reported unemployment of fifteen weeks or more, only about half as many—21 per cent—had found jobs by the following month.

The pattern of turnover among the long-term unemployed remained very similar from 1957 to 1962 in spite of sharp changes in the number of the long-term unemployed.[38] In the second quarter of each of these years an average of about three-fifths of the long-term unemployed were still looking for jobs a month after they had reported fifteen weeks or more of unemployment. About one in four had found a job, and the remainder had left the labor force.

Turnover among the very long-term unemployed is even lower. Analysis of the data for the second quarter of 1960, 1961, and 1962 shows that more than three-fifths of the very long-term jobless were unemployed for over nine months, more than a third over a year,

and more than a fifth for over a year and a half. Moreover, the rate at which they left unemployment decreased as their unemployment lengthened, an indication that the task of finding a job became more and more difficult the longer they were unemployed.[39] Further, the April, 1962, survey of the Bureau of Labor Statistics indicates that persons with a lengthy period of unemployment are prone to subsequent unemployment. Nearly half of the respondents with more than six months of unemployment in 1961 were also unemployed in April, 1962.[40]

From the discussion thus far, it is apparent that the data available on those characteristics of the long-term jobless that might be relevant to their fitness for job openings are not entirely satisfactory. The previous industrial and occupational attachment of the workers tells little about the suitability of their training and experience for jobs that are currently being filled. Nor do we know very much about the willingness or ability of the long-term jobless as a group to adjust to the demands of the labor market, although a number of case studies seem to indicate that the jobless are willing to take all possible steps in order to find jobs.[41] Preliminary findings of the Detroit study of hard-core unemployment indicate, however, that some of the long-term jobless have difficulty finding jobs because they do not know how to go about looking for work or how to evaluate their qualifications for the labor market. It was found that others were deficient in the skills, training, education, or experience necessary to qualify for existing job openings and that they "need specialized counseling to learn to understand the unique circumstances they face." Specialized legal, medical, financial, or other assistance was also found in a number of cases to be necessary to prepare workers realistically for the labor market.[42]

The temporary extended unemployment compensation studies seem to indicate that a very

---

[37] The data in the remainder of this and the following paragraph are from Bureau of Labor Statistics, *Study Paper No. 6* (n. 29), p. 35. Similar breakdowns are not available for later years.

[38] See U.S. Department of Labor, *Monthly Report on the Labor Force* (June, 1962), p. 13. Turnover in the labor-force status of the long-term unemployed is shown for the second quarter of each of the years 1957–62.

[39] *Ibid.*, p. 14.

[40] Stein, "Work History" (n. 21), p. 1407.

[41] See, for example, Richard C. Wilcock and Walter H. Franke, *Unwanted Workers* (New York: The Free Press of Glencoe, 1963), chap. 5.

[42] Bartley, "Detroit Area Manpower Development Project" (n. 32), pp. 21–22.

large majority of the long-term unemployed have a permanent attachment to the labor force. About three-fourths seem to have been in the labor force during the entire thirty-six-month period prior to filing for extended benefits, and about 94 per cent seem to have been in the labor force during at least twenty-four of these months.[43] In other words, most of them apparently are regular workers who worked whenever jobs were available.

On the other hand, a large proportion of the long-term jobless are older workers and non-whites and have relatively low levels of education. These are all groups which, if left to shift for themselves in the labor market, are severely handicapped in finding new jobs. The study of the hard-core unemployed in Detroit also identified a group of applicants "made up of individuals who are not marketable and not amenable to counseling assistance. . . ." In this group were "the retiree, the physically or psychologically handicapped who cannot be helped through some remedial program, former secondary wage earners no longer interested in employment, and applicants whose attitudes toward being independent of social agencies and self-support preclude placement assistance."[44]

IV. GEOGRAPHIC DISTRIBUTION OF LONG-TERM AND PERSISTENT UNEMPLOYMENT

The source of most of the data on long-term unemployment that have been discussed thus far is the household survey of the Department of Labor. Since these data are not generally available by state or smaller geographic areas, they cannot be used for an analysis of the location of long-term unemployment. For this purpose, we must rely on the state employment security program data available for the insured unemployed, on estimates of unemployment rates in the 150 major labor-market areas, and on special studies at particular points in time. Only a limited analysis of the data that are available is possible. As the President's Committee to Appraise Employment and Unemployment Statistics has noted concerning the use of employment security program data:

> Comparisons among States and even among areas of the same State are limited by the differences in coverage, duration of benefits, and disqualification provisions. Interarea comparisons can be ambiguous because coverage limitations have a differential effect as between different areas.[45]

The same committee has also noted with respect to data for the major labor-market areas that "the area estimates of unemployment as presently constructed have a range of uncertainty which is undesirably wide, particularly in view of the increasing operational uses being made of them."[46] Because of these limitations, some care is required in interpreting interarea patterns of long-term and persistent unemployment.

A. STATE DIFFERENCES IN LONG-TERM UNEMPLOYMENT

Table 3–3 shows the fifty-two "states," ranked in the order of the proportion of the insured unemployed who were out of work fifteen weeks or more for the years 1960–62. The proportions are monthly averages. On the basis of these data, it would appear that the problem of long-term unemployment varies considerably among the states. The per cent of long-term unemployment, which during this period averaged 19 per cent for the entire nation, varied from a high of 28 per cent in

[43] Bureau of Employment Security, BES No. U-207-4 (n. 3). The data on the labor-force status of these claimants is the least reliable part of the temporary extended unemployment compensation studies and must be used with some caution. However, the Bureau of Labor Statistics April, 1962, survey also found the long-term jobless to have relatively strong labor-force attachment. See Stein, "Work History" (n. 21), p. 1406.

[44] Bartley, "Detroit Area Manpower Development Project" (n. 32), p. 22.

[45] President's Committee to Appraise Employment and Unemployment Statistics, *Measuring Employment and Unemployment* (Washington, D.C.: Government Printing Office, 1962), p. 87.

[46] *Ibid.*, p. 194. For a detailed analysis of the accuracy of area unemployment estimates, see Joseph C. Ullman, "How Accurate Are Estimates of State and Local Unemployment?" *Industrial and Labor Relations Review*, April, 1963, pp. 434–52.

TABLE 3–3: STATES RANKED HIGHEST TO LOWEST BY PER CENT OF INSURED UNEM-
PLOYED OUT OF WORK FIFTEEN WEEKS OR MORE (1960–1962)[a]
AND BY INSURED UNEMPLOYMENT RATE (1958–1962)[b]

State	Per cent of insured unemployed out of work 15+ weeks		Rank, insured unemployment rate	State	Per cent of insured unemployed out of work 15+ weeks		Rank, insured unemployment rate
	Per cent	Rank			Per cent	Rank	
(1)	(2)	(3)	(4)	(1)	(2)	(3)	(4)
United States	19			Missouri	17	26	34
				Montana	17	26	7
Alabama	16	33	16	Nebraska	17	26	46
Alaska	13	41	1	Nevada	n.a.	n.a.	18
Arizona	12	43	33	New Hampshire	20	13	29
Arkansas	19	17	6	New Jersey	17	26	12
California	18	19	17	New Mexico	n.a.	n.a.	40
Colorado	16	33	48	New York	18	19	19
Connecticut	17	26	27	North Carolina	21	11	28
Delaware	n.a.	n.a.	41	North Dakota	25	3	21
D.C.	19	17	52	Ohio	23	5	30
Florida	12	43	38	Oklahoma	23	5	20
Georgia	12	43	32	Oregon	17	26	15
Hawaii	16	33	47	Pennsylvania	28	1	5
Idaho	13	41	24	Puerto Rico	9	47	8
Illinois	20	13	39	Rhode Island	16	33	13
Indiana	14	40	35	South Carolina	18	19	37
Iowa	18	19	51	South Dakota	n.a.	n.a.	50
Kansas	16	33	44	Tennessee	20	13	11
Kentucky	20	13	4	Texas	15	39	45
Louisiana	17	26	25	Utah	18	19	43
Maine	23	5	3	Vermont	22	10	22
Maryland	26	2	26	Virginia	10	46	49
Massachusetts	18	19	23	Washington	24	4	9
Michigan	16	33	10	West Virginia	23	5	2
Minnesota	23	5	31	Wisconsin	21	11	42
Mississippi	18	19	14	Wyoming	n.a.	n.a.	36

SOURCE: Bureau of Employment Security, *The Insured Unemployed*, various issues.

[a] A monthly average based on the months of January, April, July, and October, except that January is not included in 1960.

[b] From Table 2–7, col. 3.

Pennsylvania to a low of 9 per cent in Puerto Rico.

The states with a high percentage of long-term unemployment are not, in general, the states with high insured unemployment rates. Of the ten states with the highest percentages of long-term unemployment, only four (Pennsylvania, Washington, West Virginia, and Maine) are among the ten states with the highest insured unemployment rates. Conversely, some states with relatively high insured unemployment rates (Michigan, New Jersey, Rhode Island, Alaska) have relatively low percentages of the unemployed in the long-term unemployed group. The interpretation of these differences would have to take into account characteristics of each state's economy and is beyond the scope of this chapter, but evidently the problem of establishing suitable programs of aid varies considerably among the states.

Some clues to the distribution and concentration of long-term unemployment by state are contained in the reports of the special studies of claimants under the TEUC program of 1961–62. Seven large industrial states (California, Illinois, Michigan, New Jersey, New York, Ohio, and Pennsylvania) contained 56 per cent of the 1.6 million claimants under the program at the times of the four surveys.[47]

[47] Bureau of Employment Security, BES No. U-207-4 (n. 3), p. 49.

B. Unemployment Trends in Labor-Surplus Areas

The TEUC studies included only workers covered by unemployment insurance and do not give an accurate count of all the long-term unemployed. Additional insights into the geographic distribution of the long-term jobless can be obtained from the data on unemployment in local areas.

The problem of localized unemployment has been gaining attention since the recession of 1949, when the first of several federal programs designed to assist in the economic recovery of depressed areas was put into operation.[48] Since that time many local labor-market areas have moved in and out of the category of substantial labor surplus (unemployment at 6 per cent or higher). The number of areas in this category is closely related to the national rate of unemployment. During the period 1951–62 the average number of major labor-market areas in that category has varied from a low of fifteen in 1951 to a high of eighty-one in 1961. The average during the years 1951–56 was twenty-four, while during the years 1958–62 it was sixty. This larger number in recent years is associated with the much higher national rates of unemployment that have been experienced since 1957.

The number of smaller areas with substantial labor surplus seems to have increased greatly over the years. The trend cannot be measured exactly because the number of areas so classified depends upon their being brought specifically to the attention of the Bureau of Employment Security. Recent efforts of communities to qualify for assistance under the Area Redevelopment Act have greatly increased the number of local labor markets officially listed as areas of labor surplus. In late 1963, 786 local labor markets were listed as areas of substantial labor surplus—37 major areas, 162 smaller

areas, and 587 very small areas.[49] The pervasiveness of high unemployment areas suggests that a great deal of the localized unemployment problem is a national problem.

Because there is a large cyclical factor in the number of labor-surplus areas, it is more useful in considering the dimensions of the distressed-area problem to look at labor-market areas that have had persistently high rates of unemployment regardless of changes in the national economy.[50]

In May, 1953, only eight major labor-market areas were listed by the Labor Department as areas of substantial and persistent unemployment.[51] In November, 1963, seventeen major centers (including two major centers in Puerto Rico) were in this category.[52] Most of these areas have had high rates of joblessness (more than 6.0 per cent) since at least 1954. A recent examination of the employment history between 1957 and 1963 of a number of areas of substantial unemployment indicates that reduction in the size of the labor force through out-migration is the main form of labor-market adjustment that occurs to improve or moderate conditions of high unemployment in these areas.[53]

The seventeen major areas of persistent unemployment in late 1963 were located in six states and Puerto Rico, but twelve were in the three states of Massachusetts, Pennsylvania, and West Virginia.[54] In almost all of these communities the high unemployment is related to the decline of one or two important industries in the area. In the main, these industries are

[48] The Bureau of Employment Security resumed its program (it had been discontinued after World War II) of classifying local areas on the basis of relative labor supply. See Chronic Labor Surplus Areas (Bureau of Employment Security, U.S. Department of Labor, Washington, D.C., July, 1959), pp. 4, 45.

[49] U.S. Department of Labor, Area Labor Market Trends (November, 1963), pp. 15–50.

[50] Differences in the impact of the business cycle on various areas is also important, however, particularly in assessing the effects of programs like temporary extended unemployment compensation.

[51] See Distressed Areas in a Growing Economy (New York: Committee for Economic Development, June, 1961), p. 16.

[52] The Labor Department also listed 100 smaller areas and 462 very small areas as areas of substantial and persistent unemployment. See U.S. Department of Labor, Area Labor Market Trends (November, 1963), p. 2.

[53] U.S. Department of Labor, Manpower Report of the President, 1964 (n. 13), p. 33.

[54] U.S. Department of Labor, Area Labor Market Trends (November, 1963), pp. 15–50.

durable goods manufacturing (in particular, primary metals and metal fabrication, a few consumer goods industries, and transportation equipment, including autos), textile and apparel manufacturing, coal mining, and railroad and water transportation. Thus, the plight of most of these communities is the result of either the decline of important national markets on which their economic health depended heavily or the migration of important industries to other geographic areas. The story is similar for most of the smaller areas with chronic unemployment.[55]

During the last ten years there has been no upward trend in the proportion of the total unemployed in depressed areas (major areas of chronic unemployment). On the contrary, the proportion has declined somewhat. Unemployment in depressed areas, however, has shown a high degree of cyclical sensitivity. In the seventeen major areas, for example, unemployment exceeded the national rate by larger amounts in the 1954 and 1958 recession years than it did in other years.[56]

It is difficult to specify the portion of the total unemployed who are out of work because they are located in areas of chronic depression. The best estimate available is one based on a special study of a sample of unemployment insurance claimants for the period July, 1956, to June, 1957. It was estimated that workers in twenty-one major and seventy smaller chronically depressed areas accounted for at least one-fifth of total unemployment during that relatively full-employment period. But not all of the unemployment in even these areas is long term; much of it is the result of short-term frictional causes.[57]

C. CHARACTERISTICS OF THE UNEMPLOYED IN LABOR-SURPLUS AREAS

The major problem of depressed areas is, without doubt, a shortage of jobs. Regardless of the characteristics of the unemployed, there are no jobs for them in the areas where they live. In any attempt to help these workers find new jobs, however, whether by the importation of new industries, assistance in migration, retraining, or other methods, the characteristics of the unemployed are of some relevance.

Unfortunately, available data do not include information on some of the more relevant characteristics. We do not at present, for example, have a detailed inventory of their skills, although skill surveys have been undertaken recently in many local areas in connection with planned retraining programs. Nor do we know the level of their education, their willingness to be retrained, or their willingness to move out of the area. We do, however, have some data from a few case studies on characteristics of displaced workers in depressed areas.[58]

Further data, previously not available, on the characteristics of the unemployed in areas of substantial labor surplus are provided by a study based on special tabulations of data collected for the *MRLF* in April and May, 1959, in the nation's major labor-market areas.[59] The major differences between the unemployed in labor-surplus areas and in areas of tight or balanced labor supply, as summarized in Table 3–4, are that the unemployed in the labor-surplus areas are on the average somewhat older, are more concentrated in the prime working years of twenty-five to sixty-four, and are more likely to have been employed in factory work—particularly as semiskilled operatives—than are the unemployed in areas of balanced labor supply. Also their unemployment tends to last longer than that of other

[55] For the factors primarily responsible for the unemployment problem for each area, see U.S. Department of Labor, *Area Labor Market Trends* (August, 1963), pp. 67–97.

[56] Based on computations in "The American Economy in 1961: Problems and Policies," Council of Economic Advisers, statement before the Joint Economic Committee, March, 1961, p. B-15 (mimeographed), and on computations from data in *Area Labor Market Trends, Statistical Supplement: Unemployment in Major Areas* (July, 1962), pp. 49–53.

[57] Joseph S. Zeisel and Robert L. Stein, *The Structure of Unemployment in Areas of Substantial Labor Surplus*, Study Paper No. 23, prepared by the Bureau of Labor Statistics for the Study of Employment, Growth, and Price Levels, Joint Economic Committee (86th Cong., 2d Sess., January 30, 1960), p. 3.

[58] See, for example, R. C. Wilcock, *Impact on Workers and Community of a Plant Shutdown in a Depressed Area*, Bulletin No. 1264 (Bureau of Labor Statistics, U.S. Department of Labor, Washington, D.C., June, 1960). With experience gained through retraining programs conducted under the Area Redevelopment Act, additional information will be accumulated.

[59] Zeisel and Stein, *The Structure of Unemployment* (n. 57), pp. 1–13.

TABLE 3–4: CHARACTERISTICS OF UNEMPLOYED WORKERS IN AREAS OF SUBSTANTIAL LABOR SURPLUS AND IN AREAS OF BALANCED LABOR SUPPLY, SPRING, 1959

Characteristics	Per cent of all unemployed in various groups	
	Balanced labor supply[a]	Substantial labor surplus[b]
Personal characteristics		
Age 45 and over	28	34
Age 45–64	24	30
Men, age 25–64	36	45
Teen-agers	25	16
Married men	29	33
Married women	18	16
Nonwhites	30	22
Industrial characteristics		
Manufacturing (factory workers)	19	37
Durable goods	9	21
Nondurable goods	10	15
Blue-collar workers	46	56
Semiskilled operatives	21	31
New labor-force entrants	13	10.5
Duration of unemployment		
6 months or more	13	26
15 weeks or more	29	42

SOURCE: Joseph S. Zeisel and Robert L. Stein, *The Structure of Unemployment in Areas of Substantial Labor Surplus*, Study Paper No. 23, prepared by the Bureau of Labor Statistics for the Study of Employment, Growth, and Price Levels, Joint Economic Committee (86th Cong., 2nd Sess., January 30, 1960), pp. 1–13.

[a] Major labor-market areas whose classification remained at A, B, or C from January, 1957, to May, 1959; that is, areas with a consistently tight or balanced labor supply-demand situation.

[b] Areas whose classification fell to D, E, or F after the first quarter of 1957 and were still D or worse in May, 1959; and areas whose classification was D or worse throughout the period January, 1957 to May, 1959; that is, areas of substantial labor surplus and chronically depressed areas.

workers. At the time of the survey the proportion unemployed for over six months in the labor-surplus areas was double that of the unemployed in areas of balanced labor supply.[60]

In the broad terms used above to describe the unemployed, those in depressed areas are not greatly different from the unemployed elsewhere. In a particular area, however, the differences may be more striking. In an area that had once been dominated by a single industry, such as coal mining or textiles, the unemployed can be expected to have a narrower background of industrial experience than have the unemployed generally. In such a case, the adaptation of the worker's skills to other industries and occupations is more difficult than for the unemployed generally.

[60] For a more detailed presentation of the characteristics of workers in depressed areas, see *ibid.*, pp. 28–32.

D. ADEQUACY OF AREA UNEMPLOYMENT DATA

Increased attention to the economic problems of regional and local areas and the expansion of programs at federal and other governmental levels to bolster the economic health of these areas have highlighted the need for more accurate and comprehensive state and local labor-market information.[61]

In particular, efforts of local governments to aid the unemployed would benefit materially from more detailed knowledge of the characteristics of the unemployed, especially the long-term jobless. Data available in *The Insured Unemployed*, pertaining to four-fifths of all nonagricultural wage earners, could be

[61] See President's Committee, *Measuring Employment* (*n.* 45), pp. 191–97.

expanded at relatively little cost to provide additional geographic detail. W. L. Ginsburg has suggested that, in addition to the rate of unemployment, information on duration of unemployment, changes in labor-force status of the long-term jobless, and the composition of the unemployed should be made available periodically.[62] Clearly, more detailed information on the skills of workers in local areas will be required for the more successful administration of the retraining provisions of the Area Redevelopment Act and the Manpower Development and Training Act.

V. PROSPECTS FOR REDUCING LONG-TERM AND PERSISTENT UNEMPLOYMENT

The foregoing analysis has shown that the level of long-term and persistent unemployment is closely related to national economic trends. Prospects for reducing recent, relatively high levels of this type of unemployment depend, to a large extent, upon increasing the national rate of economic growth and minimizing recessionary swings. But a number of economic and population trends indicate that, even if these two goals are met, the problem of keeping long-term and depressed-area unemployment at low levels is likely to persist or perhaps become more difficult in the coming years.

One complicating factor is likely to be the expected rapid increase in the size of the labor force. Although the labor force in the early nineteen-sixties has not increased as fast as was expected, it is estimated that the growth for the decade of the nineteen-sixties will approximate 17 per cent as compared with the growth of only 12 per cent for the nineteen-fifties.[63] Further, while the total population during the nineteen-fifties increased faster than did the labor force, the reverse is expected during the nineteen-sixties, a factor which can be expected to make more difficult the task of keeping the labor force fully employed.

It also can be anticipated that the pace of automation and technological change will increase in the years ahead, necessitating complex and drastic labor-market adjustments. Whether this will result in higher levels of long-term and persistent unemployment depends not only on the ability of the economy to create jobs but on the ability and willingness of workers to make the required shifts in occupation, industry, and location.[64] At any rate, it seems certain that the establishment of suitable programs of aid for the long-term unemployed will remain a pressing problem for the remainder of the decade.

---

[62] Suggestion made in discussion of paper by William H. Miernyk, "The Incidence of Persistent Unemployment," *Proceedings of the Twelfth Annual Meeting* (Madison, Wisconsin: Industrial Relations Research Association, 1960), p. 46. For Miernyk's suggestions on the need for more detailed data, see p. 39.

[63] Sophia Cooper, "Interim Revised Projections of U.S. Labor Force, 1965–75," *Special Labor Force Report No. 24*, 1962, p. 1.

[64] For a more detailed discussion of the effects of labor-force and technological changes on the prospects for unemployment in the nineteen-sixties see Ewan Clague, "A Profile of Unemployment in the Early 1960's," paper presented at the 45th Economic Conference, National Industrial Conference Board, May 18, 1961. (Mimeographed.)

PART III

Programs of Aid

CHAPTER 4

Unemployment Insurance: Risks Covered and Their Financing

Merrill G. Murray*

UNEMPLOYMENT INSURANCE IS the largest and, at present, the most significant program for dealing with the needs of the unemployed. In the recession year 1961 it provided over $3.4 billion in aid to over 7 million individuals. Even in the recovery year 1962 almost $2.7 billion was paid in benefits to over 6 million unemployed persons. Unemployment compensation provides aid to the unemployed to an extent that is determined by its various provisions governing coverage, eligibility conditions, disqualifications, relationship to training, and the amount and duration of benefits. The present chapter treats all of these determinative factors except the amount and duration of benefits.

There are several important factors in determining whether the unemployment compensation program is an effective aid to the unemployed: the extent to which workers having a risk of unemployment are covered under the program; the extent to which they are able to qualify for benefits if they have a substantial attachment to the labor force; and the extent to which disqualifying conditions assure that benefits are paid only to the genuinely and legitimately unemployed. The program's relationship to training is also becoming important. Finally, the cost of the program and the way it is financed have an important bearing on whether adequate benefits are

provided and whether funds to pay the benefits are available when needed.

I. COVERAGE

Unemployment insurance is designed for workers who are dependent on an employer for their jobs and therefore face a risk of unemployment.[1] An average of approximately 47.8 million workers per month were covered by unemployment insurance in 1962. This included 41.6 million workers covered by state programs, 2.5 million federal civilian workers, 2.9 million members of the armed forces, and 0.8 million workers covered by the railroad unemployment insurance programs.[2] The total number of different persons working in covered employment at some time during the year is of course much larger than the monthly average.[3]

---

[1] The self-employed also have a risk of unemployment, such as the loss of work through failure of their businesses; but it is difficult to determine when they are unemployed. Because of this difficulty, little serious consideration has been given in this country to covering self-employed persons. Australia and New Zealand cover the self-employed, but beneficiaries are subject to a needs test in Australia and to an income test in New Zealand.

[2] *Employment and Wages of Workers Covered by State Unemployment Insurance Laws and Unemployment Compensation for Federal Employees by Industry and State, Fourth Quarter, 1962, and 1962 Average* (Bureau of Employment Security, U.S. Department of Labor, Washington, D.C.), Table 2a.

[3] This number, which cannot be known with certainty, varies from month to month and from year to year.

* Research Associate, The W. E. Upjohn Institute for Employment Research.

Unemployment insurance covers about three out of every four wage and salary workers in the country. It was estimated that in 1962 a total of 14.4 million workers (or, more strictly speaking, jobs) were not covered by any federal or state program. The principal groups excluded from coverage were employees of small firms (1.8 million workers); farm and agricultural processing workers (1.9 million); workers in domestic service (2.6 million); employees of nonprofit organizations (1.6 million); state and local government employees (6.2 million); and miscellaneous groups including "borderline employees" (totaling an estimated 0.3 million).[4]

A. EMPLOYEES OF SMALL FIRMS

The Federal Unemployment Tax Act originally covered only firms with 8 or more workers employed on at least one day in each of at least twenty weeks in a year. Some states, in their original legislation, however, covered smaller firms than the federal act did.[5] In 1937 there were ten state laws covering employers of 1 or more persons, two laws covering employers of 2 or more, six covering those of 4 or more, and one law covering employers of 5 or more. Only minor extensions occurred until, effective in 1956, the federal act was extended to employers of 4 or more in twenty weeks. The states followed suit, and several states extended their coverage to even smaller firms, so that when the extension of coverage of the federal act took effect, twenty-eight states covered firms with 4 or more employees, four states covered those with 3 or more, two states covered those with 2 or more, and eighteen states covered firms with 1 or more employees. As a result, there was an increase in coverage of 1.6 million workers. As of January 1, 1964, when several more states had extended coverage, twenty state programs covered employers of 1 or more in

varying degrees,[6] and four states covered employers of 3 or more. The estimated number of workers excluded because they worked for small firms was 1.8 million.

In discussions of extending coverage to small firms, it has been argued that it is not administratively feasible to cover them; but this has been belied by the success of the states that do cover small firms. The high administrative cost of collecting contributions in proportion to the small number covered has also been cited. It was estimated, as of December 31, 1961, that in the thirty-three jurisdictions that do not cover employers of less than 3 persons, 1.1 million smaller employers would have to be covered in order to include the 1.8 million employees now excluded from coverage.[7] This high proportion of employers to employees is probably the principal political reason that extension of coverage to small firms has been so slow. Professor Richard A. Lester has suggested another reason for failure of state legislatures to act on their own; namely, that so many state legislators are lawyers who have secretaries or assistants for whom they would have to pay contributions if employers of 1 or more were covered.[8]

It has been asserted, on the one hand, that employees of small firms have little risk of unemployment because their employers, having a personal relationship with them, will not lay them off. It is asserted, on the other hand, that the mortality among small firms is so high that they are not insurable. To see what truth there might be in either argument, the Bureau

[4] *Unemployment Insurance: State Laws and Experience*, BES No. U-198 (Bureau of Employment Security, U.S. Department of Labor, Washington, D.C., Revised May, 1963), Chart 1.

[5] Throughout this chapter, the District of Columbia and Puerto Rico are counted among the states.

[6] Alaska, Arkansas, California, Delaware, District of Columbia, Hawaii, Idaho, Maryland, Massachusetts, Minnesota, Montana, Nevada, New Mexico, New York, Oregon, Pennsylvania, Rhode Island, Utah, Washington, and Wyoming. It will be seen that these include industrial and non-industrial states, large and small states, and states in every section of the country except the Southeast.

[7] *Summary Tables for Evaluation of Coverage and Benefit Provisions of State Unemployment Insurance Laws as of December 31, 1961*, BES No. U-210 (Bureau of Employment Security, U.S. Department of Labor, Washington, D.C., July, 1962), Table 1.

[8] Richard A. Lester, *The Economics of Unemployment Compensation* (Industrial Relations Section, Department of Economics, Princeton University, Princeton, N.J., 1962), p. 126.

of Employment Security obtained special information from most of the states that cover employers of 1 or more persons.[9] In five out of the seven states that supplied such data it was found that a proportionately greater number of workers in small firms drew benefits than did those in larger firms, but duration of benefits was about the same. Also, a greater proportion of smaller than larger firms was at the maximum tax rate in seven of the nine states that supplied these data. This was partly due, no doubt, to a larger proportion of small firms staying in business only a short time. Once they have been in business long enough to get an experience rating, however, more of them obtain minimum tax rates than other firms as a result of favorable experience. It appears, accordingly, that there is some truth in both arguments for restricting coverage.

B. Farm and Agricultural Processing Workers

Agricultural workers, although declining in number, form one of the largest categories of persons not covered by unemployment insurance. Because of the great seasonal variation in their employment, it is difficult to get an accurate estimate of the number who are employed in agriculture on any particular day in the year. The Bureau of Employment Security estimated that 1.9 million wage workers were employed in farm labor and agricultural processing work during 1962. Of these, possibly a quarter of a million were in processing operations, for which coverage has been more seriously proposed because of the similarity of the work to industrial employment. Only three jurisdictions specifically cover agricultural workers: the District of Columbia (which has no agriculture); Hawaii, which covers agricultural employers of twenty or more workers; and Puerto Rico, which covers those in the sugar industry. Hawaii has a separate fund for agricultural workers. Puerto Rico brought the sugar workers (who had a separate program) under the general system on October 1, 1962, but with lower benefits than for other workers.

One of the deterrents to coverage of agricultural employment has been the lack of knowledge of the patterns of such employment. It has been contended that seasonal employment is so short and uncertain as not to be insurable. It is also argued that year round employment, as in dairies, is so steady and the demand for workers for such employment so great that there is no need for unemployment insurance for them. In order to get concrete information, several states conducted special studies of agricultural workers in 1959 and 1960. Arizona and Connecticut published the results in 1961, and New York in 1962.

Arizona found that "regular" workers were employed for an average of forty-six weeks in the year, and seasonal workers for an average of twenty-one weeks. Only one-fifth of the workers were unemployed and seeking work for more than four weeks. The duration of unemployment averaged fifteen weeks for those seeking work and eighteen weeks for those who had withdrawn temporarily from the labor force at some time in the year.[10]

The New York sample was composed of 372 regular workers and 313 seasonal workers for whom a year's work history, ending in September, 1960, was secured. Seventy-six or 21 per cent of the regular workers had less than twenty weeks of work (farm and nonfarm work combined) and would not have been able to meet the qualifying requirements of the New York law. Of the 313 seasonal workers, 226 or 62 per cent had less than twenty weeks of farm and nonfarm work in the state and would not have been able to qualify for benefits. However, if in-state and out-of-state work had been combined, only 14 of the 372 regular workers would have shown less than twenty weeks of work, and only 45 of the 313 seasonal

[9] *Unemployment Experience of Small and Large Firms*, BES No. U-195 (Bureau of Employment Security, U.S. Department of Labor, Washington, D.C., January, 1961).

[10] *Arizona: Study of Employment and Unemployment of Agricultural Workers* (2 vols.; Employment Security Commission of Arizona, Phoenix, Arizona, December, 1960).

workers would have shown less than twenty weeks.[11]

In the Connecticut study it was found that a substantial number of agricultural workers —3,951 out of 13,691—had other employment. Of this number, 1,788 or 45.3 per cent were reported as regular workers at the time of the survey. Of these, 792 had sufficient non-agricultural employment to be eligible for unemployment compensation, with an average of 9.6 weeks of potential benefits. In fact, 265 actually received benefits during the survey period.[12]

In the New York study, it was estimated that coverage would cost 3.27 per cent of payrolls for regular workers and 4.55 per cent for seasonal workers. In the Arizona study, the cost of covering all agricultural workers was estimated at 3.77 per cent, with the cost rate for regular workers only 1.40 per cent but the rate for seasonal workers 7.91 per cent.[13]

C. Workers in Domestic Service

Among uncovered workers, the second largest group—about 2.6 million—is composed of domestic workers in private homes, college clubs, and fraternities and sororities. New York and Hawaii cover some of these workers.[14] The New York law originally covered domestic workers in employing units with at least four servants for at least twenty weeks in the year and has recently extended coverage to employers of four or more at any time during the year. No great difficulty has been experienced

in covering servants in large households, and the unemployment experience was not substantially different from other types of employment. In 1961 Hawaii covered a domestic worker if he was paid at least $225 in cash during a calendar quarter.

Coverage of domestic servants has been viewed generally as the most difficult field. This would be particularly so in small households in which a domestic servant is employed only a day or two each week. There would be not only the difficulty of tax collections from housewives but also of determining when day workers who work in several households and may not seek full-time employment are unemployed. To be sure, the social security program (OASDI) has for the last dozen years covered domestic workers earning at least $50 a quarter from an employer, but this is a much simpler problem, since once taxes are collected, benefits need be determined only on an established fact—old-age, death, or, more difficult to judge, total disability. Because of the administrative difficulties that would be encountered, little serious consideration has been given to the possibility of coverage of domestic workers in private homes, although a large proportion of these workers have a greater risk of unemployment than any other group. Nor is there much prospect that domestic workers, who are unorganized, or their employers will seek such coverage.

D. Employees of Nonprofit Organizations

After employees of small firms, the most consideration has been given, particularly by the federal government, to coverage of the 1.6 million employees of nonprofit organizations. Nevertheless, there is very limited coverage of these workers. As of January 1, 1964, only three of the states—Alaska, Colorado, and Hawaii—covered nonprofit employees in general, and the District of Columbia covered scientific, literary, and educational organizations. In Colorado nonprofit organizations were covered by a bill that simply struck out the clause in the law which excluded all nonprofit workers. This bill was introduced in the

[11] *The Pattern of Farm Employment in New York State; Implications for Unemployment Insurance Coverage, 1962* (Institute of Industrial Relations and Social Security, New York University in cooperation with the Division of Employment, New York State Department of Labor and the Bureau of Employment Security, U.S. Department of Labor).

[12] *A Study of the Feasibility of Covering Farm Workers Under Unemployment Compensation* (Employment Security Division, Connecticut Labor Department, Hartford, Connecticut, July, 1961).

[13] The Connecticut study does not give similar estimates. It includes only total estimated benefits that would have been paid to workers in the sample.

[14] Eleven states cover domestic workers in college clubs, fraternities, and sororities but not in private homes.

closing hours of a legislative session. At the next session, this coverage was again modified by excluding professional workers, the clergy, and members of religious orders.

Effective in 1961, the Federal Unemployment Tax Act was extended to cover certain types of nonprofit organizations, principally fraternal societies, employee beneficiary societies, and agricultural and horticultural organizations. In 1962, six states amended their laws to conform to the federal extension. (Thirty-one states have provisions in their laws which automatically cover any employment that is covered by the federal act.)

Two large states, New York and California, have been seriously considering covering nonprofit organizations but are seeking a way to cover them, not on a contributory basis, but on the basis of reimbursement of actual costs for actual benefits paid to their former employees. The federal administration bill introduced in 1963 would revise the experience rating provisions of the federal act to permit such a method of coverage. This basis of coverage has been proposed so that nonprofit organizations will not have to build up unnecessary reserves. The unemployment rate is low in most nonprofit organizations; and on a contributory basis most organizations would have to pay full contributions, at least for a limited period, before they could get a rate commensurate with their rate of unemployment.

Those opposed to the reimbursement basis of coverage point out that most unemployment in nonprofit organizations results from budget shortages or closing of institutions and that on a reimbursement basis the institutions would have to pay the full cost of benefits at the very time they have a shortage of funds.

Under both Republican and Democratic administrations the federal government has been proposing extension of coverage to the employees of nonprofit organizations, but Congress has been reluctant to take action. Lack of action has been due principally to the arguments of the organizations that (1) they have been traditionally free from compulsory taxation (although this argument has diminished in importance); (2) they are financially hard

pressed; and (3) they have little risk of unemployment. There is little data to dispute the last claim. Although turnover is high in hospitals, this does not necessarily imply a high rate of unemployment.

E. STATE AND LOCAL GOVERNMENT EMPLOYEES

The largest group now without protection by unemployment insurance is composed of state and local government employees. Over 6 million persons are working for state and local governments, and the number is constantly growing. The federal constitution, as well as strong sentiment for states rights, prevents any federal coverage of these workers. There has been a gradual extension of coverage to such workers through state action, usually on a piecemeal basis. Coverage of state and local government workers has been slow, probably because of the lack of strong union organization among them and the common impression that government workers have little risk of unemployment. Federal workers were not provided with unemployment compensation protection until 1954, and then principally because of the pressure of postal and craft unions. The precedent of coverage of federal workers has stimulated some coverage of state and local government workers. By the end of 1963, some or all state or local government workers were covered in thirty-three states. Ten states covered their employees on a mandatory basis and seventeen provided for elective coverage. Mandatory coverage of local government employees was complete only in two states, Hawaii and Idaho, and coverage was elective in twenty-five states. As a result, only about half a million government workers had unemployment insurance protection and 6.2 million workers still had no protection. Although most have steady employment, experience under the federal employees unemployment compensation program demonstrates that government workers, especially in manual occupations, experience a considerable amount of unemployment.

F. "Borderline Employees"

Under the Federal Unemployment Tax Act, anyone who does not meet the common-law, master-servant relationship is excluded from coverage. Perhaps a quarter of a million workers are excluded from the program because they do not meet this test, although they are employed in work in which there is a real employer-employee relationship. These include commission salesmen, house-to-house canvassers, filling station operators, milk route drivers, and similar workers. Employers, in many cases in order to get employees excluded from coverage, have worked out contracts that are specifically designed so that the work will not meet the narrow common-law test. More explicit and comprehensive language is necessary in the federal act and in many of the state acts in order to cover such workers under the program. The majority of the states have such language in what are commonly referred to as the "A-B-C" tests, all of which must be met before a worker is excluded from coverage. These tests are (A) the worker is free from the direction or control of the employer in the performance of his work, (B) the service is outside the regular course or place of the employer's business, and (C) the worker is in an independent business. Similar tests are needed in the Federal Unemployment Tax Act if all states are to be expected to apply them. In fact, some of the states with the "A-B-C" test largely follow federal rulings and so nullify the language of their own laws. Only when the federal act contains the "A-B-C" test will all the states adopt it both in law and in the interpretation of the law in specific cases.

G. Summary

The prospects of providing aid to the unemployed in the presently exempted groups is not very promising. Of all these categories, coverage of state and local government employees appears most likely to grow, though at a slow pace. Some gradual extension of coverage for small firms and nonprofit organizations is probable, particularly if states are permitted to cover the latter on a reimbursement basis. Some coverage of agricultural workers may result from the recent state studies of such coverage, although there is no evidence of any prospective action as yet. The dimmest prospect is for the coverage of domestic workers in private homes.

Practically all states permit voluntary election of coverage of excluded employees, but this has been used only to a limited extent. Voluntary election is probably most commonly used by employers who operate in more than one state. These employers may have a total work force of four or more workers but may have only one or two employees in a given state. Since the employer is liable for the federal tax for such employees, he elects state coverage in order to get the allowable credit against the federal tax.

How serious are these exclusions from coverage in limiting aid to the unemployed? According to estimates of the Bureau of Employment Security, unemployed workers from covered industries totaled 2,680,000 or 73.2 per cent of the 3,660,000 unemployed in April, 1960, and 3,745,000 or 75.5 per cent of the 4,960,000 unemployed in April, 1961.[15] Unemployed workers from noncovered industries were estimated at 580,000 in April, 1960, and 765,000 in April, 1961. This represented 15.8 per cent of the total number of unemployed in April, 1960, and 15.4 per cent in April, 1961. The balance of the unemployed, 11.0 per cent and 9.1 per cent respectively for the two years, were recent entrants in the labor force. The proportion of unemployed, noncovered workers to total unemployment is thus smaller than the proportion of noncovered workers to the total number of workers—about 15 per cent as against 25 per cent. This disproportionately low number of unemployed, noncovered workers is due largely to the low rates of unemployment among two groups of this category: employees of state and local governments and employees of nonprofit organizations. While the Bureau of Employment Security estimated that about 8 per cent

15 *Selected Charts and Tables Relating to Unemployment Insurance Legislative Planning, 1961* (Bureau of Employment Security, U.S. Department of Labor, Washington, D.C.), Table C–1.

of the workers in covered industries were unemployed, the estimated rates of unemployment for the noncovered groups were: employees of small firms, 9 per cent; hired agricultural workers, 6 per cent; domestic workers, 6.6 per cent; employees of nonprofit organizations, 3 per cent; and state and local government employees, 2.6 per cent.

II. ELIGIBILITY CONDITIONS

Unemployment insurance is intended to provide protection against unemployment for workers who are regularly and continuously working or looking for work. All state laws, therefore, require an unemployed person not only to be able and available for work but also to have had a specified amount of employment or wages or both during a "base period" preceding his unemployment. This "base period" is usually a fifty-two-week period.

These eligibility conditions are unlike those for workmen's compensation, under which a worker is insured from the moment he is hired and receives full compensation even if he is injured the same day he starts work. It is necessary in unemployment insurance to have a former wage or employment requirement because unemployment cannot be tested as objectively as can an industrial accident or illness. Unemployment, to a certain extent, is a state of mind; that is, to be genuinely unemployed, a person must want to work and be able to work. If we were able to read people's minds, or if the public employment service were able to offer a suitable job to every claimant for unemployment benefits so that a "work test" could be applied, then a requirement of previous employment or earnings might be unnecessary. It might be necessary only to establish that he was separated from insured employment. However, since the "work test" can be applied to only a limited number of claimants, a test of substantial former attachment to the labor market is necessary to determine whether a worker is genuinely unemployed. It is a well-known fact that large numbers of workers, particularly students and married women, want to work only part of the year or only on part-time jobs or both. For

example, in an analysis of the work experience of the population in 1962, based on the census monthly labor-market surveys, it was found that of those who had some employment but less than fifty weeks of work during the year, 8.5 million gave as a reason for part-year work that they were taking care of the home, and 7 million the reason that they were going to school.[16]

Any test of previous employment or earnings must be arbitrary, to some extent, since some unemployed workers with short attachment to the labor market may be genuinely seeking work, and others with long labor-market attachment may be no longer seeking work. The object should be to set a qualifying period which would provide a good presumption that the worker is regularly attached to the labor market. There have been few studies of the actual work experience of covered workers to assist in establishing realistic qualifying requirements. As a result, there is more diversity in the qualifying requirements of the state laws and more guesswork as the basis for these requirements than in any other feature of unemployment insurance. This diversity also is due to differing concepts of the kinds of unemployment the program is designed to compensate. For example, some think qualifying requirements should be high enough to exclude seasonal workers; others think the requirements should be low enough to include all except casual workers.

Originally, the state laws required a multiple of the weekly benefit amount, usually sixteen. Since they also originally determined benefits as 50 per cent of full-time weekly wages, this means that they required the equivalent of eight full weeks of employment. In order to get the necessary information, all the states, except Wisconsin,[17] required weekly payroll reports of

[16] Samuel Saben, "Work Experience of the Population in 1962," *Monthly Labor Review* (January, 1963) Table 7, p. 23.

[17] Wisconsin secures wage and employment information only if a worker files a claim for benefits. Then, a form is sent to the worker's employers for whom he had worked in the preceding fifty-two weeks, with the request that they supply the necessary information. This is called "request reporting."

employers, with the wages of each worker itemized. With the record-keeping equipment available at that time, the states soon bogged down in the attempt to keep weekly records of each employee. Simpler, short-cut tests of precise earnings were therefore devised. The federal Bureau of Unemployment Compensation recommended that only reports of total earnings in each calendar quarter be secured and devised a benefit formula and qualifying requirement based on such quarterly earnings. Most states followed this recommendation. About a dozen states went further and based qualifying requirements and benefits on annual earnings. Only Wisconsin at that time retained a qualifying requirement based on weeks of employment.

As of January 1, 1964, there were five methods generally used to test previous employment or earnings. All the states required a minimum amount of earnings; in five states this was the only test applied. The four additional tests were: (1) wages in two quarters as a further test that the wages were spread somewhat, in nine states; (2) a multiple, such as 1.5, of high-quarter earnings, in ten states; (3) wages equal to a multiple of the weekly benefit amount, in eighteen states; and (4) a specified minimum number of weeks in each of which there was a minimum amount of earnings, in eleven states. Two states had variations of (2) and (4).[18]

The five states with only minimum earnings requirements showed the widest differences, the amounts required ranging from $300 to $800 in the base year. All of the nine states that required earnings in two quarters also differed in their requirements. A minimum earnings requirement, even with the additional requirement of earnings in two quarters, is perhaps the poorest test as to whether a worker has been substantially attached to the labor market, since the higher his wages have been, the shorter the period he has needed to work in order to qualify for benefits. In addition, a minimum earnings requirement becomes obsolete as

wages rise. While most of these fourteen states had adjusted the requirements upward as wages increased, they still had the basic weakness of not testing the length of labor-market attachment.

Ten states required a multiple (usually 1.5) of high-quarter earnings in the base year to assure that the worker had employment over a substantial period of time. This requirement generally is an improvement over the two tests discussed in the preceding paragraph. For example, if the worker has worked full time for thirteen weeks in the high quarter, under a 1.5 times high-quarter formula he must have worked full time for nineteen and one-half weeks in the base year. However, a worker can still qualify with only a small number of weeks of employment. Thus, if the minimum earnings requirement is low but the worker has had high weekly earnings, he could meet a 1.5 times high-quarter earnings requirement with only a few weeks of employment. For example, if the minimum earnings requirement was only $300 and the worker had earned $75 a week, he could qualify for benefits by having worked four weeks in the high quarter and two weeks in some other quarter. Even with a substantial earnings requirement, many workers could qualify with a short record of employment. This was brought out in a sample study of 6,000 workers in Oregon in 1960. Of those with less than $500 in covered earnings, 16 per cent met the test of having 1.5 times high-quarter earnings, but only 0.5 per cent had twenty or more weeks of work.[19] Yet in 1961 only one of the ten states with a multiple of high-quarter earnings requirement, Alaska, had $500 as a minimum earnings requirement, and the remaining nine states had minimum earnings requirements as low as $276.

The third additional method is to require earnings equal to a stated multiple of the weekly benefit. Under this method, the weekly benefit is a fraction—from one-twentieth to one twenty-sixth—of earnings in the quarter in which earnings are highest in the base period. The qualifying requirement is set at from twenty to

18 *Comparison of State Unemployment Insurance Laws as of January 1, 1962*, BES No. U-141 (Bureau of Employment Security, Department of Labor, Washington, D.C.), Table 17, and supplemental unpublished information.

19 *Benefit Entitlement Study* (Oregon State Department of Employment, Salem, Oregon, April, 1962).

forty-five times the weekly benefit amount so determined, depending on the state. Assuming that the worker receives a weekly benefit amount equal to 50 per cent of his earnings and works thirteen weeks in each quarter, then thirty times the benefit amount, for example, would be equivalent to fifteen weeks of employment. This assumption probably does not fit the facts in a large number of cases. For instance, a worker may have worked only a few days or weeks in his "highest quarter," and still meet the minimum earnings requirement. Also, the smaller the proportion of benefits to weekly earnings, the shorter is the period of employment required to qualify for benefits. If a state has a qualifying requirement of thirty times the benefit amount, and a worker's weekly benefit amount is $30, then he needs $900 in qualifying wages. If he has earned $100 a week, he can qualify for benefits with only nine weeks of work.

The requirement of a specified number of weeks of employment, each with a minimum amount of earnings, is obviously the best test of labor-force attachment, since it assures that a worker, no matter how high his earnings, must have been employed for the required minimum amount of time.

Wisconsin's success in relying on "request reporting" to secure reports of earnings and weeks of employment from former employers when a worker files a claim for benefits had led ten other states,[20] by the end of 1963, to adopt the method of request reporting and make weeks of employment an eligibility requirement.

The superiority of the weeks of employment test was indicated by comparisons made in the Oregon sample study previously cited.[21] In that study, 22 per cent of those failing to meet a twenty weeks of employment test met a 1.5 times high-quarter test, while only 3.5 per cent of those failing the high-quarter test met the weeks of employment test. Of persons with $500 to $1,000 in earnings, 28 per cent met the high-quarter test but only 16 per cent

met the twenty weeks of work test. With today's levels of earnings, it is obvious that present laws which use minimum earnings tests or high-quarter earnings tests are generally inadequate.

A test of twenty weeks of employment in the base year is still no guarantee that it will include all workers who are normally attached to the labor market and exclude all those who are not. In order to get a factual basis for determining the number of weeks that would be a good test, New York state made a study in 1953 of the employment patterns of covered workers in eighteen selected industries over the five-year period of 1947–51.[22] The study showed that, except in three highly seasonal industries (canneries, costume jewelry, and seasonal hotels), from 72 to 87 per cent of the workers had twenty or more weeks of employment. However, when the percentage of workers who had twenty weeks of employment in each of the five years was calculated, it was found that, except in two industries (bakeries and men's coats and suits), less than half the workers were employed twenty weeks in each year. New York, therefore, adopted a unique provision that permits a person, if he does not meet the qualifying requirement of twenty weeks in one year, to qualify on the basis of fifteen weeks of employment in the fifty-two weeks preceding the claim if he has had forty weeks of employment in the preceding *two* years.

It is not known and it is difficult to ascertain what proportion of covered workers fail to meet the state qualifying requirements. Much of the difficulty stems from the fact that many covered workers do not file claims because they know they will not qualify, and only those who file claims are counted. Although many of the uncounted are among those who have substantial attachment to the labor market but do not file claims because they know they will not qualify, by far the greater number of uncounted covered workers who do not qualify are from

---

20 Also, Wyoming in 1963 added a weeks of employment requirement to its multiple of benefit amount provision.

21 *Benefit Entitlement Study* (n. 19), p. 21.

22 *Employment Patterns of Insured Workers in Selected New York Industries, 1947–51* (Division of Employment, Bureau of Research and Statistics, State Department of Labor, Albany, New York, October 30, 1953). (Mimeographed.)

among those who are recent entrants or are intermittently attached to the labor market. These workers constitute a substantial proportion of the unemployed and are excluded from qualification by the existence of *any* requirement of wages or employment.

The Bureau of Employment Security estimated that in April, 1960, the unemployed among new entrants to the labor force numbered 400,000 or 11.0 per cent of the total unemployed and in April, 1961, they numbered 450,000 or 9.0 per cent.[23] These new entrants are mainly youths but also include others, such as married women, who are re-entering the labor market in substantial numbers. In addition, an unknown number of these had some intermittent covered employment but have not met the state qualifying requirements.

Most covered workers find it easy to meet the qualifying requirements in the state laws. In some states it may be too easy to qualify, so that some workers who are seeking employment only part of the year are able to qualify for benefits.

The changing labor market of the nineteen-sixties, along with the changing role of unemployment insurance, manifested especially by the ever-increasing duration of benefits, demands that qualifying requirements be re-examined. When the country was still in the throes of the depression of the nineteen-thirties, it was recognized that unemployment insurance could serve only as a first line of defense against long-term unemployment. Its main purpose was considered to be the provision of protection against temporary layoffs. Even seasonal unemployment was not considered, and in many quarters still is not considered, to be a compensable risk.

Technological unemployment, especially that growing out of automation, is currently receiving much attention. Since technological changes often wipe out occupations, there is increasing debate as to whether extended unemployment compensation should be provided for the long-duration unemployment that frequently results. The federal administration

in 1961 and 1963 proposed such extended benefits, to be financed by an increase in the federal unemployment tax. Whether this approach to long-term unemployment prevails or whether the states will extend the duration of their benefits to meet the needs of workers who have long-duration unemployment because of technological displacement, qualifying requirements will need re-examination. The Kennedy Administration's bill, introduced in 1963, would require employment in 78 out of the 156 weeks preceding layoff and twenty-six weeks in the immediately preceding fifty-two weeks in order to compensate only those with long and substantial attachment to covered employment. The problem of providing protection for these unemployed needs not only careful thought but also careful research as to the work patterns and characteristics of those suffering from long-duration unemployment.

III. DISQUALIFICATIONS

To be eligible for unemployment insurance, a worker must have met the qualifying requirements of the law and be able to work and be available for work. He may still be disqualified, however, if the unemployment is due to his voluntary action, except in certain cases when the action was taken with good cause. Originally, the disqualifications were limited in general to four causes: (1) voluntary quitting without good cause; (2) discharge for misconduct; (3) refusal of suitable work; (4) unemployment due to a stoppage of work directly connected with a labor dispute. Except in the case of labor disputes, and even for this cause in New York (and later in Rhode Island), disqualifications were usually in the form of postponement of benefits for a definite, usually short, period. After the worker had served the disqualification period, he was eligible for benefits if he was still unemployed.

Over the years, disqualifications have been expanded or made more stringent.[24] The

---

[23] Bureau of Employment Security, *Selected Charts and Tables* (n. 15), p. 15.

[24] See in *Employment Security Review* (Bureau of Employment Security, U.S. Department of Labor, Washington, D.C.), "Twenty Years of Unemployment Insurance in 1933–55" (August, 1955), pp. 41–46; and

period of disqualification has been lengthened in many states, often for the duration of unemployment. In addition, some states now reduce the number of weeks of benefits to which the worker is entitled by the number of weeks of disqualification; and others cancel all benefit rights. Disqualification for misrepresentation or fraud has been made more stringent: originally a fine was imposed; now all but three states have added to that penalty a disqualification from benefits for a year or longer.

Some of the states disqualify workers for additional reasons, including attendance at school, pregnancy, or absence from work to fulfill marital obligations. Finally, a varying number of states disqualify workers or reduce their benefits if they are receiving certain specific types of wage-related income. As of January 1, 1962, this included workmen's compensation (twenty-three states), old-age insurance benefits (ten states), employers' pension plans (twenty-four states), wages in lieu of notice (twenty-nine states), dismissal payments (nineteen states), and supplemental unemployment benefits (two states).[25]

In recent years, there has been considerable controversy over whether a worker should receive a pension and unemployment compensation simultaneously.[26] Criticism is leveled particularly at those who retire voluntarily and file for unemployment compensation. This became an issue in the 1961 Temporary Extended Unemployment Compensation Act, which carried a provision that reduced unemployment benefits by the amount of pension received if the pension was provided or con-

tributed to by an employer who had paid wages on which part or all of the worker's regular unemployment compensation had been based.

The reasons for disqualification from benefits and the severity of the disqualifications vary widely from state to state. Some states have designed their disqualifications on the theory that the payment of unemployment compensation should be confined to unemployment where the employer is at fault. Thus, as of January 1, 1964, twenty-one states compensated only if the good cause for quitting was connected with the work, was attributable to the employer, or involved fault on the part of the employer. The justification given for this restriction is that the employer is paying the whole cost of unemployment compensation and should not have to pay for unemployment for which he is not responsible. Most states, however, pay benefits to workers who have quit for good cause whether or not the cause is attributable to the employer.

Great variations in the laws are also due to differences of opinion as to whether the disqualification should continue until the worker is re-employed or for only a stated number of weeks. Disqualification for a limited period is based on the presumption that after a time unemployment is no longer due to the original cause but to the inability of the worker to find work. Those states that disqualify workers for the duration of unemployment do so on the theory that the employer's liability for such disqualified workers should be completely wiped out. Some of these states require, in addition, a certain amount of re-employment before the worker can again become eligible for unemployment compensation.

With respect to labor disputes, there are differences in the states as to the types of disputes to which a disqualification applies and the extent of involvement in the dispute that must exist in order for a worker to be disqualified. At the end of 1963, nine states defined labor disputes to exclude lockouts, three states excluded disputes where the employer does not live up to the labor contract, and four excluded disputes where the employer is not living up to laws relating to wages, hours,

---

"Unemployment Insurance in the USA, 1956–1960: V. Trends in Disqualifications" (August, 1960), pp. 20–23.

[25] By January 1, 1964, all but four states (New Hampshire, New Mexico, South Carolina, and South Dakota) had taken action on the question of permitting supplementation. Only Virginia did not permit supplementation.

[26] For studies of this problem see *Pensioners and Unemployment Insurance* (Division of Employment, State Department of Labor, Albany, New York, February, 1960); *Pensioners among Claimants Drawing Unemployment Compensation* (Employment Service, State of Washington, Olympia, Washington, November, 1962).

etc. Individuals were not disqualified if neither they nor any of the same grade or class of workers were participating in the dispute (forty-two states), were financing the dispute (thirty states), or were directly interested in the dispute (forty-one states).

There is no disagreement that a worker should be disqualified if he willfully misrepresents the facts in his claim; the only disagreement is with respect to the severity of the penalty. The most common provisions disqualify for the remainder of the benefit year or up to fifty-two weeks after the fraud occurred.

The remaining types of disqualification were usually enacted because of the difficulty of determining the exact period during which a worker is available for work. In thirty-seven states, as of January 1, 1964, a pregnant worker is disqualified if her unemployment falls within a stated period, such as six weeks before and six weeks after childbirth. Some laws require re-employment following childbirth before the worker is again eligible for benefits.

In considering receipt of other income, some states disqualify the worker or automatically reduce benefits if the worker is in receipt of the stated type of income. Other states make a determination as to whether or not the worker is genuinely available for work and disqualify him or reduce benefits only if he has left the labor market.

How many of the unemployed are excluded from unemployment benefits through disqualifications? Statistics have been compiled on only four types of disqualifications. Although these have been the most common causes and account for the bulk of disqualifications, they are not all the causes, and the statistics are therefore incomplete. Furthermore, many who realize that the reason for their separation from work would disqualify them from benefits do not file claims; as has been stated earlier, only those who file claims and then are disqualified are counted. Any statistics on disqualifications will thus understate the actual number of workers who do not draw benefits due to disqualification.

The largest number of disqualifications are for unavailability for work. The statistics are purely a count of those who, in filing for a particular week, claim to be, but are found not to be, able and available for work. In July–September, 1963, these totaled 290,878 or 1.4 per cent of all the weekly contacts that the offices had with the claimants. These were unemployed workers who thought they could prove that they were genuinely unemployed. Perhaps a large number of these workers were denied benefits because they were not "actively seeking work."[27]

The statistics for July–September, 1963, on the other three principal reasons for disqualification were: 165,722, or 5.22 per cent of all who filed a claim at the beginning of a new period of unemployment, disqualified for voluntary quits without good cause; 54,876, or 1.73 per cent of those who filed a claim for a new period of unemployment, disqualified due to discharge for misconduct; and 22,168, or less than 0.1 per cent of the contacts of the claimants with the local employment security office, disqualified for refusal of suitable work. The most accurate statistics are probably on those who refuse suitable work, since in these cases the worker is disqualified while he is claiming benefits and usually the job he has refused is one to which he has been referred by the public employment office. Statistics on disqualifications for voluntary quits and for misconduct are available only on workers who may have thought the reason for leaving work was not disqualifying, or thought that it was at least worth finding out whether the cause was disqualifying. Any study of appealed cases will indicate why such workers file claims. The appeal tribunals and courts frequently draw very fine distinctions. The wording of the disqualification in various state laws is identical, but in some states a cause of unemployment is found to be disqualifying, while in another state it is not found to be a reason for denial of the benefits.[28]

[27] Many states impose by law or administrative practice a further requirement that the worker, in addition to registering for work at the employment office, apply for work at other places.

[28] See "Issues Reflected in Appeals Decisions on Unemployment Benefits," monthly articles in *The*

To construct a satisfactory system of disqualifications, we need to know a great deal more than we do about the characteristics—especially the degree of labor-force attachment —of those who are disqualified. But in this area practically our only source of information comes from individual, appealed cases; we have almost no tested quantitative information.[29]

IV. PAYMENT OF BENEFITS DURING TRAINING

One of the best ways to aid an unemployed worker who cannot find a job in his own occupation or one for which his training and experience qualify him is to retrain him for work that is available. Because the emphasis in current manpower policy is on providing training, it seems desirable to go rather fully into the relationship of such training to unemployment compensation. Until recently, practically all states denied a worker unemployment compensation if he underwent training during any week of his unemployment, on the theory that the worker was not available for work. The two exceptions, the District of Columbia and Massachusetts, made training an adjunct to benefits. The District of Columbia denied unemployment compensation if a worker refused training. Massachusetts not only paid unemployment compensation during training but extended benefits for sixteen weeks if this was necessary for the worker to complete his training. The inconsistency of preventing training through denial of unemployment compensation has been increasingly discussed, with the result that by January 1, 1964, twenty-one states had provisions in their laws permitting a worker to take training while receiving unemployment compensation. A few states, through regulations or interpretations, also paid benefits during training, but several of these provided that if a worker is offered suitable employment while undergoing training, he must accept it and stop his training.

In recognition of the fact that most states deny unemployment compensation during training and also that there are limitations on the coverage of unemployment insurance, both the Area Redevelopment Act of 1961 and the Manpower Development and Training Act of 1962 provided that a worker could receive a training allowance. The amount of the allowance was set at the average unemployment compensation payment in the state.[30] The acts also provided that if a worker was seeking or receiving unemployment compensation for any week while undergoing training, he would be denied the training allowance. The training act also provided that if a state pays unemployment compensation during training, the federal government will reimburse the state for such payments.

It has not yet been clearly established in public policy if unemployment compensation should be paid during training or if it should be denied and training allowances financed by general taxation be substituted for it; and this has been the cause of much confused thinking. It has always been a principle of unemployment insurance that it is payable only to those who are available for work. If an unemployed worker is in a training course, particularly if it is full time, he may not be available for work. The question then arises whether he should be paid unemployment compensation. Many employers feel that they should not be required to finance unemployment compensation if a worker removes himself from the active labor market by undertaking training. The training

---

Labor Market and Employment Security, until its discontinuance at the end of 1963, and in *Unemployment Insurance Review*, which began publication in January, 1964, and reprints of the articles in BES No. U-180, July, 1959, and BES No. U-201, July, 1961, and BES No. U-213, January, 1963 (Bureau of Employment Security, U.S. Department of Labor, Washington, D.C.).

[29] One small study that gives information on this point is Fred Slavick, *Voluntary Quit Disqualification in Unemployment Insurance—The Iowa Experience*, Research Series No. 21 (Bureau of Labor and Management, College of Commerce, University of Iowa, Iowa City, Iowa, 1958).

[30] An amendment to MDTA in 1963 (Public Law 88–214) permits payments, in certain instances, up to $10 more than the amount of the average weekly unemployment compensation payment in the state, or the amount of unemployment compensation to which the worker is entitled if it is greater than the average compensation payment in the state.

may not fit the worker for a job in the employer's plant—in fact, it may facilitate his finding work in another plant—so why should any benefits paid during training be charged to the worker's former employer? Others argue that the employer should be willing to finance the training, since it may make the worker more employable and thereby shorten the period during which he draws unemployment compensation.

Congress has seemed to believe that unemployment compensation should be payable to the worker during weeks that he is taking training. However, when the House was considering the Manpower Development and Training Act, it was pointed out that only some of the states provided for continuance of benefits during training. Accordingly, in order that such states should not be at a financial disadvantage as compared with states not continuing benefits, the House inserted a provision that any state should be reimbursed if it paid unemployment compensation during training. The Senate, in its version of the bill, had followed the Area Redevelopment Act of 1961 by providing that the worker would receive training allowances if he was not "seeking or receiving" unemployment compensation. Under this wording, a worker could avoid filing a claim for unemployment compensation, even if he were eligible for it, and draw a training allowance. The confusion created by the problem delayed the bill for days. In the end, both House and Senate wordings were retained, although the use of the Senate language made the reimbursement feature in the House language unnecessary. This indicates the confusion surrounding the question of the relationship of unemployment compensation and training allowances. Whether training allowances should be financed through unemployment compensation or through general government funds remains to be resolved. In the meantime, the principle has been clearly established that a worker should receive income maintenance, either in the form of unemployment compensation or in some other form of allowance, during his training period. Also, it has been definitely accepted that such allowances should be related to the amounts

paid under unemployment compensation and that there should not be duplication of training allowances and unemployment compensation.

V. FINANCING

A unique feature of the American system of unemployment insurance is that it is financed almost entirely by the employer.[31]

Under the system, a federal unemployment tax of 3.1 per cent of the first $3,000 of a covered worker's annual earnings is imposed on the employer. Employers can receive credit for 2.7 per cent if they pay taxes under a state unemployment insurance law meeting federal requirements; so 2.7 per cent of the worker's earnings has become the "standard" employer contribution under state laws.

Another feature of the American system is the "experience rating" of employer contributions. Employers with favorable unemployment experience are assigned contribution rates of less than 2.7 per cent of their taxable payrolls and are given "additional credit" against the federal tax for the difference between their actual state tax rate and 2.7 per cent of their taxable payrolls.

The experience rates are assigned by different methods in the several states, the most common being the "reserve ratio" method. Under this method, the total benefits chargeable to an employer's account in the state fund are subtracted from his total contributions from the time he began to be covered by the state law; and the balance is expressed as a ratio to his average annual taxable payroll during the last one to five years. His tax rate is determined by the size of this reserve ratio. Each state has several tax schedules, depending on the size of its total fund, so that an employer with the same reserve ratio for several years may pay a different tax rate in different years if the size of the state fund has changed sufficiently to

---

[31] While originally ten states also provided employee contributions, only three states were doing so in 1963: Alabama, with employee contribution rates of 0.25–0.5 per cent; Alaska, with rates of 0.3–0.9 per cent; and New Jersey, with a rate of 0.25 per cent. In Alabama and New Jersey, the contribution is based on the first $3,000 of earnings, in Alaska on the first $7,200.

activate a different tax schedule. Since experience rating has come into operation, tax rates have always averaged less than 2.7 per cent of taxable payrolls for the country as a whole. The low point was reached in 1954 when an average of only 1.12 per cent of taxable payrolls—the first $3,000 of each employee's earnings—was paid into state unemployment insurance funds.

The states thought it possible to let employer tax rates fall so low following World War II, primarily because practically nothing was paid out in unemployment benefits during the war years. Reserves had been built up to a national average of 11.81 per cent of taxable payrolls in 1945. Since the war, and particularly since the recession of 1953–54, benefit costs have been rising, mainly as a result of higher levels of unemployment. Part of this increased cost has been absorbed by higher levels of employer taxes, but part has been absorbed by use of the high reserves that previously had been built up. Accordingly, at the end of 1962, reserves had been reduced to a national average of 5.0 per cent of taxable payrolls.

This drop in reserves has raised the question of when a reserve fund is in danger of insolvency. Recognizing that there are many factors to be considered in determining the solvency of an unemployment insurance fund, the federal Bureau of Employment Security considers it a warning signal when a state's reserves fall below 1.5 times its highest cost rate in any preceding year. In 1958, the reserves of eleven states were below this warning point. At the end of 1962, a total of twenty-three states had reserves below this point, and seven states had reserves of less than their highest cost rate.

The first and most obvious way for a state to improve its financial condition when its reserves have fallen too low is to increase taxes. Most of the states have increased taxes, so that taxes averaged 2.36 per cent of taxable payrolls in 1962. In several states, average tax rates rose to 2.7 per cent—the maximum allowable against the federal tax—and in six states they had been pushed above 2.7 per cent, the highest average

being 3.26 per cent, in Pennsylvania. Individual employer tax rates in several states are even higher, the highest possible rate being 4.5 per cent, in Michigan. However, several of the states whose finances are in the worst condition have taken no action or inadequate action to remedy their situations.

One of the inhibitions to raising adequate taxes is that a state hesitates to raise its tax rates above the 2.7 per cent credit allowable against the federal unemployment tax, because it might place its employers at a competitive disadvantage with employers in states maintaining a 2.7 per cent maximum rate. The states are especially reluctant to raise their rates now because they are paying a temporarily increased federal tax rate (3.5 per cent on the taxable wages of 1962 and 3.35 per cent on those of 1963) to finance the Temporary Extended Unemployment Compensation Act of 1961; moreover, some states still have to repay the advances made to them by the federal government under the Temporary Unemployment Compensation Act of 1958.

A state can increase its tax income, if it hesitates to raise tax rates above a certain level, by increasing the taxable wage base above $3,000. As of January 1, 1964, fourteen states had wage bases higher than $3,000, ranging from $3,300 to $7,200. In ten states the wage base had been raised to the first $3,600 a year; and in Alaska it was raised to the first $7,200. The Bureau of Employment Security has been pressing for an increase in the tax base for some time. It points out that the first $3,000 of annual earnings of each covered worker represented about 95 per cent of total payrolls in 1939 but in 1963 represented less than 60 per cent. If the relationship of taxable to total payrolls that existed in 1939 were restored, it would produce roughly 50 per cent more income at the tax levels existing in 1962. This proposal has become highly controversial.

Those opposed to increasing the taxable wage base contend that it would benefit principally "high cost" employers who should instead have their tax *rates* increased. Those favoring an increase in the tax base argue that high cost employers are not necessarily low wage employers and that the states would secure more taxes from them through an increase in the tax base. Professor Richard A. Lester has shown that even in the ten industries with the highest costs in New Jersey, the proportion of wages above $3,000 ranged from 21.8 to 45.0 per cent in 1960.[32] More research is needed to settle this argument. The federal administration bill of 1963 proposed an increase in the federal unemployment tax base to $5,200, but the states are divided as to whether there should be federal action or whether action should be left to individual states.

Another possible method of helping states with high costs to finance their systems is through some type of assistance from the federal government. Up to the time of writing (February, 1964), this has taken the form of loans (technically termed "advances") from the Federal Unemployment Account in the Unemployment Trust Fund to states whose reserves fall below specified levels. Three states—Alaska, Pennsylvania, and Michigan—had received such advances by the end of 1959. In 1960 the requirements for advances and repayments were drastically tightened so that there is little likelihood of any state (except perhaps Alaska) qualifying for an advance in the future. Even if a state might qualify for an advance in a period of extreme difficulty, this would be no permanent cure for its financial troubles, since the advance would eventually have to be repaid.

Still another method of assistance, which has been advocated for years, but without any success, is to "reinsure" states by giving them a federal "reinsurance grant" when their

[32] Lester, *The Economics of Unemployment Compensation* (n. 8), Table 13, p. 80.

reserves are below a designated level. A truer type of reinsurance was developed by the Benefit Financing Committee of the Interstate Conference in 1963. Its plan for "catastrophe reinsurance" would spread the cost of unusual risks among the states. Still another approach was included in the administration's bill for unemployment insurance introduced in 1963. This took the form of "equalization grants," that is, federal grants equal to two-thirds of a state's costs above a stated level in any year. This level was put at 2.7 per cent except in years when the average benefit cost in all states was above 2.7 per cent. In such years, the grant would be made on the basis of the excess costs in any state over the average cost in all states. This approach meets one of the arguments against "reinsurance grants"; namely, that grants would be made to states that had let their reserves become depleted through irresponsible financing. On the other hand, the proposal is still criticized on the basis that there are no adequate safeguards against states "going wild" on the benefits they provide, since the cost of such benefits above the statutory levels would be financed largely by the federal government. Those favoring the proposal argue that if a state has to pay one-third of the excess costs, this will be a sufficient curb against overliberality in benefits.

If their financing is not strengthened in the near future by federal or state action, or both, and if past high levels of unemployment continue, there is no doubt that those states whose reserves are low will be under great pressure to keep benefits below an adequate level. The method of financing unemployment insurance therefore will have an important bearing on the extent to which the program provides aid to the unemployed.

CHAPTER 5

The Adequacy of Benefits in Unemployment Insurance

Joseph M. Becker[*]

THIS DISCUSSION OF benefit adequacy proceeds on the assumption that decisions with respect to coverage and eligibility (see Chapter 4) have already been made. These crucial decisions determine whether the program is to be limited to the core of the labor force (the full-time, full-year workers with wages above a determined minimum) or whether it is to include some or all of the many classes of workers surrounding this core. Insofar as decisions on coverage and eligibility are logically prior to decisions on benefits, it is reasonable to proceed on this assumption; but what should not be overlooked is that in practice both sets of decisions are made interdependently. For example, a decision to make duration of benefits uniform is likely to be accompanied by a decision to raise the eligibility requirements; contrariwise, a decision to keep eligibility requirements low is likely to be accompanied by a decision to keep duration shorter, or to make duration variable rather than uniform.

Decisions concerning benefit adequacy depend on the answers to two questions: "What is adequacy?" and "Are present benefits adequate by this definition?" Neither question can be answered with entire satisfaction—the first because of the nature of the question itself, the second because of a paucity of data.

The first question is by its nature indefinite. Adequacy is a normative concept rooted in a

* Associate Director, Institute of Social Order, Saint Louis University.

value system, and in any large society there will be many different value systems. Reflecting these values, the concept will vary from user to user, often in unstated ways. Many a disagreement about the "adequacy" of a given benefit provision is really a disagreement about the definition of adequacy and stems fundamentally from different value systems.

I. SELECTION OF NORMS OF ADEQUACY

Norms of benefit adequacy are constituted by the objectives, the intended effects, of the payment of benefits. The main intended effects are twofold: an effect on the economy (to maintain employment) and an effect on the individual (to meet his needs).

The net effect of unemployment insurance on the level of employment is a complex one and probably varies with economic conditions. On the tax side the program can (1) regularize the demand for labor, but it can also (2) decrease the demand for labor. On the benefit side the program can (3) increase the demand for labor, but it can also (4) diminish the supply of labor. There is a general assumption among economists that the positive factors (1 and 3) outweigh the negative factors (2 and 4), at least in situations where there has occurred a sharp decrease in the demand for labor. But because the interaction of these forces is extremely complex, opposing interest groups can usually make a plausible case for contradictory predictions of what the net effect will be, at least in the long run. As a result, arguments based on this effect, rarely, if ever, prove decisive.

The effect of unemployment benefits in meeting the needs of the unemployed individual is much clearer and usually is more influential in determining legislative action. If unemployment insurance were not needed for the individual, it is not likely that it would be established solely for its effect on the general economy. On the other hand, if unemployment insurance had no effect on the level of employment, and probably even if it had a minor negative effect, we should still want the program for the help it brings to unemployed individuals. In this sense, it may be said that the primary objective of the program is to help the unemployed individual.

Since there is not sufficient space to treat both objectives thoroughly, the present discussion of benefit adequacy focuses on the primary objective only. This is in accord with the general scope of the symposium, which includes the alleviation and cure but not the prevention of unemployment; hence the discussion ignores the possible impact of unemployment benefits on production and considers only the impact on distribution.

As a form of income distribution, unemployment benefits are regulated by the two general principles of all distribution. There is the individualistic, competitive principle—"To everyone according to his contribution"—and there is the socialistic, welfare principle—"To everyone according to his need."

A given system of distribution will be characterized by the relative emphasis accorded the one or the other of these principles. The competitive market system, for example, uses mainly the first principle; while the social assistance programs use mainly the second. Such systems have a clear, easily understood logic. But unemployment compensation as a form of social insurance makes use of both principles and attempts to combine them in order to have the best of both worlds.

The combination is reflected in the very term "social insurance." As social *insurance* unemployment compensation makes use of the competitive principle and grants benefits only to those for whom (some) premiums have been paid and grants benefits (somewhat) in proportion to the premiums paid. But as *social* insurance it makes use of the welfare principle and does not attempt to match benefits exactly with premiums. As a result, it requires persons with different risks to pay the same premium, grants the same benefits to persons who have paid different premiums, and grants different benefits to persons who have paid the same premium.

Of these two aspects of social insurance, the social, or welfare, aspect has the primacy. The two are related to each other as means to end: the insurance technique is a means to the welfare end. Important though the technique is, it is subordinate to the welfare end and may never be so emphasized as to jeopardize the substantial attainment of that end.

It is sometimes said that unemployment insurance is not based on need. Stated thus, without qualification, the proposition contains a grave error. Unemployment insurance is a compulsory governmental program, and in our society we make use of governmental compulsion only when there is a clear and urgent need for it. Western political society is based on the principle of subsidiarity, which in its negative form states that a higher unit of society should not undertake to perform the functions which can be performed as well by a lower unit but should limit itself to provide the help (*subsidium*) that is needed to enable the lower unit to function at full capacity. Government should help the individual to help himself, and beyond that, as Lincoln expressed it, "Government should do for the people only what the people cannot do or cannot do so well for themselves."

Although the principle of subsidiarity can be expressed in positive form and used to justify governmental action, historically in the West the emphasis has been, as in Lincoln's formulation, on the negative form and on the limiting function of the principle. The principle of subsidiarity gives *preference* to individual responsibility and requires that the need for governmental intervention be both clear and urgent. This choice of emphasis is crucial.

It sometimes happens in public discussions of the limitations which ought to govern the amount and duration of benefits that the only limitation mentioned is the danger of malingering. This is to overlook the still more fundamental limitation, the principle of subsidiarity. Even if benefits equal to 100 per cent of wages could be paid for an indefinite period without any danger of malingering, the conclusion would not immediately follow that the program should pay such benefits. In our kind of society, before a compulsory redistribution of income can be justified, it must be established that the individuals who are to receive the benefits are in need of them. The definition of need may be very liberal, but the justification is always in terms of need. If in 1935 we had not judged that there existed a need which individuals were incapable of meeting by themselves, unemployment insurance would not have been established; and the extent of unmet need is still the fundamental norm which determines the extent to which unemployment insurance shall be further developed.

The operation of this "social" principle of need is apparent throughout the program. A judgment as to need underlies the common practice of weighting the benefit formula in favor of the lower-paid worker. A judgment as to need underlies the provision of uniform duration, minimum benefits, and—in twelve states—dependency allowances. A judgment as to need also partly explains the existence of a maximum benefit: the essential needs of most unemployed persons are judged (correctly or incorrectly) not to exceed this amount; and if the maximum benefit results, as it usually does, in the higher-paid worker receiving a smaller proportion of his wages in benefits, this is justified by the reasoning that he is not in so great need as the lower-paid worker and is more able to help himself. The possible existence of unmet need explains the launching of the benefit-adequacy studies that are analyzed later in this chapter; the studies themselves, therefore, constitute a recognition of the validity of the social principle.

But the "insurance" principle is also essential. The absence of the individual needs test from unemployment compensation constitutes one of the most satisfying characteristics of the program. In social insurance it is not each claimant's proved need, established by individual investigation, that is the norm; it is the presumed need of a general class, established preferably by an antecedent general investigation but, in any case, presumed for each individual who falls within the class.

The decision to use the norm of presumed rather than proved need is crucial and affects every aspect of the problem of benefit adequacy. Implied in the choice of presumed need is the acceptance of the fact that the program must operate in terms of averages. There will not be the close fitting of individual benefits to individual needs that is possible in a program that uses the norm of proved need. In an insurance program it must be accepted that some beneficiaries will be underpaid and some overpaid in terms of the need that brought the program into existence. (However, the extent to which beneficiaries are underpaid or overpaid can be lessened by proper classification; for example, by distinguishing between beneficiaries with and without dependents.)

To achieve what they consider the ideal program, different people will combine the social and insurance emphases in different ways. The purpose of the following analysis is not to determine the ideal combination but to see how the present combination is working out. With that information it should be possible to choose the ideal combination more intelligently. In our examination of the present system, we shall consider first the amount and then the duration of benefits. For reasons that become clear in the course of the consideration, analysis predominates in the treatment of the benefit amount, but description predominates in the treatment of the benefit duration.

II. THE ADEQUACY OF THE BENEFIT AMOUNT

In the United States the decision has been made to pay unemployment insurance benefits that vary directly with wages, with a higher benefit paid to the man who is used to a higher standard of living; in theory, though not always in practice, more taxes will have been paid into the fund for such a man. The general decision to pay benefits in some proportion to wages must be complemented by the difficult choice of a definite proportion. The proportion chosen will depend on (1) the relation to be maintained between the typical worker's living standard during employment and during unemployment and (2) the typical worker's resources apart from unemployment benefits. Our society has never stated its expectations with respect to either (1) or (2) and, therefore, has never made an explicit commitment in either area.

The benefit-adequacy studies that are discussed below can help bring about a more explicit social commitment as to what we expect in both these areas. By revealing how beneficiaries actually manage when unemployed, the studies enable us to specify with greater particularity where the system does or does not meet our expectations. Previously, we may have been uncertain about the adequacy of the system because we were unable to state even to ourselves what we meant by adequacy. When we have seen how the present system actually operates, and our implicit norms have become explicit, we shall be in a better position to decide whether to keep or change our norms.

The investigation of the adequacy of the benefit amount involves the answering of two questions: "What proportion of their wages do beneficiaries receive?" and "How well do they manage on what they receive?" The two questions are related as means to end: We settle on a certain benefit-wage proportion because we expect it to support a certain standard of living.

Because it is not feasible to investigate all possible proportions of wages in relation to all possible standards of living, this discussion is guided chiefly by the two norms (explained later) which have the widest social acceptance at the present time: Benefits should (1) equal half of wages and (2) suffice to meet essential expenditures. The wide acceptance of these norms gives them undoubted significance, but it must be kept in mind that these norms are to some extent arbitrary and that other conclusions would follow if other norms were used.

A. WHAT PROPORTION OF THEIR WAGES DO BENEFICIARIES RECEIVE?

General Estimates

There are few exact data available with which to answer the apparently simple question posed above, but rough estimates can be derived from the relation of average benefits to average wages and also from the proportion of beneficiaries who receive the maximum benefit.

The Average Benefit. In 1963 the average benefit for all states was 36 per cent of the average covered wage, a proportion that ranged among the states from 25 per cent to 48 per cent.[1] Does this mean that in 1963 most beneficiaries received the stated percentages of their wages? Not necessarily; indeed probably not. This measure of benefit adequacy must be interpreted in the light of four distinctions.

First of all, the distribution of wages among the covered population is not necessarily the same as among beneficiaries. To the extent that the average wage of beneficiaries runs lower than the average wage of all covered workers, the measure underestimates the adequacy of benefits. (A low-wage worker usually receives a higher percentage of his wages in benefits than does the average worker.) This is the more usual case,[2] but exceptions occur in some industrial states during recessions and in agricultural states in which highly paid employees from the construction industry predominate among the beneficiaries. Furthermore, even among beneficiaries the distribution of wages is skewed, so that the average is an un-

[1] Preliminary data furnished to the author by the Bureau of Employment Security, U.S. Department of Labor, April 17, 1964.

[2] A Bureau of Labor Statistics' study of those unemployed five weeks and more in 1961 found that, on the average, they had been earning about $70 per week on their last job; the comparable wage for year-round, full-time workers during 1961 was about $95. "Work History, Attitudes, and Income of the Unemployed," *Monthly Labor Review* (December, 1963), p. 1410.

certain guide to the actual number of beneficiaries whose benefits equal half of their wages.[3]

The other three distinctions concern the definition of "wages." An emphasis on the contributory principle in unemployment insurance (social *insurance*) leads to the choice of the beneficiary's average, gross, base-period wage—the wage on which taxes were paid and by which the benefits were earned. An emphasis on the principle of need (*social insurance*) leads to the choice of the beneficiary's full-time, net, recent wage—the wage on which the beneficiary's current standard of living is presumably based. These wages differ in several ways relevant to the problem of adequacy.

A beneficiary's *most recent* wage is later than his base-period wage by varying lengths of time —from a couple of months to, rarely, a couple of years. Insofar as these wages differ, the beneficiary's most recent wage will usually be higher than his base-period wage, not only because inflation may be at work but also because it is normal for workers to receive wage increases as their length of employment increases. However, it is also possible for the recent wage to be lower—for example, in the case of a pensioner working at his first post-retirement job.

A beneficiary's *full-time* wage is usually higher than his average wage because the average wage may reflect some unemployment. However, it can also be lower—for example, if the average reflects much overtime pay.

A beneficiary's *net* wage will always be lower, of course, than his gross wage by the amount of taxes (income and social security) withheld; note also that a beneficiary without dependents will receive a lower net wage than a beneficiary with dependents, even though both earn the same gross wage. The concept of net income is especially pertinent in the case of working wives. Practically all of the secondary earner (SEC) beneficiaries in the benefit-adequacy

studies analyzed below belong in this category. According to one estimate, only about half of their gross wages represent a net addition to the family income.[4] Hence unemployment benefits that are 50 per cent of their gross wages are equal to full wages in terms of net gain to the family.

In addition to the loss of net wages, the unemployed worker may experience the loss of some fringe benefits, and the question is raised whether unemployment benefits should replace this additional loss. Although desirable, it is probably not practical to replace fringe benefits. First of all, beneficiaries differ greatly in the fringe benefits to which they are entitled. Second, the function of unemployment insurance is to supply a temporary bridge between jobs, and there is no feasible way to replace the major fringe benefits (sickness and accident insurance and the opportunity to build up pension and vacation rights) on a temporary basis by unemployment benefits. The more rational arrangement, adopted by some companies, is to continue for a time the unemployed worker's rights to these fringe benefits.[5]

The application of the four distinctions generally results in a more favorable picture of benefit adequacy. To see how large a difference can result, one may compare column 5 of Table 5–1, which reflects none of the distinctions, with columns 3 and 4 of Table 5–2, which reflect all four. For example: In New York state in 1958, the average benefit was only 37 per cent of the average, gross, base-period wage of all covered workers; but in Utica at that time the percentage of beneficiaries actually receiving half or more of their full-time, net, recent wages was twice that figure. As a measure of the proportion of benefits to beneficiaries' wages the first figure, the one most

---

[3] The quantities in column 5 of Table 5–1 are not, therefore, a very reliable guide to the quantities in column 2 (still less to those in column 3) of Table 5–2.

[4] "Net Contribution of Working Wives in Texas to Family Income," *Monthly Labor Review* (December, 1962), pp. 1383–84.

[5] Although most fringe benefits are not relevant to the issue of benefit adequacy, they are relevant to the closely related issue of maintaining a differential between the rewards for working and not working. A smaller differential between benefits and wages suffices—that is, benefits may be higher—where wages are augmented by fringe benefits.

often used because it is most easily obtained, is obviously not very reliable.

The Maximum Benefit. Another rough estimate of the relationship between benefits and wages can be derived from the proportion of beneficiaries who receive the maximum benefit. Since nearly all state laws provide a benefit that is at least half of gross wages, up to the point where the maximum benefit acts as a ceiling, it is plausible to conclude that beneficiaries receiving less than the maximum benefit are receiving half or more of their gross wage and that those at the maximum are receiving less than half. In the United States during 1963, 45 per cent of all beneficiaries were eligible for the basic maximum benefit; among the states the proportion ranged from 11 per cent to 80 per cent.[6]

Although this measure is a more reliable guide than the preceding one, it also must be used with care. First of all, the figures are usually published in terms of the "basic maximum," which does not include dependents' benefits. In the twelve states which provide dependents' benefits, this measure considerably overstates the proportion of beneficiaries who, stopped by the basic maximum, are presumably receiving less than half their wages.[7] Moreover, for various reasons some beneficiaries at the maximum do, and some beneficiaries below the maximum do not, receive half of their full-time, net recent wage.[8] Nevertheless, partly because the variations above and below the maximum cancel out, the measure can be a rough indicator of the proportion of the beneficiaries receiving half or more of their net wages.[9]

A third rough estimate of the adequacy of the benefit amount is based on the proportion of total wage loss in the economy replaced by unemployment benefits. This proportion, which is itself an estimate involving many assumptions, is apparently quite low—probably less than 25 per cent. But this proportion reflects many kinds of workers and unemployment situations for which unemployment insurance is not intended. For example, it includes the non-covered workers, and among the covered workers it reflects the experience of nonclaimers, late claimers, the disqualified, and the ineligible. It also reflects the operation of the benefit duration provisions. Hence, it serves more as a reminder that the effect of benefits on the economy will always be a secondary norm[10] than it does as a guide to the appropriate weekly benefit amount. For this latter purpose it is nearly useless.

The Benefit-Adequacy Surveys

The best single source of information on the adequacy of unemployment benefits is found in the seven sample surveys completed between 1954 and 1958 by six states in co-operation with the Bureau of Employment Security.[11] The objective of each survey was to discover how a sample of the insured unemployed managed when they lost their jobs and to what extent

---

[6] See note 1.

[7] For example, the source quoted in note 1 shows Illinois as paying the (basic) maximum benefit of $38 to 67 per cent of its beneficiaries. But Illinois provides a number of different maximums, the highest at that time being $59. Illinois calculates that in 1962–63 less than 50 per cent of its beneficiaries received the maximum benefit available to each beneficiary class. As another example: The same source lists Michigan as paying a basic *maximum* benefit of $33; yet the *average* benefit paid in Michigan at that time was over $35.

[8] See Table 5–3, item 6, columns 2, 4, 6. The reasons lie partly in the benefit formulas, partly in the difference between the two definitions of wages.

[9] See, for example, in Table 5–2 the general correspondence that exists between column 3 and the complement of column 5.

[10] During the five-year period, 1958–62, annual unemployment benefits averaged only 0.58 per cent of the gross national product; the range was from 0.4 to 0.9 per cent. When the amount of taxes is subtracted from the amount of benefits paid during this period, the net cash contribution of the unemployment insurance system to private "purchasing power" is greatly reduced: the average for the period was 0.14 per cent, and the range was −0.05 per cent to 0.5 per cent. This contribution, while significant for the localities in which it occurred, is not so great as to constitute a primary norm of benefit adequacy.

[11] Copies of the surveys can be obtained from the employment security agencies of the respective states. Separate procedural reports accompany the surveys and can be obtained from the same source. There is available a summary of the first six surveys, prepared by Saul J. Blaustein and Daniel N. Price of the Bureau of Employment Security, *Unemployment Insurance and the Family Finances of the Unemployed* (BES No. U-203, July, 1961). For an analysis of the surveys, including Utica, see Joseph M. Becker, *The Adequacy of the Benefit Amount in Unemployment Insurance*, published by the W. E. Upjohn Institute for Employment Research (Kalamazoo, Michigan, May, 1961).

TABLE 5–1: SELECTED BENEFIT-WAGE RELATIONSHIPS PREVAILING IN STATE AT TIME OF BENEFIT-ADEQUACY SURVEYS

State and year of survey	Method of computing benefit	Amount of benefit		Average benefit as per cent of average covered wage	Maximum benefit as per cent of average covered wage	Per cent of beneficiaries in receipt of maximum benefit
		Minimum	Maximum			
(1)	(2)	(3)	(4)	(5)	(6)	(7)
Florida (1956)	1/13–1/26 of high quarter wages	$ 8	$26	32%	40%	42%
South Carolina (1957)	1/21–1/26 of high quarter wages	8	26	37	45	29
New York (1957)	67%–51% of average weekly wage	10	36	35	41	42
Oregon (1958)	1/26 of high quarter wages	15	40	41	47	60
Missouri (1958)	1/25 of high quarter wages	8	33	34	41	55
New York (1958)	67%–51% of average weekly wage	10	45	37	49	36

SOURCES: *Handbook of Unemployment Insurance Financial Data, 1938–1958*, Rev. Edition, April, 1960. *BES No. U-191*, July, 1960. *Statistical Supplement, Labor Market and Employment Security.* (All issued by Bureau of Employment Security, U.S. Department of Labor.)

they were helped by their unemployment benefits. The samples were drawn from the following labor markets: Pittsburgh, Pennsylvania (August, 1954); Tampa-St. Petersburg, Florida (October, 1956); Anderson-Greenville-Spartanburg, South Carolina (March, 1957); Albany-Schenectady-Troy, New York (April, 1957); Portland, Oregon (March, 1958); St. Louis, Missouri (April, 1958); Utica, New York (fall of 1958).

The benefit formulas in use in these states at the time of the studies are shown in Table 5–1.[12] Three of the states used a weighted formula, which is more liberal to low-wage earners. Oregon, using the fraction one twenty-sixth, made no allowance for unemployment in the high quarter. None of the survey states provided dependents' benefits—an unfortunate limitation in the surveys' coverage. Changes have occurred, of course, in the provisions of these and of nearly all the states since the time of the survey; but the changes do not invalidate the conclusions of our discussion, which is directed to determining not how many states have or had adequate benefits but simply what is the nature of an adequate benefit. As remarked above, in the treatment of the benefit

amount the emphasis is analytical rather than historical.

The first six studies followed an identical procedure; the seventh introduced some variation. In each of the first six studies a sample of about 300 claimants was interviewed intensively, and a detailed accounting of each claimant's income and expenditure during the year was secured in order to measure the change in living standards between his most recent period of employment and his most recent period of unemployment.

Each of the six samples was restricted to claimants who had been unemployed for six weeks or more (the average duration of their unemployment was about seventeen weeks) and who were still drawing unemployment benefits. Not represented, therefore, were the short-term unemployed and those who had exhausted their benefits. Claimants unemployed for six weeks or more represent, on the average, somewhat more than half of all claimants.

Only two basic family situations were represented—the worker living alone (S)[13] and the four-person family. The families in the sample were limited to those in which only

[12] The results of the Pittsburgh survey, which was a pilot study, are not fully compatible with the other surveys and are not included in the tables analyzed here.

[13] "S" is shorthand for "single" but does not necessarily mean unmarried: it excludes unmarried persons living with their families and includes the few married persons living separated from their families.

TABLE 5–2: ASPECTS OF BENEFICIARY EXPERIENCE SELECTED FROM SIX BENEFIT-ADEQUACY SURVEYS, 1956–1958[a]

Sample survey by beneficiary type[b]	Per cent of beneficiaries whose benefits were half or more of their wage		Average benefit as per cent of average net wage	Per cent of beneficiaries with maximum benefit	Beneficiary net wage as per cent of family net income	Benefits as per cent of essential expenditures (adjusted)[c]	Total expenditures during unemployment	
	Gross wage	Net wage					Per cent change from period of employment	Per cent in excess of income
(1)	(2)	(3)	(4)	(5)	(6)	(7)	(8)	(9)
Tampa, Fla. ('56)								
S	28	65	46	21	96	95	−7	40
P	27	} 53	34	67	91	60	−5	57
SEC			27	24	71	52	−4	19
Anderson, S.C. ('57)								
S	51	84	56	37	92	118	−16	29
P	34	47	45	41	77	85	−10	30
SEC	41	75	53	27	39	108	−4	13
Albany, N.Y. ('57)								
S	51	72	54	46	90	114	+6	42
P	26	41	45	51	80	79	−10	45
SEC	64	91	62	12	36	100	+10	23
Portland, Ore. ('58)								
S	52	79	58	42	91	118	−15	28
P, 1E	20	35	45	74	88	94	−25	39
P, 2E	30	49	48	80	67	96	−18	33
SEC	42	79	58	11	34	112	−9	16
St. Louis, Mo. ('58)								
S	34	58	48	49	94	106	−17	42
P, 1E	15	26	38	73	83	80	−20	43
P, 2E	18	26	42	76	65	95	−19	18
SEC	40	67	50	33	38	105	−9	12
Utica, N.Y. ('58)								
A	46	79	63	12	89	145	−15	10
B	40	74	57	28	82	109	−9	16
C	40	74	57	39	59	124	−4	10
D	63	92	65	3	34	135	−7	2

SOURCE: See n. 11.

[a] All benefit data refer to the benefit rate established during base-year employment. All wage and income data refer to the most recent period of employment, and net is equivalent to gross minus social security and income taxes.

[b] See text, pp. 85, 87 for explanation of code.

[c] See text, p. 91 for explanation of adjusted essential expenditures.

the head and/or his spouse was an earner. There were, therefore, three possible family situations: The beneficiary as the primary and only earner (P,1E); the beneficiary as the primary earner, but having a working wife (P,2E); the beneficiary as the wife, a secondary earner (SEC).

The "weekly wage" shown in the tables is the average wage, gross and net, actually received during the beneficiary's most recent period of employment. It represents, therefore, the best available measure of loss during unemployment —each beneficiary's own recent, full-time wage.

The Utica, New York, survey (1958) differed from the other six surveys in several respects. It used a larger sample (772), which was not limited to particular classes of claimants but was drawn from all classes. It restricted the comparison of income and expenditures to two months—the most recent month of unemployment and the most recent month of employment. And it classified beneficiaries into four types, labeled simply A, B, C, and D. For our purposes these four can be taken as roughly equivalent to the categories of the other surveys: S; P,1E; P,2E; and SEC.[14]

What proportion of the beneficiaries received half or more of their wages? The answers provided by the benefit surveys are shown in Table 5-2, columns 2 and 3, and in Table 5-3, columns 2, 4, and 6.

Quite different answers can be given, even for states with similar benefit formulas, in terms of net or gross wages, for periods of prosperity or recession, and for beneficiaries with or without dependents. Consider the two extreme examples: In Albany, in the prosperous year of 1957, 91 per cent of the SEC beneficiaries received half or more of their net wages; but in St. Louis, in the recession year of 1958, only 15 per cent of the P,1E beneficiaries received half or more of their gross wages (Table 5-2, cols. 2 and 3).

[14] The four classes in the Utica study were defined as follows: A, individuals living alone; B, families with no one else employed during the beneficiary's unemployment; C, families with one or more other members employed during the beneficiary's unemployment, the beneficiary being the head of the family; D, same as C, except that the beneficiary was not the head of the family.

It is evident from a comparison of the Albany with the Utica survey that the condition of low or high unemployment is not necessarily the dominant factor. Despite the fact that the Utica survey took place in a period of higher unemployment, its results are more favorable, primarily because in the time between the two surveys New York's maximum benefit was raised from $36 to $45 (Table 5-1, col. 4).

The largest and most constant differences are those associated with different family types. Whether it is a period of recession or prosperity and no matter how beneficiaries are classified (by age, sex, wages, or duration of unemployment), one fundamental difference shows through—that single and secondary beneficiaries fare better than primary beneficiaries. Of the beneficiaries without dependents, the secondary beneficiaries fare somewhat better than the single ones; and of the primary beneficiaries, those with additional earners fare somewhat better than those with only one earner.

Column 5 of Table 5-2 contains the single most important clue as to why the experience of the primary beneficiaries was the least favorable. They were the ones whose benefits were most often limited by the maximum benefit. The striking difference made by a higher maximum in the case of primary beneficiaries, is seen in the contrast between Albany and Utica in terms of either column 2 or column 3.

Table 5-3 provides more detailed information for three of the surveys.[15] The table shows the percentage of beneficiaries who received benefits that were adequate according to the two norms of adequacy used in this analysis. The beneficiaries are classified by various personal characteristics and subclassified by family type. Family types are reduced to two—beneficiaries with dependents (P,1E and P,2E) and beneficiaries without dependents (S and SEC)— because the samples are too small to support further division and because these are the most significant classes.

Columns 2, 4, and 6 show the percentage of

[15] These surveys were the only ones for which the original punch cards were still available when this chapter was in preparation.

TABLE 5–3: BENEFICIARIES WHO RECEIVED ADEQUATE BENEFITS[a] AS PER CENT OF ALL BENEFICIARIES, IN DESIGNATED CLASS BY SELECTED CHARACTERISTICS FOR THREE SAMPLE SURVEYS

Beneficiary characteristic	St. Louis, Mo. (1958)		Albany, N.Y. (1957)		Utica, N.Y. (1958)	
	Norm of wages	Norm of expenditures	Norm of wages	Norm of expenditures	Norm of wages	Norm of expenditures
(1)	(2)	(3)	(4)	(5)	(6)	(7)
1. *Family Type*						
All types	44	45	67	51	80	73
S	58	58	72	69	79	89
P, 1E	26	28	33	19	74	62
P, 2E	26	42	56	28	74	69
SEC	67	60	91	71	92	79
Dependents	26	32	41	22	74	65
No dependents	62	59	83	70	89	81
2. *Sex*						
Male						
All types	30	39	44	43	73	69
Dependents	23	31	36	23	72	64
No dependents	46	59	61	85	78	84
Female						
All types	70	57	87	51	94	80
Dependents	57	38	63	21	91	76
No dependents	72	59	90	55	94	80
3. *Age*						
Under 25 years						
All types	38	43	78	52	90	76
25–65 years						
All types	44	45	66	51	80	71
Dependents	26	30	41	21	73	65
No dependents	62	60	82	72	91	79
Over 65 years						
All types	75	75	67	50	78	66
4. *Unemployment Duration*						
Average and Longer						
All types	46	50	63	52	78	71
Dependents	26	37	38	20	72	62
No dependents	64	62	78	71	85	81
Below Average						
All types	41	40	70	50	84	75
Dependents	25	26	44	24	76	69
No dependents	60	55	88	69	94	83

Beneficiary characteristic (1)	St. Louis, Mo. (1958) Norm of wages (2)	Norm of expenditures (3)	Albany, N.Y. (1957) Norm of wages (4)	Norm of expenditures (5)	Utica, N.Y. (1958) Norm of wages (6)	Norm of expenditures (7)
5. Wages						
Average and Above						
All types	20	37	52	44	65	68
Dependents	15	28	35	21	66	63
No dependents	31	56	72	72	64	84
Below Average						
All types	68	54	82	57	97	77
Dependents	48	39	56	24	95	71
No dependents	78	60	89	67	98	80
6. Maximum Benefits						
At Maximum						
All types	37	42	37	42	63	71
Dependents	22	30	22	17	64	69
No dependents	62	63	58	81	53	88
Below Maximum						
All types	54	49	82	56	85	73
Dependents	35	35	61	27	79	64
No dependents	63	56	90	67	91	81
7. Norm of wages						
Adequate[a]						
All types		60		63		77
Dependents		49		36		71
No dependents		65		71		84
Inadequate[a]						
All types		33		28		49
Dependents		26		13		46
No dependents		49		61		57
8. Norm of expenditures						
Adequate[a]						
All types	58		83		87	
Dependents	40		68		81	
No dependents	68		85		92	
Inadequate[a]						
All types	32		50		65	
Dependents	18		34		60	
No dependents	53		78		75	

SOURCE: Original punch-card data of benefit-adequacy surveys.
   [a] Adequate by norm of wages: 50 per cent or more of recent, full-time, net wages. Adequate by norm of expenditures: 100 per cent or more of adjusted essential expenditures; for definitions see text, pp. 83–84, 91.

beneficiaries who received half or more of their net wages. Item 2 (sex) may be used to illustrate how the table is read: In St. Louis 30 per cent of all males received adequate benefits; 23 per cent of all males with dependents received adequate benefits; 72 per cent of all females without dependents received adequate benefits. (In the St. Louis and Albany surveys, since the sample beneficiaries do not reflect the relative size of any given type in the total claimant population, the percentages for each type are more significant than for "all types.")

A much larger proportion of female than male workers received adequate benefits. Females generally receive lower wages than males and are consequently less limited by the maximum benefit. It is noteworthy that, whereas in Albany the difference between male and female was 43 percentage points, in Utica, which provided a higher maximum, the difference was only 21 percentage points (item 2, cols. 4 and 6).

No significant pattern emerges from the classification of these "adequate" beneficiaries by either age[16] (item 3) or duration of unemployment (item 4).

A very clear pattern, however, emerges from classification according to wages (item 5). On the average, 37 percentage points separate high-wage from low-wage beneficiaries. The classification of beneficiaries into those at and below the maximum (item 6) produces a similar pattern, a reflection of the wage differences.[17] It is in this combination of inadequate benefits with high wages, along with a concentration of beneficiaries at the maximum, that there exists the chief opportunity for an *insurance* system to liberalize its benefits. To achieve a notable improvement in adequacy, the system need only carry its own logic—the payment of benefits as a percentage of wages—up to a higher maximum.

[16] Since there were relatively few cases in the categories below twenty-five and above sixty-five years of age, these percentages are less reliable than the others.

[17] It is noteworthy that, except in Utica, differences of family types show through even the strong correlations of wages and maximum benefits.

B. How Well Do Beneficiaries Manage on the Benefits They Receive?

For one who assumes that one-half or more of wages is the correct proportion, there is no need to proceed beyond this point of the analysis; by definition the data already examined suffice for the conclusion that such and such a percentage of beneficiaries received "adequate" benefits. However, one who wishes to investigate the correctness of the assumption must proceed further and ascertain how the claimants who received this proportion of their wages actually fared.[18]

The last three columns of Table 5-2 throw some light on the actual experience of beneficiaries. Column 8 shows that, at least in periods of prosperity, the beneficiaries did not greatly reduce their expenditures while unemployed. The reductions were larger in the St. Louis and Portland surveys, which were conducted during a recession period; but in Utica, despite the recession, the reductions continued to be small. At all times, and everywhere, the smallest reductions in expenditures occurred among the SEC families.

Column 9 is a measure of the strain on the beneficiary's family resources to maintain a given level of expenditures. It shows the extent to which families drew on savings or went into debt. As measured by this criterion, the strain of maintaining family expenditures was least among the SEC families. These families, therefore, were not only the most successful in maintaining expenditures, but they were able to do so with the least strain.

Not shown in the table, but reported in the

[18] For this question, as for the first question, the best answers are provided by the benefit-adequacy surveys. The few other available studies of the unemployed are not restricted to the insured unemployed and refer, moreover, to exceptional situations for which unemployment insurance is not intended to be an adequate answer. Such studies cannot form the basis for concrete decisions as to what the benefit formula in unemployment insurance ought to be. Some useful information relating to the long-term insured unemployed should emerge from the investigations conducted by thirteen states into the financial experience of their temporary extended unemployment compensation claimants; but at the present writing (April, 1964), this information is not yet available.

studies, is the proportion of beneficiaries who had recourse to relief programs. This proportion is of particular interest, because one of the oldest proposed criteria of adequacy is that benefits should be sufficient to keep the unemployed "off relief." By this norm benefits were clearly adequate. On the average, less than 5 per cent of all beneficiaries received relief in kind and an even smaller percentage received cash relief. This description holds not only for the states in which the unemployed were ineligible for general assistance but also for New York and Oregon, where they were eligible.[19]

Column 7 is perhaps the most important part of the table. Of all the criteria that have a substantive character (as distinguished from the purely mechanical proportion-of-wage criterion) the one that is most often proposed, in other countries as well as in the United States, is that benefits should suffice to meet the "essential expenditures" of the unemployed worker until he finds another job.

The definition of essential is elastic and can be given many meanings. In the first five surveys it was given the meaning of "non-deferrable" and defined to include the four items of food, housing, clothing, and medical care. The Utica survey used the criterion of "recurrent" expenditures, defined to include food, housing, medical care, installment payments, and all other regularly required expenditures such as the support of someone living outside the household. Column 7 shows the percentages of beneficiaries of each type whose benefits were sufficient to meet essential expenditures thus defined.

[19] This finding is supported by other studies. Two of these found that only about 2 per cent of the long-term unemployment insurance beneficiaries appeared on the relief rolls. See "Exhaustions of UC Benefits and Public Assistance Cases Opened Because of the Loss of UC Benefits," a report of the Pennsylvania Governor's Advisory Committee on Unemployment Compensation, 1959; see also "Debts and Dependency" in *A Case Study of a Permanent Plant Shutdown*, Special Committee on Unemployment Problems (U.S. Senate, 86th Cong., December 21, 1959). A third study, a survey of the elderly unemployed in the Trenton, New Jersey, labor market during the 1958 recession, found that less than 1 per cent were on relief (*Age 60 Plus*, Division of Employment Security, N.J. Department of Labor and Industry, July, 1959, p. 71).

Note that benefits are compared with "adjusted" essential expenditures. The adjustment factor, found in column 6, is the ratio of the beneficiary's wage to the family income. As an example, consider the secondary worker in Albany. Since she contributes only 36 per cent of her family's income while she is employed, it is logical to expect her unemployment benefit to support that proportion, rather than the whole, of her family's expenditure while she is unemployed.[20]

Measured by this important criterion, benefits were adequate for the average beneficiary without dependents (except in Tampa) and were inadequate for the average beneficiary with dependents (except in Utica).

Table 5–3, which enables us to go from averages to individual experience, corroborates these conclusions. In St. Louis, Albany, and Utica the majority of the beneficiaries without dependents received adequate benefits; but only in Utica did the majority of beneficiaries with dependents receive adequate benefits (Table 5–3, cols. 3, 5, and 7).

With respect to the first six items of Table 5–3, the general impression conveyed by columns 3, 5, and 7 is very similar to that conveyed by columns 2, 4, and 6: The norm of essential expenditures seems to lead to much the same conclusions as does the norm of wages.

Items 7 and 8 of the table, however, along with Figure 5–1, reveal that the results of the two norms are far from identical. Figure 5–1 shows the number of claimants who received benefits that were adequate or inadequate as measured by each of the two norms. Block A shows the claimants whose benefits were adequate by both norms, and block D shows those whose benefits were inadequate by both norms. Blocks B and C show the claimants whose benefits were adequate by one norm but not by the other, and these two blocks include about one-third of the beneficiaries.

Some of the relationships between the blocks

[20] When the figures are published without this adjustment—as they usually are—they seem to show that the benefits of secondary workers are the least adequate of all the claimant groups, and this is the reverse of the fact.

Figure 5-1

Norm of Wages Compared with Norm of Essential Expenditures

Adequacy measured by norm of wages

Adequacy measured by norm
of essential expenditures

	Adequate (161)	Inadequate (206)

St. Louis, Missouri
(367)

(d = Beneficiaries
with dependents)

St. Louis

A Adequate (166): 97 < 23d / 74 ; 69 < 35d / 34 B

C Inadequate (201): 64 < 24d / 40 ; 137 < 102d / 35 D

Adequacy measured by norm
of essential expenditures   (181)   (90)

Albany, New York
(271)

(d = Beneficiaries
with dependents)

A Adequate (139): 114 < 16d / 98 ; 25 < 8d / 17 B

C Inadequate (132): 67 < 28d / 39 ; 65 < 54d / 11 D

Adequacy measured by norm
of essential expenditures   (562)   (137)

Utica, New York
(699)

(d = Beneficiaries
with dependents)

A Adequate (500): 433 < 205d / 228 ; 67 < 47d / 20 B

C Inadequate (199): 129 < 84d / 45 ; 70 < 55d / 15 D

Sources and notes: The same as for Table 5-3.

92

are shown in percentage form in Table 5–3, items 7 and 8. These items are answers to a general question: "Of those whose benefits were adequate by one norm, what per cent received benefits that were adequate by the other norm?" The use of the table is illustrated by the following data drawn from the St. Louis survey.

Item 7: Of those whose benefits were adequate by the wages norm (received half or more of their full-time, net, recent wage), 60 per cent found the benefit adequate to cover essential expenditures. Of all those with dependents whose benefits were adequate by the wages norm, 49 per cent found the benefit adequate to cover essential expenditures. Of all those without dependents whose benefits were inadequate by the wages norm, 49 per cent found the benefit inadequate to cover essential expenditures (51 per cent, therefore, found even this benefit adequate).

Item 8: This item is read as the reverse of Item 7. Of those whose benefits were sufficient to cover their essential expenditures, 58 per cent received half or more of their net wages (therefore 42 per cent managed on less than half of their wages). Of those with dependents whose benefits were not sufficient to cover essential expenditures, only 18 per cent received half or more of their net wages. (The 82 per cent of this group who did not receive a benefit equal to half their wage represent a very important claimant class, which could easily be helped within the logic of the present system by simply arranging to pay them half their wages.)

As would be expected, the lack of correlation between the two norms is more marked in the case of claimants with dependents. In Albany, for example, of the claimants with dependents whose benefits equaled half of their wages (item 7), only 36 per cent found that benefits covered their share of the family's essential expenditures; the corresponding figure for claimants without dependents was 71 per cent.

The explanation of the general correspondence between the two norms in the other items (1–6) of Table 5–3 is to be found in the fact that blocks B and C of Figure 5–1 tend to cancel each other, so that the *net* effect of applying

one norm or the other tends to be similar. In terms of the net figures the similarity can be quite close. In St. Louis, for example, 44 per cent of the beneficiaries received adequate benefits as measured by the wage norm, and 45 per cent received adequate benefits as measured by the norm of essential expenditures (item 1, cols. 2 and 3).

The extent of correlation between the two norms is important because they are related as means to end: A given proportion of wages is expected to enable (most) beneficiaries to meet their essential expenditures. To the extent that this intended correlation does not exist in fact, it is necessary either (1) to accept the resulting imperfections on the ground that, as remarked before, social insurance necessarily deals in averages and cannot achieve the precise adjustment of benefits to need that is achieved in the social assistance programs; or (2) to improve the correlation through devices that distinguish—by objective, nondiscretionary criteria—between classes of beneficiaries, for example, between beneficiaries with and without dependents; or (3) to abandon reliance on social insurance in favor of a program of social assistance.

C. Benefit Amount: Summary and Conclusions

Measured either by the norm of wages or by the norm of essential expenditures, the majority of the beneficiaries without dependents received adequate benefits while the majority of the beneficiaries with dependents did not. Since these two groups of beneficiaries divide the general claimant population about equally, it seems likely that only about half of all beneficiaries in the states surveyed received adequate benefits. This generalization does not hold for the Utica survey, in which a majority of beneficiaries of all types received adequate benefits.

With the help of the benefits, most beneficiaries, with and without dependents, managed not only to avoid the relief rolls but even to maintain their expenditures close to the level established before unemployment. They did so, however, only at the cost of a significant worsening of their net asset position.

The findings of the benefit-adequacy studies confirm the reasonableness of the traditional half-of-wages norm if one accepts as reasonable that the majority of those who receive benefits equal to half their wages should be able, with such benefits, to meet essential expenditures as defined in the surveys. Within the limits set by the maximum, benefits should represent at least 50 per cent of full-time, net, recent wages. The present practice of paying 50 per cent of average, gross, base-period wages would seem to be an acceptable approximation to this norm and is, of course, administratively more convenient. The use of the gross instead of the net wage is one way of compensating for the fact that a beneficiary's average, base-period wage is frequently lower than his full-time, recent wage.[21]

As to the maximum benefit, the evidence of the benefit-adequacy surveys would seem to argue for a maximum benefit that is at least 50 per cent of the average covered wage in the state. Only in the Utica survey did a majority of the primary workers receive half or more of their full-time, net, recent wage; and the New York maximum benefit at that time was 49 per cent of the average covered state wage. The other states surveyed had maximums that were lower relative to the covered state wage.

In 1962 the Interstate Conference of Employment Security Agencies recommended as a standard for all the states that "the maximum basic weekly benefit [without dependents' benefits] equal at least one-half of the statewide, gross average weekly wage in insured employment." As of March 31, 1963, only 6 per cent of covered workers were in states which met this standard. However, 39 per cent were in states whose basic maximum benefit equaled over 45 per cent of the state average wage; and 26 per cent were in states which paid dependents' benefits and therefore paid a maximum benefit

to some claimants that was higher than the state's basic maximum.

A strong case exists for improving the position of the primary beneficiaries relative to the single and secondary beneficiaries. Two methods are available for achieving this objective. It can be accomplished to a considerable extent by increasing the maximum benefit. Since the primary beneficiaries tend to have higher than average wages and therefore tend to cluster at the maximum, they will benefit more than the others from any increase in the maximum. This method is in accord with the "insurance" character of the program. The objective can also be achieved by some system of dependents' benefits, a method more in accord with the "social" character of the program.[22] The best method or combination of methods to improve benefit adequacy will be that which increases the compensation of those whose benefits are inadequate without, at the same time, overcompensating those whose benefits are already adequate. (It may be well to recall here the warning voiced earlier that the norms of adequacy used in this analysis are themselves debatable.)

Table 5–4 compares the available methods in terms of this twofold objective.[23] Part A of the table answers the questions: "Of those who needed additional help (their benefits were inadequate by one of the norms), what proportion would probably have been helped by some increase in the maximum benefit (because their benefits were currently at the maximum)? What proportion would have been helped by a system of dependents' benefits?" Part B

---

21 Compensation is needed especially where, as in Oregon, no allowance is made for possible unemployment in the base period and where the beginning of the base period may antedate the beginning of the benefit period by two years.

22 There are two main systems from which to choose: the flat amount system (currently in use in Alaska, Connecticut, District of Columbia, Maryland, Massachusetts, Nevada, Ohio, Rhode Island, Wyoming) and the variable maximum system (currently in use in Illinois, Iowa, Michigan). In the latter system no benefit is paid beyond the established percentage of wages—for example, 50 per cent—but beneficiaries with dependents are paid this percentage up to a higher maximum.

23 Table 5-4 must be used cautiously because of the smallness of the sample cells. It can illustrate the general effects of various decisions, but it cannot provide detailed guidance for making the decisions. Further, it should be recalled that, except for Utica, the data for "all types" is not so representative as the data for each of the family types taken separately.

Part A: Percentage of those in need of help who would be helped by a higher maximum or by dependents' benefits

Sample survey by family class (1)	In need by the norm of wages[a]		In need by the norm of expenditures[b]	
	Helped by a higher maximum (2)	Helped by dependents' benefits (3)	Helped by a higher maximum (4)	Helped by dependents' benefits (5)
St. Louis, Mo. (1958)				
All types	65.5	66.0	61.2	62.7
Dependents	77.4	100	74.6	100
No dependents	43.4	0	38.7	0
Albany, N.Y. (1957)				
All types	63.3	68.8	39.4	62.1
Dependents	67.7	100	54.9	100
No dependents	53.6	0	14.0	0
Utica, N.Y. (1958)				
All types	40.1	74.4	21.9	70.3
Dependents	53.9	100	29.6	100
No dependents	22.9	0	3.5	0

Part B: Percentage of those helped by a higher maximum or by dependents' benefits who would not need the help

Sample survey by family class (1)	Helped by a higher maximum		Helped by dependents' benefits	
	Not in need by the norm of wages[a] (2)	Not in need by the norm of expenditures[b] (3)	Not in need by the norm of wages[a] (4)	Not in need by the norm of expenditures[b] (5)
St. Louis, Mo. (1958)				
All types	36.6	42.3	25.5	31.5
Dependents	22.2	30.4	25.5	31.2
No dependents	61.5	62.8	0	0
Albany, N.Y. (1957)				
All types	36.7	42.2	40.1	21.9
Dependents	22.2	16.7	40.1	21.9
No dependents	58.3	80.0	0	0
Utica, N.Y. (1958)				
All types	62.6	71.4	73.9	65.5
Dependents	63.8	69.2	73.9	65.5
No dependents	52.9	88.2	0	0

SOURCE: Original punch-card data of benefit-adequacy surveys.

[a] Norm of wages: 50 per cent of full-time, net, recent wage.

[b] Norm of expenditures: 100 per cent of essential expenditures during unemployment; for definitions see text p. 91.

answers the question: "Of those who would have received a higher maximum or dependents' benefits, what proportion would not have needed the help?"

Part A: Proportion Helped of Those Needing Help. The following data drawn from the St. Louis survey illustrate the use of the table. In the case of beneficiaries with dependents, 77.4 per cent of those whose benefits were less than half of their net wages probably would have been helped by a higher maximum; 74.6 per cent of those whose benefits were insufficient to cover their essential expenditures probably would have been helped by a higher maximum. All of these beneficiaries, of course, would have been helped by a system of dependents' benefits. In the case of beneficiaries without dependents, 43.4 and, of course, 0 are the respective percentages. In St. Louis there would have been little to choose between dependents' benefits or a higher maximum. In Utica and Albany dependents' benefits would have had a more favorable effect than would a higher maximum, at least as judged by the norm of essential expenditures.[24]

Part B: Proportion Not Needing the Additional Help They Would Have Received. In Utica both dependents' benefits and a higher maximum would have "overpaid" a large percentage of the beneficiaries. Dependents' benefits, however, would have "overpaid" to a somewhat lesser degree (65.5 per cent as against 71.4 per cent). In Albany, also, dependents' benefits would probably have resulted in fewer "overpaid" beneficiaries. For primary workers there would have resulted little difference between a higher maximum and dependents' benefits (16.7 per cent as against 21.9 per cent), but for single and secondary workers the difference would have been considerable (80 per cent as against 0 per cent). In St. Louis, also, insofar as there is any difference, dependents' benefits would have "overpaid" to a lesser degree.

In summary: According to the norms of adequacy used in this analysis, a state with a benefit formula at least as liberal as that of New York at the time of the Utica survey would probably be paying an adequate weekly benefit. To reach this minimum level of adequacy, states with a less liberal formula would probably need to raise their maximum benefit, or introduce a system of dependents' benefits, or both. Although a system of dependents' benefits would be the most direct means of overcoming the program's most obvious deficiency—the failure to provide adequate benefits for the primary worker—an increase in the maximum benefit also would overcome this deficiency to a considerable extent. The findings of the benefit-adequacy studies would support a decision to move simultaneously on both fronts by means of a system of variable maximums; but they do not furnish adequate information on what the schedule of maximums should be in such a system.

III. THE DURATION OF BENEFITS

The problem of benefit duration must be approached somewhat differently from the problem of benefit amount. In the case of benefit duration usable norms of adequacy (those that command a sufficiently broad social consensus to be significant) are not available, nor does there exist a body of data on the duration of benefits that is comparable to the six surveys analyzed in the discussion of the benefit amount. Hence, the following discussion of benefit duration uses an alternative approach: it reviews the history of benefit duration and, against that background, analyzes some of the principal current issues.

A. HISTORY OF DURATION PROVISIONS

Regular Unemployment Insurance Program

In unemployment insurance the history of duration has been notable equally for a process of continuous extension and for the absence of any clear norms governing the process.

Figure 5–2 shows the changes that have occurred in the maximum duration[25] from 1937

---

[24] For simplicity of treatment, only the norm of essential expenditures is used in these and the remaining illustrations.

[25] There are three principal measures of duration. (1) The legal maximum potential duration is the longest period for which any beneficiary can draw benefits (it sets the limits of potential benefits for

Figure 5-2

Maximum Duration: Weighted Average and Range, 1937-1963

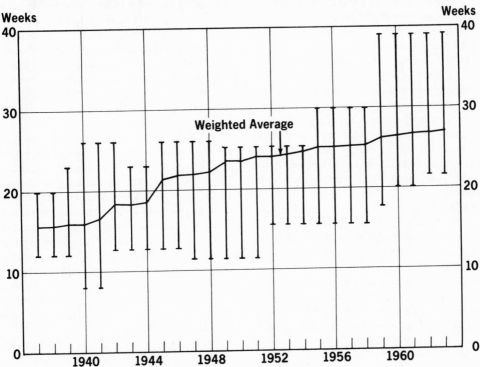

Source: Comparison of State Unemployment Insurance Laws, Bureau of Employment Security.

(the earliest date by which all the states had enacted unemployment insurance laws) through 1962. The figure shows the average[26] and the range of the maximum. During this period the average maximum duration rose, without any reverses, from 15.6 to 26.9 weeks, an increase of 72 per cent. The rise did not occur evenly. Nearly three-quarters occurred in the first half of the period, indeed one-fourth

potential beneficiaries); in this discussion it is called simply *maximum duration.* (2) The personal maximum potential duration is the maximum duration available to actual beneficiaries (in uniform duration states this is identical with the legal maximum); in this discussion it is called simply *potential duration.* (3) Personal actual duration is the number of weeks actually drawn by beneficiaries; in this discussion it is called simply *actual duration.* These three measures of duration appear together in Figure 5–3.

[26] The average of all the states weighted by the proportion of covered workers in each state.

occurred in the two-year period preceding the reconversion (1944–45).

In the decade 1945–55 the average climbed steadily closer to the upper range, which had stabilized at about twenty-six weeks. The states below twenty-six weeks kept moving toward that limit, while the states already at twenty-six weeks showed no inclination to go beyond.

During 1955 the upper range again began to rise, as first Pennsylvania and then a number of smaller states went beyond twenty-six weeks. In 1959 there was a great leap, but its importance must not be exaggerated, since it was taken by only one small state (Oklahoma). The rise in the average in the last few years has been caused more by movement in the lower than in the upper range.

A few small extensions of duration that

occurred in 1963 and early 1964 are not shown in the figure. By the spring of 1964 only two states were left in which the maximum duration was less than twenty-six weeks. These were South Carolina and South Dakota, which together have only 1.3 per cent of all covered workers. Currently, therefore, practically all (98.7 per cent) of covered workers can become eligible for twenty-six weeks of benefits.

The upper range dropped only once; this occurred in 1943, when California reduced its maximum from twenty-six to twenty-three weeks for the period of the war. The lower range dropped twice—in 1940 (Kentucky) and in 1947 (Arizona). The average has never dropped.

While the maximum duration was lengthening, the waiting period was shortening. A shorter waiting period represents an increase in available protection for all claimants except exhaustees. The waiting period progressively shortened from three weeks to two weeks to one week. By 1955 no state required claimants to wait more than one week before receiving benefits, and four states had no waiting period at all. The number of states without a waiting period increased to five by 1957 but declined again to four in 1964.

As compared with a lengthening of the maximum duration, a shortening of the waiting period has both an advantage and a disadvantage. The shortening of the waiting period helps more of the claimants. An increase in the maximum helps only exhaustees—indeed, only those exhaustees eligible for the maximum number of weeks. A shortening of the waiting period, however, increases the effective duration of benefits for all claimants except exhaustees.[27] On the other hand, a

decrease of one week in the waiting period is for this very reason much more costly than an increase of one week in the maximum duration, and it represents assistance to claimants who are presumably in a situation of less urgent need than are the claimants who have exhausted their benefits. Seen from this point of view, a given amount of available funds will purchase a greater good if spent on lengthening the maximum than if spent on shortening the waiting period further.

The adequacy of the duration formula is not determined solely by the maximum duration; the "duration ratio" is equally important. This ratio is the ratio between a given amount of covered work (as measured by weeks worked or dollars earned) and the weeks of benefits to which the worker thereby becomes entitled. In states which have uniform duration, the duration ratio is in effect supplied by the qualifying requirement: any claimant admitted to benefits is entitled to the maximum duration. In states with variable duration, a separate provision determines the weeks of benefits for which each claimant is eligible.

The provisions that determine the duration ratio are complex and vary greatly among the states. Their net effect, however, is reflected in a single statistic—potential duration, that is, the number of weeks of benefits for which actual beneficiaries are eligible. Figure 5–3 shows the national average potential duration for the period 1946[28] through 1963. The average potential duration is always less than the average maximum, because in the states with variable duration, the duration ratio does not permit all beneficiaries to qualify for the maximum. As is evident from Figure 5–3, however, the general trend of potential duration has been similar to that of the maximum, following the latter steadily upward. In 1963 over two-thirds of all

---

[27] The shortening of the waiting period has implications also for the adequacy of the benefit *amount*. The shortening represents, in effect, an increase in the weekly benefit amount of all beneficiaries except exhaustees. The increase is inversely proportional to the length of the beneficiary's unemployment and directly proportional to the length of the state's waiting period. By way of illustration consider two beneficiaries. One is unemployed four weeks in a state with a two-week waiting period. The other is unemployed five weeks in a state with a one-week waiting period. Each state shortens the waiting period by one week.

As a result, the first beneficiary receives 50 per cent more benefits during his period of unemployment, and the other beneficiary receives 25 per cent more. It is as though their weekly benefit amounts had been increased 50 per cent and 25 per cent respectively. This increase is generally overlooked in discussions of the historical changes that have occurred in the weekly benefit amount.

[28] Data on potential duration are not available for the years prior to 1946.

Figure 5-3

Potential Duration and Actual Duration, 1937-1963

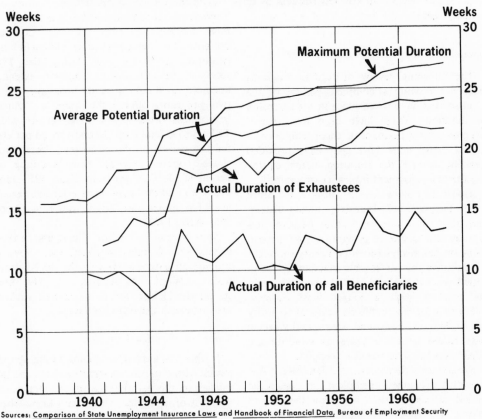

Sources: <u>Comparison of State Unemployment Insurance Laws</u> and <u>Handbook of Financial Data</u>, Bureau of Employment Security

claimants were eligible for twenty-six or more weeks, and the average potential duration stood at twenty-four weeks, not far below the average maximum of twenty-seven weeks. The closeness of these two measures indicates that duration ratios have permitted the great majority of covered workers to qualify for the maximum. The current distribution of the states around these averages, that is, the extent to which the states currently differ in their maximum and potential duration, may be seen in Table 5-6, pp. 104-5, columns 3 and 4.

One of the major choices to be made in the area of duration is between the systems of uniform and variable duration. Each system has its own logic, its own set of advantages and disadvantages, and neither has been able to win

the field. Some of the states have shifted at various times from one system to the other. For example, Ohio, the first state to have uniform duration, changed to variable duration in 1949 and returned to uniform duration in 1959.[29] Pennsylvania changed from variable to uniform duration in 1954 and back to variable duration in 1964. Table 5-6 shows the states as they were at the end of 1962; between then and the spring of 1964, however, three states (North Dakota, Pennsylvania, Tennessee) changed from uniform to variable duration. The number of states with uniform

[29] Technically, Ohio has variable duration, but, practically, it has uniform duration: under its benefit formula 99 per cent of the claimants become eligible for the maximum duration.

duration reached sixteen with 35 per cent of all covered workers in 1959, but was down to nine with 24 per cent of all covered workers as of January, 1964.

Special Programs of Extended Duration

The foregoing review of regular programs does not provide a complete picture of the changes that have taken place in the extension of duration. There have been four federal programs—one permanent, three temporary—and a dozen state laws that have provided benefits beyond the duration limits of the regular unemployment insurance program.[30]

Railroad Unemployment Insurance. Since 1938 the railroad industry, under federal legislation, has been operating its own unemployment insurance program. The railroad program has always provided twenty-six weeks of duration for all eligible claimants, but in recent years it has provided extended duration for workers with a longer work history. Workers with ten to fifteen years of seniority are eligible for thirty-nine weeks, and workers with fifteen or more years of seniority are eligible for fifty-two weeks of benefits.

Servicemen's Readjustment Allowances. Anticipating prolonged unemployment during the period of readjustment following the end of World War II and recognizing that returned servicemen would not be eligible for regular unemployment insurance benefits, Congress in 1944 adopted the servicemen's readjustment allowances program. Under this program, which was in operation until 1952, veterans were eligible to draw up to a maximum of fifty-two weeks of benefits during two years after their discharge. The benefits were paid through the regular unemployment insurance offices. Experience under this program led Congress to the conclusion that fifty-two weeks was too long a duration; and subsequent programs enacted to pay unemployment benefits to ex-servicemen

provided no more than twenty-six weeks of duration.[31]

Temporary Unemployment Compensation and Temporary Extended Unemployment Compensation. During the 1958 recession Congress established the temporary unemployment compensation program and during the 1961 recession it established the temporary extended unemployment compensation program. These two programs offered the states a financial inducement (loans under TUC, grants under TEUC) to extend their duration by 50 per cent for the period of the recession. Twenty-two states[32] offered extended benefits during the period of the TUC program (June, 1958–June, 1959), and all the states made extended benefits available under the TEUC program (April, 1961–June, 1962).

State Recession Benefits. Beginning in 1958, a number of states amended their laws to provide an extension of benefits during statewide recessions. As of January 1, 1964, seven states, with 21.2 per cent of the covered workers, provided such extended protection.

Causes of Duration Extension

It would be a mistake to think of the upward march of the maximum duration from the late thirties to the early sixties as the methodical progress of a pilgrim, who always knew where he was going and who climbed steadily closer toward a clearly defined goal. It was rather the sporadic progress of a wanderer, who had never clearly glimpsed the top of the mountain he was climbing, but stumbled upward by uneven steps, pushed and pulled by a variety of forces, always willing to go a bit further and "see what it's like up there."

Among the many factors which accounted for the continued extension of duration, four were dominant. Of these, two were continuous (the need of the unemployed and the ability of the fund to meet that need) and two were

---

[30] In addition, duration has been extended by various private programs of unemployment benefits; see Chapters 6 and 7. In the railroad industry, in special situations, payments resembling unemployment benefits can be made for up to five years.

[31] In the permanent program enacted in 1958 (Ex-Servicemen's Unemployment Act), Congress made the claimant eligible for whatever duration was provided for in the state in which he drew benefits.

[32] Seventeen states took advantage of the federal loans, and five others financed their own extended-benefit programs.

occasional (increases in unemployment rates and federal pressures).

It became evident that the original tax of 3 per cent and even the lesser taxes that followed experience rating would buy more duration than had been calculated. It was evident, also, that more duration was needed, because benefits were being exhausted by large numbers of persons who seemed in every respect proper subjects for a social insurance system (they had been and would probably continue to be regular, full-time members of the work force). These were the two fundamental, persistent forces at work throughout the period, the one permitting and the other inducing an extension of benefits. Extension of the maximum duration was the least costly form of liberalization (the added weeks were used by a relatively small number of beneficiaries, especially in the variable duration states) and yet it directly helped those who presumably were most in need of help, the long-term unemployed. The actual advances in maximum duration occurred when particular circumstances in particular states combined with these two persistent forces to bring about amendments to state laws.

Among these particular circumstances, one of the most influential was the occurrence of periods of heavy unemployment. The marked increase in the maximum in 1944–45, for example, is primarily explainable in terms of the reconversion period and the heavy unemployment that reconversion was expected to bring. (Also, state reserves had grown greatly during the war.) Other smaller but marked rises were connected with the recessions of 1949, 1954, and 1958. In recent years concern over so-called prosperity unemployment has also contributed to the liberalization of duration provisions. The economy has experienced rapid structural changes that have increased the difficulty of worker adjustment and consequently lengthened the duration of unemployment, even in times of prosperity.

Another particular circumstance, usually connected with the unemployment rate but constituting an independent influence, was federal pressure. From time to time the federal government proposed either to enact minimum duration standards or to pay extended benefits out of its own funds to exhaustees under the state systems. Such proposals were made at the inception of the program and were repeated at intervals in varying forms. The federal influence on the programs is not to be measured by the few occasions when the federal proposal to act was realized (servicemen's readjustment allowances, temporary unemployment compensation, temporary extended unemployment compensation). Throughout the life of unemployment compensation the possibility of federal action has been a potent factor in inducing the states to enact more liberal duration provisions.

Although the above four factors were the principal ones at work, they were supplemented by a multitude of other factors that operated from time to time in various states. Sometimes an increase in duration was made in lieu of a more costly increase in the benefit amount or was part of a bargained package that included some tightening of disqualifications. It has happened on occasion that a legislature wanted to "do something for labor" (in one state the legislature had just passed a right-to-work law), and an increase in the duration of unemployment benefits seemed the most useful and the least costly action. Again, in one gubernatorial contest, when the challenger heard that the incumbent was proposing an increase in the maximum duration from thirteen to twenty weeks, he phoned the printer, where his own legislative program was being readied, and had his proposal changed to read twenty weeks also (it had previously read sixteen weeks). It can be said, in general, that the history of the extension of duration has not been the story of a carefully planned development resting on clearly perceived principles.

B. THE ADEQUACY OF BENEFIT DURATION

Despite the substantial liberalization of duration provisions, some beneficiaries still exhaust their benefits, that is, use up all the benefits for which they are eligible. The existence of these exhaustees inevitably raises the question of the adequacy of the program's duration provisions.

TABLE 5-5: SELECTED DATA ON THE DURATION AND EXHAUSTION OF UNEMPLOYMENT INSURANCE BENEFITS IN THE UNITED STATES, 1940-1963[a]

Year	All beneficiaries			Exhaustees				Insured unemployment rate
	Potential duration (weeks)	Actual duration (weeks)	Actual as per cent of potential duration	Number (000)	As per cent of covered employment	As per cent of all beneficiaries	Actual duration (weeks)	
(1)	(2)	(3)	(4)	(5)	(6)	(7)	(8)	(9)
1940		9.8		2,590	12.1	50.6		
41		9.4		1,544	6.6	45.6	12.1	
42		10.0		1,078	4.0	34.9	12.6	
43		9.0		194	.6	25.5	14.3	
44		7.7		102	.3	20.2	13.8	
45		8.5		254	.8	18.1	14.5	
46	19.8	13.4	68	1,986	6.9	35.7	18.5	
47	19.5	11.1	57	1,272	4.2	30.7	17.8	3.1
48	21.1	10.7	51	1,028	3.9	27.7	18.0	3.0
49	21.4	11.8	55	1,935	5.8	29.1	18.7	6.2
1950	21.1	13.0	62	1,853	5.8	30.5	19.3	4.6
51	21.4	10.1	47	811	2.5	20.4	17.9	2.8
52	22.0	10.4	47	931	2.7	20.3	19.3	2.9
53	22.1	10.1	46	764	2.1	20.8	19.2	2.7
54	22.4	12.8	57	1,769	4.8	26.8	20.0	5.3
55	22.7	12.4	54	1,272	3.6	26.1	20.3	3.4
56	23.0	11.4	50	980	2.7	21.5	20.0	3.1
57	23.4	11.6	50	1,138	2.9	22.7	20.5	3.7
58	23.5	14.8	63	2,505	6.3	31.0	21.7	6.6
59	23.6	13.1	56	1,675	4.4	29.6	21.7	4.3
1960	24.0	12.7	53	1,603	4.1	26.6	21.4	4.7
61	23.9	14.7	62	2,371	5.9	30.4	21.8	5.7
62	23.9	13.1	55	1,638	3.9	27.4	21.6	4.4
63	24.1	13.3	55	1,654	3.1	25.4	21.6	4.3

SOURCE: Bureau of Employment Security, U.S. Department of Labor.
[a] Cols. 2, 4, and 9 do not take into account data prior to 1946; such data are not available.

Table 5-5 presents some data that are relevant to the question. It shows the weeks of benefits that were available (col. 2), the extent to which this available duration was actually used (cols. 3 and 4), and the extent to which duration was exhausted (cols. 5-8). Column 9 provides a convenient measure of general economic activity.[33]

It is clear that the provision of benefits does not automatically result in their being used. On the average, not much more than half of the available duration was actually used (col. 4). Although this ratio has not fallen as potential duration has increased, because actual duration has risen along with potential duration, most of the rise in actual duration has been due to the rise in the duration of the exhaustees (col. 8), which is included in col. 3.

Exhaustions are greatly affected by the general state of business: The number of exhaustions during recessions is about double the number at other times (cols. 5 and 6). But exhaustions are not simply a recession phenomenon. The considerable number of exhaustions that occur even in periods of prosperity obviously reflect causes of a more constant nature.

[33] One should not be misled by the apparent similarity in the ratios of columns 6 and 9: although the denominator is the same, the numerators are very different. The numerator in column 6 is the cumulative number of different beneficiaries who exhausted their benefits sometime in the course of the year; in column 9 the numerator is the average number of beneficiaries who were drawing benefits at any one time during the year. Column 6 measures a static pool of exhaustees, column 9 a flowing stream of beneficiaries.

Columns 6 and 7 measure different aspects of the exhaustion problem. Column 6 refers to all those who had an insurance policy and shows what proportion of these policyholders found the insurance inadequate. This proportion is an indication of the general size of the problem but is not a direct measure of adequacy. Column 7 refers only to those who had occasion to use their policy and shows what proportion of these found their insurance inadequate. This proportion is called the exhaustion ratio.

The exhaustion ratio declined markedly during the early years of the program, when business conditions were improving at the same time that the maximum duration was being extended. In more recent years, although duration has continued to be extended, the ratio has ceased to decline—probably because counterinfluences in the economic sphere have brought about an increase of the long-term unemployed.

The exhaustion ratio provides the most usable criterion of adequacy, but the usefulness is limited by the difficulty of determining its proper value. In addition to fundamental difficulties rooted in political philosophy, there is the technical difficulty that the same exhaustion ratio has a different significance in a state with variable duration than in one with uniform duration (the former will include a larger proportion of the short-term unemployed), or in states with different qualifying requirements (the easier the requirements, the greater the number of exhaustees who will come from the fringes of the labor force).

Table 5–6 illustrates the extent to which the states differed in their duration experience.[34] For the reasons just given, these differences are difficult to interpret, and their significance is ambiguous. There is, however, a highly suggestive inverse correlation between the length of potential duration (col. 4) and the

exhaustion ratio (col. 8) and a highly suggestive direct correlation between the unemployment rate (col. 10) and the exhaustion ratio. Both correlations reinforce the observations made earlier, that the mere provision of longer duration does not automatically result in its being used and that the major factor determining benefit use is the general condition of a state's economy.

That there are exhaustees is not in itself a proof, much less a measure, of the program's inadequacy. Given the nature of unemployment insurance as a temporary bridge between jobs (Chapter 13), it is inevitable that for some claimants even the maximum duration that can be provided by such a program will be insufficient. The measure of inadequacy is that number of exhaustees who would regain their normal status of being employed if they were carried by the program somewhat longer (the "somewhat" must be within the limits set by the nature of an insurance program). To apply this measure effectively, that is, to form a reasonable judgment as to how soon how many of the exhaustees would find their way back to employment if they were carried somewhat further by the unemployment insurance program, one must know the relevant characteristics of the exhaustees.

Numerous, though rather thin, surveys of exhaustees have been conducted during the past eight years. Seventeen surveys by as many states were made during the period 1954–56, and another sixteen were made during the period 1956–59.[35]

In these surveys questionnaires were mailed to a sample of exhaustees at intervals of two months and four months after the exhaustion of benefits. Each recipient was asked to classify himself as working (employed), looking for work (unemployed), or neither (out of the labor force).

---

[34] A number of legislative changes were made in the duration provisions after 1962. The major changes were: North Dakota, Pennsylvania, and Tennessee went from uniform to variable duration; North Dakota, Tennessee, and Virginia increased maximum duration to twenty-six weeks; Colorado lowered its maximum to twenty-six weeks. The corresponding data for the other parts of the table for the period after 1962 were not available at the time of writing (April, 1964).

[35] The findings are presented in individual state reports and are summarized in two mimeographed publications of the Bureau of Employment Security, U.S. Department of Labor, Washington, D.C.: "Experience of Claimants Exhausting Benefit Rights Under Unemployment Insurance, 17 Selected States" and "Major Findings of 16 State Studies of Claimants Exhausting Unemployment Benefit Rights."

TABLE 5-6: SELECTED DATA ON THE DURATION AND EXHAUSTION OF UNEMPLOYMENT INSURANCE BENEFITS, BY STATE, 1962 (1964)

State	Per cent of all covered workers	All beneficiaries			Exhaustees				Insured unemployment rate
		Maximum duration[a] (weeks)	Potential duration (weeks)	Actual duration (weeks)	Number	As per cent of covered labor force	As per cent of all beneficiaries	Actual duration (weeks)	
(1)	(2)	(3)	(4)	(5)	(6)	(7)	(8)	(9)	(10)
52 states	100.0	27[b]	23.9	13.1	1,638,359	3.9	27.4	21.6	4.4
Alabama	1.3	26	23.4	14.4	28,800	5.5	38.7	21.1	5.0
Alaska	.1	26	25.2	18.2	3,238	9.8	30.4	24.5	10.8
Arizona	.6	26	22.7	11.2	7,881	3.1	23.0	19.1	3.9
Arkansas	.7	26	21.8	11.6	14,140	4.9	28.1	19.0	5.9
California	9.7	26E	23.9	13.7	179,587	4.5	25.5	22.5	5.4
Colorado	.9	26	28.5	14.0	7,655	2.0	23.8	21.7	2.9
Connecticut	1.8	26E	21.8	13.2	27,568	3.6	29.8	19.9	3.5
Delaware	.3	26	21.8	11.8	5,159	4.2	28.0	20.5	3.4
D.C.	.6	34	26.8	13.3	5,396	2.0	31.5	19.5	2.0
Florida	2.3	26	19.6	11.2	39,416	4.2	37.1	16.5	3.8
Georgia	1.9	26	18.7	10.0	36,819	4.9	35.2	15.1	3.4
Hawaii	.4	U26E	26.0	13.8	5,098	3.0	21.4	26.0	3.9
Idaho	.3	26E	18.3	11.3	6,569	5.2	31.0	15.5	4.9
Illinois	6.5	26E	21.0	12.3	100,172	3.8	31.9	19.0	3.2
Indiana	2.7	26	18.4	10.2	49,348	4.5	34.9	14.4	3.2
Iowa	1.1	26	20.3	12.1	13,248	3.0	27.9	16.9	2.5
Kansas	.9	26	22.4	11.3	9,692	2.7	25.0	19.8	2.8
Kentucky	1.1	28	22.9	13.2	21,231	4.7	30.8	21.3	5.7
Louisiana	1.3	26	22.8	18.6	30,488	5.7	45.5	20.6	4.9
Maine	.5	U26	26.0	12.0	6,259	3.2	16.3	25.7	5.5
Maryland	1.7	U26	26.0	14.0	26,929	3.9	24.9	26.0	4.4
Massachusetts	3.8	30	24.9	13.1	63,736	4.2	25.3	22.4	4.9
Michigan	4.2	26	22.5	10.5	83,342	4.8	28.4	18.5	4.5
Minnesota	1.7	26	22.2	14.5	23,848	3.3	27.0	22.1	4.0
Mississippi	.7	26	22.4	12.6	13,284	4.8	29.6	20.3	5.0
Missouri	2.4	26	22.7	11.3	29,808	3.1	22.8	20.2	4.0

Montana	.3		21.8	12.7	5,949	5.4	31.6	19.3	4.9
Nebraska	.6	26	21.6	11.9	6,398	2.7	25.5	17.9	2.5
Nevada	.2	26	21.8	11.4	3,570	3.8	23.6	19.3	4.2
New Hampshire	.4	U26	26.0	10.4	2,558	1.6	12.6	25.9	3.5
New Jersey	3.9	26	23.3	13.4	80,015	5.1	28.7	20.9	5.2
New Mexico	.4	30	28.5	14.3	5,095	3.2	23.8	25.2	4.0
New York	12.2	U26	26.0	14.3	152,502	3.0	19.6	26.0	4.8
North Carolina	2.3	U26E	26.0	10.3	29,254	3.2	18.5	24.5	3.8
North Dakota	.2	26	24.0	15.6	1,953	2.9	18.0	24.0	5.2
Ohio	5.8	U26	25.9	13.8	71,461	3.0	24.5	26.0	4.2
Oklahoma	.9	39	27.2	14.9	14,528	3.8	32.9	23.1	4.5
Oregon	.9	26	23.6	13.1	16,768	4.2	24.9	21.5	4.9
Pennsylvania	7.2	30E	30.0	15.5	121,866	4.2	24.0	30.0	6.3
Puerto Rico	.6	U12	12.0	10.0	29,071	11.8	64.6	12.0	6.6
Rhode Island	.6	26	22.8	11.0	10,397	4.3	23.8	19.9	5.0
South Carolina	1.1	22	20.5	12.2	16,816	3.8	36.0	19.7	3.1
South Dakota	.2	24	19.2	10.6	2,557	3.1	30.9	14.7	2.7
Tennessee	1.6	26	21.4	14.0	36,328	5.4	37.2	21.0	5.3
Texas	4.4	26	19.6	12.0	73,372	4.0	41.7	16.5	2.8
Utah	.5	36	24.6	11.8	5,036	2.6	21.9	19.1	3.3
Vermont	.2	U26E	26.0	14.0	2,584	3.5	22.6	26.0	4.8
Virginia	1.8	26	16.6	9.8	24,350	3.3	39.0	13.7	2.1
Washington	1.5	30	27.4	14.0	26,749	4.3	21.6	25.2	6.0
West Virginia	.8	U26	26.0	12.7	15,700	4.9	24.6	25.0	6.8
Wisconsin	2.1	34	c	c	19,962d	4.5	14.9e	c	3.0
Wyoming	.2	26	21.5	13.1	3,535	5.3	30.2	18.3	4.8

SOURCES: Bureau of Employment Security; Wisconsin Unemployment Compensation Department.
a As of April 1, 1964. U indicates uniform duration. E indicates extended duration available when triggered by unemployment level.
b Weighted average; does not include triggered extended benefits.
c Comparable data not available for Wisconsin.
d Complete, not "per employer," exhaustions.
e Estimated beneficiaries in 1962: 134,000.

In the earlier set of surveys, which were conducted in generally favorable economic conditions, it was found that two months after exhaustion about one-third of the exhaustees were employed, and four months after exhaustion between one-third and one-half were employed. During the later set of surveys economic conditions were less favorable, and slightly smaller percentages of the exhaustees were found to be employed after two months (between one-fourth and one-third) and after four months (about two-fifths).

If the duration of benefits had been extended for another two to four months, the unemployment insurance program might have served as a bridge between jobs for about those proportions of the exhaustees.[36] With respect to the other exhaustees, who also would have been paid benefits during the additional weeks and would still be unemployed at the end of the benefit extension, the original question recurs: How soon are how many of them likely to be re-employed?

These surveys also give the number of exhaustees who reported that they were out of the labor market. In the 1954–56 surveys, an average of less than 15 per cent (the range was from 6 to 25 per cent) so reported two months after exhaustion, and less than 20 per cent (the range was from 8 to 27 per cent) so reported four months after exhaustion. In the 1956–59 surveys, the range was from 5 per cent to 16 per cent after two months and from 7 per cent to 20 per cent after four months.

The reliability and significance of the survey data on the extent to which exhaustees leave the labor force are open to some question. The difference between being unemployed and being out of the labor force, as these terms are understood in the unemployment insurance system, is difficult to define, let alone determine by means of a mailed questionnaire answered by the claimant himself.

The pattern of withdrawal from the labor force shown by census data is considerably different from that shown by the post-exhaustion surveys. The census figures on gross changes in the labor force show that even in prosperous years about 19 per cent of the unemployed, on the average, leave the labor force each month.[37] Among women the proportion is greater— about 31 per cent. Moreover, these proportions generally hold for the long-term as well as the short-term unemployed,[38] and hence seem to be usable for a comparison with the experience of exhaustees. Consistent with this general picture is the census finding that of all those who work during a year, even a prosperous year, only about 37 per cent of the women (about 64 per cent of the men) work at full-time, full-year jobs.[39]

Some differences between the two sets of data are to be expected, because the characteristics of all the unemployed, as sampled by the census, are presumably not identical with those of unemployment insurance exhaustees. For example, there are probably fewer part-time and part-year workers among unemployment insurance exhaustees. But the differences in the proportions leaving the labor force are so considerable that they point up the difficulty of getting accurate labor-force information from a mailed questionnaire and emphasize the desirability of securing more detailed data through a more intensive investigation. Although the post-exhaustion surveys have produced a great deal of valuable information about the unemployed who are not being cared for by the unemployment insurance system, especially the long-term unemployed, they do not suffice to construct general norms for the adequacy of duration in unemployment insurance. For that, a more intensive kind of survey is needed, an investigation in depth. Two such intensive surveys have been made in recent years, both in Michigan.

The first survey, conducted by Professor Ronald S. Johnson of the University of

---

[36] This is on the assumption, not to be made lightly, that the respondents were in the labor market by unemployment insurance standards during the entire period of their non-employment.

[37] "The Extent and Nature of Frictional Unemployment," Study Paper No. 6, prepared by the Bureau of Labor Statistics for the Joint Economic Committee of Congress, November 19, 1959, p. 35.

[38] *Ibid.*, p. 36.

[39] Carl Rosenfeld, "Work Experience of the Population in 1960," *Monthly Labor Review* (December, 1961), p. 1328.

Michigan,[40] investigated a sample of Detroit exhaustees during the period 1948–49 and classified them according to the degree of their attachment to the labor force and the likelihood of their re-employment. Johnson came to the conclusion that only 53 per cent of the exhaustees studied were clearly regular members of the labor force with good chances of re-employment and that at least 16 per cent, most of them women, may have received benefits improperly because they had dropped out of the labor force even before the exhaustion of their benefits.

The Michigan Unemployment Compensation Commission conducted a post-exhaustion survey at about the same time, 1949, by means of the usual mailed questionnaire. The commission reached the conclusion that only 2–3 per cent of exhaustees might have drawn benefits improperly while out of the labor force. The marked difference between this conclusion and that reached by Johnson's intensive study would seem to indicate that the results of less intensive surveys must be interpreted with caution.

Another intensive survey was made by Professor William S. Devino of Michigan State University.[41] Devino investigated a sample of exhaustees in the Lansing labor market during the 1958 recession. Three-fourths of the exhaustees in that labor market came from the auto industry, nine-tenths of them were males, and nine-tenths were under fifty years of age. Direct comparison with the Johnson study is not feasible because Devino did not use Johnson's classifications of labor-force status and because the composition of the two samples differed. In the kind of exhaustee population sampled by Devino, persons with a secure attachment to the labor market would be expected to predominate. Devino found that three months after exhaustion 35 per cent of the exhaustees were re-employed, 60 per cent were still unemployed,

and less than 5 per cent had left the labor force. Six months after exhaustion the corresponding proportions were 63 per cent (here the unusual character of the sample shows most clearly), 31 per cent, and 6 per cent. The experience of this sample is probably the typical experience of the unemployed in a cyclically sensitive, durable goods manufacturing industry during a recession. As such, it provides support for the proposal discussed below under the heading "Regular Cyclical Benefits."

The most ambitious attempt to survey the characteristics of exhaustees was made in connection with the TEUC program. When Congress passed the law, it did so with the provision that a detailed report be made of the characteristics of TEUC beneficiaries and it appropriated a million dollars to carry out the necessary investigation. The Bureau of Employment Security required all state agencies to interview samples of these beneficiaries throughout the country at four different times, in the spring and fall of 1961 and in the winter and spring of 1962. Altogether, about 175,000 interviews were conducted. Although the results of this tremendous survey, the largest single research task ever undertaken by the Bureau of Employment Security, have not yet been published completely or analyzed in detail, the data that are available suffice for some general conclusions.[42]

Since the TEUC beneficiaries exhausted their regular benefits during a recession, the samples would be expected to include a large proportion of regular, full-time members of the work force. This expectation was realized.

Over three-fifths of the TEUC claimants were what might be called principal earners, that is, individuals living alone and primary workers in families.[43] In over two-thirds of these families, no one else was working.

---

[40] *A Study of People Who Have Exhausted Unemployment Benefits in an Active Labor Market* (Bureau of Business Research, University of Michigan, Ann Arbor, Michigan, January, 1951).

[41] *Exhaustion of Unemployment Benefits During a Recession* (Labor and Industrial Relations Center, Michigan State University, East Lansing, Michigan, 1960).

[42] The findings quoted are taken from the fourth report, *Family Characteristics of the Long-Term Unemployed*, TEUC Report Series No. 4 (Bureau of Employment Security, U.S. Department of Labor, Washington, D.C., January, 1963).

[43] Probably some of the "secondary" earners should be included among the principal earners, because about 15 per cent of them reported dependents. In this survey the meaning of the term "secondary earner" is obscure. The term was used to designate a person who answered

Men, who comprise about two-thirds of the civilian labor force, made up about three-fifths of the TEUC claimants. Among the claimants about 60 per cent of the men and about 70 per cent of the women were in the prime working years, ages twenty-five to fifty-four. Pensioners constituted only 14 per cent of all claimants.

Fifty per cent of the claimants had worked in manufacturing industries, and 70 per cent had worked in blue-collar occupations. Three-fourths said that they had been in the labor force, either employed or unemployed, during each of the thirty-six months prior to filing for TEUC benefits.

The over-all impression is that these are the types of claimants to be expected during a recession. They are temporarily unemployed in the sense that most of them, without making any drastic change in their personal situation, will find employment when the recession ends. To that extent they are proper claimants under the unemployment insurance system. In general, findings on TEUC support the conclusion that some extension of benefits is desirable during the temporary declines in employment associated with recessions.

There is evidence already, and closer analysis may reveal more, that some benefits were paid under circumstances not strictly within the purview of an unemployment insurance system. There is also considerable evidence that the states differed significantly in their TEUC experiences. All this evidence will be useful in designing the structure of the next, probably permanent, program of recessionary extended benefits; for example it may point up the desirability of allowing each state more freedom in adapting such a program to its own economy.

Of the 2.8 million TEUC claimants, 1.7 million, or 60 per cent, exhausted their extended benefits. This is a much higher exhaustion ratio than obtains in the regular unemployment

insurance program.[44] Does it signify that benefits were not extended far enough? Or since the majority of these exhaustees were still not employed at the end of their extended benefits, does it signify that unemployment benefits are not the proper remedy for this kind of unemployment? Part of the answer may be supplied by a detailed analysis of TEUC exhaustees, including the post-exhaustion studies being made by thirteen of the states;[45] but even then, in all probability, we shall be unable to determine exactly the proper relationship of unemployment insurance to this type of claimant.

C. Future Developments

In the absence of widespread agreement on norms to govern benefit duration, any conclusions drawn in this area necessarily must have a high content of personal judgment. Hence the following observations on future developments in benefit duration are intended primarily as a participation in the dialogue that must go on until a broader consensus emerges.

In any consideration of duration it is useful to distinguish between what may be called regular and extra-regular benefits and, within each of these, to distinguish two subtypes. For convenience in discussion, the four types are assigned the following descriptive titles: (1) regular, (2) regular cyclical, (3) extra-regular insurance, (4) extra-regular assistance.

Regular Benefits. The program of regular benefits is that program which operates at all times and in all places (not only during reces-

---

in the negative when asked whether he or she was the family's "main support." The classification represents only the worker's opinion of his or her status in the family and has no necessary connection with the actual importance of his or her earnings in the family's total income.

[44] Among the states the range of variation in the TEUC program was from 41 per cent to 92 per cent; in the regular unemployment insurance program in 1962 the range was from 13 per cent to 46 per cent.

[45] The 13 states are: Arizona, California, Georgia, Illinois, Indiana, Louisiana, Maryland, Michigan, New York, Ohio, Oregon, Pennsylvania, and Vermont. Tennessee made a survey of its own exhaustees and found that "approximately 75 per cent of all the TEUC claimants in Tennessee exhausted their extended insurance, and 45 per cent of these were still unemployed, or employed only part time, or temporarily employed at the 16th week after they had exhausted their TEUC benefits." (Ernest J. Eberling, "Extension of Benefit Payments," *Employment Security Review* [December, 1962], p. 12.)

sions or in depressed areas) and pays benefits up to a maximum of twenty-six weeks. The cutoff at twenty-six weeks is not altogether arbitrary. In much of the literature dealing with duration, one finds the opinion advanced that the present program cannot be pushed very far beyond twenty-six weeks without a change in its nature and the loss of some of its advantages. The International Labor Office study takes this position,[46] as do numerous specialists in this country.[47] There seems to be a tendency for the maximum duration to level off at twenty-six weeks (Figure 5–2); currently there is a ceiling at about this level. The Kennedy Administration, in its 1961–62 proposals (H.R. 7640), distinguished between what happens up to twenty-six weeks and what happens thereafter. The same distinction was made in the 1962 Report of the Committee of Inquiry into the Unemployment Insurance Act of Canada.

Over the years, duration in the regular program has been lengthened so that by the spring of 1964 over 98 per cent of the covered workers were in states with a maximum duration of twenty-six weeks, and the average worker who actually became unemployed was eligible for about twenty-four weeks of benefits. The same forces that brought about the liberalization of the program in the past are still operative. The conclusion would seem to follow that this regular program may safely be left to the evolutionary processes at work within the separate states.

It is likely that the issue of variable versus uniform duration will also be left to the determination of the individual states. Each system has advantages and disadvantages, and the final choice between them depends very much on each state's own economy and on the other provisions of the state's unemployment in-surance program, especially the provisions regulating eligibility, disqualifications, and the maximum duration. Hence it would be rash to say that any one choice is the best for every situation.

A likely development in this area is that the variable duration states will continue to raise their qualifying requirements and minimum duration, and the uniform duration states will add extended benefits available only to claimants with a longer history of attachment to the labor force. The net effect will be for the variable duration states to approach uniform duration more closely at the lower end of the duration spectrum, while the uniform duration states are introducing variability in the upper part of the spectrum.

Regular Cyclical Benefits. A likely development in the near future is the extension of the regular program to pay longer benefits during cyclical downturns. The development has both logic and precedent on its side. Since the purpose of unemployment insurance is to provide a bridge between jobs, it is logical to extend the bridge somewhat for everybody when jobs generally are harder to find. As precedents, there are the TUC and the TEUC programs, and there are currently (April, 1964) eight states[48] which provide extended benefits up to thirty-nine weeks when unemployment in the state rises above a designated level.

Should there be federal participation in any of these regular cyclical benefits? From the viewpoint of the financial burden involved, there is no compelling reason why each state could not finance its own benefits. The tax necessary to finance cyclically extended benefits (on the average probably less than 0.2 per cent of covered wages) would be a small part of total unemployment insurance taxes, and these taxes are a small part of total labor costs.[49] If there had been no federal temporary extended unemployment compensation, many more states

[46] *Unemployment Insurance Schemes,* Studies and Reports, New Series No. 42 (Geneva, Switzerland: International Labor Office, 1955), p. 179.

[47] See Eveline M. Burns, "New Guidelines for Unemployment Insurance," *Employment Security Review* (August, 1962), p. 8; Richard A. Lester, *The Economics of Unemployment Compensation* (Princeton, N.J.: Princeton University, 1962), p. 127; and Harry Malisoff, *The Financing of Unemployment Insurance Benefits* (Kalamazoo, Michigan: The W. E. Upjohn Institute for Employment Research, 1963), p. 1.

[48] These states are indicated by an "E" in Table 5–6, col. 3.

[49] Even Michigan could have avoided its present financial difficulties if it had levied an unemployment insurance tax averaging 0.5 per cent higher over the life of the program; or if it had increased the taxable wage base commensurate with increasing wage levels.

probably would have had their own programs in operation by this time. However, precedent and the desire to assure universal state action make some federal participation very likely.

With this likelihood in view the Interstate Conference of Employment Security Agencies (ICESA) in 1962–63 prepared a possible program of extended cyclical benefits by which the federal government would offer to match state payments of extended benefits during state recessions. Such a program would have some of the advantages of both federal and state action. Federal matching would put enough financial pressure on the states to assure general participation and would mean at least partial sharing of costs among the states. On the other hand, there would remain some of the discipline that accompanies state financial responsibility and, more importantly, there would remain state flexibility in tailoring the program to meet the conditions of each state's economy and unemployment insurance system.

In the ICESA proposal the extended benefits were limited to half the claimant's regular benefits up to a maximum of thirteen additional weeks or a total of thirty-nine weeks. This extension would carry most beneficiaries through most recessions yet would not create too great a financial burden for the regular unemployment insurance program. The burden would be felt less by the most hard-pressed employers if the additional taxes required by the costs of these extended cyclical benefits were not experience rated. Under these conditions there would be partial pooling of costs as between states and complete pooling as between employers within a state.

Even outside of recession periods, there can be long-term declines in particular industries and areas and as a result there can be unemployed persons for whom the regular duration of unemployment insurance is insufficient. There is a growing number of these long-term unemployed, many of whom are clearly in the labor market and not all of whom can or should be immediately offered an opportunity of retraining or relocation. Can the duration of unemployment insurance be extended in these cases? The desirability of

helping the long-term unemployed before they are reduced to the status of relief recipients is obvious; what is not so obvious is the extent to which the unemployment insurance program can be used to serve this need. Perhaps the solution will be found in two steps, each representing a further departure from the structure of the present program.

Extra-regular Insurance. An extension of benefits from twenty-six to thirty-nine weeks may be provided somewhat along the following lines. First of all, such non-recession extended benefits may be limited in some way, probably to workers with a fairly substantial attachment to the labor market.[50] A further limitation has been suggested, that only workers who are their own or others' sole support should be eligible for these extended benefits; but this limitation has much less backing. Second, the definition of suitable work may be somewhat enlarged, and beneficiaries may be put under more pressure to make necessary changes in their economic situation. Third, the source of funds may be other than an experience-rated payroll tax, and the burden of the taxes, however they are raised, may be shared between the state and federal governments—perhaps through an arrangement of matching grants.

Extra-regular Assistance. There are good reasons for thinking that most persons unemployed for more than thirty-nine weeks in normal times are in a special situation that will not be changed by merely the extension of unemployment insurance benefits. On the other hand, there may be some cases in which it will seem unwise to rush into an elaborate program of relocation or retraining; given a little more time, the beneficiaries may find their way back into employment. Could unemployment benefits properly be granted in these cases for a still longer period?

The problem of paying benefits beyond thirty-nine weeks, perhaps up to fifty-two weeks, thus far has not presented itself in a pressing form. When it does, it may be answered by an as

---

[50] In the federal proposal (H.R. 7460) extended benefits were limited to workers with 78 weeks of work out of the preceding 156 weeks. Both Utah and Wisconsin require additional weeks of work in the base period if the worker is to qualify for benefits beyond 26 weeks.

yet only dimly perceived program intermediate between the social insurance and the social assistance programs we now know. In addition to the limitations applied to the twenty-six–thirty-nine week beneficiaries, an income limitation might be applied to the thirty-nine–fifty-two week group. Ignoring any assets that the beneficiary may have, such a program might examine the applicant's income needs and income resources and fix a benefit accordingly. The measure of need for income would probably have to be similar to that used in the relief programs.

Since such a program would probably draw its funds from general revenues, it might be open to more persons than only those previously covered by unemployment insurance. It might include all those who could offer proof, perhaps in the form of withholding-tax receipts, of a substantial history of previous employment.

Under such a program, which would cover the gray area between insurance and relief, the condition of being able and available for work would be more obvious, the definition of suitable work would be still more enlarged, and the beneficiaries would be under more pressure to take any reasonable steps to improve their employability. This program, like that of extra-regular insurance, might be a joint federal-state program and operate in terms of matching grants.

Our knowledge of the labor market is not sufficiently comprehensive to enable us to say with certainty whether or not the payment of unemployment benefits up to thirty-nine weeks, or up to fifty-two weeks, is desirable. The answer will depend to some extent on available alternative provisions for the long-term unemployed. Developments in public and private pension programs, in private unemployment benefit programs, in public works programs, in public relief programs, in both private and public retraining programs—all these will help establish the parameters within which lie the solutions of the problem of the long-term unemployed.

CHAPTER 6

Supplementary Unemployment Benefits
Joseph M. Becker,
Virginia Kyner Boman*

I. INTRODUCTION

CLOSELY CONNECTED WITH the subject matter of the two preceding chapters are the programs of supplementary unemployment benefits (SUB), which are private arrangements to supplement the amount and duration of state unemployment insurance benefits.[1]

It helps in understanding supplementary unemployment benefit programs to see them in relation to the other private programs which attempt to meet the problem of irregular income caused by irregular employment. The major types of these programs are shown in Table 6-1, where they are classified according to three characteristics: the expected permanency of the employer-employee relationship, the time at which the guarantee of income becomes effective, and the claimant's employment status.

If the employer, at the time of hire, guarantees to maintain the employment relationship for a given period of time, the plan is of the A-type. Strictly speaking, programs of the A-type seek to prevent unemployment rather than to

* Research Associate, Institute of Social Order, Saint Louis University.

[1] For several years after the birth of SUB there was considerable debate as to whether SUB was a form of wage payment and therefore disqualified the recipient from receiving unemployment insurance at the same time. The states answered this question in various ways at the beginning, but by 1964 only Virginia continued to prohibit the payment of unemployment insurance to recipients of supplementary unemployment benefits.

aid workers who have become unemployed. Whether the guarantee is expressed in terms of wages or of weeks of employment is immaterial. The guarantee may be for a day (call-in pay), for a week (weekly hours guarantee and the short-workweek benefit), or for a year (the traditional "guaranteed annual wage").

The guarantee may be for longer than a year. The 1962 Kaiser contract with the steelworkers' union, for example, contains the equivalent of a guarantee against certain kinds of unemployment during the life of the contract. Indeed, the guarantee may be for an indefinitely long period. Thus, by the terms of the 1961 contract between the Southern Pacific Railroad and the Order of Railroad Telegraphers, nearly all telegraphers are guaranteed employment until their retirement. (And in some industries in Italy and France governmental pressure on the employer has at times made it almost impossible to lay off a worker once he is hired.)

It is the expected termination of the employment relationship that distinguishes the programs in column B. In some B-type programs, benefits are paid whether or not any unemployment results from the termination of employment. The employee is considered to have a kind of property right to the job, and the benefit is paid as a consideration for the loss of the property right. Programs to provide severance pay and early pensions belong in this category.

In other B-type programs, unemployment is a necessary condition for the receipt of benefits.

TABLE 6–1: TYPES OF PRIVATE INCOME MAINTENANCE PLANS

Time at which guarantee becomes operative	Nature of employment relationship		
	Expected to continue (A)	Expected to end (B)	Expectation uncertain or irrelevant (C)
I. At time of hire	1. Daily call-in pay 2. Weekly wage guarantee; short-workweek benefits 3. Guaranteed annual wage		
II. At time of layoff a. Unemployment not a necessary condition		4. Severance pay 5. Early pension ————— 6. Most railroad dismissal plans	8. Extended layoff benefits
b. Unemployment a necessary condition		7. Some SUB plans	9. Vested "SUB" plans 10. Unemployment insurance 11. Most SUB plans

In this category belong certain limited SUB plans (No. 7) such as that in the women's garment industry whereby benefits are paid only when the employer goes out of business, and several recent (1963) railroad plans (between the Clerks and the Southern Pacific Railroad, and between the Telegraphers and the B & O) in which railroad unemployment insurance is supplemented for a year[2] if unemployment results from the permanent abolition of a position.

There are other railroad unemployment benefit plans (No. 6) which do not fit precisely in either category and are therefore placed in the table between "A" and "B." In these plans, which operate only in special situations (the merger or abandonment of railroads, or the permanent abolition of a position), a man need not be completely unemployed to receive a benefit, but his earnings plus the benefit may not exceed his former wage from the railroad.

In programs of the C-type, it is irrelevant whether the separation from employment is temporary or permanent; but in all except one of these programs the claimant must be unemployed in order to be eligible for benefits.

[2] For the four succeeding years the plan is similar to the other railroad plans in No. 6.

The one exception is the aerospace industry's plan of extended layoff benefits—a hybrid requiring a category of its own. Although this plan does not necessarily envisage a permanent break in the employment relationship (beneficiaries retain their seniority rights) and therefore is properly classified in column C, functionally it is more closely related to the severance pay plans of column B and for that reason is discussed with those plans in Chapter 7.

In other programs of the C-type, the claimant must be unemployed to be eligible for benefits. Some of these plans are of the vested or individual-account type, such as currently exist in the glass, clay, and tile industries. In these plans the employer regularly sets aside a given amount in the name of the employee, who may draw on this account under stated conditions when he is unemployed. These are essentially savings plans having no element of sharing or insurance.[3] Although frequently described as SUB plans, they belong to a different category, since they do not necessarily supplement any

[3] Beginning in 1935, General Motors Corporation for several years operated a loan plan that has an affinity with this general category. The company loaned money, free of interest, to laid-off employees, and the employees did not have to repay the company unless they were recalled to work.

other unemployment benefit, and their provisions are in no way connected with the amount, duration, eligibility, or disqualification provisions of the public unemployment insurance program.

Private unemployment insurance plans in the United States date back at least to 1831.[4] They never spread widely and experienced only a limited growth; the likelihood of any further development was seemingly ended by the advent of public unemployment insurance in 1935. Beginning in 1955, however, they experienced a significant revival in the form of private supplements to the public insurance program.

Historically, the SUB plans grew out of the efforts of the steel and auto unions to achieve a guaranteed annual wage. The United Steelworkers of America made a guaranteed annual wage one of their proposals to the steel industry in the negotiations of 1943. Since this was wartime, the proposal was referred to the National War Labor Board. Although the board denied the request, it initiated an investigation whose results were eventually published in what has come to be known as the "Latimer Report."[5] It was in this report and especially in a subsequent report written by Latimer for the United Steelworkers[6] that there occurred the metamorphosis of the guaranteed annual wage into SUB.

In effect, Latimer concluded that a guaranteed annual wage would be too expensive for the steel industry at that time but suggested that a less expensive and in some ways a more satisfactory plan would be to supplement the benefits paid by the public unemployment insurance system. These supplementary benefits would be paid out of a pooled, non-vested fund consisting of employer contributions. As compared with a guaranteed annual wage, this SUB plan not only would be less expensive

but would have the advantage of providing maximum protection when protection was most needed—at the time of layoff. In a guaranteed annual wage plan the protection provided is greatest at the time of hire and continually diminishes as the year, or other guaranteed period, draws to its close. But in a SUB plan the period of protection continually moves out ahead of the employee and is available to its full extent whenever unemployment occurs.

It was in the auto industry that SUB actually was born. In 1955 the UAW succeeded in negotiating this type of plan first with Ford and then with the other auto companies. The United Steelworkers negotiated an essentially similar plan, although with some significant differences, in the can industry in 1955 and in the steel industry in 1956. In subsequent years some additional SUB plans of the non-vested type (listed in Table 6–2) were negotiated by other unions in other industries.

II. EXTENT OF SUB PLANS

SUB plans of the non-vested, pooled-fund type covered over 2.5 million employees in 1962. The known coverage of the plans listed in Table 6–2, which is not altogether complete, was 2,560,000. About 70 per cent of these workers were employed in the steel, can, aluminum, auto, agricultural implement, and rubber industries. About the same proportion belonged to three unions: the United Steelworkers, the United Auto Workers, and the United Rubber Workers. Altogether, companies in at least nineteen different industries have negotiated SUB plans with twenty-three different unions.

Some unions, notably those of the steel, auto, and rubber workers, have negotiated SUB plans for most of their memberships. Other unions, which appear not to have considered SUB a major collective-bargaining objective, have negotiated such plans for only part of their memberships. For example, locals of the IAM and IBEW, which bargain for some workers in the steel, can, auto, and agricultural implement industries, have adopted the steel-

[4] Bryce M. Stewart, *Unemployment Benefits in the United States* (New York: Industrial Relations Counselors, Inc., 1930), p. 80.

[5] Murray W. Latimer, *Guaranteed Wages* (Washington, D.C.: Government Printing Office, 1947).

[6] *A Guaranteed Wage Plan for the Workers in the Steel Industry* (Washington, D.C.: U.S. Wage Stabilization Board, Case no. D–18–C [no date]).

ato plan in some companies, while in other ompanies they have adopted the glass-type avings plan or negotiated no plans at all.

About 72 per cent of covered workers are in lans that are basically of the auto-steel type; aese are shown under A of Table 6–2. Other lans have distinctive features some of which re especially tailored to the nature of the adustry; these are shown under B.

Although SUB plans have not spread widely nce the major ones were negotiated, interest as not died, as is evidenced by continuing new evelopments. For example: The 1962 conention of the IUE adopted a bargaining proram that included a demand for supplementary nemployment benefits covering both total nemployment and short workweeks. In the erospace industry the UAW and the IAM ave sought to replace the industry's extended ayoff benefit plan (see Chapter 7) with a SUB plan of the auto-steel type. In 1963 an rbitrator's award established a SUB plan for he Brotherhood of Railway Clerks with the outhern Pacific Company; later that year the Order of Railroad Telegraphers negotiated a

similar plan with the Baltimore and Ohio Railroad.

III. PROVISIONS OF SUB PLANS OF THE AUTO-STEEL TYPE

To make possible a more detailed examination of experience under SUB programs, the rest of this chapter concentrates on the two principal plans, those in the auto and steel industries. Thus the following description of the essential features of SUB plans covers only the type of plan in part A of Table 6–2.

A. CURRENT PROVISIONS

Although SUB plans of the auto-steel type vary considerably in detail, their major provisions are similar, as may be seen in Table 6–3. Since the plans provide for the supplementation of state unemployment insurance benefits, it is convenient to describe their provisions in the familiar unemployment insurance terms of coverage, eligibility, disqualification, amount and duration of benefits, financing, and administration.

ABLE 6–2: ESTIMATED COVERAGE OF THE MAJOR NON-VESTED SUPPLEMENTAL UNEMPLOYMENT BENEFIT PLANS AS OF AUGUST, 1962

A. Plans basically similar to auto and steel plans		
ndustry or company	Union	Approx. no. covered
Auto, agricultural implement, misc.	United Automobile, Aerospace and Agricultural Implement Workers of America	875,000
Steel, can, aluminum	United Steelworkers of America	723,000
Auto, agricultural implement, steel, misc.	International Union of Electrical, Radio and Machine Workers	47,000
Auto, agricultural implement	International Brotherhood of Electrical Workers	n.a.
Can, aluminum, agricultural implement, misc.	International Association of Machinists	10,000
Aluminum	Aluminum Workers International Union	24,000
Can	International Longshoremen's and Warehousemen's Union	n.a.
Rubber and plastics	United Rubber, Cork, Linoleum and Plastic Workers of America	130,000
Cement	United Cement, Lime and Gypsum Workers	10,000
Harbison-Walker Refractories Co.	Oil, Chemical and Atomic Workers; United Brick and Clay Workers; United Stone and Allied Products Workers of America	2,000
Thirteen other refractories	United Brick and Clay Workers	5,000
California Food Employers	Retail Clerks International Association	26,000

TABLE 6·2 (*continued*)

B. Plans with distinctive provisions

Industry or company	Union	Distinctive provisions	Approx. no. covered
Women's and children's garments	International Ladies' Garment Workers' Union	Eligibility: Layoff caused by closing of business by employer.	386,000
U.S. Borax and Chemical Corp.	International Chemical Workers Union	Eligibility: Layoff caused by general curtailment of operations; benefits not payable until 90 days after layoff.	1,100
Armour and Company	United Packinghouse Workers; Amalgamated Meatcutters and Butcher Workmen	Eligibility: Layoff caused by permanent shut-down of department or plant; employee waiting for transfer to another plant.	n.a.
Southern Pacific Company	Brotherhood of Railway Clerks	Eligibility: Layoff caused by permanent abolition of position.	6,000
Baltimore and Ohio Railroad	Order of Railroad Telegraphers	Benefit amount: 70 per cent of wages. Financing: No trust fund.	3,000
General Electric Co.	Three electrical unions (I.U.E., I.B.E.W., U.E.); various other unions	Supplements duration only: One week of benefits for each six months worked.	172,000
Westinghouse Electric Corp.			100,000
Atlantic and Gulf Coast shipping	National Maritime Union	Maximum duration: Eight weeks for any single period of unemployment.	36,000
New York photo-engravers	International Photo-Engravers' Union	Must report to employment office two days a week and remain for one hour.	2,800
California and Hawaiian Sugar Refining Corp.	Sugar Refining Employees Union	Financing: No trust fund.	1,250
Men's Hats, Inc., Baltimore	United Hatters, Cap and Millinery Workers International Union	Contribution: Six per cent of gross wages. Benefit: $10 for a maximum of ten weeks.	n.a.

SOURCES: (1) Bureau of Labor Statistics: Supplemental Unemployment Plans Negotiated January, 1955–August, 1962. (Mimeographed.) (2) Collective bargaining contracts. (3) California Department of Industrial Relations, "Supplemental Unemployment Benefit Plans," *California Industrial Relations Reports*, April, 1960. (4) Bureau of National Affairs, Inc., *Collective Bargaining Negotiations and Contracts*, 1955–1962 (Washington, D.C.).

Coverage. In any one company typically all employees for whom a union bargains are covered by the SUB plan. An exception is found in the can industry, which has a marked seasonal pattern and specifically excludes seasonal workers. (The steel industry uses eligibility requirements to achieve something of the same effect.)

Eligibility. To be eligible for SUB, an employee must be part of the employer's regular work force; this is currently defined as having one or two years of service. "Service" includes all weeks during which an employee retains seniority with the company, even though in some weeks he may not actually work or receive any pay.

As a general rule, to be eligible for SUB a claimant must also be eligible for unemployment insurance. This requirement assures that the unemployed person is registered with the public employment service and has satisfied the other conditions for receiving state benefits. There are a number of exceptions to this general rule, however, and the number has grown.

The most important exception is that exhaustion of state benefits does not of itself

TABLE 6–3: MAJOR PROVISIONS OF SUB PLANS OF THE AUTO-STEEL TYPE
AS OF JUNE 30, 1963

Provisions	General Motors plan	U.S. Steel plan
Eligibility	1 year's service.[a]	2 years' service.[a]
Benefit duration		
Ratio	1 week's benefit per 2 weeks worked or paid.	1 week's benefit per 2 weeks worked or paid.
Maximum	52 weeks.	52 weeks.
Benefit amount		
Regular benefit		
With unemployment insurance	62% of weekly earnings plus $1.50 for each of not more than 4 dependents *minus* unemployment insurance and other compensation.[b] Maximum: $40.	24 times hourly earnings plus $1.50 for each of not more than 4 dependents *minus* unemployment insurance and other compensation.[c] Maximum: $37.50 plus $1.50 for each of not more than 4 dependents.
Without unemployment insurance	62% of weekly earnings plus $1.50 for each of not more than 4 dependents *minus* estimated unemployment insurance and other compensation.[d] Maximum: $40.	24 times hourly earnings plus $1.50 for each of not more than 4 dependents *minus* other compensation. Maximum: $60 plus $1.50 for each of not more than 4 dependents.
Short-week benefit	50% or 65%[e] of hourly wage rate times hours less than 40 not worked (*minus* any unemployment insurance received).	Regular hourly wage times hours less than 32 not worked (*minus* any unemployment insurance received).
Benefit reduction		
Amount	When fund is less than approx. 8% of maximum financing.	When fund is less than 35% of maximum financing.
Duration	When fund is less than approx. 50% of maximum financing.	No reduction.
Financing		
Maximum monthly contribution	5 cents per man-hour worked or paid; plus costs of short-workweek benefits in some circumstances.	4.5 cents cash plus 5 cents contingent liability per man-hour worked.
Maximum financing	About $544 per employee.[f]	About $250 per employee.[g]

[a] Definition of "service" varies somewhat among companies. Other eligibility requirements are discussed in text.

[b] Other compensation: earnings from company and earnings in excess of $10 from sources other than company.

[c] Other compensation: amount of earnings in excess of amount disregarded in determining unemployment insurance benefit.

[d] Estimated unemployment insurance: unemployment insurance benefit receivable if claimant were not ineligible for specified reasons. In the Ford and Studebaker contracts estimated unemployment insurance is not deducted if reason for ineligibility is exhaustion of state benefits.

[e] The 65 per cent applies if the short week is scheduled for the purpose of adjusting production to customer demand; the 50 per cent applies to unscheduled short weeks.

[f] Maximum financing is determined by multiplying the average benefit (including the average weekly medical insurance premium) by 16; this estimate assumes an average benefit of $30 and an average insurance premium of $4.

[g] Maximum financing for any month is determined by multiplying 12.5 cents by the total number of hours worked by all employees in the first 12 of the preceding 14 months. This estimate assumes the average employee worked 2,000 hours, which is probably in excess of the actual average.

render a claimant ineligible for SUB. This exception is necessary in order that SUB benefits may supplement unemployment insurance duration. Some of the other exceptions are primarily attempts to circumvent minor obstacles posed by technical provisions of unemployment insurance laws, for example, those regulating the benefit year. Other exceptions are closely related to the disqualification provisions and are noted below.

Disqualification. As in the unemployment insurance program, a claimant for SUB may be disqualified because of a voluntary quit, a discharge, a strike, or a refusal of work. With some few exceptions, moreover, the definition and interpretation of these causes of unemployment make the disqualification provisions of SUB stricter than the corresponding provisions of unemployment insurance.

In SUB plans all voluntary quits are permanently disqualifying and the unemployment insurance concepts of "good cause" and temporary disqualification do not apply.

The strike disqualification in SUB plans can be very broad. In the steel industry, for example, it applies even to situations in which production is interrupted because of a strike by transportation or utility workers, or a strike by members of the claimant's union at a different plant, or even a strike at the plant of another company. Thus, during the 1959 steel strike members of the steelworkers' union who were laid off in the can industry because of a lack of steel were denied SUB.

There are some provisions in SUB plans which are more liberal than the corresponding provisions in unemployment insurance. In the auto and steel plans for example, if work is offered by the claimant's own employer, and if it is work which he has the option to refuse under the collective bargaining agreement, such a refusal does not disqualify him for SUB even though the work is suitable by unemployment insurance standards and he may be disqualified by the unemployment insurance agency. In some plans a claimant may receive SUB even though he is disqualified for the receipt of unemployment insurance because he has earned more in a week than the allowable

limit. In the steel plan there is a provision which permits SUB to be paid to a worker who is disqualified for unemployment insurance benefits because he becomes disabled during his layoff.

Because of such differences between the two programs, an unemployed worker may receive both SUB and unemployment insurance or either form of benefit alone.

Amount and Duration of Benefits. In general SUB plans provide for a benefit which, if unemployment insurance is also received, equals 60 or 62 per cent of regular straight-time earnings (this equals over 70 per cent of take home pay), with additional benefits paid to a claimant with dependents. There is a maximum benefit, which in steel is higher for claimants with dependents but in autos is the same for all claimants.

The duration of benefits is determined by the number of credit units an employee has accumulated. He acquires one-half credit unit for each week of work or pay,[7] up to a maximum number of units (generally fifty-two) at any one time; normally one credit is cancelled for each benefit payment. The system works like a bank account, each employee putting in and taking out credit units according to his own pattern of work.

All plans provide that benefits be reduced in amount or duration or both if the fund for supplementary unemployment benefits is below a specified level. In order to protect workers with greater seniority, who may not be laid off until the fund is low, the reduction generally occurs earlier and is greater for employees with lower seniority.

Financing. SUB plans are financed through employer contributions, which are stated in terms of a given number of cents per man-hour worked, as described earlier.[8] Most plans provide that the necessary contribution be

[7] In determining an employee's credit units, most plans credit all weeks for which compensation is received, including paid leave for vacation, union duty, etc. Contributions to the fund, however, are based only on man-hours actually worked. For simplicity, the expression "man-hours worked" is sometimes used in the text and tables to cover both situations.

[8] See note 7.

made in cash. In the steel plan, however, part of the contribution is made in the form of contingent liability, which accumulates and is convertible into cash when there is insufficient money in the fund to pay benefits.

When the SUB fund is at the required level, which is defined in various ways but can be expressed most simply as a specified number of dollars times the number of employees, the fund is at maximum financing. The employer's monthly obligation is limited to the stipulated number of cents per man-hour or the amount necessary to bring the fund up to maximum financing, whichever is less. Some plans provide for an automatic decrease in maximum financing if average SUB payments and, therefore, costs decrease—for example because of an increase in unemployment insurance benefits.

Administration. SUB plans are administered by the company. Except in the case of a short-workweek benefit an unemployed person must apply for a benefit and present evidence of the receipt of unemployment insurance. The company makes the determination of eligibility, but the determination may be appealed to a bipartite board. Costs of administration are generally borne by the company.

Funds for supplementary unemployment benefits are held by a trustee, who may invest them in certain prescribed ways. The trustee's fee is paid from this fund.

B. DEVELOPMENT OF PROVISIONS

Current SUB provisions represent a development of the original plans. Over the years a number of significant changes have been made, many of them involving fundamental issues, and most of them having a liberalizing effect.

Eligibility and Disqualification

Some eligibility provisions of SUB plans in the auto and steel industries were revised in 1961 and 1962. Both plans increased the number of exceptions to the general requirement that to receive SUB a claimant must be eligible for unemployment insurance. One issue between labor and management was the provision that permits a worker to receive SUB when he has refused a job which he has an option to refuse under the collective bargaining contract. In the auto plans this provision, which previously had been limited to certain skilled workers, was extended more broadly in 1961. The steel plan had this provision from the beginning; in the 1962 negotiations, employers sought to have it removed but were unsuccessful.

Another issue between the steelworkers' union and basic steel companies in 1962 was the disqualification for SUB if a layoff is caused by a disruption of production because of a strike of transportation or utility workers. The union sought to have this disqualification removed but was not successful.

Because the period of unemployment insurance disqualification varies among the states, the UAW has sought to have supplementary benefits paid six weeks after any disqualifying act, even if state benefits are not paid. American Motors was the only auto company which agreed to this provision, which became effective September 6, 1961.

Benefit Formula

Many issues are involved in the construction of a benefit formula in SUB programs: the duration of benefits, the proportion of the wage loss to be compensated—including the treatment of wages as net or gross and the relation to be maintained between workers with and without dependents—the maximum benefit, the relationship between SUB and unemployment insurance benefits, the reduction of benefits when the supplementary benefits fund is low, and short-workweek benefits. These issues have been the subject of continuing debate, and the debate has resulted in changes.

Duration of Benefits. In the original SUB plans of the auto, agricultural implement, and rubber industries, benefits were limited to twenty-six weeks (except that an additional thirteen weeks could be credited during the life of the TUC and TEUC programs). Beginning in 1962, the duration of benefits was increased to fifty-two weeks in the auto[9] and

[9] In the Studebaker plan the maximum duration was not changed. Studebaker differed from the other auto companies in two additional respects: the benefit rate was about 55 per cent of wages and the maximum benefit was $35.

agricultural implement industries, and in 1963 was increased to thirty-nine weeks in the rubber industry. Maximum duration was fifty-two weeks in the original plans of the steel, aluminum, and can industries.

Benefit-Wage Ratio. In all the original agreements, except those of the can companies and the Aluminum Company of America, the benefit amount was calculated as a percentage of net wages (65 per cent of after-tax straighttime weekly wages). Since the net wage of a worker with dependents is larger than that of a worker without dependents, this method of calculation automatically provided a larger benefit to claimants with dependents.

In 1962 and 1963 two changes were made which had the effects of simplifying calculation and increasing the benefit amount. The benefit amount in all plans is now calculated as a percentage of gross wages (60 or 62 per cent), and a separate allowance for dependents is added ($1.50 for each of not more than four). For workers with or without dependents, 60 or 62 per cent of gross wages is generally more than 65 per cent of net wages; the separate allowance for dependents maintains a differential between workers with and without dependents which is roughly equal to that produced by paying each group 65 per cent of take-home pay.

The benefits of some workers may amount to less than the stated 60–62 per cent of wages because of the limiting effect of the maximum benefit, or because there is no unemployment insurance benefit to be supplemented, or because of the operation of the reduction table. In recent years liberalizing changes have been made in all three of these limitations.

Maximum Benefit. The level of the maximum benefit is influenced by two considerations that pull in opposite directions. One consideration operates to keep the maximum down: a maximum benefit prevents workers in states that pay low unemployment insurance benefits from draining the fund at the expense of workers in states that pay high benefits. The other consideration operates to move the maximum higher: the typical worker covered by a SUB plan is a high-wage worker and

needs a high maximum if his benefit is to equal 60–62 per cent of his wages.

The latter consideration has exerted the stronger influence, and the SUB maximum has risen. In the steel industry the maximum was increased in 1962 from $25 (plus $1.50–$6.00 for dependents) to $37.50 (plus $1.50–$6.00). In the auto industry the maximum (the same for workers with or without dependents) was increased from $25 to $30 in 1958, to $40 in 1962, and to $50 in 1964.

SUB without Unemployment Insurance. As noted above, SUB is paid in some circumstances even though unemployment insurance is not paid. The various plans pay different amounts of supplementary benefits in this situation, but no plan pays the full 60–62 per cent of gross wages.

In most auto plans, SUB continues unchanged when the unemployment insurance benefit ceases, so that upon exhaustion of the state benefit the beneficiary experiences a sharp drop in income. For such a beneficiary the drop is sharper in a state with high benefits than in a state with low benefits.

This provision was changed in the Studebaker plan in 1960 and in both the Ford plan and the various plans of the agricultural implement industry in 1961. In these plans, the maximum benefit of $40, about one-third of the average wage in the auto industry, may be paid after unemployment insurance benefits are exhausted. The 1963 rubber agreement also provides for a maximum benefit of $40 (plus $2 for each of four dependents) payable to unemployment insurance exhaustees.

The steel plan has always provided a higher maximum benefit for unemployment insurance exhaustees. The current (1963) maximum is $60 (plus $1.50–$6.00 for dependents), which equaled 47–52 per cent of average weekly earnings in basic steel in 1963.

Reduction of Benefits. All SUB plans provide for some reduction in the amount and/or duration of benefits when a fund is at a specified level below the maximum. The auto, agricultural implement, and rubber plans protect the fund mainly by reducing benefit duration; they do not reduce the benefit amount until he fund is quite low. The auto agreement originally provided that when the fund was less than 85 per cent of maximum funding, credit units were to be exchanged for benefits in a ratio greater than one for one, depending on seniority and the level of the fund. Under the 1962 agreement the critical point was lowered from 85 per cent to approximately 50 per cent.

The steel and can plans originally provided for a reduction of the benefit amount when the fund was less than 75 per cent of its maximum level. As a result of this provision, reduced benefits were paid by the major steel companies in almost two-thirds of the months between 1958 and early 1962.[10] Management agreed with labor that this provision was too conservative, and the 1962 steel agreement provided that benefits should not be reduced until the fund was less than 35 per cent of its maximum level.

Short-Workweek Benefit

A significant addition to SUB plans in the auto, agricultural implement, steel, cement, and rubber industries was made in 1961 and 1962 in the form of short-workweek benefits. Strictly speaking, the short-workweek benefit is not a form of SUB but a form of weekly wage guarantee. As such, it represents a move along the original road from which the SUB programs diverged, the guaranteed wage. But since the short-workweek benefit is paid out of the SUB fund and in both origin and operation is connected with SUB, it has a place in this chapter.

Short-workweek benefits are of two types to fit the two kinds of short workweeks: (1) scheduled (those intended to adjust production to a decrease in customer demand) and (2) unscheduled (all others, such as those due to breakdowns, lack of materials, faulty planning, etc.).

In the case of unscheduled short workweeks, the steel and the cement plans provide full hourly pay for hours not worked up to thirty-two hours; the auto, agricultural implement,

and rubber plans provide half pay for hours not worked up to forty hours.

SUB for *scheduled* short workweeks is available in the auto but not in the steel industry. There is less need for the provision in the steel industry, which in any case is prevented by the regular contract from scheduling less than a thirty-two-hour week. In the auto industry those who work scheduled short weeks are paid 65 per cent of their hourly wage for hours not worked up to forty hours. Thus far, scheduled short workweeks in the auto industry have been only a small fraction of all short workweeks, and labor has been protesting that management's interpretation of "scheduled" is too limited.

In pressing for the short-workweek benefit, the UAW was motivated by two considerations. First, it was moving closer to a long-cherished objective: to obtain for the hourly-rated employee the kind of income continuity that the salaried employee has. The short-workweek benefit represents an appreciable advance toward a weekly salary.

Secondly, the union was satisfying a growing complaint among its members. Some of the auto companies had been using a flexible week, that is, had been employing their work force for a reduced number of hours in the week. Instead of working a smaller force full time they had been working a larger force part time and thus substituting the partial unemployment of all for the total unemployment of some. From the viewpoint of the employer, the short workweek has a number of advantages: He can maintain his work force, avoid the costs[11] attendant upon layoffs followed by recalls, and cut his unemployment costs, both unemployment insurance and SUB.

From the viewpoint of the workers, however, especially those with longer seniority, the flexible week had its drawbacks. The partially employed workers were usually ineligible for unemployment insurance and SUB, and in the

---

10 "Explanation of 1962 SUB Amendments," United Steelworkers, April 2, 1962. (Mimeographed.)

11 In addition to administrative costs there are the temporary inefficiencies that result from the reorganization of production and from the "bumping" that ensues when employees exercise their seniority right to move to other jobs.

case of those who worked only a couple of days their income was no greater than it would have been if they had not worked at all but had drawn unemployment insurance and SUB.

Not all union members had the same attitude toward the short workweek. Members with less seniority, the ones most likely to be laid off, saw the flexible workweek as a method of sharing the work; they tended to favor it if it produced an income significantly greater than the unemployment benefits they would receive if they were not working at all. Employees with more seniority saw the flexible week as a method of "sharing the misery," and they tended to oppose it.

The benefit for a scheduled short workweek represents a compromise that has something for everybody. Although it adds to the employer's cost of scheduling a short workweek and thus tends to lessen his use of the device, it also diminishes the union's objection to the short workweek and hence increases the employer's freedom to use the device when he chooses.[12] For the employee with little seniority a short workweek plus a short-workweek benefit is obviously preferable to a complete layoff; and the employee with long seniority may consider the loss of 35 per cent of a day's gross wage compensated by an extra day of leisure.

Financing and Administration

To support the more liberal benefits provided by the 1961–62 negotiations, the funds of most plans have had to be strengthened. All the auto companies have raised the maximum financing level of their plans. In 1962 the Chrysler company began to make extra contributions to a special reserve fund; these additional contributions can go as high as 5.7 cents per man-hour. Studebaker also became liable at this time for extra contributions under certain conditions. The steel companies have increased their contributions to the SUB fund from 5 cents per man-hour (3 cents cash, 2 cents contingent liability) to 9.5 cents per

man-hour (4.5 cents cash, 5 cents contingent liability). In the steel plans the maximum financing level also has been raised.

Among the new provisions in the steel plan is one that restricts the opportunity of an employer to save on contributions and to this extent lessens his incentive to stabilize employment. If the fund exceeds maximum financing, accrued liability may no longer be canceled and a minimum contribution of 4.5 cents in the form of contingent liability is required under all circumstances. If the contribution is not needed for SUB, it is payable to the Savings and Vacation Fund;[13] if it is not needed there, it accrues to the Contingent Liability Fund Reserve.

Some administrative procedures have been changed. Originally a recipient was required to report each week to the company and present his unemployment insurance check as proof of his receipt of unemployment insurance. If he cashed it prior to the visit, he was ineligible for SUB. Most plans now accept proofs other than the unemployment insurance check, and some permit claims, after the first one, to be processed by mail.

In the auto plan the costs of administration were paid from the SUB fund originally, but are now borne directly by the company. This change seems to have stemmed from disputes between the union and the company over expenditures.

IV. EXPERIENCE UNDER SUB PROGRAMS

A. Experience in the Steel Industry

Protection Available. Two fundamental measures of the effectiveness of the SUB program are the proportion of workers who are insured (have the required seniority) and the number of weeks for which they are insured (the number of their credit units). The measures are applicable not only to the unemployed but also to the employed; for SUB

---

[12] Under the current arrangements, a scheduled short workweek is likely to involve only slightly greater direct dollar costs than would the alternative procedure of the laying off of some employees.

[13] The operation of this fund is designed to encourage retirement at age sixty-five.

plans, like any form of insurance, are valuable even to those who are not actually experiencing the calamity they are insured against.

The proportion of workers who are insured varies inversely with changes in employment. The proportion insured declines as the company hires new employees with little seniority and increases as the company lays off employees, usually those with the least seniority. Although the steel industry does not have a marked seasonal pattern,[14] it has experienced significant secular and cyclical movements. Employment in steel has been in a decline for the last decade and the proportion of workers eligible for some SUB benefits has therefore been increasing. It is estimated that in the last several years the proportion has been about 90 per cent, even during times of highest employment.

This estimate relates to the labor force, employed as well as unemployed. For the unemployed alone the proportion is of course smaller. The union has made estimates for two dates. On May 1, 1958, at the bottom of the 1958 recession, 67 per cent of those on layoff were eligible for SUB when their layoff started; on May 31, 1960, at the beginning of the 1961 recession, 62 per cent were eligible.

An important measure of the adequacy of supplementary unemployment benefits is the number of weeks of benefits for which workers are eligible—that is, the number of credit units they have. Exact information on this point is not available. There is no "benefit year" in SUB as there is in unemployment insurance, but workers continuously take from and add to their stock of credit units as though it were a bank account. Since the steel companies do not keep a current record of each worker's account the amount of insurance currently in effect can only be estimated. Since employees with long seniority experience less unemployment, and since the proportion of such employees has been increasing as employment has decreased, and since any employee who has worked fairly steadily for two or three years will

build up the maximum number of credit units, a conservative estimate would seem to be that in recent years the majority of employees were insured for the full fifty-two weeks.

Extent of Use. To measure the extent to which the available protection was actually used, it is necessary to ascertain the number of beneficiaries and the amount and duration of their benefits.

Data on the number of beneficiaries are available for only one week in each quarter. Table 6–4, which is based on the experience of nine companies whose reports to the union were available, shows the proportion of employees who were receiving SUB in the indicated weeks.[15] The data cover the business cycle of 1960–62, and the difference between the low point in March, 1960 (.7 per cent), and the high point in March, 1961 (16.3 per cent), is a reflection of the cyclical sensitivity of the steel industry.

TABLE 6–4: SUB BENEFICIARIES IN NINE BASIC STEEL COMPANIES[a] AS PER CENT OF WORK FORCE ON SELECTED DATES

Date	Number of benefici- aries	Per cent of work force
First calendar week ended in:		
March, 1960	2,808	.7
June, 1960	14,290	3.8
September, 1960	40,271	10.6
December, 1960	59,300	15.6
March, 1961	61,789	16.3
June, 1961	29,605	7.8
September, 1961	14,455	3.8
December, 1961	12,830	3.4
March, 1962	8,461	2.2

SOURCE: Quarterly reports by companies to United Steelworkers of America.

[a] In 1961 the nine companies had a work force estimated by the union at 380,000, which represented about 52 per cent of all steelworkers covered by the SUB plan.

14 In the can companies there is a strong seasonal movement and a distinct group of seasonal workers, but these workers usually do not acquire eligibility under the SUB plan.

15 Although the number of individuals who receive SUB in the course of a year is not known, it is, of course, much higher than the number of recipients in any one week. It is known, for example, that in the entire labor force the number of persons who experience some unemployment in the course of a year is 2–3 times larger than the greatest number unemployed in any one week of the year.

Table 6–5, based on the experience of eleven companies during the four years for which data are available, shows the relationship between SUB and unemployment insurance benefits. During this period SUB represented an average addition to unemployment insurance benefits of about 50 per cent. The low percentages in 1961 are explainable partly by increased unemployment insurance benefits but chiefly by lower supplementary benefits, which, in turn, are explained by the operation of the reduction table. During most months of 1961 the majority of steel companies paid reduced SUB because their reserve funds were below 75 per cent of maximum financing.

The average SUB payment varied considerably from state to state. This is because the unemployment insurance benefit, especially the maximum, varies from state to state and the supplementary benefit necessarily varies to the same extent but in the opposite direction. In 1962, for example, the average SUB benefit paid by one company was $14.74 in California, $22.07 in Ohio, and $29.23 in Alabama.[16]

An adequate description of duration experience would require knowledge of the distri-

[16] These state differences are more important to autoworkers than to steelworkers because, as already noted, in most auto plans SUB payments remain unchanged in amount after unemployment insurance is exhausted.

TABLE 6–5: AVERAGE SUPPLEMENTARY UNEMPLOYMENT BENEFITS AND UNEMPLOYMENT INSURANCE RECEIVED BY STEELWORKERS IN ELEVEN BASIC STEEL COMPANIES,[a] DECEMBER, 1958–JUNE, 1962

Date	With state benefits				Without state benefits
	Average UI	Average SUB[b]	Total	Percentage by which SUB supplemented UI	Average SUB[b]
(1)	(2)	(3)	(4)	(5)	(6)
First calendar week ended in:					
1958					
Dec.	$33.06	$18.22	$51.28	55	$32.77
1959					
Mar.	33.12	15.35	48.47	46	30.52
June	32.85	16.42	49.27	50	33.75
Sept.	35.46	24.16	59.62	68	50.11
Dec.	31.79	23.17	54.96	73	48.17
1960					
Mar.	32.03	20.87	52.90	65	50.58
June	36.91	18.75	55.66	51	48.69
Sept.	39.36	22.26	61.62	57	51.52
Dec.	39.29	22.06	61.35	56	51.52
1961					
Mar.	39.51	13.42	52.93	34	27.62
June	38.64	13.01	51.65	34	28.12
Sept.	37.29	13.57	50.86	36	30.36
Dec.	37.82	15.69	53.51	41	34.46
1962					
Mar.	37.57	17.82	55.39	47	37.49
June	39.43	17.88	57.31	45	39.21

SOURCE: Quarterly reports by steel companies to United Steelworkers of America.

[a] Figures are for 11 companies, which employed 56 per cent of all covered steelworkers, with the following exceptions: December, 1958, 8 companies; June, 1959, 10 companies; September, 1959, 4 companies; December, 1959, 5 companies; September, 1961, 10 companies; June, 1962, 8 companies.

[b] Figures include full benefits and benefits reduced because of the condition of the SUB fund.

bution of benefit payments according to duration intervals, the extent to which SUB supplemented the duration of unemployment insurance, and the extent to which SUB beneficiaries exhausted their benefits. There is no direct information on any of these three aspects of duration, but some inferences can be drawn from the data in tables 6–6 and 6–7.

Table 6–6 shows the number of benefits paid with and without unemployment insurance. If it is assumed that nearly all of the SUB payments without unemployment insurance were made to beneficiaries who had exhausted their benefits and that most of these beneficiaries were eligible for the maximum duration in the state program—both very reasonable assumptions—then column 3 shows payments made for periods longer than the unemployment insurance maximum. The length of that

maximum—and therefore the meaning of column 3—varied during the period covered by the table. From March, 1960, through March, 1961, the typical unemployment insurance maximum duration was twenty-six weeks, but during two other periods thirteen additional weeks of unemployment insurance benefits were generally available to SUB claimants. The TUC program was in operation from June, 1958, through June, 1959, and the TEUC program from April, 1961, through June, 1962. During these latter periods the payments in column 3 generally represent unemployment that had lasted longer than thirty-nine weeks.[17]

[17] During these periods of temporarily extended benefits the quantities in column 3 understate the extent to which SUB is likely to be needed to supplement the duration of regular unemployment insurance benefits.

TABLE 6–6: SUB PAYMENTS WITH AND WITHOUT UNEMPLOYMENT INSURANCE, FIVE BASIC STEEL COMPANIES,[a] BY QUARTER, DECEMBER, 1958–JUNE, 1962

Date	Number of SUB payments with UI	SUB payments without UI	
		Number	Number as per cent of Col. 2
(1)	(2)	(3)	(4)
First calendar week *ended in:*			
1958			
Dec.	19,444	2,819	13
1959			
Mar.	11,236	1,020	8
June	3,090	634	17
Sept.	b	b	b
Dec.	b	b	b
1960			
Mar.	2,320	222	9
June	11,479	173	1
Sept.	33,578	780	2
Dec.	45,984	2,955	6
1961			
Mar.	41,429	11,275	21
June	26,923	81	c
Sept.	11,701	1,287	10
Dec.	9,935	1,804	15
1962			
Mar.	7,210	563	7
June	8,879	640	7

SOURCE: Quarterly reports by steel companies to United Steelworkers of America.
[a] These five companies employed approximately 29 per cent of all USW members covered by SUB plans.
[b] The steel strike was in progress and no supplementary benefits were paid.
[c] Less than 1 per cent.

It is clear that in the relatively prosperous year of 1960 the duration of SUB payments exceeded twenty-six weeks in very few cases. By March, 1961, however, a substantial number of SUB payments were made beyond twenty-six weeks, and at the end of both the 1958 and 1961 recessions there were considerable numbers of SUB payments beyond thirty-nine weeks. The very sharp drop in the number of payments of supplementary unemployment benefits without unemployment insurance (col. 3) between March and June, 1961, probably reflects the impact of the TEUC program, which began in April of that year.

It would be desirable to know the proportion of beneficiaries who exhausted their supplementary benefits.[18] Unfortunately, only scattered data are available on this important facet of SUB experience, and the significance of even these data is obscured by several limitations. The data do not reveal the length of unemployment represented by each exhaustion (in the data an exhaustion after one week of unemployment is indistinguishable from an exhaustion after fifty-two weeks of unemployment); they do not reveal the number of different individuals who exhausted benefits (in the SUB program it is easy for the same individual to exhaust repeatedly); and there is no way of identifying the relevant "beneficiary population" to which the number of exhaustees must be referred if an exhaustion rate is to be calculated.

Table 6–7, column 3, shows the number of exhaustions for a recent period in nine basic steel companies representing 53 per cent of covered steelworkers. From September, 1960, through August, 1961, a period which included the 1961 recession, there were 24,027 exhaustions (there were fewer individual exhaustees). During this same period the work force of these companies was about 380,000, not all of whom were eligible for SUB. Hence, in that period of heavy unemployment something over 6 per cent of all steelworkers found duration of SUB insufficient—either because they were eligible for only a few weeks of benefits or because their unemployment was very long term. In more normal periods, when unemployment is lower, the percentage is probably half this size.

[18] Exhaustions indicate that the program was inadequate for certain individuals but do not necessarily indicate that the program was inadequate in terms of its own objectives. Unless a program is geared to pay benefits indefinitely, there comes a point at which exhaustees are no longer its concern. An exhaustion ratio acquires significance only in relationship to a program's objectives. This relationship was discussed in the preceding chapter.

TABLE 6–7: EXHAUSTIONS OF BENEFITS IN SUB BY EMPLOYEES OF NINE BASIC STEEL COMPANIES[a] AS PER CENT OF BENEFICIARIES, BY QUARTER, MARCH, 1960–FEBRUARY, 1962

| Date | Number of beneficiaries during first calendar week of quarter | Number of exhaustions | | |
| | | Quarterly total | Weekly average | Col. (4) as per cent of Col. (2) |
(1)	(2)	(3)	(4)	(5)
3/60–5/60	2,808	460	35	1.2
6/60–8/60	14,290	1,484	114	.8
9/60–11/60	40,271	3,862	297	.7
12/60–2/61	59,300	6,188	476	.8
3/61–5/61	61,789	6,793	523	.9
6/61–8/61	29,605	7,184	553	1.9
9/61–11/61	14,455	3,208	247	1.7
12/61–2/62	12,830	3,673	283	2.2

SOURCE: Quarterly reports by companies to United Steelworkers of America.

[a] In 1961 the nine companies had an estimated work force of 380,000 representing about 53 per cent of all covered workers in basic steel.

The proportion of SUB beneficiaries who found duration insufficient is, of course, much larger. The proportion cannot be determined accurately from the data in the table because column 2 is a considerable understatement of the number of different beneficiaries who drew benefits in the quarter; also, not all the exhaustees in column 3 "come from" the beneficiaries of the corresponding date in column 2, but from some earlier period. A reasonable estimate would be that over the period covered by the table the proportion of beneficiaries who exhausted their benefits ranged from about 10 per cent in prosperous periods to about 20 per cent in recession periods.

Column 5 compares two weekly flows: the flow of beneficiaries in column 2 and the flow of exhaustees in column 4. They are to be thought of, not as coming one from the other, but as two streams flowing side by side, the former consisting of those beneficiaries for whom the program was still adequate, the latter consisting of those for whom the program had just proved inadequate. Over a sufficiently long period of time their relative size provides some indication of the adequacy of the duration provisions of the program. In the period covered by the table, the stream of exhaustees averaged about one-hundredth the size of the stream of beneficiaries. It must be remembered, of course, that the stream of exhaustees is flowing into a more or less stagnant pool and that this pool is the most significant measure of the adequacy of duration. Unfortunately, we do not know the size of the pool because, although we know the flow into it, we do not know the flow out of it.

Costs. Over the five-year period during which benefits were paid under the original plans, September, 1957, through June, 1962, benefits totaled about $227.5 million and contributions totaled about $321.8 million.[19]

---

[19] These figures are projections of data from seventeen companies, which, as of 1961, employed 62 per cent of covered steelworkers (about 450,000 out of about 726,000). The figure for contributions is net, being total cash contributed and contingent liability accrued, minus contingent liability canceled when funds were above maximum financing. Canceled liability amounted to $7.3 million.

Table 6–8, which is based on the experience of four companies employing approximately 43 per cent of covered steelworkers, shows how benefits and contributions varied over time. The relevance of the business cycle to SUB is clear. Although substantial amounts of benefits were paid even in prosperous years, benefits were considerably higher during recessions. The table also shows that the program operates to some extent countercyclically: the heavier burdens of contributions fall in the more prosperous years.

The man-hour costs of the program in terms of contributions and benefits varied among the firms. The great majority of firms made the full five-cent contributions in nearly all the months. However, during the first five to nine months of 1960 all firms saved something in contributions. During this period even companies which had previously paid reduced benefits because of the low level of their funds found themselves paying less than the full five cents in contributions. The explanation of the paradox is to be found in the strike which shut down the steel industry from July 14 to November 5, 1959. This long strike had the effect of lowering the base (man-hours worked) on which maximum financing is calculated and thus of decreasing the contributions needed to achieve maximum financing.

The man-hour cost of benefits can only be approximated because the companies do not report the number of man-hours for which contributions are made. However, since nearly all companies paid less than the full five-cent contribution during some months of the period August 1, 1956, through July 31, 1962, and since benefits were less than contributions, it follows that the cost of benefits during this period was something less than five cents per man-hour for practically all the companies.

Data available for seventeen companies provide the basis for more detailed estimates. Six of these companies, which employed 17 per cent of covered workers, did not have to convert any of their contingent liability into cash to pay benefits; their benefit costs, therefore, must have been less than 3 cents per man-hour (the maximum cash contribution). Among

TABLE 6–8: SUB CONTRIBUTIONS AND PAYMENTS OF FOUR MAJOR STEEL COMPANIES, 1956–1962

(In thousands of dollars)

Company	Aug. 1, 1956, through July 31, 1957	Aug. 1, 1957, through July 31, 1958	Aug. 1, 1958, through July 31, 1959	Aug. 1, 1959, through July 31, 1960	Aug. 1, 1960, through July 31, 1961	Aug. 1, 1961, through June 30, 1962	Total, entire period
Company A							
Contributions	$17,392	$13,417	$13,812	$6,312[cd]	$10,546	$11,028	$72,507
Benefits	–0–	14,411[a]	10,247[b]	4,951	20,422	4,671	54,702
Company B							
Contributions	9,427	7,595	7,083	3,568[cd]	5,386	6,145	39,204
Benefits	–0–	5,357[a]	8,911[b]	1,389	9,930	3,324	28,911
Company C							
Contributions	5,318	3,704	4,549	3,227[cd]	3,086	3,622	23,506
Benefits	–0–	2,601	5,381[b]	1,627	6,844	1,670	18,123
Company D							
Contributions	3,227	2,570	2,888	–0–[cd]	1,980[d]	2,208[d]	12,873
Benefits	–0–	1,115[a]	1,797[b]	303	2,659	671	6,545

SOURCE: Company reports to union.

[a] Benefit payments began September 1, 1957.

[b] Includes Ohio benefits which could not be legally paid prior to May, 1959.

[c] Covers strike period of no contributions, July 14, 1959, through November 5, 1959, and post-strike period of reduced contributions.

[d] Company had reached maximum financing and therefore paid reduced contributions or none.

these six companies benefit costs ranged from about 0.5 cents to just under 3 cents per man-hour. The other eleven firms, which employed 45 per cent of covered workers, had to convert some of their liability into cash to pay benefits. Among these companies benefit costs ranged from slightly more than 3 cents to slightly less than 4 cents per man-hour.

The combination of the steel strike and the provisions for reduced benefits kept contributions and benefits lower than they otherwise would have been. If contributions had been made at the full five-cent rate, it is certain that all seventeen companies could have paid full benefits throughout the period; probably they could have done so even within the limits of the contributions that actually were made.

B. EXPERIENCE IN THE AUTO INDUSTRY

The experience of the auto industry with SUB cannot be described in exactly the same way as experience in steel because the available

data are somewhat different. The description of auto experience, however, follows the same general order: protection available, protection used, and cost of providing the protection.

Protection Available. The proportion of the labor force which is eligible for SUB varies inversely, as has been noted, with the growth and decline of the labor force. Although no continuous data are available on the proportion of the work force eligible for SUB, the following example is probably typical of recent years. Among Ford workers in September, 1960, when employment was relatively high and the proportion of workers eligible for benefits presumably relatively low, 92 per cent had the requisite one year of seniority.

The extent of protection (number of credit weeks) available to laid-off employees is not known with any exactness, but some scattered pieces of evidence were secured from interviews with the companies. It appears that among the large groups of workers who are laid off during retooling periods nearly all have the credit units necessary to cover the few weeks involved. In one company about 85 per cent of all those laid off in 1960 had the requisite one year of seniority and about 70 per cent had twenty-six credit units. It can be conservatively estimated that of all autoworkers laid off after the SUB program was functioning fully, more than two-thirds had some credit units.

Companies maintain a list of employees who are on extended layoff; typically a company carries an employee on the list for one or two years, or for the length of his seniority. Occasionally an estimate is made of the proportion on the list who are eligible for SUB. Data for one company indicate that of those on extended layoff in the period 1960–61 an average of one-half or more continued to be eligible for some SUB payments. The pro-portion varied, month by month, from 60 to 80 per cent in 1960 and from 33 to 85 per cent in 1961.

It should be noted that potential duration is decreased when the fund is at specified levels below the maximum; for during these periods more than one credit unit must be exchanged for one week's benefit. From the time the funds were well established until the end of 1961, this lessening of potential duration never occurred in the case of three companies, occurred during about half the months in the case of one company, and occurred during all the months in the case of another company.

Extent of Use. Table 6–9 reflects the experience of five major firms in the auto industry from the beginning of the SUB plan through

TABLE 6–9: APPROXIMATE PERCENTAGE[a] OF COVERED WORKERS DRAWING BENEFITS IN SUB PROGRAMS OF FIVE AUTO COMPANIES, BY YEAR, 1956–1961

Company	1956	1957	1958	1959	1960	1961
Company A						
Range	1–19	1–23	4–41	2–46	1–26	2–38
Average	9[b]	6	19	11	19	13[c]
Company B						
Range	12–58	5–34	31–67	8–48	12–52	11–65
Average	32[b]	12	41	19	20	34[d]
Company C						
Range		14–30	2–20	0.1–11	0.1–31	0.4–46
Average		19[e]	12	3	4	11[c]
Company D						
Range		1–29[f]	3–27	1–4	2–16	3–42
Average		20[f]	24	2	6	30
Company E						
Range	2–7	1–7	8–29	3–11	2–10	2–17
Average	4[b]	3	19	7	5	8[c]

SOURCE: Company reports to union.

a Each monthly figure is for the last pay period (seven consecutive days beginning on Monday) of the month. Except for Company E, the rates represent employees on layoff with credit units as a percentage of the approximate work force (the number of the employed plus the unemployed with credit units). In the case of Company E, "employees on layoff" do not include those on temporary layoff. See *n.* 20 for certain limitations affecting all the rates of this table.

b Average of eight months.

c Average of eleven months.

d Average of ten months.

e Average of five months.

f Because of a provision in the Indiana unemployment insurance law none of these employees who were entitled to benefits actually received benefits in 1957. See Table 6–10.

1961. The table shows the approximate[20] proportion of the work force that was receiving SUB benefits as of a given week in each month.

That employment in the auto industry is cyclically sensitive is evident from the swings in the annual average ratios. Employment has also fluctuated seasonally because of periodic retooling and because demand for autos usually decreases during the last four or five months of the model year. The seasonal pattern is apparent in the fact that the upper range of the ratios for all companies is high in every year, even in good years. Seasonal unemployment also explains the relatively smaller range of Company E's ratios: the unemployment which was omitted from Company E's data (see note 20) was largely seasonal unemployment. The ratios of Company E are also some measure of the relative importance of unemployment due to a reduction in force as contrasted with less serious forms of unemployment.

Supplementary unemployment benefits have not been confined to short-service employees. If the following data, which show the experience of the Ford company in 1960, are typical, the distribution of beneficiaries and of benefits has been fairly proportionate among seniority groups. This surprising result is largely

Years of seniority	Per cent of work force	Per cent of total beneficiaries	Per cent of total benefits
Less than 1	8	0	0
1–4	21	22	25
5–9	26	30	38
10–19	23	29	25
20+	22	19	11

explained by the marked seasonal pattern in auto employment: during the model changeover even older men are laid off for at least a short

period. Thus the workers with twenty or more years of seniority are proportionately represented among the beneficiaries, although they draw a disproportionately small share of the benefits.

The auto plan originally provided that benefits be reduced in amount if the fund dropped below 13 per cent of maximum financing. Only one of the funds ever fell this low, so practically all benefits paid have been full benefits. As pointed out in the case of steel, the average SUB payment varied considerably from state to state. In 1961, for example, the average supplementary unemployment benefit paid by one company was $7.12 in California, which had a high unemployment insurance maximum, $19.54 in Michigan, which had a middle-range average unemployment insurance maximum, and $29.00 in Texas, which had a low unemployment insurance maximum.

The average SUB payment has increased over time. The average for the various companies has risen from $13–$14 in 1957–58, to $18–$19 in 1959–61, to $28–$32 in 1962–63. The rise has occurred partly because wages have risen and partly because the benefit formula has been liberalized.[21]

Apparently, few beneficiaries have felt the limitation imposed by the maximum benefit. The Ford company estimated that only 6 per cent of its beneficiaries drew the maximum benefit ($25) in 1958, and about 5 per cent drew the maximum ($30) in 1960. It is uncertain how typical this Ford experience was. Beginning in 1962 the auto companies (except American Motors) have reported this statistic to the union. For the year 1962 the proportion of beneficiaries drawing the maximum benefit ranged from 2.5 per cent to 12 per cent for the various companies.

Some data on the duration of unemployment and of SUB payments are available for the recession year of 1958 and for the relatively good employment year of 1960. During 1958 in the auto industry as a whole 45 per cent of

[20] In the case of all companies the rates are, to some extent, an overstatement of the actual use made of the program: The numerator of the rate is overstated because it includes the unemployed with credit units who were disqualified or for some reason did not apply for SUB, while the denominator is understated because it does not include the unemployed without credit units. In the case of Company E, however, there is a counterbalancing factor which makes the rates a net understatement: the numerator of the rate does not include those beneficiaries who are on temporary layoff.

[21] In 1958 the maximum was increased from $25 to $30; in 1962 the maximum was increased from $30 to $40, and the calculation of the weekly benefit amount was liberalized.

those who experienced unemployment were out of work for fifteen weeks.[22] Judging from this fact and from the large amount of total benefits paid in that year (see Table 6–10), the average duration of SUB payments was substantial. In one company in 1958 about one-third of recipients exhausted their benefits, and the average duration of payments was twenty weeks.

In 1960 the duration of payments was generally short. In one company, only 5 per cent of the layoffs were for twenty-six weeks or more, while 77 per cent were for less than six weeks. In another company about 5 per cent of beneficiaries received benefits for twenty-one or more weeks, while the average duration for all beneficiaries was six weeks. In the latter company 8 per cent exhausted benefits and the average duration of these exhaustees was fifteen weeks. It would seem, therefore, that in a good year like 1960 supplementary unemployment benefits were needed to supplement the duration of unemployment insurance (typically

twenty-six weeks) in only about 5 per cent of the cases. In a recession year like 1958 the proportion, of course, would be higher.

Costs. The maximum liability of the auto companies for contributions to SUB was 5 cents per man-hour. As the plan worked out, actual contributions over the period 1956–1961 amounted to less than 5 cents for three companies and to the full 5 cents for the other two companies.

Companies A and E of Table 6–10 had generally similar experiences. About two and one-half years of full contributions—from January, 1956, through May, 1958—were necessary for the funds to reach the level required for maximum financing. Subsequently, in the period June, 1958, through November, 1961, these companies contributed less than 5 cents per man-hour in about half of the months, and in some of these months made no contributions at all. Their average cost per man-hour from 1958 through 1961 did not exceed 3.5 cents and was probably about 3 cents.

Company C's cost was also less than 5 cents after August, 1959, when the fund reached

[22] Sophia Cooper, "Work Experience of the Population in 1959," *Monthly Labor Review* (December, 1960), p. 1280.

TABLE 6–10: SUB CONTRIBUTIONS AND PAYMENTS OF FIVE AUTO COMPANIES, 1955–1961

(In thousands of dollars)

Company	1955	1956	1957	1958	1959	1960	1961	Total[a]
Company A								
Contributions	22,135	34,881	32,924	12,906	6,373	33,482	12,685[b]	155,386
Benefits	0	1,545	4,121	16,313	22,483	8,853	21,470	74,895
Company B								
Contributions	0	12,306	10,625	3,616	6,496	7,259	3,794[c]	44,096
Benefits	0	1,899	1,603	8,134	9,741	5,224	13,385	39,987
Company C								
Contributions	0	258	955	1,329	2,303	2,547	569[b]	7,961
Benefits	0	0	62	199	51	168	754	1,234
Company D								
Contributions	0	264	571	373	493	658	459	2,818
Benefits	0	0	0	221	855	1,717	393	3,185
Company E								
Contributions	1	21,309	14,403	6,935	9,744	9,830	7,047[b]	69,270
Benefits	0	788	1,275	12,455	5,665	5,479	8,174	33,835

SOURCE: Reports by companies to union.
[a] Because of rounding, totals may not equal the sum of the separate items.
[b] Through Nov., 1961.
[c] Through Oct., 1961.

maximum financing. The figures available are not precise enough to estimate the probable cost per man-hour. Companies B and D experienced relatively severe unemployment and, except for a few months, apparently made the maximum contribution throughout the entire period.[23]

Since both contributions and benefits are geared to man-hours, they tend to vary inversely, so companies are not subject to maximum financial strain during periods of high benefit payments. Table 6–10 illustrates this counter-cyclical character of the program. In 1958 benefits for the various companies were four to ten times higher than in 1957, but contributions were between one-half and two-thirds less. In 1961 benefits were from one-half to two and one-half times higher than in 1960, but contributions were between one-fourth and two-thirds less.

In general, SUB funds were adequate to meet the demands made upon them. Full benefits, both in amount and duration, were paid by companies A, C, and E throughout the entire period; company B reduced duration during a part of the period and company D during the entire period. For companies A and E total benefits were slightly less than one-half of total contributions; for company C they were less than one-twelfth. By contrast, benefits in company B were nine-tenths of contributions. The SUB fund of company D was finally bankrupted when the company closed its main plant. In terms of cents per man-hour worked, benefits paid averaged about 2 cents for companies A and E, about 4.5 cents for company B, and 5 cents for company D.

Company D experienced considerable unemployment for much of the period during which the plan was in operation. Duration was reduced and in some months benefit payments were suspended altogether. The fund never reached maximum financing, and when the company permanently closed its operation

23 In the 1962 contract, company B was made liable for an additional contribution to a reserve fund. This special contribution amounted to 1.14 cents through September, 1962, and 3.42 cents through September, 1963.

in the United States in 1964 there was insufficient money in the fund to pay more than a few weeks of benefits and none for separation payments. This experience points up the weakness inherent in an insurance plan which has a small base. A SUB plan of a multi-plant company would have been in a stronger position to meet the demands caused by the closing of a plant.

V. APPRAISAL OF SUB

The SUB program may be appraised on two levels—the one more immediate, the other more fundamental. That is, we may ask simply whether the program has met its objectives, and we may go on further to ask whether the objectives themselves are desirable. These are distinct inquiries.

If we accept SUB as an existing institution and prescind from the issue of whether it ought to exist, the task of appraisal consists in answering the question: Has it worked—has it done what it set out to do? The general answer to this question is that in the auto and steel industries SUB plans have worked very well. They have achieved their major objectives, and if they have produced any offsetting undesirable effects, these have not been great enough to be obvious.

In the auto and steel programs nearly all workers have had the necessary seniority and have been eligible for some benefits. Most of those who were eligible enjoyed substantial protection. On the average, SUB supplemented the unemployment insurance benefit by at least 50 per cent. The liberalizing changes made in the plans in 1961 and 1962 have probably resulted in an average supplementation closer to 70 per cent.

SUB functioned to supplement the duration of unemployment insurance benefits only in the steel plan and only to a minor extent. (Until 1962 SUB duration in the auto plan did not exceed duration of unemployment insurance.) This was predictable since the great majority of the unemployed are unemployed for less than the maximum duration of unemployment insurance. SUB would have had to supplement duration more in this period if duration in unemployment insurance had not been extended on an emergency basis during the TUC and TEUC programs.

The adequacy of the duration provisions of SUB plans has not been a major problem. The proportion of beneficiaries who exhausted SUB after drawing the maximum number of benefits seems to have been quite low, even under the old twenty-six-week maximum in the auto industry; and it will be even lower under the new fifty-two-week maximum. The present maximum duration is not likely to be extended further in this type of plan.

Recipients of benefits were not limited to low-seniority workers but apparently were scattered widely among the work force. This broad participation in the benefits of the program seems to have widened labor's appreciation of it and lessened the kind of opposition that was shown by the skilled members of the UAW in 1955, when SUB was being negotiated. At that time these workers preferred an immediate wage increase rather than future supplementary benefits that they never expected to draw.

In general, the major SUB funds have withstood the strain of periods of heavy unemployment. In the auto industry, however, one company with experience less favorable than the others had to strengthen its fund, and the fund of another company proved completely inadequate to meet the catastrophe of a complete plant shutdown. In steel, a few small firms were occasionally unable to pay more than 5 or 10 per cent of the full benefit. The auto industry continues for the most part to function within the original limit of 5 cents per man-hour; in the steel industry the limit of future costs has been raised to 9.5 cents per man-hour.

It is an interesting, but largely speculative, question whether SUB plans have had any effect on the level of unemployment.[24] In theory, they can influence both the demand for and the supply of labor. The benefits that are paid represent some additional expenditure

on consumer goods; under most conditions this helps to sustain the demand for labor. Contributions to the programs represent an additional labor cost, which has two effects on the demand for labor. First, it reinforces the employer's incentive to regularize the production process. In the auto industry, supplementary benefits have probably contributed to the trend toward the more stable production pattern that has characterized the industry in the postwar period. The short-workweek benefit especially is acknowledged by both labor and management to have resulted in a decreased use of the short workweek and thus to have helped bring about a more stable production schedule. In the steel industry, whatever effect the SUB program may have had in reducing layoffs was diminished by the 1962 contract changes.[25] Secondly, SUB and the short-workweek benefit may have contributed to the recent tendency of employers to work a smaller labor force for longer hours, and this may or may not be a desirable effect.

SUB influences the supply of labor chiefly by maintaining the work force intact during temporary layoffs. This desirable effect is only partially dependent on SUB, however, for in high-wage industries workers cling tenaciously to their seniority and gladly leave other jobs when they receive their call-back notices. An undesirable effect of SUB may be that it decreases necessary labor mobility. SUB programs are likely to come into being in industries affected by serious unemployment problems, some of which call for movement of labor out of the industry.[26] Since unemployment benefits under such a program may equal the wages paid in other available jobs,[27] they may have

---

[24] The effects of SUB on the level of employment are both small and uncertain and hence are of secondary importance to an appraisal of the program. The principal norm of appraisal is the effect of the program on the security of the individual worker.

[25] See p. 121.

[26] One function of SUB is to maintain an employer's work force intact during periods of temporary unemployment. At the time when the program was introduced in the auto industry this function received considerable attention. Later, emphasis shifted somewhat to its other function—to provide a bridge to a new job for the worker permanently displaced.

[27] A Detroit taxicab driver told one of the authors that he and his wife had previously worked for the Chrysler auto company and that their combined earnings in their new jobs—he drove a cab and she worked as a waitress—were just half of what they had earned together at Chrysler.

the effect of delaying needed adjustments in the labor force.

The effect of the program on the employer's freedom to direct the work force has not been significant in either direction. There have been situations where the availability of SUB seems to have induced employees to prefer a temporary layoff rather than move to lower-paying jobs[28] or to insist that layoffs be by "reverse seniority," that is, that those with the highest seniority be laid off first. Such instances have been few, however, and even when they have occurred have constituted no problem for industrial efficiency. In other situations, the availability of SUB has increased the freedom of employers to make temporary layoffs according to the requirements of efficiency rather than according to rigid seniority rules.

If it is assumed that SUB programs have been achieving their objectives, a question may be asked at a more fundamental level of appraisal. Is it a good thing that the program has been functioning successfully? That is, should there be a SUB program at all? The answer to this question depends largely on the function that is assigned to the unemployment insurance program and the relationship that is envisioned between SUB and unemployment insurance.

If one assumes that unemployment insurance is inadequate—by whatever norm of adequacy one has selected as proper to a public program[29] —there is obviously a function for SUB to perform: it can make up for the deficiencies of the public program. If this is its only justification, the SUB plan is, at best, a necessary evil that can be rendered unnecessary by the simple expedient of making the public program "adequate."

If one assumes that unemployment insurance is adequate—again, by whatever norm of adequacy one has selected as proper to a public program—there remains a function, but a different function, for SUB to perform. SUB can supply a "middle-layer" of protection. There is a political philosophy that favors a three-layer approach to the provision of security: The government supplies only the first layer of protection, limited to essentials; private groups supply a second, supplementary, layer; the individual supplies the final layer suited to his own particular needs and resources. According to this philosophy, the role of supplementary unemployment benefits is to supply a degree of protection that is beyond what is possible for the individual and proper for the government to provide.

Whether, or why, this political philosophy is sound are questions which extend beyond the scope of this essay. But if, as a matter of fact, the role of unemployment insurance is currently limited to supplying "essentials," and if it is likely to continue to be thus limited, a role for SUB plans undoubtedly exists. They can particularize the provision of security. In industries with special needs and above-average resources —that is, in industries that are willing and able to pay for more protection—they can be used to provide benefits that are beyond the current scope of the public program.[30]

As contrasted with unemployment insurance, SUB has the usual disadvantages and advantages of private action in relation to public action. The principal disadvantage of SUB is its restriction to those industries which can afford it. This is the general disadvantage of a system of private property as contrasted with a system of common property. In particular situations, the choice between the two systems must be made by weighing disadvantages against compensating advantages.

---

[28] There have been instances of union pressure on employers not to report such job refusals to the unemployment insurance office lest the employee be disqualified for benefits. In the case of one large corporation, a strike was prolonged, after all other issues had been settled, until the company agreed not to make such notifications to the unemployment insurance office.

[29] Chapter 5 supplies some evidence for judging the truth of this assumption; but even Chapter 5 is only a partial treatment of adequacy, omitting as it does all consideration of the possible effects of unemployment insurance on production (see pp. 79–80).

[30] The Ford–UAW negotiations in 1955 reached a point where the total cost of the "package" had been determined and there remained only the choice between SUB and some alternative equal gain. Since the union preferred SUB to any alternative and since the company could afford it, the case for the program was complete.

Besides any general political advantage there may be in keeping private groups active,[31] there are two concrete economic advantages. SUB, like other private programs, can be adapted to fit the particular needs of particular industries; the variety of plans exemplified by tables 6–1 and 6–2 probably marks only the beginning of this development. Furthermore, since the entire cost of SUB is borne by the particular company establishing it, the program automatically keeps companies in these high-wage, highly organized industries under the discipline of competitive costs. Each increase in SUB must, *ceteris paribus*, result in lower profits, lower wages, or higher prices demanded of the consumers of the company's product.

For nearly a decade the private system of SUB plans has been operating alongside the public system of unemployment insurance. Has this experience under the SUB plans, with their higher benefits and longer duration, thrown any light on the feasibility of paying similar benefits under the unemployment insurance program? (Couched in terms simply of feasibility, the question prescinds from any issues of political philosophy.)

This question cannot be answered on the basis of information currently available. The programs of supplementary unemployment benefits and unemployment insurance are too different for experience in the one to be applied directly and simply to the other. SUB is confined to a more homogeneous work force with higher-than-average wages, has stricter eligibility requirements, has stricter disqualifications in the crucial areas of the voluntary quit and the strike, is under the closer surveillance and control of the employer, and is under the discipline of a stricter kind of experience-rating system. In order to make proper allowance for these differences more detailed knowledge of experience with SUB plans is needed than is now available. When such knowledge is available, however, it may well reveal reasons for

and methods of liberalizing unemployment insurance benefits beyond the limits we have been accustomed to set for the public program.

It was hoped in some quarters and feared in others that SUB would cause employers to favor higher unemployment insurance benefits[32] and would cause labor leaders to lose some of their interest in the public program. A brief investigation, consisting of interviews with labor and management leaders, produced no evidence that any significant change had occurred in the position of either. If SUB continues to expand, however, the anticipated changes may begin to appear on both sides.

After a period of comparative quiescence the supplementary unemployment benefits idea has shown signs of renewed growth. Although it will probably never cover a majority of the work force, it is likely to continue to spread. Supplementary unemployment benefits are most likely to appear in highly organized industries with high unemployment and high wages. High unemployment increases the marginal utility of unemployment insurance as against alternative gains to be sought in collective bargaining. High wages facilitate the introduction of a SUB program in two ways: they induce a demand for such benefits and they permit the demand to be satisfied. Workers with high wages, feeling the limiting effect of the unemployment insurance maximum benefit, seek to supplement this benefit in order to obtain the same proportion of their wages in unemployment benefits as do workers with lower wages. Their demand for a SUB program can

---

[31] For a fuller discussion of the crucial role of the private group, see Joseph M. Becker, S.J., *Shared Government in Employment Security* (New York: Columbia University Press, 1953), chap. I.

[32] Since unemployment insurance benefits are tax free, while supplementary unemployment benefits are not, an employer can pay a given amount of unemployment benefits to his employees at a lesser cost. Moreover, an employer who offers supplementary benefits and is already paying the maximum unemployment insurance tax in his state will have the costs of his supplementary benefits diminished by the whole of any increase in unemployment insurance benefits and will not experience any increase in his unemployment insurance costs. Finally, the likelihood that a supplementary unemployment benefits program will be demanded by his work force unless unemployment insurance benefits are increased may diminish an employer's resistance to higher and longer insurance benefits.

be satisfied because an industry able to pay high wages is likely to be able to afford the extra cost of the program.

As supplementary unemployment benefits spread, their relationship to the guaranteed annual wage is likely to come under renewed discussion. Since these two benefits are not exact substitutes for one another but are distinct programs fitted to perform distinct functions, labor may seek to add the guaranteed wage to supplementary unemployment benefits. An employee protected by both programs would be guaranteed a year of employment measured from the time of hire and a year of high unemployment benefits after separation from employment. The main obstacle to such a development is the possibility that the operation in tandem of the two programs will constitute a serious drag on the demand for labor and on labor mobility.

CHAPTER 7

Private Programs of Aid for the Permanently Terminated Worker

*Geraldine M. Beideman**

I. INTRODUCTION

THIS CHAPTER IS concerned with the efforts of private industry to alleviate the hardships of employees who are subjected to the most serious threat of unemployment, the permanent separation from a job. Severance pay and early retirement plans constitute the major part of these efforts and are treated at length. Other programs of a similar nature are described briefly where they touch on severance pay plans; these include some railroad dismissal plans, special supplementary unemployment benefit arrangements, and other income maintenance plans shown in columns B and C of Table 6–1. This chapter also touches briefly on the special services which some employers provide for permanently displaced workers.

The payment of money benefits to a permanently terminated worker may have two purposes: to supply him with some income and to compensate him for the loss of his investment in his job. Severance pay and early pension plans may accomplish both purposes but they have the latter as their specific purpose.

Today the loss of a job can be very much like the loss of a valuable piece of property. A job carries with it not only a money wage but also many work-connected advantages. Among the indirect compensations available to employed workers are paid vacations and holidays,

* Research Associate, The W. E. Upjohn Institute for Employment Research.

paid sick leave, group life insurance and medical care plans for workers and their families, and pension plans. Employees also accumulate a number of tangible job rights and privileges, such as seniority, that ensure the worker's security in his job and influence his opportunities for advancement.

Moreover, the longer an employee works for a firm, the greater are his expectations for continued employment tenure. The more service he accumulates with one company the smaller may be his chances for employment with another; the skills a worker acquires on a job, which may make him valuable to his employer, particularly in mass production industries, may not improve his employment opportunities elsewhere. It is to compensate the permanently terminated worker for the loss of these benefits, rights, and expectations, as well as for the loss of wages, that private programs such as severance pay and early retirement benefits are designed.

II. SEVERANCE PAY PLANS

Compensation for workers who are permanently dismissed from their jobs is known by a number of names; among them are "dismissal pay," "dismissal compensation," "termination pay," and "separation pay." "Severance pay," the name under which the plan will be discussed here, is one of the most commonly used terms today. But whatever the name of the program, the generally accepted definition of the benefit has remained fairly constant over the years. One student of the program has defined it as follows:

Dismissal compensation may be defined as the payment of a specific sum, in addition to any back wages or salary, made by an employer to an employee for permanently terminating the employment relationship primarily for reasons beyond the control of the employee.[1]

A. THE NATURE OF THE PLANS

The severance pay plans in existence vary from company to company and industry to industry, depending upon the circumstances the plans were set up to meet. There are, however, certain general features which are common to most of the arrangements.

One such feature is that the severance benefits are paid only to workers whose release is considered to be permanent. Another is that the reason for the termination must be among those stipulated in the plan. Still another usual characteristic is that the benefits which workers receive vary with the wages they have been paid and the length of time they have been with the company or in the industry. Also, it is typical for workers to relinquish in exchange for the severance awards their seniority and other job rights and various employment-connected benefits they received while they were working. What particularly distinguishes this benefit from other private plans to help displaced employees is that terminated workers do not have to remain unemployed in order to collect severance pay. Along with these similarities go many differences which are discussed in the following sections.

B. GROWTH OF THE PLANS

In the period antedating compulsory unemployment insurance several hundred firms voluntarily paid severance benefits to employees who were being released. Most of these plans were adopted during the nineteen-twenties and

nineteen-thirties. Some of the programs grew out of the movement in the nineteen-twenties to establish good policies and practices in employee relations. As the Depression deepened in the nineteen-thirties, more companies introduced plans to take care of the workers who were released when businesses closed or drastically curtailed their activities.

Generally, these early arrangements were outside the collective bargaining process, and the payments made under the various formal and informal plans most frequently went to white-collar workers. Labor's preoccupation during those years typically was with other, more important, issues, and unions in only a few industries pressed for severance pay.[2]

Labor's interest in severance benefits, however, was spurred somewhat during World War II. In part, this concern stemmed from the general trend of that period toward expanding employee benefits. Apparent, also, was the concern about the displacement of workers once war production declined. Consequently, a few plans were negotiated in the early nineteen-forties. Since World War II the growth in the number of negotiated severance pay plans has been slow but steady.

Although severance pay plans predate most other means of employee protection, such as life insurance, medical care, and pension plans, their growth over the years has been comparatively slow. Presumably, labor considered that the benefits provided by the other programs met more pressing needs.

Jobless benefits provided under the federal-state system of unemployment insurance, and, in quite recent years, the start of some private unemployment benefit plans as well, have tended to obscure the need for compensating permanently terminated workers. These other programs meet the most immediate needs of such workers and thus lessen the pressure for compensating them more fully for their lost jobs. Another factor restricting the growth of severance pay plans has been the tendency of

---

[1] Everett D. Hawkins, *Dismissal Compensation* (Princeton, N.J.: Princeton University Press, 1940), pp. 5–6.

[2] *Ibid.*, pp. 19–42, 144–86. According to Hawkins, most of the pre-World War II negotiated severance pay plans were in the textile, garment, railroad, and newspaper-publishing industries.

private benefit plans to favor those employees who remain on the job.

Now that many of the important employee benefit programs are fairly well established, however, the remaining gaps have become increasingly obvious. Consequently, the interest in employee security is being directed toward ways of compensating the workers who are separated from their jobs.

Available information indicates that the number of severance pay plans, while small, is growing. According to surveys by the Bureau of Labor Statistics, the proportion of major union agreements that contained severance pay provisions increased from 5 per cent in 1944 to 8 per cent in 1949 and to nearly 16 per cent by 1956.[3] A union spokesman estimated in 1960 that about 25 per cent of all union agreements contained severance pay provisions,[4] and preliminary data for 1963 indicate a figure closer to 30 per cent. Similar growth patterns have been demonstrated in studies made by the National Industrial Conference Board, Inc.[5]

Information about the number of workers protected by the plans is even less full and less precise than is information about the plans. A 1960 estimate by a labor representative indicated that about 35 per cent of workers under union agreements were covered by severance pay provisions as compared with 25 per cent a few years earlier.[6] A 1961 study of severance pay plans in New York showed that almost a third of the workers employed under union contracts in that state were protected by severance pay.[7] There are, of course, workers who are protected by severance pay plans outside collective bargaining.

C. CIRCUMSTANCES DETERMINING THE KINDS OF PLANS

The contingencies against which severance pay plans help protect permanently released workers, the characteristics of the workers, and the threats of unemployment they face determine to a large extent the considerable variations in these plans. Moreover, plans may be progressively modified as new kinds of job threats are recognized.

The severance pay plans which are being designed now are quite different in scope from those that were adopted in the nineteen-twenties and nineteen-thirties. The programs that are being initiated today reflect the changes in the structure of the labor market and in industrial processes and demonstrate corresponding inventiveness and adaptation to new conditions. Perhaps the most graphic way of presenting the different kinds of plans currently in force is to show them against the background of risks against which they offer protection.

Mergers, Acquisitions, and Consolidations. Company mergers, acquisitions, and consolidation of operations, for a long time characteristic of business practices in some industries, have accounted for the initiation of many severance pay programs. The railroad and newspaper industries offer good examples of the start of such arrangements under collective bargaining.

The Washington Job Protection Agreement, signed in 1936 by representatives of the carriers and the twenty-one unions which bargain with railroads, was a significant early step in providing protection for workers who were displaced when two or more carriers merged or consolidated their operations or services.[8] The agreement climaxed many years of effort by the Interstate Commerce Commission, the Congress, and various other government agencies to help the financially hard-pressed railroad industry reduce costs by such co-operative activities as car pooling and the joint use of railway

[3] *Collective Bargaining Clauses: Dismissal Pay,* Bulletin No. 1261 (Bureau of Labor Statistics, U.S. Department of Labor, Washington, D.C., 1957), pp. 1–2.

[4] "Severance Pay Plans," *Readings in Unemployment.* Printed for the use of the Special Committee on Unemployment Problems, United States Senate (Washington, D.C.: Government Printing Office, 1960), p. 1295.

[5] See the board's analyses in *Studies in Personnel Policy,* Nos. 1, 50, 141, 174, and 178, published in 1946, 1954, 1959, and 1960, respectively (New York).

[6] "Severance Pay Plans" (*n.* 4).

[7] *Severance Pay in Union-Management Agreements in New York State,* Publication No. B–138 (New York State Department of Labor, New York, July, 1962), pp. 1, 5.

[8] Hawkins, *Dismissal Compensation* (*n.* 1), pp. 157–75.

terminals and repair shops. The agreement reduced union objections to these cost-saving devices by furnishing the means for protecting workers who would be displaced.

The agreement provided an income-protection system which offered displaced workers a choice between two kinds of benefits, "co-ordination allowances" and "separation allowances." While both essentially represented payment for job loss, the conditions under which they were paid differed. Workers not employed by their home road or in the co-ordinated operation but who did not resign and therefore retained a relationship with their company could draw the co-ordination allowances. Indicative of their status as being on "layoff," these workers continued to have such job-connected benefits as free transportation and hospitalization, and their pension rights were protected. They forfeited these benefits as well as their allowances if they failed without good reason to respond to call-back notices, if they resigned, or if they were discharged for cause.

In these respects the co-ordination allowances did not resemble severance pay, but in one other respect they did. Displaced workers did not have to remain unemployed in order to be eligible for the allowances. Any earnings they received from employment outside the railroad industry did not affect the amount of their allowances. If they found other jobs in the railroad industry, however, their allowances were reduced by the amount that their combined wages on the new jobs and their allowances exceeded their former railroad pay.

The amount of the co-ordination allowance depended upon how long a worker had been employed by his company and the wages he had earned. A worker having one year of service was entitled to six monthly payments, for example, while one having fifteen or more years on the job would receive sixty monthly payments—that is, payments for five years. The monthly payments amounted to 60 per cent of prior earnings.

Workers who chose to resign at the time of the co-ordination received separation allowances instead. Signifying the break in the employment relationship, these workers relinquished their company benefits and other job rights in exchange for lump-sum payments. The separation allowances were considerably smaller than the co-ordination allowances. Terminated workers having one year of service were entitled to three months' pay; those with fifteen years of service received twelve months' pay.[9]

In the years that followed the signing of the Washington agreement, the Interstate Commerce Commission made a number of decisions modifying the original provisions and, in some ways, changing the character of the program. One change was to take into account any benefits paid under statutory unemployment insurance programs in calculating the monthly allowances. At the time of the 1936 agreement, it will be remembered, public unemployment insurance systems were not yet operative. Another change required that appropriate reductions be made in the monthly allowances for earnings from all employment, not just railroad employment.[10] Thus, the monthly allowances have come to take on some of the characteristics of unemployment benefits, even when they are paid to workers who are permanently released from their jobs. In recent years, the railroad program has undergone still other modifications and extensions, some of which are described later in this chapter.

Among newspapers, as among railroads, mergers or the discontinuance of operations have long constituted an important job threat to employees. As a measure against this threat, the American Newspaper Guild had severance pay as one of its early objectives in collective bargaining.[11]

That this early interest in protection against the threat of job elimination has continued over the years is manifest by the guild's success in negotiating severance provisions in local union agreements. A comparatively recent

[9] *Ibid.*
[10] Interstate Commerce Commission, *Finance Docket No. 15820.* Decided January 16, 1952.
[11] A 1938 survey of 102 guild agreements showed that in 96 cases some dismissal notice or compensation was given members. Hawkins, *Dismissal Compensation* (*n.* 1), pp. 182–83.

study of severance pay provisions in New York union agreements showed that all the contracts of the American Newspaper Guild provided for severance pay.[12] The newspaper plans have not been limited to the same extent as the railroad plans to unemployment caused by mergers, acquisitions, or consolidations. The guild plans especially have tended to cover all kinds of permanent layoffs and, in some cases, even certain kinds of discharges. Guild members receive severance pay based on their salaries and length of service, with the awards ranging from as little as two weeks' pay for one year of service to as much as sixty weeks' pay after twenty-nine and one-half years of service.[13]

Discontinuance of Businesses. The closing of a business, the shutting down of a company plant, and the moving of operations from an old location to a new one, all have spurred the development of severance pay arrangements.

The garment industry is one which is particularly vulnerable to the hazard of firms going out of business. Unlike the reasons for the displacement of workers in a number of other industries—the introduction of new kinds of equipment and new processes—the major reason in the garment industry has been the discontinuance of business.[14]

The garment workers who are discharged when companies close down are not necessarily permanently displaced. In garment-production centers such as New York and Los Angeles there is a ready demand for experienced workers because of the labor needs in new and expanding businesses. Older workers and those with marginal skills, however, may find it hard to

get new jobs in spite of available job opportunities. In areas where only a few garment-making firms are located, the re-employment process is, of course, more difficult for all the released workers.

The International Ladies' Garment Workers' Union (ILGWU) and employers in the industry have established a nationwide severance pay plan to help workers who are displaced when companies close. Interest in severance pay arrangements for such workers began early in the nineteen-fifties. By 1960 most of the locals had negotiated plans with employers or employer associations, and late in 1960 the local plans were merged to form a nationwide, industry arrangement. From the beginning, the local ILGWU plans were funded by employer contributions based on a percentage of their payrolls; with the merging of the plans the local funds were consolidated into one national fund, called the ILGWU Supplementary Unemployment Severance Benefits Fund (SUSB).

As is implied by the name, SUSB, the national plan provides for supplementary unemployment benefits as well as severance pay. Under the earlier plans, ILGWU members who were released when their firms closed down received severance benefits in line with their earnings and the length of their service with the company. Some of these workers found new jobs fairly soon and therefore experienced relatively little in the way of wage loss. Those who had difficulty finding new work, however, experienced not only job loss but also a substantial loss in wages. The purpose of the broadened benefits under the national plan was to help protect the released employees against both of these contingencies.[15]

When a firm goes out of business, severance benefits are paid to displaced workers in a lump sum. If a worker does not find another job at once, she can draw supplementary unemployment benefits as well. Under SUSB the benefits are awarded on the basis of average earnings and length of service. The most any

---

[12] *Severance Pay in Union-Management Agreements* (*n.* 7), pp. 9–10.

[13] "Severance Pay Provisions in California Union Agreements," *California Industrial Relations Reports,* No. 20 (Division of Labor Statistics and Research, California Department of Industrial Relations, San Francisco, California, April, 1960), pp. 9–10.

[14] Thomas Kennedy, *Automation Funds and Displaced Workers* (Graduate School of Business Administration, Harvard University, Cambridge, Massachusetts, 1962), pp. 162–64. Hawkins, however, reported that worker displacement resulting from new kinds of equipment and other kinds of labor-saving devices was the job hazard against which garment workers sought protection in the nineteen-twenties and nineteen-thirties, *Dismissal Compensation* (*n.* 1), pp. 152–55.

[15] "Broad Severance," *Business Week,* October 29, 1960, p. 88. Also see Kennedy, *Automation Funds* (*n.* 14), pp. 166–68.

employee may receive in severance and un-employment benefits combined, however, is $1,600, severance pay accounting for $400, and supplementary unemployment benefits, for $1,200.[16]

Accrued vacation pay is provided in addition to the severance benefits. It is indicative of the vested right to the severance benefits that, if a worker dies before she receives her pay, the monies are paid to her estate.

During World War II concern about plant shutdowns stimulated the steelworkers to take an interest in severance pay plans. The concern was centered on foreseeable postwar conditions: the likelihood of widespread employment cut-backs after the war and the possibility that steel companies would concentrate production in the modern plants built after the start of the war and close the older, obsolete facilities. The first severance pay contracts in the steel industry were negotiated by the United Steelworkers of America in 1947. As with the ILGWU plan, the steel plan provisions governing the pay-ment of benefits have reflected the serious threat to workers' jobs in the closing of plants or the severe curtailment of some intraplant operations. Payments are generally restricted to workers affected by these developments. If a displaced worker exercises his seniority rights and thereby displaces another employee, however, the latter is entitled to severance pay if he meets the other qualifications. Three years' employment is required for benefits. Severance pay is related both to length of service and to earnings, and the benefits range from four weeks' pay for workers having less than five years of service to eight weeks' pay for workers having ten or more years of service. In contrast to the garment plan, where a separated worker can receive both supplemen-tary unemployment benefits and severance pay, under the steel plans he must choose one or the other. The separation of the two pro-grams in the steel plans presumably represents an attempt to distinguish between temporary and permanent layoffs.[17]

Technological Advances. Technological changes long have spurred workers' interest in maintaining job security or, if that could not be achieved, in obtaining income security. Efforts to retain the security of jobs through such means as work rules, prohibitions against terminations except for cause, and similar restrictions have been one approach to the threat of worker displacement by technological innovations. Another has been to compensate the workers who are released when technological improve-ments are instituted. Jules Backman offers the latter approach as the desirable social answer to innovation:

> Any program adopted must be designed to protect the workers—not to preserve the job. To the extent that the number of jobs is frozen, technological changes would be impeded.[18]

Severance pay programs offer one way of protecting the worker, not the job, and have been called "a device for adjusting the conflict between society's interest in technological progress and the worker's claim to protection against hardship caused by the loss of his job."[19]

Severance pay has been used in different ways by a number of industries where technological changes have led to worker displacement. Some of these approaches are described below.

A union contract provision for severance pay may originate because of a specific tech-nological change; the provision may later be broadened to relate to other innovations, both imminent and as yet unforeseen. The 1958 and 1961 contracts between the Columbia Broadcasting System, Inc., and the International Brotherhood of Electrical Workers are examples of this kind of development. One of the important issues in the 1958 strike of the IBEW against CBS radio and television facilities was the union's demand for improved severance pay protection; eight weeks' pay represented the maximum benefit provided. Of particular concern at that time was protection for techni-cians who would be released when transmitters

---

[16] *Severance Pay in Union–Management Agreements* (*n.* 7), pp. 29–30.

[17] *Ibid.*, p. 34.

[18] "Cushioning the Impact of Technological Change," *Labor Law Journal* (September, 1962), p. 745.

[19] John H. Fanning, "The Challenge of Automation in the Light of the National Law," *Labor Law Journal* (October, 1960), pp. 880–81.

were converted to remote control, an immediate threat. Reductions in "live" productions and the increased use of video tape productions were also resulting in employment curtailments. The 1958 settlement extended the severance pay provision to three months' pay for all workers laid off as a result of the use of new processes or equipment; workers released for other reasons would continue to be held to the old schedule of benefits. In addition, transmitter operators were to receive nine months' notice that their jobs were to be eliminated: this provision in effect was a form of the guaranteed annual wage noted in column A of Table 6–1.

At the time of the 1961 negotiations the transmitters already had been converted to remote control. Moreover, the union's position had come to be that technological advances accounted both directly and indirectly for all reductions in the work force. In the resulting contract, therefore, the distinction between technological and other reasons for layoff and the consequent two schedules of severance payments were abandoned. A revised severance pay provision granted an increase in benefits—up to a maximum of fifteen weeks' pay for ten or more years of service—to all workers laid off or discharged except when the release was caused by dishonesty, drunkenness, or gross insubordination.[20]

In the meatpacking industry, also, labor and management have attempted to meet the problem of worker displacements resulting from new processes and equipment. In the 1959 negotiations, Armour and Company and the two unions, the Amalgamated Meat Cutters and Butcher Workmen and the United Packinghouse Workers of America, recognized jointly "that the meatpacking industry is undergoing significant changes in methods of production, processing, marketing and distribution."[21] In

order to permit Armour to effect a modernization program and still protect the workers, the agreement provided for a labor-management committee to study the problem and offer recommendations for its solution.[22]

The 1961 Armour agreement that eventually evolved provided for an elaborate system of job and income security—a guaranteed annual wage, supplementary unemployment benefits, severance pay, and early retirement benefits— for employees when plants or departments were closed down as modern plants were built or workers were displaced by new equipment. Among the provisions was a ninety-day advance notice of shutdown and guaranteed earnings during that time to workers who would be affected. After that period, eligible workers intending to stay in the labor market had their choice of two separate kinds of benefits, technological adjustment pay and severance pay. Displaced workers wanting to remain with the company and transfer to a new location could draw technological adjustment pay until the transfer occurred or their eligibility for it expired. Technological adjustment pay was a special form of supplementary unemployment benefit; total benefits amounted to $65 weekly, including unemployment insurance and earnings the employees might receive from any other work. The time during which workers might draw technological adjustment pay depended upon how long they had worked for Armour. Recipients were considered as employees on layoff; evidence of the continued employment relationship was to be found in the fact that Armour continued to pay the group insurance premiums for these workers.

Displaced workers who chose not to transfer or who could not qualify for technological adjustment pay might be entitled to severance pay. The severance arrangement negotiated in 1961 was considerably more liberal than that

---

[20] Background information was provided by an IBEW representative of Local 45, Hollywood, in the course of an interview on September 6, 1962. The 1958 contract provision is detailed in "Severance Pay Provisions in California Union Contracts" (n. 13); the 1961 contract provision is contained in *1961 Agreement, Columbia Broadcasting System, Inc., and International Brotherhood of Electrical Workers (AFL–CIO)*, Section 5.11, p. 49.

[21] "Developments in Industrial Relations," *Monthly Labor Review* (October, 1959), p. 1109.

[22] Joint committees of this kind have been suggested as a valuable interim measure. They can develop programs which are applicable to specific industries or companies. And without the pressures which are exerted when collective bargaining is in process, they can help work out mutually satisfactory programs. See Backman, "Cushioning the Impact of Technological Change" (n. 18), p. 753.

which was in effect previously. Under the 1961 agreement, benefits were stepped up for the longer service employees. The ten-year man was eligible for 10 weeks' pay; the twenty-year man, for 27.5 weeks' pay; the twenty-five-year man, for 35.5 weeks' pay; and the thirty-year man, for 47.5 weeks' pay.[23]

In the Hawaii stevedoring industry the increasing mechanization of loading and unloading ship cargo has stimulated the development of generous severance pay arrangements for longshoremen in order to encourage work force reductions. Not only released workers but also selected workers, called "substitute layoffs," who leave voluntarily, are entitled to severance benefits. The agreement between the International Longshoremen's and Warehousemen's Union (ILWU) and the stevedoring companies combines two types of severance benefits. One of these is based upon the actuarial equivalent of the employee's vested pension benefits, and the other is an additional benefit which increases with the worker's age and the length of his service. Workers drawing severance benefits under this arrangement forfeit their pension rights.[24] Severance benefits are paid from an industrywide fund made up of contributions from the stevedoring companies.[25]

The ILWU has also negotiated severance pay plans with the sugar and pineapple industries in Hawaii. These plans are intended to protect workers who are permanently laid off because of innovations in processing as well as changes in marketing and in market demand. Reflecting the special character of the Hawaii work force, the arrangements provide that pineapple industry employees who repatriate to their homeland—usually Japan, the Philippines, or Taiwan—receive extra allowances.

Unlike the plan in the pineapple industry, the provisions in the plan of the Hawaii sugar industry do not contain the repatriation bonuses;

the plan does, however, provide escalated allowances for older employees. Workers age forty through forty-nine receive a 10 per cent increase in severance pay, and those age fifty through fifty-four receive a 35 per cent increase. Neither industry plan, incidentally, stipulates a maximum limit on the amount of the awards, and severance payments often exceed $10,000.[26]

The railroad industry plans offer another example of ways in which severance benefits have been used in an attempt to resolve the automation-versus-jobs issue. A number of individual carriers, who have been seeking to eliminate jobs, have negotiated various income continuation arrangements with the unions concerned. The 1936 Washington Job Protection Agreement—originally applying only in the case of mergers and consolidations of two or more carriers—has been the model for the new contracts which extend to unemployment caused by technological changes. Some of them have adopted without change the original agreement (as modified by subsequent Interstate Commerce Commission rulings); others have established plans which are different in several significant respects.

The 1961–62 contracts between the telegraphers and the Southern Pacific, the Chicago and Northwestern, and the New York Central railroads provided the traditional benefits (a lump-sum separation allowance of up to twelve months' pay or a furlough allowance of 60 per cent of prior wages for up to five years). More recently (1963), the Southern Pacific and clerks and the Baltimore and Ohio and telegraphers adopted a plan generally similar to the Washington Job Protection Agreement but different in one respect. The furlough allowance begins like a SUB plan: The unemployed worker must apply for a railroad unemployment insurance benefit as long as one is available to him (the maximum period is one year) and the carrier supplements this benefit in an amount which will provide an aggregate unemployment benefit of 70 per cent of prior weekly wages. Thereafter, up to four years, the furlough allowance is 60 per cent of prior wages.

[23] "Developments in Industrial Relations," *Monthly Labor Review* (November, 1961), pp. 1246–47.
[24] *Severance Allowance Provisions in Contracts* (Honolulu: Hawaii Employers Council, August 31, 1962), p. 3.
[25] "Memorandum of Agreement between I.L.W.U. Local 142 and the Undersigned Stevedoring Companies of Hawaii," November 22, 1961. (Mimeographed.)
[26] *Severance Allowance Provisions in Contracts* (n. 24), pp. 4, 7.

Though modernization programs and the introduction of technological changes are often thought of as applying to old-line industries, such as the railroads, some workers in a newer transportation industry—the airlines—also have been subjected to technological hazards. The displacement of the flight engineers offers a graphic example of the serious impact of technological change—the switch from piston-type to jet-propelled airplanes—on a fairly new industry.[27]

The 1958 contract between United Air Lines, Inc., and the Flight Engineers International Association offered one solution to the displacement problem. Flight engineers could enroll in a company-provided training course for flight proficiency; those successfully completing the course would be assigned to turbojet aircraft and permitted to relieve other cockpit crew members. Engineers deciding against taking the training and those failing to qualify after enrollment would be entitled to severance pay of $20,000.[28] The 1962 negotiations between Trans-World Airlines and the union took a similar course; severance pay for flight engineers ranged from $10,000 for those with low seniority to $39,000 for long-service engineers.

Sometimes an established employee benefit is extended to provide protection against additional risks. In the automobile industry the 1958 agreement amended the existing SUB provision to furnish severance benefits as well. To some extent, this amendment grew out of the SUB funding mechanism. With the benefit funds relatively solvent at the time of the 1958

negotiations, it was financially possible to divert some of the monies to a benefit program for workers being permanently released. Perhaps as important as the availability of funds in stimulating the United Auto Workers' interest in severance pay was the growing concern about worker displacement. Where once the main income security threat to workers in the automobile industry had come from short-term layoffs, by the late nineteen-fifties the threat was seen to be in the growing trend toward permanent layoffs. Not only were technological changes accounting for reduced labor needs, but the closing of some plants and the relocation of others also were causing the permanent release of many long-service workers.[29]

D. RELATIONSHIP BETWEEN SEVERANCE PAY
AND UNEMPLOYMENT BENEFIT PLANS

Severance pay, of course, is only one of the programs that pay money benefits to displaced workers. The public and private unemployment benefit plans described in earlier chapters also make monetary awards to terminated workers; and so, too, do a number of other private industry arrangements which combine some of the features of severance pay with those of unemployment benefits.

In the case of private programs it is difficult to draw very distinct lines between severance pay plans and unemployment benefit plans, because the private programs, adapted as they are to individual industry situations, do not fit into one particular mold. In general, though, unemployment benefits in the private plans—as in the public unemployment insurance system— are paid only to workers who are out of jobs, whereas severance benefits are paid even to workers who go on to new jobs immediately. Severance payments typically represent compensation for the breaking of the employment relationship, whereas private unemployment

[27] In "Fourth Man Out—Background of the Flight Engineer-Airline Pilot Conflict," *Labor Law Journal* (August, 1962), pp. 649–57, Albert A. Blum has suggested that the job competition resulting from technological displacement of flight engineers was intensified by the struggle between the Flight Engineers International Association and the more powerful Air Line Pilots Association.

[28] *1958 Agreement between United Air Lines, Inc., and Flight Engineers in the Service of United Air Lines, Inc., as represented by UNA Chapter, Flight Engineers International Association, AFL–CIO,* Section X, Paragraph B, 4. As of the latter part of 1962, the company had had very little experience with the severance pay arrangement; according to a United Air Lines representative, only six employees had been terminated up to that time.

[29] In the April 1, 1963, *Newsweek* article, "Unemployment in America" (p. 68), it was reported that in 1953, about 917,000 auto workers were required to build 7.3 million vehicles, but ten years later only 723,000 were required to build 8.3 million vehicles.

benefit plans usually make payments to persons who essentially are on layoff. Thus, severance pay characteristically protects workers against the risk of job loss—the loss of accompanying job rights and benefits—as well as loss of wage income. In contrast, private unemployment benefit plans—like the public program—typically protect workers only against the risk of income loss.

Private plans co-ordinate these job-loss and wage-loss concepts in their benefit programs in different ways, some of which are commented on below. Noted, too, are the various relationships which exist between severance pay and the public unemployment insurance benefits.

Supplemental Unemployment Benefits. In some industry and company benefit programs, workers can draw both SUB and severance pay. In the rubber industry, for example, the severance awards that are eventually paid to workers are not reduced by any SUB payments they may have received.[30] The garment industry plan also allows workers to draw both SUB and severance benefits.

On the other hand, in the automobile industry severance benefits are reduced by the amount of SUB paid. There, the use of the same fund for both benefits probably accounts in part for the avoidance of overlapping payments. In the steel industry, where severance benefits are paid only to workers released when plants close down or certain operations are discontinued, those who receive the termination payments are not entitled to SUB.[31]

Extended Layoff Benefits. Extended layoff benefits plans, which were originally developed in the course of the 1960 negotiations in the aerospace industry, combine some of the features of severance pay with those of SUB. In these plans, benefits are paid to employees whose layoff has lasted for four weeks. These benefits are like severance pay in that the workers do not have to be unemployed in order to draw them. They are like SUB in that the

workers are considered to be on layoff and retain their seniority rights for as long as five years; moreover, recipients who are unemployed can draw state unemployment insurance benefits along with their extended layoff benefits. The purposes of extended layoff benefits, as stated in the union contract, demonstrate the dual nature of the plan:

> Among the purposes for which the benefits . . . are provided are to help pay living expenses by supplementing and not replacing unemployment compensation, and to help compensate for loss of job security, vacation and sick leave accrual, and insurance benefit coverage.[32]

Because it is frequently difficult at the time of layoff to tell whether the terminations will be long term or short term, neither severance pay nor SUB seemed to meet the particular protection needs of aerospace employees. Because the prospects for recall often are unpredictable, the firms would have little interest in holding a labor reserve. Yet the industry was concerned about protecting the previous service rights of employees who would be called back.

Extended layoff benefits are paid in a lump sum, partly to hold down administrative costs but also to encourage labor mobility. Because of the indefinite nature of the layoffs the companies are not interested in maintaining a reserve labor force.

The benefits are based on length of service, and are payable at the rate of $75 for each year of employment up to a maximum of fifteen years. Thus, the top award is $1,125 for employees having fifteen or more years of employment. Aerospace companies assume liability up to a fixed maximum of $150 per employee for the payment of extended layoff benefits and accrue this liability at the rate of 3 cents for each straight-time hour that is worked. If benefits are paid at a time when the company liability is below the maximum, the amount of the extended layoff benefit payments

---

[30] "Developments in Industrial Relations," *Monthly Labor Review* (June, 1963), p. 707.

[31] *Severance Pay in Union–Management Agreements* (*n. 7*), pp. 30–31, 34.

[32] *Agreement between North American Aviation, Inc., and International Union, United Automobile, Aerospace, and Agricultural Implement Workers of America, September 30, 1962,* Article XXIV—Extended Layoff Benefits, Section 2. Similar agreements are in effect in most of the other major aerospace firms.

is reduced in proportion to the liability that has been attained.

Income Extension Aid Plan. This plan, negotiated by General Electric Corporation and the International Union of Electrical Workers, is very similar to a number of the agreements in the electrical manufacturing industry. The Income Extension Aid Plan provides both a special form of supplementary unemployment benefits and severance pay. Workers who are on layoff and are still unemployed after they have exhausted their state unemployment insurance benefits are entitled to weekly payments amounting to one-half of their former pay; the number of weekly payments that they can receive is based upon one payment for each six months of service. Thus, this is a supplementary unemployment benefit in that it supplements the duration of state unemployment insurance. Laid-off workers can choose instead to be paid their entitlement in a lump sum; this option represents severance pay because the workers drawing the benefits forfeit their recall rights and other benefits except for any vested pension rights they may have. Whenever company plants are closed, the terminated workers always receive their income extension aid in a lump sum—again, a severance payment.

Unemployment Insurance. Most states allow workers receiving severance pay also to draw their full unemployment insurance benefits. Eighteeen of the states,[33] however, either deny unemployment insurance benefits to recipients of severance pay or reduce the amount of their unemployment benefits. In these states the disallowance or reduction in insurance applies not only to the week in which the severance payment is made but also to the number of weeks of wages that the severance payment represents. The rationale for this denial or reduction of benefits is that severance pay is considered to be a continuation of wages. What is not considered in this reasoning is the important function of severance pay as com-

pensation for lost job rights. Not considered, either, is that the workers previously chose to forego direct wage increases in order to have the protection of severance pay if they should be permanently discharged.

Until recently, California was among the group of states disallowing or reducing the insurance of severance pay recipients. Since July 1, 1963, however, the California Department of Employment has paid full unemployment insurance benefits to claimants receiving severance pay. This change occurred when an Attorney General's opinion concerning employee benefits designed to supplement unemployment insurance was interpreted as applying to severance benefits as well. As a result of this interpretation, severance pay now is considered to be a private unemployment benefit and not a continued wage payment.[34]

E. An Appraisal of Severance Pay Plans

It is not possible to provide an appraisal of these plans in the strict sense because the requisite norms of adequacy are not readily available. The difficulty of establishing such norms in the case of severance pay plans stems from the variety of plans and of workers covered, the industry differences in the risks of displacement, and the absence of information about experience under existing plans. All that can be done here by way of evaluation is to show the wide variations in the protection afforded by existing programs, indicate some of the limitations of this form of benefit, and assess the eventual direction that severance pay plans may take.

Only a minority of workers are covered by severance pay plans, and the existing plans vary considerably in the amount of protection they provide for this minority. The ILGWU plan, for example, limits benefit payments to situations where firms go out of business. The steel

---

[33] Alabama, Arizona, Arkansas, Connecticut, Indiana, Maine, Minnesota, Missouri, Montana, Nebraska, New Hampshire, North Carolina, Ohio, Oregon, Pennsylvania, Virginia, West Virginia, and Wisconsin.

[34] For fuller details, see the communication from the Director of Employment to Assemblyman George A. Willson in *Assembly Daily Journal, California Legislature, 1963 Regular Session* (April 25, 1963), pp. 2526–28.

industry plans operate only when a plant or one of its major departments closes down. By contrast, most American Newspaper Guild plans cover almost all kinds of terminations.[35] As indicated earlier, however, once severance pay plans are adopted, they are often broadened to cover other contingencies besides those in the original plans. For example, the Columbia Broadcasting System-IBEW plan at first gave special consideration only to technologically displaced workers but later extended this consideration to include most workers terminated involuntarily.

The money benefits under severance pay plans vary considerably from company to company, and the variations are found both for long-service and for short-service workers. The meatpacking, steel, auto, electrical, and ILGWU plans provide examples of such variations for both thirty-year workers and five-year workers.

In the meatpacking industry the thirty-year worker receives 47.3 weeks of pay. In the steel industry he receives only 8 weeks of pay. In the automobile industry he receives 37.5 weeks of pay, but that benefit is reduced by any supplementary unemployment benefits he has received. Under some electrical industry plans he receives only 15 weeks of pay because the plan provides for only one-half his weekly earnings for each year of service. Under the ILGWU plan the $400 maximum placed on severance awards means that the long-service worker drawing top pay in the industry cannot receive more than about 4 weeks of pay.

In the meatpacking industry the five-year worker receives 5 weeks of pay. In the steel industry he receives 6 weeks of pay. In the automobile industry he receives $3\frac{1}{8}$ weeks of pay minus any supplementary unemployment benefit he has received. In the electrical industry he receives $2\frac{1}{2}$ weeks of pay. The ILGWU worker receives $1\frac{1}{4}$ weeks of pay.

While industry comparisons such as these can be made, the adequacy of the different awards does not depend solely upon the amount of money that is paid. The re-employment opportunities may be better for workers in one industry than in another or in one labor-market area than in another. The job rights and work-connected benefits which one group of workers loses may be more valuable than those lost by other workers. The degree of risk to which long-service employees are exposed also affects the benefit picture. The objectives of the plans also may vary, thus affecting the size of the awards. In the ILGWU plan, for example, the severance benefit is not intended as income continuation pay during spells of unemployment; instead it compensates the worker for the loss of a job and, incidentally, for any decrease in earnings she may experience while she is getting used to a new job. If the ILGWU member does not go to work on another job immediately, another program, supplementary unemployment benefits, comes into play. Some other plans, in contrast, incorporate the income continuation feature as well as job-loss compensation in their benefit formulas.

Under most severance pay plans terminated workers lose most fringe benefits concerned with health and welfare. A few plans, however, provide for benefits like continued group health and life insurance, medical and hospital care, and funeral expenses. The TWA severance pay plan for flight engineers, for example, provides that engineers who are terminated continue to be eligible for coverage under the company's group life and medical insurance plans.[36] The Welfare and Retirement Fund of the United Mine Workers of America is another example of the extension of fringe benefits to terminated workers. Unemployed mine workers, even those who are ineligible for pensions, can receive hospital and medical expenses for themselves and their families during the first year of their unemployment. If a miner dies within one year after the termination of his employment, the fund pays his funeral expenses and survivors' benefits and continues for that year the hospital and medical benefits for his survivors.[37]

---

[35] Excepted usually are those where dismissal is for gross misconduct or is self-provoked in order to obtain the severance pay, or where the employee fails to maintain his guild membership.

[36] See "Developments in Industrial Relations," *Monthly Labor Review* (January, 1963), p. 71.

[37] Kennedy, *Automation Funds* (n. 14), pp. 31–33. Until July 1, 1960, the men and their dependents were

Under most plans, however, terminated workers lose such health and welfare benefits; the severance pay itself is considered to be compensation for the loss of protection. This thinking is exemplified in the Armour and Co. program, which distinguishes between workers whose employment connection is continued under technological adjustment pay and workers whose employment is definitely terminated; the former continue to be covered by insurance paid by the company, and the latter receive only severance pay.

Some plans, like the newspaper guild plans[38] and the ILGWU plan,[39] recognize workers' vested rights to severance pay and award the benefits to survivors of deceased workers. Somewhat more prevalent and of growing importance as benefits which terminated workers retain are the vested rights to their accumulated pension credits. This vesting may entitle workers either to regular retirement benefits at the normal retirement age or to reduced benefits starting at an earlier age. Usually, in order to retain these vested pension rights, the worker must have attained a prescribed age—forty or fifty, for example—and have worked for the firm for a specified time—such as ten or fifteen years—before his termination. Under some plans these vested rights are retained regardless of the reason for termination, as in the case of workers in the automobile industry; in other industries, such as steel, the workers must have been on layoff for an extended period or have been released when a plant or department closed.[40]

A slow but steady growth of severance pay

plans is likely, and the future will probably see a moderate expansion of the present limited coverage. One reason for expecting this expansion is the developing interest in income security, which is the result of rising job attrition and management's continued search for improvements in efficiency.

Future plans undoubtedly will be characterized by the same variety of experimentation that is found in present plans. It is likely too that there will be increasing numbers of private industry programs which co-ordinate severance pay with other income security programs in order to meet a variety of layoff situations. The trend toward funding income continuation arrangements and using common funds to meet a number of contingencies very possibly will encourage the further development of such combination programs. Another circumstance that favors flexible programs is the growing difficulty of determining at the time layoffs occur whether they will be short term or permanent.

There also would seem to be in prospect an easing of the restrictions on the payment of unemployment insurance to severance pay recipients. Political interest has not yet been focused on the removal of these restrictions because, so far, only a relatively few workers have been affected by the prohibitions that exist in eighteen of the states. With an increase in the number of workers affected, there are likely to be mounting legislative pressures to allow the payment of unemployment insurance along with severance pay. A further aid to the removal of these restrictions is the development of combination programs to aid workers laid off for short periods, for indefinite periods, and permanently. As more and more industry programs integrate severance pay with supplementary unemployment benefits and with other kinds of layoff benefits, it will seem increasingly illogical to allow the payment of unemployment insurance to recipients of some private-plan benefits and to disallow it in the case of others.

Growing pressures for some income tax relief to recipients of severance pay may also be expected. The present tax treatment of the benefits as wages earned in the year they are paid reduces the net award materially and thus

---

entitled to these benefits for an indefinite period, but the steady depletion of the fund necessitated a curtailment of this more liberal policy.

[38] "Severance Pay Provisions in California Union Agreements" (*n.* 13), pp. 9–10. Continuation of the practice was confirmed by contact with M. I. Gershenson, Chief of the Division of Labor Statistics and Research.

[39] *Severance Pay in Union–Management Agreements* (*n.* 7), p. 30.

[40] *Digest of Selected Pension Plans under Collective Bargaining, 1961* (Division of Labor Statistics and Research, California Department of Industrial Relations, San Francisco, California, November, 1962), pp. 38–41, 54–57.

subverts the purpose of the program. Some terminated workers receiving large severance awards can choose to have the benefit payments stretched over a period of time in order to avoid an excessive tax. While this option is by no means common, there is a growing trend, especially when the severance payments are large, toward paying the benefits in installments. This not only offers certain tax advantages to the recipients but also helps to avoid the early dissipation of the benefit.[41]

As severance pay plans increase in number and coverage, the cost of the benefit can be expected to rise. At present, severance pay expenditures are generally quite modest as compared with the costs of other benefit programs. Fringe benefit cost surveys made by the Chamber of Commerce of the United States show that company costs for severance payments have averaged only 0.2 per cent to 0.3 per cent of payroll during the past several years. The costs to individual companies paying severance benefits to sizable numbers of workers have, of course, been significantly higher.[42]

Any assessment of the future of severance pay plans must recognize that many industries and companies will not be financially able to provide this benefit for their terminated employees. It must be recognized too that some of the remedial measures necessary to maintain the income of displaced workers and to secure their re-employment represent too large a task to be assigned as the reponsibility of any one firm or industry.[43]

III. EARLY RETIREMENT BENEFITS

Because of the special difficulties that older persons have in finding new jobs, the plight of the older terminated worker is more serious than that of the somewhat younger man.[44] Characteristically, the number of older workers among the chronically unemployed is greater than their proportion in the general population. The situation for workers in the fifty-five and over age groups has been described as a "no man's land" because the workers are too old to find jobs and yet too young to qualify for pensions.[45] Indeed the results of a number of studies suggest that "retirement" when it finally can be achieved is an escape from unemployment.

Provisions in private pension plans which allow workers to retire earlier than the customary retirement age—usually sixty-five—benefit not only the displaced older workers whose chances of re-employment are slim, but also younger employees, whose jobs may be saved

---

[41] For some workers' views on the tax aspects of severance pay, see William Haber, Louis A. Ferman, and James R. Hudson, *The Impact of Technological Change* (Kalamazoo, Michigan: The W. E. Upjohn Institute for Employment Research, September, 1963), p. 24.

[42] See *Fringe Benefits, 1961; Fringe Benefits, 1959; Fringe Benefits, 1957; Fringe Benefits, 1955* (Washington, D.C.: The Chamber of Commerce of the United States). The SUSB Fund of the ILGWU is financed by employer contributions of 0.5 per cent of payroll; this contribution so far has been sufficient to pay both severance benefits and supplementary unemployment benefits. The high costs that a company can expect when severance payments are made to considerable numbers of released workers is indicated by the experience of the Sioux City Armour plant, which terminated 797 employees when the plant closed, on June 16, 1963. Some of the checks totaled more than $8,000. Under the Armour plan the smallest amount that any worker could receive was five weeks' pay; at the average weekly meatpacking rate of $100.30, the minimum payment was slightly more than $500. See "Union Attacks Armour Program to Retrain Victims of Automation," *Wall Street Journal* (August 26, 1963).

[43] An example of the development of new concepts concerning the encouragement of private measures to prevent or alleviate unemployment was a bill introduced in the 1963 session of the California legislature. The bill proposed the allowance of unemployment insurance tax offsets to employers who established severance pay, supplementary unemployment benefits, retraining, and similar programs (Assembly Bill No. 607, January 30, 1963). The measure was referred to an interim committee for consideration as part of a comprehensive review of unemployment insurance financing.

[44] Arthur M. and Jane N. Ross, "Employment Problems of Older Workers," *Studies in Unemployment*, printed for the Special Committee on Unemployment Problems, United States Senate (Washington, D.C.: Government Printing Office, 1960), pp. 97–120; Margaret S. Gordon, "The Older Worker and Hiring Practices," *Monthly Labor Review* (November, 1959), pp. 1198–1205. See also the study made by A. J. Jaffee and J. R. Milavsky of the labor force and the financial situation of unemployed men from ages fifty-five to sixty-four in New York State during 1957 and 1958. The findings were presented at Columbia University in 1960 in a paper titled, "Unemployment, Retirement, and Pensions."

[45] Jaffee and Milavsky, "Unemployment, Retirement, and Pensions" (*n.* 44), p. 19.

by the retirement of the older workers. It is necessary, of course, that the displaced workers receive enough in pension benefits to be able to "afford" to retire.

A. DEVELOPMENT OF EARLY RETIREMENT PROVISIONS

An increasing number of private pension plans are incorporating early, nondisability retirement features. A comparatively recent study of pension plans made by the Bankers Trust Company showed the liberalization of provisions for early retirement to be one of the most pronounced trends in pension planning. The proportion of plans having early retirement provisions increased from 70 per cent in 1953–55 to 88 per cent in 1955–59. A significant increase also was recorded in plans allowing voluntary early retirement.[46]

A more recent study of insured pension plans made by the Connecticut General Life Insurance Company showed a similar trend. According to the findings, 90 per cent of the 900 plans in the survey contained early retirement options in 1961 as compared with 77 per cent in 1957.[47]

A California study of negotiated pension plans in 1961 substantiated this trend. About nine out of every ten of the plans reviewed contained early retirement provisions.[48]

Most pension plans allow for early retirements, but generally they also pay actuarially reduced benefits to these retirees: The benefits are computed in the same way as the normal benefits and are then reduced to reflect the longer periods over which benefits will be paid and the shorter periods of fund accumulation. Recent studies of pension plans indicate that comparatively few—perhaps 13 or 14 per cent—pay normal or above-normal benefits to persons retiring early. These special benefit arrangements are limited, moreover, to retirements

dictated by specific conditions such as the release of older workers when a plant is closed or when a work-force reduction occurs.[49]

Still another private pension benefit arrangement is gaining in popularity, the "level income" option. Under this option, a larger benefit is paid before the social security benefits begin and a smaller benefit is paid afterward. Thus the worker's total pension remains about the same throughout his retirement period.

In spite of the spread of private pension plans in recent years, however, the protection is far from universal. Less than one-half of the workers in private industry were covered by these arrangements in 1961, according to one recent study.[50] Moreover, not all of the persons covered can qualify for the pension benefits. They may not have worked long enough under the plans to satisfy the length of service requirements or they may be too young to meet the age requirements at the time they are terminated. The California study showed minimum age requirements for early retirement generally to be at least fifty-five, and many called for age sixty or sixty-two. Only a very few plans allowed early retirement under special circumstances at age fifty. In only a few plans did length of service requirements specify less than ten years of employment; most of the plans called for at least fifteen or twenty years of work. Some comparatively new pension plans, however, in calculating the necessary years required to qualify for early retirement take into account service with the firm prior to membership in the plan.[51]

B. KINDS OF EARLY RETIREMENT PROVISIONS

Initially, the prevailing reason for early retirement provisions was to allow aging

---

[46] *1960 Study of Industrial Retirement Plans* (New York: Bankers Trust Company, 1960), pp. 8–11.

[47] Alfred M. Skolnik, "Growth of Employee Benefit Plans, 1954–61," *Social Security Bulletin* (April, 1963), p. 15. See also Harry E. Davis, "Recent Changes in Negotiated Pension Plans," *Monthly Labor Review* (May, 1962), pp. 528, 530–31.

[48] *Digest of Selected Pension Plans under Collective Bargaining* (n. 40), pp. 34 ff.

[49] About 14 per cent of the plans studied by the Bankers Trust Company and nearly 13 per cent studied by the California Department of Industrial Relations paid special benefits to early retirees under certain circumstances.

[50] Skolnik estimated coverage at 45.3 per cent of workers in private industry. Skolnik, "Growth of Employee Benefit Plans" (n. 47), p. 7.

[51] *Digest of Selected Pension Plans under Collective Bargaining* (n. 40).

workers to retire in advance of the prescribed age if they were physically or mentally unable to perform their work adequately. In recent years, however, the objectives of retirement systems have been broadened to include older employees who, although still able to work, are no longer in demand. Depending upon the uses made of the advance retirement provisions, there tend to be within the same company or industry systems different schedules of benefit payments and different eligibility requirements.

Voluntary Early Retirements. A worker who feels that he is no longer able to keep up the pace of work may be allowed to retire ahead of time. A worker on layoff may, if he wishes, retire instead of waiting indefinitely to be recalled. These kinds of voluntary retirements are permitted by an increasing number of pension systems—perhaps two out of three.

When the worker retires early of his own accord, he usually receives a reduced benefit, the actuarial equivalent of the pension he would have been paid if he had retired at the normal age. If the normal benefit at age sixty-five is $2.50 a month for each year of service, that amount would be reduced by 0.5 per cent for each month under age sixty-five that the retirement took place. The man with twenty years of service would receive a $50 monthly pension if he waited to retire until he was sixty-five years old. If he retired at age sixty, however, his pension would be 30 per cent less, or $35 a month. This private pension income, moreover, could not be bolstered by social security benefits until the retiree was at least sixty-two years old. In an effort to maintain the same total amount of pension income throughout the retirement period, an increasing number of private retirement plans are incorporating level income options in their benefit provisions.

Encouragement of Early Retirements. Some company and industry retirement systems not only allow but encourage older employees to retire early. Under certain circumstances, these systems pay normal or above-normal benefits to early retirees. While the number of such arrangements is still relatively small, there has been a developing trend in recent years to provide these financial incentives—often called

"nudge factors"—for older workers to leave their employment. Characteristically, these programs are found in industries where labor needs are declining, where workers are displaced because plants are being closed or moved to new locations, and where income protection is exchanged for modifications in work rules.

The coal mining industry offers an early example of this development. Under the Welfare and Retirement Fund, which was set up in 1946, members of the United Mine Workers of America are able to retire at age sixty if they have had twenty years of employment in the industry and meet other eligibility requirements.[52] Hospital and medical benefits are available to pensioners and their families in addition to the retirement benefits.

Long-service employees of some firms are able to retire ahead of schedule under special early retirement provisions when plants are closed down or facilities moved to new locations. Under such conditions, workers can usually retire at an earlier age than the workers who retire voluntarily, and these displaced workers customarily receive higher benefits than those paid the voluntary retirees. The Armour plan, for example, allows workers who have been with the firm twenty years or longer and who are at least fifty-five years of age to retire with benefits which are one and one-half times their full pensions if plants or departments in which they are employed close down. When such a worker reaches age sixty-two and can begin to draw reduced social security payments, his private pension benefit drops back to the normal amount. If an Armour worker retires of his own choice, however, he must be at least sixty years of age. Moreover, his pension benefit is reduced actuarially from the normal amount.[53]

Several company plans in the steel industry pay normal pension benefits for life to persons

[52] Kennedy, *Automation Funds* (n. 14), pp. 31–34. For some years pensions of $100 a month were paid. Beginning in 1961, however, the monthly benefits were reduced to $75 because of the worsening financial condition of the fund.

[53] *Digest of One-Hundred Selected Pension Plans under Collective Bargaining, Spring, 1961,* Bulletin No. 1307 (Bureau of Labor Statistics, Department of Labor, Washington, D.C., January, 1962), p. 8.

retiring early because of the shutdown of the plants or departments in which they work. To qualify, these workers must be fifty-five years of age or older and must have had at least twenty years of service.[54]

The West Coast longshoring industry offers one example of the use of early retirement benefits to obtain labor's co-operation in the installation of mechanized equipment and processes.[55] In exchange for allowing the shipowners and stevedoring companies a relatively free hand to mechanize, to eliminate restrictive work practices, and to introduce new methods, the International Longshoremen's and Warehousemen's Union (ILWU) gained for its members a number of benefits. Important among them was early retirement pay.

The regular pension plan negotiated between the Pacific Maritime Association (PMA), representing the employers, and the ILWU does not allow retirement before age sixty-five. The Mechanization and Modernization Fund, established as a part of the 1960 PMA-ILWU agreement, supplements the regular pension system by making it possible for workers to retire as early as age sixty-two. Longshoremen who were union members at the time the contract was signed are entitled to compensation for the work rules which were relinquished when the ILWU agreed to the modernization and mechanization program. The loss of accumulated rights for longshoremen when they reach age sixty-five if they have worked on the docks for twenty-five years has been valued at $7,920.[56]

Instead of waiting until he is sixty-five years old to obtain this payment, however, the twenty-five year man may retire as early as age sixty-two and draw all or part of the $7,920 sum in monthly payments of $220. Whatever amount is still due him when he reaches age sixty-five is paid in a lump sum. At this time his regular pension and full social security benefits also begin. Obviously, if he retires at sixty-two he uses up all his "vested rights" by

the time he reaches age sixty-five. If he retires at age sixty-four, however, and hence draws only twelve months of early retirement pay, he is entitled to a lump-sum amount of $5,280 a year later. If a worker dies after he has retired, his beneficiaries are paid the amount still due him—as though it were a piece of property. If he becomes disabled or dies before retirement but after twenty-five years of service, he or his beneficiary receives the $7,920. Workers having less than the twenty-five years of service are entitled to smaller amounts.[57]

The longshoremen's agreement also contains a special provision for compulsory early retirement; workers with twenty-four, twenty-three, or twenty-two years of service can be involuntarily retired at either sixty-two, sixty-three, or sixty-four years of age. In these cases, the retirees receive an extra $100 monthly, or a total of $320, presumably to help make the compulsory retirement more palatable. Their rights are vested, however, in the $7,920 figure only, and the remaining payments which may be outstanding when they reach age sixty-five are the same as those for the men who retire voluntarily.[58]

C. Costs of Early Retirement Plans

Retirement plans are the most costly of the employee benefit arrangements. According to Skolnik, retirement plans in 1961 received the largest proportion of total benefit plan contributions—40 per cent; in firms studied by the Chamber of Commerce, pension plan contributions for 1961 amounted to 4.9 per cent of their payroll.[59] Systems which provide early retirement benefits amounting to more than the actuarial equivalent of normal retirement pay are even more costly. Yet actuarially reduced pension benefits may provide little

54 Davis, "Recent Changes" (n. 47), p. 531.
55 See "Sharing Automation Savings," *Business Week*, October 29, 1960, p. 80.
56 Kennedy, *Automation Funds* (n. 14), pp. 70–101.

57 *Digest of Selected Pension Plans under Collective Bargaining* (n. 40), pp. 70–71. The right starts vesting after fifteen years of service and is fully vested after twenty-five years.
58 Max D. Kossoris, "Working Rules in West Coast Longshoring," *Monthly Labor Review* (January, 1961), pp. 6–7.
59 Skolnik, "Growth of Employee Benefit Plans" (n. 47), p. 8; *Fringe Benefits, 1961* (n. 42).

incentive for older workers to forfeit their accumulated job rights and interests in favor of younger workers or to permit the introduction of mechanized or automated processes.

Some firms consider the cost of normal or above-normal retirement benefits to be a worthwhile investment. The expenses of early retirement benefits are at least predictable, as against the unpredictable expenses connected with the continuation of restrictive work rules or with the reduction of the work force by attrition.

Funding a pension plan, however, is a long-range endeavor undertaken to furnish retirement income to workers when they reach retirement age. Whether or not the system can be adapted to take care of early retirements depends in part upon the volume of the early retirements and their timing. A trickle of workers retiring ahead of time would present quite a different cost picture from that of a sizable and steady number of workers retiring early.

The kind of pension funding which has been developed in the West Coast longshoring industry suggests that a separate system to finance early retirements might be devised to meet special situations of worker displacement. In that way, not only would the objectives of the regular pension system be kept intact, but there would also be a control on the financing of the plan. The benefits and the qualifications under the two systems could be distinct, reflecting the different purposes of each of the systems.[60]

D. RELATIONSHIP OF EARLY RETIREMENTS TO SOCIAL INSURANCE PROGRAMS

The federal social security program has moved more slowly in providing for early retirement than have some private pension plans, perhaps in part because of the somewhat different objectives of each. Although the public system essentially continues as a regular retirement program, beginning in 1961 the social security program has allowed both men and women to qualify for retirement payments as early as age sixty-two with actuarially reduced benefits.[61]

The early retirement provisions in the private industry plans, however, are often designed so that the benefits furnished dovetail with those paid under the public system. Extra benefits are paid until the retirees can qualify for social security, when the private pension benefits drop back to normal. Some of the plans in the meatpacking industry, for example, pay above-normal benefits until workers reach age sixty-two and can qualify for reduced social security payments. In some of the plans in the automobile industry, early retirees receive supplemental benefits until they reach age sixty-five and can qualify for full social security benefits.

The relationship between pension benefits and those paid under the public system of unemployment insurance is considerably more complex. Traditionally, public and private retirement plans have been thought of as furnishing basic income maintenance to workers who have retired from the labor force. Unemployment insurance, in contrast, has been considered to be a program for providing income maintenance to workers who have lost their jobs but are still in the labor market. In the early days of unemployment insurance, it was extremely uncommon for retirement benefits to be paid to older workers who were released from their jobs but were not ready to quit working. The traditional distinction between pensions and unemployment benefits is reflected today in the unemployment insurance laws of a number of states.

---

[60] For a discussion of the relative advantages of some special kinds of funds, see Kennedy, *Automation Funds* (*n.* 14), especially pp. 348–52. The growing use of funds for employee benefit programs is noted in Sumner H. Slichter, James Healy, and E. Robert Livernash, *The Impact of Collective Bargaining on Management* (Washington, D.C.: The Brookings Institution, 1960), pp. 381–84, 477–81.

[61] The California Labor Federation is on record as favoring optional retirement under the Social Security Act at age sixty with normal benefits increased by 25 per cent. The federation gave as its reason the displacement of manpower by automation and mechanical procedures. See Resolution No. 265 in *Resolutions, Part 2, Daily Proceedings* (Fourth Convention of the California Labor Federation, AFL–CIO, Long Beach, California, August 20, 1962).

These laws provide for paying retirees the difference between the weekly jobless benefits and the weekly prorated retirement benefits—social security or private plan benefits or both.[62] An important concept expressed in these laws as well as in discussions favoring such legislation is that persons receiving retirement benefits are presumed to have retired from work. Certainly it is justifiable to consider that the person who retires of his own accord has withdrawn from the labor force, at least at that time. But the man who receives early retirement pay because his job has been eliminated, or the man whose company requires him to retire when he reaches the prescribed age is in a quite different situation from that of the man who chooses to stop working.

While this chapter does not permit a full discussion of the complex relationship between unemployment insurance and pension benefits, it should be noted that private pension income is usually not so high that it makes withdrawal from the labor force attractive or, in many cases, even feasible. It would appear that as early retirement comes to be used increasingly to aid older displaced workers, state unemployment insurance statutes will be modified to recognize that a man may "retire" from a job but still not "retire" from the labor market.

E. THE OUTLOOK FOR EARLY RETIREMENT
PROVISIONS

As in the case of severance pay, an increase of early retirement plans is in prospect. The steady shift in emphasis from job security to

income security in collective bargaining argues for the extension of this benefit. So, too, does the mounting social pressure against the restrictions which work rules place upon economic change. With early retirement provisions already incorporated in the collective bargaining agreements of a number of pattern-setting industries, other industries can be expected to follow suit. Moreover, there is growing recognition of the gap in our social security system which causes the plight of the older jobless worker who has used up all his unemployment insurance benefits but is too young to qualify for social security. Where it is feasible to do so, private industry plans will be developed to fill this gap.

Beyond the spread of early retirement benefit protection to workers still not covered, there is the likelihood of a broadening of some of the features of early retirement plans. The normal or above-normal early retirement benefits that are now provided by a number of plans are generous in comparison with the actuarially reduced benefits in other plans; but the benefits are still usually not high enough to serve their purpose as "nudge factors"—that is, providing incentives for early retirement. Thus, if the early retirement benefits are to meet the objectives for which they are designed, there must be some increase in allowances.

Part of this increase may take the form of a continuation of group life insurance and medical care protection for early retirees and their families, with the company or industry paying a part or all of the costs. In recent years there has been a steady increase in the number of retirees covered by health and welfare plans, but the great majority still do not have this protection.

Another prospect is a lowering of the age and length of service requirements for displaced workers retiring early. The growing recognition of the "no man's land" of older jobless persons, who cannot find new work but are too young to retire, may well prompt more liberal eligibility requirements.

It can be expected that in the next few years management and labor will experiment with various early retirement provisions related to

---

[62] States which reduce the unemployment insurance benefit awards of persons who receive retirement pay are Alabama, Arkansas, Colorado, Connecticut, Delaware, Idaho, Illinois, Indiana, Iowa, Louisiana, Maine, Michigan, Minnesota, Missouri, Montana, Nebraska, New Hampshire, New York, North Dakota, Ohio, Oklahoma, Oregon, Pennsylvania, South Dakota, Tennessee, Texas, Utah, West Virginia, and Wisconsin. Also, the federal Temporary Extended Unemployment Compensation Act of 1961 called for reducing the weekly extended benefit whenever the claimant received a pension contributed to or provided by a base-period employer. However, while the weekly benefit was reduced, the amount of the total award remained unchanged; thus, such a claimant could draw temporary extended unemployment compensation benefits for a longer period than could other claimants.

particular industry situations. The future growth of such provisions, however, will be somewhat limited. Some firms and industries do not have a pressing need for this particular device; others cannot afford it. It seems, therefore, that programs to encourage early retirements will be confined to special situations of worker displacement.

IV. INDUSTRIAL RELATIONS PRACTICES IN AID OF THE UNEMPLOYED

In addition to the income security programs discussed above, labor and management groups have been experimenting with various other ways of easing the problems of the permanently terminated worker. Some of these efforts have been one-time measures for special displacement situations. Others have been broader in scope and have had considerable continuity.

Special employment services have been provided by some firms to help released employees find new jobs when plants close down or the work force is cut. Experience with this measure indicates that success depends in part upon prevailing labor-market conditions in the area and also upon the occupational demand for the kinds of workers being released. The amount of lead time available for planning the placement efforts and making referrals for job interviews also governs the effectiveness of the measure. Often, too, careful co-ordination with the public employment service has aided the company placement efforts.

Many firms give employees advance notice of permanent release. Such warning tends to lessen the shock of dismissal and allows the worker some opportunity to arrange his personal finances and to look for another job. The advantages of advance notice of dismissals are ably demonstrated in Louis A. Ferman's study of workers' adjustment to job loss.[63]

Some of the released workers who were contacted in the course of the study commented that they would not have embarked on major expenditures, such as taking a vacation or buying a new car, if they had had any warning that the firm was going to close down. Others regretted having turned down jobs in other companies before they knew that their company was going out of business.

Among other industrial relations practices designed to soften the impact of terminations are joint labor-management efforts to ease the displacement problems. The co-operative efforts of Armour and Co. and the Meat Cutters and Packinghouse Workers have been referred to earlier. Other companies and unions, including some in the automobile and steel industries, also have set out to give constructive consideration to worker displacement and other industrial relations problems.

A somewhat broader labor-management effort, not limited to developments in a single company or industry, was initiated early in 1962 by the U.S. Industries, Inc., and the International Association of Machinists. The joint Foundation on Automation and Employment, Inc., was established to develop effective and workable ways of easing automation's impact on displaced workers. Initial research projects of the foundation include study of the desirability of the shorter workweek and examination of the steps taken in Europe to resolve problems connected with employee displacement in the Common Market countries.[64]

The problem of helping workers who are permanently terminated, always a complex one, has been intensified by the rising job attrition of recent years. Because no generally satis-

---

[63] Death of a Newspaper: The Story of the Detroit Times (Kalamazoo, Michigan: The W. E. Upjohn Institute for Employment Research, April, 1963), pp. 12, 34. Recommendations for "adequate lead time"

and "open reporting to the employees" were among the measures advocated in the report by the President's Advisory Committee on Labor–Management Policy, The Benefits and Problems Incident to Automation (Washington, D.C.: Government Printing Office, January 11, 1962), p. 6.

[64] The purpose of the foundation and the blueprint of research efforts are outlined in "The Challenges and Opportunities of Automation," address by John I. Snyder, Jr., co-chairman of the foundation, before New York University's Fifteenth Annual Conference on Labor, June 12, 1962.

factory solution for compensating displaced workers has been found, the situation calls for experimentation with numerous approaches. In the search for ways to resolve the problem, private industry has the advantage of flexibility to devise different approaches and to test different means under a variety of conditions of worker displacement. Some of the solutions for coping with this complex problem of helping permanently released workers may result from the experimentation that is being done by private industry.

CHAPTER 8

Area Redevelopment
*William H. Miernyk**

I. INTRODUCTION

THE FAILURE OF the American economy to achieve "full" employment in recent years has led to various policy prescriptions for reaching the goals enunciated in the Employment Act of 1946. Some economists have attributed recent high-level unemployment to inadequate demand. Others have stressed the supply side of the labor-market equation. They have argued that the major cause of unemployment is the inability of the work force to adapt to structural changes in the economy, partly because of institutional barriers.[1] Both approaches treat unemployment in aggregate terms; they fail to differentiate among various types of unemployment.[2] And the nation's policy-makers have not been persuaded that either approach fully explains the recent high level of joblessness. As a consequence, public policy has not been wedded to a single line of attack on unemployment.

The major purpose of the 1964 tax cut was to stimulate demand with the objective of reducing unemployment. As James Tobin has pointed out, however, the demand stimulant, while necessary, is by no means sufficient to eliminate long-term unemployment.[3] A variety of policies have been proposed or adopted to aid specific groups of the unemployed. The discussion in this chapter is limited to one of these policies—aid to depressed areas. It is thus concerned with one type of unemployment, chronic localized unemployment, which is part of the broader class of *structural* unemployment.[4]

The first postwar recession, 1948–49, was relatively mild and of short duration. By the end of 1949 recovery was underway, and by mid-1950 economic activity had again reached a high plateau. The impact of the recession was far from even, however. Some areas and some industries were hit much harder than others. And when recovery came, it also was uneven. The national unemployment rate dropped to a peacetime low during the early nineteen-fifties, but it remained high in a number of industrial and mining areas. In 1955, a year of rapid recovery from the second postwar recession, a dozen of the nation's major labor-market areas reported unemployment rates of 10 per cent or more. And in a number of smaller areas the unemployment rate was in excess of 20 per cent.[5]

* Director, Bureau of Economic Research, Institute of Behavioral Science, University of Colorado.

[1] See, for example, *Higher Unemployment Rates, 1957–60: Structural Transformation or Inadequate Demand*, Subcommittee on Economic Statistics, Joint Economic Committee (Washington, D.C.: Government Printing Office, 1960).

[2] For an excellent discussion of the various types, see *Unemployment: Terminology, Measurement, and Analysis*, Subcommittee on Economic Statistics, Joint Economic Committee (Washington, D.C.: Government Printing Office, 1961).

[3] "Tax Cut Harvest," *The New Republic* (March 7, 1964), p. 16.

[4] Structural unemployment, as the term is used here, means long-term unemployment resulting from all types of structural changes in the economy. It can be caused by shifts in demand, the relocation of industry, changing technology, and other changes which result in the displacement of labor. Use of the term does not mean acceptance of the *structural transformation* hypothesis discussed in the study referred to in note 1.

[5] William H. Miernyk, *Depressed Industrial Areas—A National Problem* (Washington, D.C.: National Planning Association, 1957), pp. 10–11.

The persistence of localized unemployment became an object of congressional concern as early as 1955, and various committees or subcommittees in the Senate and House of Representatives held hearings on the causes of high-level unemployment during periods of "full employment" in the nation as a whole.[6] These investigations, as well as studies by a number of independent scholars, revealed that thousands of workers were victims of the kinds of change that are inherent in a dynamic economy. Migration of industry, depletion of resources, technological change, shifts in demand, and increased foreign competition were among the forces creating hard-core unemployment in many local areas.

In an earlier day it had been widely believed that such unemployment was self-liquidating. It was assumed that as economic activity in a community declined wages would be depressed. This was supposed to attract new employers to these localities and at the same time stimulate the outmigration of workers who would search for employment elsewhere. During the nineteen-fifties, however, a series of local labor-market studies revealed that displaced workers —especially those who are middle-aged or older—are much less mobile than was commonly believed in the past.[7] There was growing recognition that market forces alone would not eliminate hard-core localized unemployment. Community leaders realized that positive steps would be required to halt the economic decline in some areas. Thus the earliest redevelopment programs were initiated by local groups. In a few cases local organizations were able to obtain at least a modest amount of state aid.

A. State and Local Industrial Development Activities

The most ambitious attempt to provide state aid to depressed areas was the Pennsylvania Industrial Development Authority Act (PIDA) of 1956. The PIDA was authorized to make loans, covering as much as 30 per cent of the cost of projects, to local industrial development agencies in Pennsylvania. A modest revolving fund of $5 million was set up to get the program started.

Another example of redevelopment efforts at the state level is the New Hampshire Industrial Park Authority, established in 1955. The Authority assists in the development of prepared industrial sites by means of a revolving fund, which is replenished each time a site is sold. A somewhat different approach—the establishment of industrial building authorities —was followed in Maine and Rhode Island. The Maine authority was established in 1957, and that in Rhode Island a year later. Essentially, these authorities pledge the credit of the state to guarantee mortgage payments on new industrial plants.[8]

A detailed discussion of local development and redevelopment activities is beyond the scope of this chapter. There are literally thousands of organizations throughout the nation engaged in activities which come under the general heading of redevelopment. Local efforts are not limited to depressed areas, however. Indeed, some of the most aggressive local development organizations are in communities which have experienced rapid growth and periodic labor shortages, at least in certain skills. When Donald Gilmore made his study, in the late nineteen-fifties, he found that there were 312 local redevelopment and renewal agencies in the nation devoted specifically to such activities as urban renewal. He found further that there were 135 area development associations, each covering several communities within a state, engaged in industrial development and related activities. These figures did

---

[6] See Miernyk, "The Incidence of Persistent Unemployment," *Proceedings, 12th Annual Meeting, Industrial Relations Research Association* (December 28, 1959), p. 32.

[7] *Ibid.*, p. 28. See also Leonard P. Adams and Robert L. Aronson, *Workers and Industrial Change* (Ithaca,

New York: Cornell University Press, 1957), and references cited on pages 1 and 23 of that work; and William Haber, *et al.*, *The Impact of Technological Change* (Kalamazoo, Michigan: The Upjohn Institute, September, 1963), pp. 35–43.

[8] For further discussion of redevelopment activities at the state level, see Donald R. Gilmore, *Developing the "Little" Economies*, Supplementary Paper No. 10 (New York: Committee for Economic Development), pp. 49–56; and Miernyk, *Depressed Industrial Areas* (*n.* 5), pp. 32–36.

not include chambers of commerce or local planning groups which also participated in development programs.[9]

In a few cases local development programs were successful from the community point of view. Enough new jobs were created in or attracted to these communities to bring local labor markets into balance. But it soon became apparent that local efforts, even when coupled with state aid, were unable to halt the rise of chronic localized unemployment in the nation as a whole.[10] Although some communities were dropped from the Department of Labor's list of "areas of substantial labor surplus," others were added. And some remained on the list throughout the nineteen-fifties.[11]

From a national point of view local development activities may be at least partly self-defeating. To the extent that such activities create new jobs, they aid both the communities involved and the national economy; but state and local agencies use a substantial part of their limited resources for promotional purposes, and their programs often have led to the relocation of jobs from one part of the country to another.

Those responsible for state and local development necessarily—and understandably—have a limited point of view. They do not think in terms of the *national* unemployment problem; their focus is on the state or community which they serve. If investment can be stimulated which will create new jobs and add to both the local and the national job totals—well and good. But the real object is to add to the job total in the state or community, and if this involves job losses elsewhere—that is unfortunate. State and local industrial development is a competitive game; and to the winners belong the spoils.

9 Gilmore, *Developing the "Little" Economies* (n. 8), pp. 80–85 and 158–62.

10 This is not a criticism of such activities or of the individuals involved. Many public-spirited citizens have given selflessly of their time, and the residents of many communities have raised surprisingly large amounts of money for redevelopment activities. In very few cases, however, have such efforts been able to stem the rising tide of local unemployment, although it can be said that in the absence of state and local development programs conditions in many depressed areas would be worse than they are today.

11 Miernyk, "The Incidence of Persistent Unemployment" (n. 6), pp. 13, 16–17.

B. LIMITED FEDERAL AID

Under the Employment Act of 1946 the federal government was committed to a policy of maintaining "full" employment. But the act is a statement of general principles; it does not contain specific provisions for dealing with such problems as persistent localized unemployment. Various *ad hoc* efforts were made by federal agencies during the nineteen-fifties, however, to come to the aid of surplus labor areas. The most important of these aids were the policy of granting preferential treatment to depressed areas in the award of defense contracts and efforts to stimulate new investment in communities with an excess labor supply by granting the privilege of accelerated tax amortization to firms which would locate or expand in these areas.

Government Procurement Policies. Early in 1952 Defense Manpower Policy No. 4 was announced by the Office of Defense Mobilization—the first major effort to channel government contracts to surplus labor areas. Under this policy the government divided its procurements into two parts. The major part of each procurement was formally advertised, and a contract awarded to the lowest qualified bidder. But some portion of government orders, particularly textile mill products, was set aside for negotiated bids with employers in surplus labor areas. Initially, employers in these areas were forced to meet the lowest bid. But high-cost employers in depressed areas were often unable to meet competitive bids, and as a consequence the policy was amended to permit such employers to be awarded contracts on the basis of the average of all bids submitted.[12]

Manufacturers in relatively low-cost areas objected to Defense Manpower Policy No. 4 almost from the start. And by November, 1953, the pressure of their protests led to revision of the policy. Thereafter, contracts could be negotiated on the set-aside portion of procurements only if firms in surplus labor areas could meet the lowest price bid. The program of "set-asides and bid matching"

12 For further details, see Miernyk, *Depressed Industrial Areas* (n. 5), pp. 38–39.

was nevertheless effective to a limited extent. In fiscal 1962, for example, $142.5 million, or 0.5 per cent of total military procurement, consisted of labor-surplus area and industry set-asides.[13]

Accelerated Amortization. The policy of preferential procurement has been at best a stop-gap measure, although it has had the effect of slowing down the rate of decline in employment in some of the nation's labor surplus areas. A program with somewhat more lasting consequences was designed to encourage investment by granting the privilege of accelerated tax amortization to qualified firms. Certificates of necessity, permitting rapid tax write-offs, were granted to firms engaged in defense work. Under this program seventy-four such certificates were issued to firms which established plants in depressed areas. Once in operation, these plants employed a total of 17,480 workers.[14]

Both the preferential procurement and rapid amortization programs were applicable only to defense activities. Indeed, Frederick H. Mueller, then Assistant Secretary of Commerce for Domestic Affairs and subsequently Secretary of Commerce in the Eisenhower Administration, stated emphatically that it was against the policy of the Department of Commerce to recommend tax amortization certificates for firms in depressed areas unless the proposed investment was directly related to the nation's defense goals.[15] Thus these efforts to create jobs in depressed areas were limited. The justification for whatever aid could be granted was that it contributed to the nation's defense goals, not that it created employment per se in depressed areas.[16]

The preferential procurement and accelerated amortization programs helped bolster the sagging local economies of some of the nation's depressed areas. But only a limited number of goods needed by the military were manufactured in labor-surplus areas. Also, this program was based upon administrative rulings rather than on legislative action. It was thus particularly sensitive to counter-pressures from manufacturers in other areas. Finally, the preferential procurement program did not add to total output. It was merely an effort to allocate work, to a limited extent, on the basis of community needs. The same volume of goods would have been produced in the absence of this program.

Accelerated amortization undoubtedly helped stimulate some new investment and thus had an expansionary effect. Moreover, the direction of plant expansion could be partly controlled. The object was to stimulate growth in areas where there was an abundant labor supply and to discourage expansion in already congested areas. But since this program was tied directly to defense needs, it could not be a completely effective attack on the problem of localized unemployment. A much broader approach was needed—one which was based upon the view that chronic localized unemployment is a national rather than a local or regional problem and which recognized that a national policy would be required to cope with a problem that was becoming increasingly serious throughout the decade of the nineteen-fifties.[17]

---

[13] *Background Material on Economic Aspects of Military Procurement and Supply*, Joint Economic Committee (March, 1963), p. 36.

[14] *Proposal to Promote Industrial Development in Local Areas of Chronic Unemployment Through Granting the Rapid Tax Amortization Privilege to Manufacturers Locating Facilities in These Areas and/or to Local Development Organizations*, ARA, Economic Analysis Division, Memorandum (July 12, 1962), p. 3.

[15] U.S. Congress, Senate Subcommittee on Labor of the Committee on Labor and Public Welfare, *Hearings, Area Redevelopment*, 84th Cong., 2nd Sess., 1956, Part II, p. 836.

[16] Another approach, even more restricted in application, was the location of government offices in areas

of substantial labor surplus. Examples are the Internal Revenue Service offices in Massachusetts and West Virginia. While not linked to the defense effort, this approach also has rather obvious limitations. *Ibid.*, p. 336.

[17] For support of the position that the problem of depressed areas is national in scope and thus one which requires a co-ordinated federal program, see the "Policy Statement" by the National Planning Association Committee on Depressed Areas in Miernyk, *Depressed Industrial Areas* (n. 5), pp. v–ix. Opposition to a program of federal aid to depressed areas came from various conservative groups. For a typical expression of this position, see Guy Waterman, "Adjustment to Localized Unemployment," *American Economic Security* (Washington, D.C.: Chamber of Commerce of the United States, November–December, 1956), pp. 25–39. For other references to the extended debate over federal aid to depressed areas, see "The Incidence of Persistent Unemployment" (*n.* 6), p. 32.

II. AREA REDEVELOPMENT IN GREAT BRITAIN

Localized unemployment is not uniquely an American phenomenon. Other advanced industrial countries—including some which have maintained remarkably low average levels of unemployment—have experienced pockets of hard-core joblessness. Before turning to a discussion of the national program of area redevelopment in the United States, it might be instructive to examine briefly the experience of another industrialized nation which has launched a vigorous attack on localized unemployment.

The British program of aid to depressed areas was started in the nineteen-thirties, at a time when there was chronic mass unemployment in the nation as a whole. In 1934 Parliament enacted the Special Areas Development and Improvement Act, which provided for public works and preferential treatment in the award of defense contracts to firms in depressed areas. Under the Special Areas Reconstruction Agreement Act, passed in 1936, financial assistance was provided to firms willing to locate facilities in the special areas.[18]

In 1937, the Royal Commission on the Distribution of the Industrial Population, better known as the Barlow Commission, was established to make an exhaustive study of the causes of localized unemployment. In its report the commission concluded that the problem was national in character and that its solution "must be sought along the lines of national inquiry and national guidance."[19] By the time the Barlow report was issued, however, war clouds had appeared on the horizon. Under the stimulus of rearmament, the level of unemployment began to recede—slowly at first, but more rapidly as mobilization

was stepped up. Within a relatively short time Great Britain's major concern was not unemployment but how best to use its manpower capabilities in the successful prosecution of the war.

Even before the end of hostilities, Parliament was concerned about the return of mass unemployment under peacetime conditions. In May, 1944, the government issued a White Paper outlining the steps it would take if postwar unemployment became a serious problem. Prominent among these was a series of provisions for dealing with localized unemployment.[20]

The White Paper was a policy statement only, but it was followed after the war by legislation to ensure effective full employment. The first of these laws was the Distribution of Industry Act, passed in 1945. Under this law, and a 1950 amendment to the special areas act, the Board of Trade was authorized to provide limited assistance to firms willing to locate facilities in areas of above-average unemployment. Some firms responded to the inducements to expand in depressed areas, but not enough of them to stop the rising level of unemployment in some older mining and industrial communities. Most firms appeared to be willing to forego the modest government aid available and preferred to locate their new facilities in congested industrial areas such as London and Birmingham.

Until 1947 the government could offer only inducements. In that year, however, the Town and Country Planning Act was passed. Under this law industrial development certificates were required for the construction or expansion of industrial buildings. These were granted by the Board of Trade, which used this authority to limit the expansion of industry in congested areas while urging such expansion in Scotland and Wales, where unemployment continued to be a troublesome problem. Thus negative controls over the distribution of industry were established, and the expansion of industry in depressed areas was somewhat accelerated.

The next significant piece of legislation was

[18] For further details on the prewar program of aid to depressed areas in Great Britain, see the following articles by Miernyk: "British and American Approaches to Structural Unemployment," *Industrial and Labor Relations Review* (October, 1958), pp. 3–19; and "Labor Market Lessons from Abroad," *Labor Law Journal* (June, 1962), pp. 429–38.

[19] *Report of the Royal Commission on the Distribution of the Industrial Population*, Cmd. 6153 (1940), p. 201.

[20] *Employment Policy*, Cmd. 6527 (London: H.M.S.O., May, 1944), published by the Macmillan Company in 1945.

the Local Employment Act of 1960.[21] This law authorized the Board of Trade to engage in a number of redevelopment activities. It was given authority to acquire land and buildings, to construct buildings for prospective industrial tenants, and to make loans or grants to establishments which appeared to be capable of providing permanent employment. This was the most significant area redevelopment legislation in Great Britain since the Distribution of Industry Act of 1945.

During the first three years that the new law was in operation, the Board of Trade supported 406 projects in development areas, involving government expenditures of £80.3 million or about $225 million. As a result of this activity, an estimated 89,500 new jobs were created. The average government expenditure per new job came to £897 or about $2,516.[22]

Between March, 1961, and March, 1962 (the reporting period under the Local Employment Act), unemployment in Great Britain rose fractionally while there was a corresponding fractional decline in the development districts. This might have been due in part to the transfer of some unemployment from the development districts to other areas through migration. But the creation of an estimated 27,000 new jobs in the districts that year also contributed to the shift in unemployment rates.

The following year there was a mild recession in Great Britain. Nationally, unemployment increased 35 per cent, and the unemployment rate rose to 2.1 per cent as compared with 1.5 per cent in the preceding year. In the development districts, however, unemployment went up 42 per cent. The unemployment rate, which had been 3.6 per cent in the 1962 reporting period, rose to 5 per cent. It is estimated that

Board of Trade activities produced 27,000 new jobs that year, the same as in the preceding reporting period. But total unemployment in the districts rose by more than 46,000.[23] It appears that the development districts are more sensitive than the British economy as a whole to cyclical unemployment.

The local employment program has been strongly supported by both of the major political parties in Great Britain. There have been some suggestions, however, that British employment policy might be too narrow. Essentially, this policy consists of two parts: (a) monetary and fiscal policies, designed to maintain adequate effective demand, and (b) the local employment program, designed to create new jobs in development districts through efforts to control the location of industry. It has not been suggested that these policies be abandoned but that they be supplemented. Proposals have been advanced to increase the mobility of labor. This would be accomplished by more vigorous retraining programs to increase occupational mobility and by subsidized travel and housing for workers willing to move out of the development districts.[24]

III. AREA REDEVELOPMENT IN THE UNITED STATES

A. LEGISLATIVE HISTORY OF THE AREA REDEVELOPMENT ACT

Early in 1955 the Senate Committee on Labor and Public Welfare appointed a subcommittee, under the chairmanship of Senator Matthew M. Neely of West Virginia, to investigate the causes of high-level localized unemployment.[25] Later

---

[21] The Distribution of Industry Act was amended in 1958 to permit the Treasury to make loans and grants to firms in depressed areas; but the machinery established to administer the program was unwieldy, and few significant gains resulted from this change in the law. See "Foreign Experience with Structural Unemployment and Its Remedies," *Studies in Unemployment* (Washington, D.C.: Government Printing Office, 1960), pp. 416–17.

[22] *Third Annual Report by the Board of Trade* for the period ended 31st March, 1963 (London: H.M.S.O., July, 1963), p. 8. Dollar equivalents were computed by averaging the 1960–63 exchange rates for the pound.

[23] *Ibid.*, p. 12.

[24] For typical expressions of these views, and the analysis on which they are based, see Laurence C. Hunter, "Employment and Unemployment in Great Britain: Some Regional Considerations," *The Manchester School* (January, 1963), pp. 21–38; Hunter, "Unemployment in a Full Employment Society," *Scottish Journal of Political Economy*, X, 289–304; and H. W. Richardson and E. G. West, "Must We Always Take Work to the Workers?" *Lloyds Bank Review* (January, 1964), pp. 35–48.

[25] U.S. Congress, Senate Subcommittee to Investigate Unemployment of the Committee on Labor and Welfare, *Hearings, Causes of Unemployment in the Coal and Other Domestic Industries*, 84th Cong., 1st Sess., 1955.

that year the Joint Committee on the Economic Report conducted an investigation of low-income families. Testimony dealing with localized unemployment played an important part in these hearings, which provided a wealth of information on the causes of chronic unemployment in the nation's depressed areas and on some of the social and economic consequences.[26]

During the same session of Congress, the first of a series of bills to provide federal aid to depressed areas was introduced by Senator Paul H. Douglas of Illinois. This bill (S.2663) would have established an independent Depressed Areas Administration, which would have been authorized to make loans to firms willing to locate or expand in surplus labor areas. It would have provided also for technical assistance to the communities involved and for supplementary unemployment compensation to displaced workers willing to undergo retraining for new jobs.

During the second session of the 84th Congress, Senator Douglas introduced a substitute bill, under the original designation, which was somewhat broader in scope. It would have provided aid to both industrial and rural redevelopment areas, and would have liberalized the loan provisions in the original bill. This bill was passed in the Senate toward the end of the 84th Congress by a two-to-one majority. But despite numerous concessions to conservative opponents, it failed to get through the House of Representatives.

Between 1956 and 1961 depressed-area legislation was introduced in every session of Congress; in some sessions there were several competing bills. Spokesmen for the Eisenhower Administration in the House and Senate introduced versions of legislation which the administration was to support. Meanwhile, Senator Douglas, joined by other Democratic senators and a few liberal Republicans, continued to press for legislation which would have provided both more generous financial aid than the administration-supported bills and

a separate Area Redevelopment Administration. Two of the bills sponsored by Senator Douglas and his associates passed the Senate and the House only to be vetoed by President Eisenhower.

B. THE SPECIAL COMMITTEE ON UNEMPLOYMENT PROBLEMS

The Special Committee on Unemployment Problems, established by the Senate during the closing days of the 86th Congress, was instructed to make a "full and complete investigation and study of unemployment conditions in the United States, giving particular consideration to areas of critical unemployment for the purpose of determining what can be done to alleviate such conditions. . . ."[27] The committee was not empowered to report a bill nor was it given other legislative jurisdiction. It was given the responsibility, however, of bringing together available data on unemployment in the nation and of hearing the testimony of witnesses on various aspects of the unemployment problem.

Hearings were held in Washington, D.C., where witnesses presented an overview of the problem, with numerous references to the specific problem of chronic localized unemployment. Field hearings were held in such states as Pennsylvania, Michigan, Illinois, Kentucky, West Virginia, Indiana, and Oregon—each of which contained one or more areas of substantial unemployment at that time. The field hearings provided graphic evidence of the extent of localized unemployment and of the hardships which such unemployment engendered.[28]

The special committee concluded its investigation with a series of recommendations, including one that "highest priority be given to the enactment of an effective area redevelop-

---

[26] U.S. Congress, Subcommittee on Low-Income Families of the Joint Committee on the Economic Report, *Hearings, Low-Income Families*, 84th Cong., 1st Sess., 1955.

[27] Senate Resolution 196, 86th Cong., 1st Sess.

[28] U.S. Congress, Senate Special Committee on Unemployment Problems, *Hearings, Unemployment Problems*, 86th Cong., 1st Sess., November 1959–January 1960. See also *Readings in Unemployment* (Washington, D.C.: Government Printing Office, 1960), and *Studies in Unemployment* (Washington, D.C.: Government Printing Office, 1960).

ment program."[29] While the minority members disagreed with the majority on a number of points, they agreed in their conclusion that "it is a matter of prime importance that an area redevelopment bill be enacted and that it contain means for stimulating local effort."[30]

C. THE AREA REDEVELOPMENT ACT OF 1961

During the presidential campaign of 1960, John F. Kennedy had promised that if elected he would urge Congress to provide federal aid to areas of substantial labor surplus. And the first piece of major legislation which he signed into law, on May 1, 1961, was the Area Redevelopment Act.[31]

The ARA is part of a broader program proposed by the Kennedy Administration, and continued by President Johnson, to reduce persistent unemployment in the nation as a whole. There is a major difference between this program and the state and local development activities discussed in an earlier section. State and local organizations judge the success of their programs by their effects on state or local employment and unemployment. Under these programs gains in some areas might be at the expense of other areas. The ARA, however, was not intended to be a device for shifting jobs. Indeed, this is specifically precluded by the act: "Under the provisions of this act new employment opportunities should be created by developing and expanding new and existing facilities and resources rather than by merely transferring jobs from one area of the United States to another."[32]

The Area Redevelopment Act was the first step in a program which recognizes that persistent unemployment is a national rather than a local or regional problem. The objective of the ARA is to create *new* jobs. If jobs can be added in depressed areas without reducing employment elsewhere, both the communities involved and the nation will gain.

This is the criterion by which the success of the ARA is to be judged.

The Area Redevelopment Act established the Area Redevelopment Administration in the Department of Commerce. It set up an advisory policy board made up of five cabinet members and the administrators of the Housing and Home Finance Agency and of the Small Business Administration. A national public advisory committee on area redevelopment, made up of twenty-five members representing labor, management, agriculture, state and local governments, and the public, was also provided for.

An area can be designated as a "redevelopment area" by the Secretary of Commerce if at the time of designation the rate of unemployment (excluding seasonal or other temporary unemployment) is 6 per cent and if the annual average rate of unemployment in the area has been either:

50 per cent above the national average for three of the four preceding calendar years; or

75 per cent above the national average for two of the three preceding calendar years; or

100 per cent above the national average for one of the two preceding calendar years.

Provisions were established for the designation of areas which do not meet the above requirements but where there is an unusually high proportion of low-income families and where there is substantial and persistent unemployment or underemployment. As of December 31, 1963, 1,076 areas were designated as eligible for ARA assistance. They represented an estimated 20 per cent of the nation's population, and accounted for an estimated 27 per cent of the nation's unemployed.[33]

D. THE AREA REDEVELOPMENT ACT IN OPERATION

The principal forms of aid provided by the law are loans to business establishments, loans or

---

[29] *Report of the Special Committee on Unemployment Problems* (Washington, D.C.: Government Printing Office, March 30, 1960), p. 122.

[30] *Ibid.*, p. 182.

[31] Public Law 87–27, May 1, 1961.

[32] *Ibid.*, Sec. 2.

[33] *Area Redevelopment Chartbook, May 1, 1961–December 31, 1963* (Area Redevelopment Administration, Department of Commerce, Washington, D.C.), p. 3.

direct grants for the construction of public facilities which will contribute to economic growth in the affected communities, technical assistance, and provisions for the retraining of displaced workers.

Loans. The ARA is authorized to make loans for any industrial or commercial project in a depressed area, including the construction of new buildings and the remodeling or expansion of existing buildings. Loans cannot be made, however, to provide a firm with working capital or to assist an establishment in moving from one area to another. The ARA must also be assured that the project is designed to provide more than temporary employment, that funds are not available from other sources, and that there is reasonable assurance of repayment. Loans must be repaid within twenty-five years, and assistance provided by the ARA cannot exceed 65 per cent of the aggregate cost of the project. At least 10 per cent of the total cost must be borne by the state in which the loan is made or by any political subdivision of the state. And at least 5 per cent must come from nongovernmental sources in the form of equity capital or of loans repayable only after all federal loans have been repaid. Finally, before a loan can be considered by the ARA, a local redevelopment group in the area involved must submit an over-all economic development plan (OEDP) which meets the approval of the ARA. To finance these loans, Congress authorized a revolving fund of $200 million. Half of this is earmarked for aid to industrial and mining areas and the other half for aid to "rural" low-income areas in which there is substantial unemployment or underemployment.

Loans for Public Facilities. Loans may be made directly to any state or political subdivision of the state to assist in financing the purchase or the development of land or public facilities within a redevelopment area if it can be shown that this will stimulate economic activity in that area. Such loans may be made for a period of forty years. The rate of interest is to be one-quarter of one per cent greater than the rate paid by the ARA to the Treasury. The law stipulates that the total of all such loans

shall not exceed $100 million at any given time.

Grants for Public Facilities. Recognizing that it might be burdensome for communities in economic distress to repay loans for the construction of some types of public facilities (e.g., roads, sewers, water systems), Congress authorized the ARA to make direct grants for land acquisition or development for public use. The project for which the grant is made, however, must be one which will contribute to the development of the community by stimulating economic activity which will provide more than temporary employment. The limit on grants of this kind is $75 million.

Technical Assistance. Congress also authorized an annual appropriation, not to exceed $4.5 million, to provide technical assistance to redevelopment areas. These funds are intended to support various kinds of studies and surveys of the areas in need of assistance to determine their economic potentialities and to provide expert advice to local development groups. The studies may be made by members of the ARA staff or by specialists engaged by the ARA.

Occupational Training. Firms which might consider locating or expanding in depressed areas must be assured of an adequate labor supply. To retrain workers for new occupations, Congress authorized annual appropriations, not to exceed $4.5 million, for the establishment and operation of vocational training programs. An additional $10 million annually has been authorized for subsistence payments during retraining of eligible workers who have exhausted their unemployment compensation.

E. Additional Forms of Aid

Two other forms of aid, which are not necessarily limited to redevelopment areas, may be provided under the terms of the Area Redevelopment Act. Title I of the Housing Act of 1949, as amended by the Area Redevelopment Act, authorizes the administrator to provide financial assistance to local public agencies engaged in renewal activities, including the renewal of blighted industrial and commercial areas. The law also permits urban planning

,rants to depressed areas.   Financial aid may
ie granted provided the community is able to
ibtain funds from other sources covering at
east one-fourth of the cost of the planning
iroject.

The program launched under the Accelerated
'ublic Works Act, signed by President Kennedy
in September 14, 1962, should also be men-
ioned, since operational responsibility under
his act has been given to the Area Redevelop-
nent Administration.   The provisions of this
ict will not be discussed at this point, however,
iince the issue of public works is discussed in the
'ollowing chapter.

When a community no longer meets the
criteria for aid under the ARA, it is not eligible
for further assistance.   The loss of eligibility,
however, will not in any way affect the validity of
contracts previously entered into, and does not
preclude further aid if at some time in the
future the unemployment rate in the area rises
and it once again meets the eligibility requirements.   As of March 6, 1964, thirty-nine areas
which had received ARA assistance had been
terminated, and another thirty-six had been
notified that the termination of designation was
pending.[34]

IV. EXPERIENCE UNDER THE AREA REDEVELOPMENT ACT

Experience under the ARA through April 30,
1964, is summarized in Table 8-1. This
table does not include activities under the
Accelerated Public Works Program.[35] A total
of 478 redevelopment projects was authorized
during this period. Expenditures committed
by the ARA amounted to $227.2 million, and
28,100 persons were actually employed directly

on ARA projects.   It was estimated that this
number would increase to 66,800 direct new
jobs when projects then underway reached
planned levels of operation.[36] Assuming an
employment multiplier of 0.65, the ARA has
estimated that this investment will eventually
result in the addition of about 110,000 direct
and indirect new jobs.[37] During this period
the ARA invested $9.7 million in 305 technical
assistance projects and supported 657 training
projects at a cost of slightly more than $16.8
million.   Almost 30,000 trainees were involved
at an average cost of $560 per trainee, exclusive
of administration costs.   The total investment
through April 30, 1964, amounted to $253.7
million.   Based on the above projection of
direct new jobs, the cost per job would amount
to about $3,800.

A. EVALUATION OF THE AREA REDEVELOPMENT PROGRAM

It is much too early to make anything but
the most tentative evaluation of the area
redevelopment program.   The problem of
chronic localized unemployment did not appear
overnight.   The economic forces creating depressed areas have been operating for a long
time, and it would be unreasonable to expect
substantial mitigation of the problem, much less
a solution, in the short time the ARA has been
in operation.   But area redevelopment legislation was strongly opposed by conservative
groups, notably the U.S. Chamber of Commerce, and the ARA has been under steady

34 ARA News Release 64–44, March 6, 1964.
35 As of January 1, 1964, the ARA had administered
4,646 accelerated public works projects. The value of
these projects, based on the reported percentage of
completion, was estimated at $285.4 million. On-site
employment in December, 1963, amounted to $29,237.
See *Accelerated Public Works Program, Directory of
Approved Projects* (Area Redevelopment Administration, Department of Commerce, Washington, D.C.,
February, 1964), pp. 8–9.

36 The job estimates are based on figures reported to
the ARA by firms which have received ARA support.
The agency has not been in operation long enough to
make final tests of the reliability of these estimates.
Comparisons have been made of anticipated jobs and
actual employment on fifty-seven projects which have
been operating for a year or more.   Job estimates
originally reported amounted to 8,943.   Actual employment on these projects at the end of January, 1964,
came to 9,376.   Much broader coverage and several
years of experience will no doubt be required before
final tests can be made.
37 For a general discussion of the employment
multiplier see Charles M. Tiebout, *The Community
Economic Base Study*, Committee for Economic
Development, Supplementary Paper No. 16, pp. 46–50
and the references cited on page 49.

TABLE 8-1: ARA APPROVED PROJECTS, BY TYPE OF PROJECT, AS OF APRIL 30, 1964

(Dollar amounts in thousands)

States	Industrial and commercial loans			Public facility loans/grants			Technical assistance		Training			Total activity by state[a]		
	No.	Investment	Jobs	No.	Investment	Jobs	No.	Investment	No.	Investment	Trainees	No.	Investment	Jobs
Alabama	11	$1,976	894	13	$1,641	1,356	2	$31	11	$408	1,032	37	$4,056	2,250
Alaska	6	2,426	301	3	1,793	675	9	211	8	202	225	26	4,632	976
Arizona	1	351	95	—	—	—	5	112	4	246	215	10	709	95
Arkansas	8	11,208	1,673	12	4,494	3,031	6	227	28	739	1,205	54	16,668	4,704
California	7	1,518	351	1	458	100	4	140	1	44	24	13	2,160	451
Colorado	1	380	72	—	—	—	3	81	6	92	116	10	553	72
Connecticut	4	4,831	1,738	—	—	—	5	73	11	431	1,037	20	5,335	1,738
Delaware	—	—	—	—	—	—	—	—	—	—	—	—	—	—
Florida	5	3,797	674	—	—	—	6	89	2	62	107	13	3,948	674
Georgia	13	3,136	1,657	9	3,346	1,052	11	363	4	170	343	37	7,015	2,709
Hawaii	2	627	90	1	190	300	—	—	4	45	92	7	862	390
Idaho	5	2,257	290	—	—	—	1	36	4	44	47	10	2,337	290
Illinois	10	2,190	1,119	2	692	775	7	582	24	768	1,482	43	4,232	1,894
Indiana	10	3,901	1,415	6	1,776	1,640	2	83	5	387	522	23	6,147	3,055
Iowa	—	—	—	—	—	—	1	50	1	21	20	2	71	—
Kansas	2	35	15	—	—	—	—	—	4	38	58	6	73	15
Kentucky	21	5,636	1,773	12	13,486	3,636	12	279	47	689	1,431	92	20,090	5,409
Louisiana	11	8,974	2,221	—	—	—	2	17	1	29	30	14	9,020	2,221
Maine	12	9,792	3,528	1	83	200	6	125	16	150	494	35	10,150	3,728
Maryland	4	1,082	772	2	753	1,075	4	32	9	330	511	19	2,197	1,847
Massachusetts	9	3,013	370	2	587	500	7	388	19	516	444	37	4,504	870
Michigan	11	6,673	1,170	5	1,329	596	14	692	45	1,768	2,764	75	10,462	1,766
Minnesota	16	2,410	581	3	3,217	261	19	1,145	11	367	1,197	49	7,139	842
Mississippi	6	2,020	697	2	392	680	4	113	—	—	—	12	2,525	1,377
Missouri	3	1,344	316	3	1,759	335	7	130	6	224	425	19	3,457	651
Montana	1	188	62	2	388	94	9	203	17	261	667	29	1,040	156
Nebraska	—	—	—	—	—	—	—	—	—	—	—	—	—	—
Nevada	—	—	—	1	75	5	2	43	4	91	250	7	209	5
New Hampshire	3	263	87	—	—	—	2	104	—	—	—	5	367	87

State														
New Jersey	3	1,844	280	—	—	—	3	117	642	25	1,473	31	2,603	280
New Mexico	4	823	133	1	118	200	6	128	398	14	817	25	1,467	333
New York	7	3,570	573	2	375	183	4	226	97	3	140	16	4,268	756
North Carolina	7	2,243	935	1	175	b	6	190	607	42	972	56	3,215	935
North Dakota	—	—	—	1	26	17	1	15	190	13	295	15	231	17
Ohio	8	885	294	1	167	195	4	254	331	20	549	33	1,637	489
Oklahoma	15	5,643	1,507	7	12,215	1,650	7	93	876	46	2,028	75	18,827	3,157
Oregon	1	1,307	212	4	1,704	444	6	69	32	2	85	13	3,112	656
Pennsylvania	23	7,575	3,564	15	3,251	2,204	16	764	1,414	43	2,397	97	13,004	5,768
Rhode Island	1	286	110	2	569	1,300	1	37	674	7	791	11	1,566	1,410
South Carolina	4	2,197	507	3	509	750	1	24	74	3	57	11	2,804	1,257
South Dakota	1	381	65	—	—	—	2	61	122	8	222	11	564	65
Tennessee	7	1,513	553	12	2,283	3,067	5	169	587	25	721	49	4,552	3,620
Texas	16	3,290	1,306	2	664	607	11	257	286	21	375	50	4,497	1,913
Utah	5	2,019	504	—	—	—	3	52	—	—	—	8	2,071	504
Vermont	2	119	80	—	—	—	1	c	12	1	96	3	119	80
Virginia	2	101	180	1	26	125	3	52	80	6	250	7	191	305
Washington	7	1,021	215	2	446	206	14	410	1,338	44	2,836	27	1,957	421
West Virginia	12	5,044	1,442	15	30,186	2,906	20	531	740	36	786	91	37,099	4,348
Wisconsin	2	4,513	282	3	183	181	8	272	—	—	—	49	5,708	463
Wyoming	3	3,381	308	—	—	—	1	49	—	—	—	4	3,430	308
American Samoa	1	1,011	130	—	—	—	3	18	35	1	20	5	1,064	130
Guam	—	—	—	—	—	—	—	—	—	—	—	—	—	—
Puerto Rico	9	8,084	1,360	—	—	—	2	58	151	5	340	16	8,293	1,360
U.S. General	—	—	—	—	—	—	32	975	—	—	—	32	975	—
Inactive Totals	4	1,003	—	—	—	—	—	—	—	—	—	4	1,003	—
U.S. TOTALS[d]	326	$137,880	36,501	152	$89,353	30,346	305	$9,674	$16,810	657	29,988	1440	$253,717	66,847

SOURCE: U.S. Department of Commerce, Area Redevelopment Administration.

[a] Number and investment cover all projects: financial assistance, technical assistance and training. Jobs are for financial assistance projects only.

[b] Anticipated jobs included in companion industrial loan.

[c] Less than $1,000.

[d] The sums of the dollar amount for states will not add to the U.S. total because project and state totals are rounded in thousands; the sums of the number of technical assistance projects for states will not add to the U.S. totals because projects extending across state lines are shown in each state.

attack from these groups since it started to operate.[38]   It has also been criticized by others, not generally considered to be in the conservative camp.[39]   Some of the major issues raised by the critics will be considered in the following tentative appraisal of the ARA.

A number of questions might be asked: First, is area redevelopment necessary? What problems have been faced by the ARA? Is it following the right approach to area redevelopment? What has the ARA accomplished? The rationale for an area redevelopment program is that some workers who are displaced by structural changes in the economy are immobile.   A corollary assumption is that some depressed areas have a heavy investment in social capital, which should not be allowed to go to waste.   Given these assumptions, society stands to gain from the creation of *new* jobs in surplus labor areas.

As noted earlier in this chapter, a number of empirical studies have supported the thesis of worker immobility. Some workers, for a variety of reasons, do not respond to the pull of market forces. This is not always because workers are unwilling to move but also because they recognize that age and lack of education or training limit their chances of finding employment elsewhere. Noneconomic forces also contribute to the immobility of some displaced workers. Home ownership, attachment to friends, and family or other community ties are often the cause of unwillingness to move.

The social capital argument does not apply to every depressed area; but there are many communities with a substantial investment in public facilities, and the abandonment of these would involve losses to society. This is not to argue that every depressed area should be rehabilitated. Judgments have to be made on a case-by-case basis. Redevelopment of an area should be attempted only if the social gains will be greater than the losses to society which abandonment of a community would entail.

Even if the above assumptions are granted, area redevelopment is not a simple matter. One of the more obvious limitations is the "voluntary" nature of area redevelopment in this country. Unlike the British Board of Trade, which can exercise negative control over the location of industry, the ARA can use only the positive inducements of industrial and commercial loans, public facility loans or grants, and technical assistance. The community itself must take the initiative. Unless the leaders of a community are able to organize, raise their share of the required capital, and prepare an over-all economic development plan, the ARA is helpless to come to its assistance.

What are some of the more specific handicaps under which the ARA has operated? Space limitations preclude extended discussion, but some of the more significant problems can be mentioned briefly. First, an area redevelopment program can be fully successful only if there is "full" employment in the economy as a whole. The American economy has not approached this condition since 1957. And there are some, including the author, who would argue that we have not had full employment since the Korean War.

Secondly, too much has been expected of the ARA even by many who strongly endorse area redevelopment. To achieve needed support in Congress, coverage of the proposed area redevelopment program was expanded through successive pieces of legislation. As a result, more than one-third of the nation's counties, comprising about one-fifth of its population, can qualify for ARA assistance. The British program, by way of contrast, is largely limited to mining and industrial areas. In 1963 the British special areas accounted for only about 12 per cent of the nation's work force. In addition to having greater administrative authority, the Board of Trade can concentrate its efforts on smaller areas than those designated by the ARA.

There have been delays in processing applications for assistance under the ARA. The

[38] While the U.S. Chamber of Commerce has opposed federal aid to depressed areas, many local chambers of commerce supported the legislation and continue to support the activities of the ARA.
[39] See, for example, Sar A. Levitan, *Federal Aid to Depressed Areas: An Evaluation of the Area Redevelopment Administration* (Baltimore, Md.: The Johns Hopkins Press, 1964).

oint federal-state-local program ensures participation at the local level, but it makes the process of channeling investment funds into local areas a cumbersome one. There have been further delays engendered by the requirement that the ARA work through delegate agencies such as the Small Business Administration. While the ARA Administrator must make the final determination on loan applications, he cannot do so until these have been processed by the Small Business Administration.

There is also the matter of "competing area interests." Perhaps the most important example, although there are others, is that involving Appalachia. This is a region including parts of eight states extending from Pennsylvania to Alabama, and from Maryland to Kentucky. The President's Appalachian Regional Commission (PARC), headed by Undersecretary of Commerce Franklin D. Roosevelt, Jr., was established to study the problems of this region. The ARA provided staff and financial support for the study. The commission has recommended a five-year development program which might involve $3 billion in federal grants and loans. Some critics of the ARA have suggested that regional programs should supplant the present area redevelopment approach. But the PARC proposal is directed toward the improvement of transportation, resource development, community renewal, and educational facilities. ARA activities would be co-ordinated with a massive program of public development. It would have the responsibility for stimulating growth in the private sector. There is no logical contradiction between the two approaches; indeed, they are complementary. Establishment of regional programs would not be a substitute for present ARA activities. The important thing would be to see that there is co-ordination of all programs which have the common goal of providing useful and productive employment to those who are now jobless.

One final problem will be mentioned: criticism of the ARA for supporting service activities, such as tourism, instead of concentrating on manufacturing or other goods-producing activities. This criticism is difficult to understand in view of long-range employment trends. Employment in the service sector has been rising while there has been little change in the level of manufacturing employment over the past decade. The ARA has been given a mandate to create *new* jobs, and its best bet is to do so in expanding sectors. If the ARA is to succeed it must have freedom to generate employment in any sector where there are prospects for permanent new jobs.

B. CONCLUSIONS

Given the above problems, what can be said about the ARA's performance to date? First, and most important, it is too early to make a final appraisal of the area redevelopment program. It is worth repeating that a similar program has been operating in Great Britain since the end of World War II, under much more favorable economic and administrative conditions, without fully solving the problem of chronic localized unemployment. But the British program continues to receive strong support.

The area redevelopment program in the United States should be given a fair trial. Mistakes have been made, and ARA officials are willing to concede this. But there has been sufficient progress to warrant continuation of the program. Within a short time it is anticipated that about seventy communities which have received ARA assistance will no longer be eligible for further assistance. Since 1961 the unemployment rate in the combined redevelopment areas has dropped more rapidly than in the nation as a whole.[40] While this cannot be attributed entirely to area redevelopment activities, since the effects of outmigration also must be considered, it is evidence that the ARA has made progress in its attack on localized unemployment.

The area redevelopment program has not been in operation long enough to permit a realistic appraisal of its potential, but there has been some congressional disenchantment. In 1963

[40] *Economic Growth in American Communities,* Annual Report of the Area Redevelopment Administration (Washington, D.C.: Department of Commerce, 1963), p. 6.

the Senate voted to increase the ARA's appropriation, but this measure did not pass the
House. Instead, authority to make public
facility grants was terminated and loan funds
available to the ARA were curtailed. Congress
will vote on the measure again in 1964, but as
this is written the outcome is uncertain. This
uncertainty is a handicap to the ARA, and to
communities in need of assistance. Without
additional appropriations the program will
expire in June of 1965. This would be unfortunate, since the program will not have had
a fair trial by that time.

The attack on unemployment was stepped up
in 1964. The tax cut was an effort to stimulate
over-all demand. And the President announced
an active manpower policy to assist specific
groups of the unemployed.[41] He requested
continuation and expansion of the area redevelopment program as part of this policy.
Given the structural changes which affect
specific localities, vigorous redevelopment efforts will be required if unemployment is to be
reduced to the minimum levels of seasonal,
cyclical, and frictional unemployment that
are associated with the operation of a free
market economy.

[41] *Manpower Report of the President* (Washington,
D.C.: Government Printing Office, March, 1964),
pp. xiii–xix.

CHAPTER 9

Public Works and Work Relief

Roger A. Freeman*

ON SIGNING THE Public Works Acceleration Act of 1962, President Kennedy called the new law "a significant milestone in our efforts to strengthen the economy and provide a greater measure of economic security to the unemployed." It was, indeed, the first act of Congress since the nineteen-thirties which aimed to create a large number of jobs and to revitalize the economy by a general expansion of public construction. Although the program is just beginning at the present time of writing and it is too soon to judge performance under the 1962 legislation, it will be useful to examine the major issues involved in such a program. This chapter, therefore, after reviewing previous experience in the United States, discusses some perennial problems connected with public works.

When Representative John A. Blatnik introduced H.R. 10113, the bill that later passed the House, he declared: "Of all the devices in the arsenal of public policy designed to cope with unemployment, a public works program is the only one that directly and immediately opens up employment opportunities." He added: "A public works program is not only the direct way to full employment. It is also the most economical one. More jobs are created per dollar of additional public expenditure for goods and services than are created per dollar of tax reduction."[1]

The victory did not come easily, nor by a wide margin. President Kennedy's proposals were the subject of hearings in both Houses at which mostly friendly witnesses were heard. The Senate passed a much-amended public works bill on May 28 (44–32, with 24 not voting) and the House Public Works Committee reported a similar measure less than a week later, overriding a strongly dissenting minority opinion. When informal nose counts in the House suggested the absence of a sufficient number of affirmative votes, action was postponed until the week before Labor Day. After several concessions by the sponsors and much "arm twisting" by the White House and the majority leadership, the bill was scheduled for August 28 and passed 221–192, with 24 not voting.

As it advanced through the congressional machinery the program gradually shrank. The President had submitted a plan that called for $2.6 billion and granted him broad authority. The Senate sharply restricted presidential powers and reduced the amount to $1.5 billion; the House cut it further to $900 million. In the end the 87th Congress appropriated only $400 million, but the 88th Congress appropriated the remainder.

The new law authorizes the President to allocate funds for direct federal construction as well as for grants-in-aid to state and local governments for up to 50 per cent—and in certain cases up to 75 per cent—of the total cost of a planned structure. A project may be located either in a "redevelopment area," so

* Research Associate, The Hoover Institution on War, Revolution, and Peace, Stanford University.
[1] U.S. Congress, House Committee on Public Works, *Hearings, Standby Capital Improvement Act of 1962*, 87th Cong., 2nd Sess., p. 11.

designated by the Department of Commerce (there are presently over 900 such areas, commonly called depressed areas), or in a community whose unemployment rate has been at least 6 per cent for nine of the preceding twelve months (there are presently over 100 such communities). Only construction projects which can be promptly started and substantially completed within twelve months are eligible. Most of the work will be in the areas of water and sewer plants, recreational facilities, streets, and public buildings, excluding schools.

Some feel that the passage of a watered-down public works bill shortly before elections was largely a pacifying gesture by a Congress which had given a cold shoulder to such other contracyclical proposals as a quick tax cut and extended unemployment benefits. The authorized amount certainly will permit only a modest rate of acceleration in public construction, which has risen an average of almost $1 billion annually since the end of World War II. It will not make a significant impact on the 4 million unemployed, the $80 billion construction industry, or on the $550 billion American economy. But it could portend more for the future. Many believe that the 1962 act was merely the first step in a program through which the government will eventually provide hundreds of thousands of additional job opportunities. The question is now whether sentiment for public works expansion to increase employment opportunities is gaining ground and may command more attention in the years ahead than it has for a long time.

I. WHY PUBLIC WORKS?

At first glance, the case for public works expansion in times of heavy, protracted unemployment appears to be overwhelming and self-evident. Social insurance and public assistance can meet the immediate problem of supplying men and their families with money for their essential needs—food, shelter, clothing, medical care—but they do not lift from them the bane of involuntary idleness. Able-bodied men who are forced into leisure for many months or even years deteriorate mentally and

physically. Their self-respect crumbles, their skills fade. Work habits, ambition, positive attitudes toward society, moral principles, and even family cohesion erode, and the bread winner loses face with his neighbors and the members of his household.

Why should able-bodied, involuntarily jobless men who are supported from public funds be left idle for long periods? Why should they not be offered an opportunity—or be required—to earn their keep? Why should not the taxpayers get a tangible and lasting return on their outlay? What better opportunities are there for producing goods which are not directly competitive with the products of other workers' labor, whose production would not jeopardize the job security of others, goods which are not in sufficient demand and would not be forthcoming without a public works program but offer unquestioned value to the community, which pays for them whether it gets them or not? Moreover, may not the expenditures for public works perform a pump-priming function and revitalize the entire economy? Or at least build up the infrastructure of chronic labor-surplus areas and thus rehabilitate their sagging economies?

Finally, the building of public structures has long been a popular method of rulers to keep idle hands from leading to dangerous thoughts which might incite violent action. "Even the building of the Great Pyramid of Egypt and the beautification of the Acropolis under Pericles have been attributed to a desire to make work for the unemployed masses."[2] Public works played a prominent role in the antidepression campaign of the New Deal and set a million hands or more into motion which otherwise might have been idle. Views differ on how much they helped to revitalize the economy.

The study of contracyclical policy intensified in the nineteen-thirties and developed into a veritable science after the passage of the Employment Act of 1946, which called upon the national government "to promote maximum

[2] Arthur D. Gayer, "Public Works," *Encyclopaedia of the Social Sciences*, XI (New York: The Macmillan Co., 1937), 694.

employment, production and purchasing power."

But the student who searches for evidence of contracyclical public works action in the postwar period is in for a disappointment: whatever here was of action—as distinguished from words, written or spoken—was little, late, and ineffective. The economic fraternity, after much analysis, contemplation, and controversy, was obviously disenchanted with the results of public works expansion in the nineteen-thirties and turned to more sophisticated fiscal and monetary techniques for dealing with downturns in the business cycle. There was more or less general agreement that a high rate of gross national product growth was the best way of assuring full employment and that governmental policy should aim "to change the climate rather than to ration raindrops."

To be sure, reports dealing with contracyclical strategy still tend to include public works in a checklist of possible remedial measures. But the authors' hearts do not seem to be in such proposals. The Joint Economic Committee, while approving the President's plans for public works acceleration in March, 1962 ("the proposal would add an important supplement to the arsenal of weapons for fighting recessions"), qualified:

This does not mean that we favor reliance on massive or long-term public works as an effective contracyclical program. On the contrary, our studies have led us to share the general view that such programs are likely to be too slow in starting and too late in ending.[3]

The attention given to public works acceleration proposals in the 1962 session of Congress suggests that the cited "general view" may be weakening and public works action may be gaining favor. Two explanations are possible:

1. Officials who run for elective office and have to watch the ballot box tend to feel more kindly than professional economists toward public works when unemployment is high. General fiscal and monetary techniques may pack more punch than do public works in reviving a sagging economy, but their effect on unemployment is harder to explain. The "man in the street" often is not fully aware of the size and impact of taxation on economic growth nor does he appreciate what the operations of the Open Market Committee, a lowering of margin requirements, more liberal depreciation rules, or changes in discount rates may be doing for him. But he can see the excavations, the rising walls and huge sign boards "Public Works Project of the X Government to Provide Employment." This obtrusive visibility duly impresses him that his government is truly doing something for the unemployed. Besides, there is something immensely satisfying about building permanent structures, as August Heckscher so well described in "Public Works and the Public Happiness."[4] Of the many ways in which Franklin Roosevelt tried to end the great depression, none are as well remembered as the PWA and the WPA.

2. Experience during the early nineteen-sixties weakened faith in the all-redeeming virtue of gross national product growth. President Kennedy voiced a common fear when he warned, "We could have a great boom and still have the kind of unemployment they describe."[5] The increase in the number of long-term unemployed was particularly disturbing. With almost half a million men jobless for over half a year, with technological change proceeding rapidly, and with an unprecedented, impending wave of new entrants (the postwar babies) into the labor force, it seemed to many that more had to be done than to make jobless men eligible for relief under the program of Aid to Families with Dependent Children, which was not designed for and ill fits that purpose.

The record of recent decades, however, provides little assurance that we have thus far developed an effective technique for the alleviation of mass unemployment through public works acceleration. Experience to date

[3] *Annual Report of the Joint Economic Committee, Congress of the U.S., on the January, 1962, Economic Report of the President* (March 6, 1962), p. 92.

[4] *Saturday Review*, August 4, 1962.

[5] *Wall Street Journal*, October 12, 1961, reporting the presidential news conference held on October 11, 1961.

justifies little confidence in this approach to the unemployment problem.

II. THE UNIMPRESSIVE RECORD OF PUBLIC WORKS ACCELERATION

Growing joblessness in the wake of World War I led to the convening of the President's Conference on Unemployment, which recommended, among other things, an expansion of public works. No action ensued and prosperity soon returned anyway—to end abruptly in 1929.

A. THE GREAT DEPRESSION

Within six weeks of the stock market crash President Hoover began action to stimulate construction in order to prime the economy. Federal building volume was then quite small, and an expansion of significant size seemed more feasible and promising in the private and state-local sectors:

Average Annual New Construction 1925-1929

	Million $	Per cent	Per cent of GNP
Federal, direct	113	1%	.1%
Federal, aid to states	83	1%	.1%
Federal, total	$196	2%	.2%
State and local	2,136	18%	2.2%
Private	9,265	80%	9.6%
All new construction	$11,597	100%	12.0%

SOURCE: *Construction Volume and Costs 1915-1956, A Statistical Supplement to Construction Review.*

The President's appeals to business executives, state governors, and mayors received only a modest and temporary response. As the depression continued, private construction shrank to a trickle—a low of $1.2 billion in 1933—and state and local building fell to less than $1 billion a year.

Federal construction expanded rapidly in relative terms, climbing from $235 million in 1929 to $313 million in 1930 and $506 million in 1931. ("Federal construction" throughout

this chapter includes both federal direct construction and federal aid to state and local governments for construction.) But these amounts were too small to make a tangible impact on an economy in a state of collapse. Congress, therefore, appropriated an additional $300 million for federal public works in July 1932, and authorized $1.5 billion in construction loans; a year later it empowered the President to spend up to $3.3 billion for emergency public works.

Federal construction continued to expand and reached a peak of almost $2.4 billion in 1936. This was ten times its volume in 1929 but amounted to an increase of only a little over $2 billion. It compensated for a mere fraction of the shrinkage in other construction and did not help much to offset the decline in the gross national product from $104 billion to $56 billion.

It did put men to work. Site employment of the PWA, at its peak in 1934, exceeded half a million men, and all employment, direct and indirect, created by federal construction spending has been estimated at an average of three-quarter million between 1934 and 1938.[6] McKean and Taylor placed federal direct construction employment (not including work relief) at an average of 3 per cent of the total unemployment in 1934–38 and indirect employment (suppliers, etc.) at another 4.5 per cent.[7]

Under conditions of utter national distress, therefore, when a fourth of the country's labor force was walking the streets, when private construction had all but ceased, and when the size of the budget deficit was deemed irrelevant, the federal public works effort managed to provide jobs for between half a million and a million men.

The record of the nineteen-thirties disillusioned many observers about the efficacy of

[6] John K. Galbraith and G. G. Johnson, Jr., *The Economic Effects of Federal Public Works Expenditures 1933–1938* (National Resources Planning Board, 1940), p. 46; and Eugene C. McKean and Harold Taylor, *Public Works and Employment from the Local Government Point of View* (Chicago: A Report of the W. E. Upjohn Institute for Community Research, Public Administration Service, 1955), p. 115.
[7] McKean and Taylor (n.6), p. 116.

ublic spending in halting an economic decline t a time when the environment is not favorable o an increase in private capital spending. Federal outlays in the fiscal years 1933 through 938 were twice as large as in the preceding six ears. Almost all of this increase was deficit inancing. But unemployment declined only rom an average of 12.4 million in 1932 to 9.9 million in 1938. It finally yielded under the demands of World War II, when federal spending reached almost $100 billion a year nd deficits exceeded $50 billion annually. Contrary to the expectations of most economists, unemployment did not again become a problem until 1949.

B. The Postwar Recessions

The four postwar recessions—in 1949, 1954, 1958, and 1961—were neither as deep nor long-lasting as some of the depressions in the pre-World War I period or in the nineteen-thirties. Much of the credit is commonly given to the 'built-in" stabilizers. Clearly, the declines were not halted or measurably shortened by prompt and effective public works acceleration.

When unemployment approached a rate of 6 per cent in the spring of 1949, the U.S. Public Works Administrator, General Philip B. Fleming, prepared, at the request of the Director of the Budget, a plan for stepping up the public works pace and absorbing workers laid off by a decline in private and state-local construction, should total unemployment reach five million. But unemployment did not reach the five million mark, non-federal construction kept on rising, and federal construction continued its gradual recovery from the war lull without a noticeable spurt. The economy recovered anyway, prospered in the Korean build-up, but reversed itself after demobilization.

The 1954 recession presents a close similarity to events in 1949. When the unemployment rate reached 5.7 per cent in April, 1954, the Council of Economic Advisers established a Public Works Planning Unit under General John S. Bragdon, former deputy chief of Army Engineers. This unit was transferred to the White House Office in 1955 and subsequently drafted numerous acceleration plans. None of the plans was carried out, and the unit was quietly dissolved five years later. The volume of private as well as state-local construction continued to expand through the recession and unemployment period of 1954, while federal construction declined by $700 million from 1953 to 1954 and by another $600 million from 1954 to 1955.

During the 1957 recession federal public works activity was sharply increased. Civil works more than doubled, and the total federal construction volume increased by almost $2 billion between 1956 and 1958. But this was largely coincidental. The budget for the fiscal year 1958, submitted in January, 1957, long before any signs of an economic downturn appeared, had scheduled an even greater works expansion than took place after the unemployment wave hit the country. It aimed to meet facility needs, not to absorb unemployment.

The President referred to widespread unemployment when asking for increased federal allocations to the interstate highway system early in 1958, and Congress granted them promptly. Highway fund allocations to the states were raised from $362 million in the third quarter of 1957 to $643 million in the third quarter of 1958. But they reached $1.1 billion in the third quarter of 1959, when unemployment had been declining and the economy moving upward for over a year. How much they contributed to recovery has remained controversial.

The staff report to the Joint Economic Committee concluded after extensive hearings on "Employment, Growth, and Price Levels" in 1959: "The 1957/58 recession offers persuasive evidence of the ineffectuality of increasing public expenditures to deal with recession. Although enacted early in the recession, many of these increases did not in fact occur until recovery was well along." [8] During the recession of 1961, when unemployment rose to its

[8] *Staff Report on Employment, Growth, and Price Levels*, prepared for consideration by the Joint Economic Committee (86th Cong., 1st Sess., 1959), p. 264.

highest level since the nineteen-thirties, no material increase took place in federal construction, and all other construction remained stable.

C. ARE PUBLIC WORKS AN EFFECTIVE CONTRACYCLICAL TOOL?

Much searing comment has been made on the inadequate contracyclical action by the national government at times when the storm signs were up. But little of the criticism was directed at the absence of effective public works acceleration, which was held to be of limited utility. Economists, with the experience of the nineteen-thirties in mind, generally agreed with the views expressed by two congressional committees. In 1944: "The federal government should be fully prepared to participate in *holding* construction at a level that can be sustained without courting sudden deflation in the industry."[9] And in 1952: "The function of public works was redefined in the narrower terms of *leveling out the swings in the construction industry* with the limited objectives of achieving a better use of construction resources and *neutralizing* the effect of construction as only one factor in the general economic cycle."[10]

Two conferences of the National Bureau of Economic Research, sponsored by the Committee for Economic Development, in Princeton in 1953 and 1954, dealt extensively with matters indicated by the subsequent report, *Policies to Combat Depressions* (Princeton University Press, 1956). One of the fourteen papers covered "Self-liquidating Public Works," a small segment of total public construction. There were only a few other fleeting references to public works. "The selection of subjects," commented the editor, "reflects, in part, the planning committee's estimate of relative importance."

The National Planning Association published a volume *The Employment Act, Past and Future: A Tenth Anniversary Symposium* (1956), in which

not one of the thirty-five contributors discussed the potential of public works. The Special Committee on Unemployment Problems of the U.S. Senate asked fifteen eminent scholars to prepare papers for a volume *Studies in Unemployment* (86th Congress, 2nd Session, 1960). None dealt with public works. However, the committee itself did include advance authorization and acceleration of public works among its recommendations.

The Joint Economic Committee held extensive hearings on *Employment, Growth, and Price Levels* in 1959. None of the twenty-three study papers is devoted to public works, nor does the comprehensive index to the 3,486 pages of testimony contain any reference to the subject.

Even the construction industry's journal *Engineering News Record* stressed "the limited value of public works construction as a depression reliever" in a strongly negative editorial, "Public Works No Panacea" (January 7, 1960).

The American public appears to agree with the economists. When asked in a Gallup Poll (August 5, 1962) about their preference between a tax cut and government spending for public works if the government were to take action to improve the business situation in the country, 59 per cent voted for a tax cut, 28 per cent for public works. But 71 per cent opposed a tax cut if it meant the government would go further into debt.

Two major studies within the past decade have dealt more thoroughly with the use of public construction for antirecessionary purposes. Miles L. Colean and Robinson Newcomb focused, as their book's title indicates, on *Stabilizing Construction.*[11] They carefully evaluated the possibility of expanding public construction in times of sharp decline in private construction. They concluded that public works could not be expanded enough to compensate for a large decline in private investment and that "public works is not a tool which ordinarily can or should be used at an early stage of a decline, whether the decline is a minor one or the precursor of a major depression."[12]

[9] *Postwar Economic Policy and Planning, Seventh Report of the House Special Committee on Postwar Economic Policy and Planning* (House Report 852, 79th Cong., 1st Sess., 1944), p. 2. Emphasis supplied.
[10] *The Sustaining Forces Ahead*, materials prepared for the Joint Committee on the Economic Report (82nd Cong., 2nd Sess., 1952), p. 66. Emphasis supplied.

[11] New York: McGraw-Hill Book Co., 1952.
[12] *Ibid.*, pp. 289–90.

They believe that "public works should not be used unless construction itself is down seriously and has been down for possibly a year."[13]

The most thorough study of the contracyclical potential of public works was conducted under the auspices of the W. E. Upjohn Institute for Community Research by Eugene C. McKean and Harold C. Taylor. In the foreword to their book *Public Works and Employment from the Local Government Point of View*, William Haber summarized their conclusions:

> Their findings raise serious doubts as to the potency of timed public works in alleviating the evils of cyclical contraction. The authors also question whether this method is the most effective way to deal with unemployment relief. Even allowing for the full effect of the multiplier and pump-priming, they conclude that a program to stabilize state and local public works would influence the course of the economy to an insignificant degree.[14]

The authors are also doubtful about the effectiveness of public works expansion by the federal government and suggest "that the needy unemployed can be reached in far greater numbers by general assistance and work relief programs than by public works programs."[15]

In summary: There appears to be a broad consensus among scholars and practitioners who have devoted much study to the subject that the potential of public works to absorb a significantly large number of the unemployed

[13] *Ibid.*, p. 301.
[14] Public Administration Service, Chicago, Illinois, 1955, p. v.
[15] *Ibid.*, p. 233.

in a recession, or to stem the recession itself, must be rated low and ranks far behind the potency of general fiscal and monetary methods of revitalizing the economy and providing employment. Ewan Clague, director of the Bureau of Labor Statistics, expressed the prevailing opinion: "As a result [of the experience in the nineteen-thirties] more thought was given after World War II to the idea of establishing long-range public works programs and maintaining *stability* in these programs rather than attempting to use them to *counterbalance* changing business conditions."[16] The postwar period produced greater stability in public works and in other construction than in unemployment rates or in the economy as a whole. This explains, in part, why public works were used so little as a contracyclical tool. But there are many other limitations to the effective use of public works.

III. POTENTIAL AND LIMITATIONS OF PUBLIC WORKS ACCELERATION

Although construction is one of the most conspicuous activities of government, its leverage on the nation's economy is not as great as is widely believed. Public construction equals slightly over 3 per cent of gross national product and provides direct jobs for about 1.5 per cent of the civilian labor force. Even if we consider the multiplier effect, this is a narrow base from which to absorb a significant part of

[16] *Encyclopaedia Britannica*, XXII (1961), 688b. Emphasis added.

New Construction in 1962 (est.)	billion	per cent of GNP
Total	$61.2	11.1
Private	43.7	7.9
Residential	25.1	4.5
Other private	18.6	3.4
Public	17.6	3.2
Defense	1.7	.3
Civil	15.9	2.9

Civil Public Construction in 1962 (est.) (by source of funds)	billion	per cent
Total	$15.9	100.0
Federal	4.7	29.2
Direct	2.2	13.8
Grants-in-aid	2.5	15.4
State and local	11.2	70.8

Computed from: *Construction Review*, November, 1962.

unemployment that has been running at 5 per cent or more of the civilian labor force for five years.

A. JURISDICTION AND FINANCING

Authority over public construction is widely dispersed and jealously guarded. Excluding defense work, which cannot well be timed to coincide with the business cycle, state and local governments constructed in 1962, 86 per cent of all public works and supplied 71 per cent of the funds. They have been increasing their capital outlays—by boosting taxes and debts—at a spectacular rate. But they are not likely to do so in a major downturn. Voters don't feel like approving bond issues and increasing debts at a time of general belt-tightening.

In 1954 I testified before the Joint Economic Committee:

> State and local officials generally feel that it is their responsibility to take care of the needs in those areas which are traditionally state and local functions. . . . But they regard the maintenance of maximum employment and a high level of production—to the degree to which this is a government obligation—as a responsibility of the federal government . . . they are not very likely to engage in advance action to raise their rate of spending to prevent a potential lack of buying power. The level and trend of the national economy are a national problem which requires a national solution.[17]

Most of the funds for public works acceleration in an economic downturn would have to be provided by deficit federal financing.

To employ a significantly large percentage of the jobless on public construction would call for a dramatic increase in the rate of federal activity. Federal civil work funds (direct and aid) would have to be doubled to offset a 10 per cent decline in private construction and more than doubled to compensate for a one percentage point increase in the unemployment rate.[18]

Congress does not easily or quickly vote new funds of that magnitude. Not that a budgetary deficit as such is much of a deterrent, particularly when business is slow. Deficits have been the rule rather than the exception for one-third of a century. But more thought is being given to the cost of new programs and to the size of deficits since the balance of payments and the international value of the dollar have become matters of concern. Questions are being raised whether more idle men could be put to work by using available funds for programs other than public works expansion.

Most public works activities are in fields which traditionally have been state and local responsibilities. The range and size of federal operations in those fields were sharply expanded in recent decades, usually in order to cope with some sort of emergency, either war or depression. Such measures often are not repealed after the emergency has passed; they tend to become permanent and to shift the balance in our federal system increasingly toward the national government. Congressmen who are ideologically opposed to ever-growing concentration of governmental power deem such further centralization too high a price to pay. They may not be able to halt or reverse the trend, but they can delay action long enough to make it useless in fighting an economic downturn.

In order to reduce or eliminate such delays inherent in the congressional authorization and appropriation process, proponents of public works acceleration have suggested that the President be granted "standby authority." Such plans meet resistance from members of Congress of both parties who have had personal experience with the use to which presidential power may be put in the allocation of funds and the location and timing of projects. The minority is afraid that some legislators or certain localities will be rewarded by the approval of projects for voting "right" and others punished for a dissenting vote or for electing the "wrong" man. The majority floor

---

[17] U.S. Congress, Joint Committee on the Economic Report, *Hearings, January 1954 Economic Report of the President*, 83rd Cong., 2nd Sess., 1954, p. 489.

[18] Private construction, at $44 billion in 1962, equaled about nine times the federal civil public works volume. At an average rate of 100 jobs for every

$1 million spent in construction, it would require an additional $7 billion to employ 700,000 workers, equal to 1 per cent of the civilian labor force.

leader for the Public Works Acceleration Act found it necessary to put through the Senate an unprecedented unanimous-consent request: "That the RECORD reflect it to be the sense of the Senate that this bill be administered on a basis that will be free of any partisan favoritism by any agencies of government having responsibilities under it." Since the act charges the President with making the allocations, this request was almost like asking the President to kindly observe his oath of office.

Colean and Newcomb commented a decade ago:

> The real question is not whether public works can be handled administratively or economically. It is whether they can be handled politically. Much leeway must be given the executive if the task is to be handled well. Yet the Congress is understandably hesitant to give much leeway: leeway means opportunity for abuse. It means opportunity for the executive to put pressure on the Congress. It means giving up more of the control over the purse strings. It may be necessary at times, but it is dangerous. The Congress does not want to do this if it can be avoided.[19]

B. NEEDED: MORE PLANS AND BLUEPRINTS?

Lack of ready plans and specifications in the nineteen-thirties delayed many construction projects for which funds and manpower were available. So the demand arose for a "shelf" of plans to be prepared in advance and held in readiness at all times. Federal departments have been planning their capital improvements for six years ahead ever since 1942. The Housing Act of 1954 (sections 701 and 702) authorized planning grants and advances, and the Public Works Planning Unit of the White House tried for some years to stimulate more long-range planning by state and local governments. A Census Bureau survey in 1960 revealed plans in different stages of readiness for 88,174 capital projects by state and local governments, with a construction value of $30 billion.

Close study suggests that long delays often

[19] Colean and Newcomb, *Stabilizing Construction* (n. 11), p. 305.

are caused not by the absence of a plan, but by the existence of several plans or ideas concerning what should be built. Few highways, schools, or water projects have been long retarded merely by a lack of blueprints; but some have been postponed for years while local fights were raging over where the road should run, who needed how much water, whether the school should have a gym or a swimming pool, whether present facilities were efficiently used to provide a good education, whether the new school ought to follow the 8-4 or the 6-3-3 plan, or whether the school should be located in the center of a homogeneous population or on the boundary between different socio-economic or ethnic settlements.

It usually requires far more time to resolve conflicting ideologies or interests than to draft and file an engineering plan. The nature of the problem is less technical than political— local dependence upon the consent of the governed, of those who will use and pay for the facilities.

Many hold that such parochial attitudes should not be permitted to block the building of needed structures. Others deem such expressions of local autonomy to be at the heart of self-government in a free society. Views differ on whether the time loss is too high a price to pay.

Attempts to achieve voluntary co-ordinated national-state-local public works planning have conspicuously failed. Federal agencies from 1954 to 1960 effectively resisted efforts at co-ordination by General John S. Bragdon, then Special Assistant to the President for Public Works Planning. Again, at congressional hearings in 1962, they objected to the creation of an office of Public Works Co-ordinator. The sponsors of the 1962 legislation quietly dropped the proposed new office when the bills were readied for floor action.

General Bragdon was no more successful with appeals to state and local governments for co-ordinated, comprehensive, long-range public works planning. Counties, cities, and school and special districts are usually willing and eager to co-operate with their neighbors and with state and federal agencies in regard to building plans. But they want to reserve the final decisions to themselves. Few want to be truly co-ordinated.

But even home rule has its price. Federal grants to states are usually conditioned upon the existence of a "state plan," prepared by a "single state agency," and subject to the approval of the federal department allocating the funds. State aid to localities often places review of local plans under the jurisdiction of a state board or agency. There are now co-ordinated plans in some functional fields such as highways and hospitals, but there often is no formal co-ordination between them. The lines of command and responsibility (as well as professional allegiance) tend increasingly to run vertically—federal-state-local—rather than horizontally, at each level of government. The system of buying compliance could be expanded and bring about comprehensive planning for all types of public works, subjecting local plans to the jurisdiction of state agencies and state plans to the approval of a national agency. Such far-reaching centralization runs counter to widely held concepts and is not likely to materialize, at least not for a long time to come.

C. PUBLIC FACILITY NEEDS

The need for public facilities is so vast that we shall never run out of projects that should be achieved. Addressing the Municipal Finance Officers Association in 1954, I talked about "A Hundred Billion in State and Local Public Works."[20] Soon after, the Department of Commerce compiled various surveys, estimates, and demands and concluded that $204 billion in state and local construction was needed over the succeeding ten years. Bringing that survey up to date, the department recently estimated state and local public works needs between 1962 and 1970 and the required rate of increase in the volume of construction as follows:[21]

[20] Published in *Municipal Finance*, August, 1954.
[21] William G. Jordan, "Requirements for State and Local Public Works Construction, 1962–1970," *Construction Review* (September, 1962).

	Requirements 1962–1970 (billions)	Rate of increase needed in average annual volume over actual 1961 volume
Highways	$57.4	+ 12%
Water and Sewage	39.1	+162%
Education	31.3	+ 8%
Hospitals and Institutions	25.1	+153%
Other	23.0	+ 23%
	$175.9	+ 38%

Some estimates of facility needs at all levels of government, including the federal, in the next nine to ten years run as high as $300 billion.

Public construction has been gradually expanding and totaled close to $18 billion in 1962. It will not, at its present or projected pace, meet the cited demands. *Architectural Forum* (February, 1960), predicted a construction total of $205 billion in the nineteen-sixties if present trends continue. So there is ample room for expansion.

Facility needs are vast, but it is not easy to find the type of public works that fits the timing and other requirements of contracyclical action which can be expanded and contracted—or preferably started and terminated—on short notice. The great engineering works, such as major dams and water supply systems, bridges, harbors, and expressways, are not sufficiently flexible to be fitted into such schedules. Almost every major type of public construction involves one or several weighty substantive issues of public policy which lead to extended arguments, tend to prolong the decision-making process, and render prompt action of significant magnitude difficult or impossible. A few examples may illustrate the point.

Everyone agrees that there is a need for more and better roads. Highway building has been rapidly increasing, particularly since the enactment of the interstate highway program, which is 90 per cent federally financed. But the extent of recently disclosed scandals suggests that either methods have been inadequate or growth was too rapid for its own good. Even one of the system's greatest boosters, Representative Blatnik, head of the congressional investigation, had to admit that "on the basis of the record, here is grave doubt that the federal dollar has been buying a dollar's worth of properly built highway."[22] Controls are now being tightened to prevent further abuse. But the lesson for future crash programs in construction is unmistakable.

The public schools offered a great potential for expanded construction in the early nineteen-fifties when the Office of Education reported a shortage of 370,000 classrooms. A record volume of building has changed the picture, and the deficiency was reported down to 127,000 in the fall of 1961. Attendance growth, which averaged 1.2 million pupils a year in the nineteen-fifties, will be 600,000 annually in the second half of the nineteen-sixties. Construction has been running at the rate of 70,000 new classrooms each year since 1956, which is considerably above the average annual requirements (including "backlog") in the nineteen-sixties, which President Kennedy placed at 60,000 classrooms annually in his education messages of February 20, 1961, and February 6, 1962. Classroom construction for the lower levels of education almost certainly will decline as enrollment growth slackens. Although facility needs in higher education are large and growing, the combined construction volume in all education is unlikely to expand in the nineteen-sixties at the rate at which it grew in the nineteen-fifties.

Congress has been debating on school construction for many years but has taken no action. It may be significant that the representative of the Housing and Home Finance Agency (HHFA) at the hearings on the 1962 public works bill assured the committee that none of the funds would be spent on schools and that the bill's sponsor, Representative Blatnik, took pains to emphasize that point repeatedly in the House of Representatives.

Public and private investment in urban renewal could be vastly enlarged. A report of the National Planning Association in June, 1962, suggested an increase in the annual volume by $25 billion for the next twenty years. But the present federal program for urban renewal and slum clearance is probably the most cumbersome and intricate of all such programs. Dissension within the community and friction between the agencies involved are the rule and are usually intense and protracted. Rare is the project without a lag of several years between the first draft and the start of construction. Whether the program, in its present form, best serves its ends and could be improved by pouring in far larger amounts was seriously questioned in two recent studies by Thomas F. Johnson and Oscar H. Steiner, both former HHFA officials; and the underlying concept of city planning was devastatingly criticized by Jane Jacobs in *The Death and Life of Great American Cities*.[23]

Mass transit is another field in which an outlay of many billions of dollars has been suggested. Nobody doubts that the extent of urban traffic congestion calls for vigorous action. But there is far from unanimous agreement that rail transit necessarily offers the best solution. Most experts agree that not enough passengers would use the system to pay for its cost and that most or all of the capital investment would have to be provided from tax funds. This subsidization is held to be desirable and necessary by many city planners, if city streets are not to become choked. But other traffic experts have voiced doubt that such large subsidies are justified for a mode of transportation which the public has been deserting by the millions and which might be used by only a small percentage of the commuters for a few hours each week. If the inhabitants of an area feel that they need a rail transit system, then they can vote a bond issue and a tax subsidy as the residents of the San Francisco Bay Area did in November, 1962. But it is less certain that the taxpayers of the whole nation should be called upon to foot the bill for a selected few who choose to live a long distance from their place of work.

---

[22] "AAHSO Warned of Payola," *Engineering News Record*, October 19, 1961.

[23] Thomas F. Johnson, James R. Morris, and Joseph G. Butts, *Renewing American Cities* (Washington, D.C.: The Institute for Social Science Research, 1962); Oscar H. Steiner, *Our Housing Jungle and Your Pocketbook* (New York: University Publishers, 1960); Jane Jacobs, *The Death and Life of Great American Cities* (New York: Random House, 1961).

D. Construction Repairs and Maintenance

Repair and maintenance projects are free of many of the characteristics which tend to hamper or obstruct the use of public works for contracyclical purposes: they require no extensive, time-consuming preparations for planning, authorization, and financing (bond or current); they usually call for few if any blueprints and need little lead time; and they seldom cause community dissension over location, type, or magnitude. Above all, they are flexible. Most projects are small and can be started, expanded, contracted, or terminated on short notice. Colean and Newcomb have emphasized the potential of expanding repairs.[24]

Construction maintenance and repair, particularly on highways and streets, public buildings, recreation facilities, etc., were used widely to create job opportunities during the nineteen-thirties but were seldom resorted to after the demise of the WPA. Many people feared that such a program offered too much opportunity for a boondoggle. They could envision armies of men leaning on their shovels. It is true that projects of this type are difficult to control, particularly when funds come from a central government. Also, such work lacks the glamour and the drama of creating great new structures.

On balance, however, construction repair and maintenance have much to recommend extension of their use. Virtually all the available funds can be applied to direct wages on location because little has to be spent for equipment and materials and nothing on site acquisition. (Those non-labor items account for one-half or more of the cost of major public works projects.) The variety of potential work is great: filling street holes and smoothing road surfaces; cutting brush and improving the landscape along roads; fixing up sidewalks and gutters, docks and piers; planting trees; cleaning up slums and deteriorated urban areas; rehabilitating run-down public buildings and playgrounds, etc. Such chores are waiting to be done almost everywhere, and projects of

[24] Colean and Newcomb, *Stabilizing Construction* (*n.* 11), pp. 40, 294–95.

moderate size can be placed wherever long-term unemployed men, particularly those of low or no skill, are to be put to work. Interest in such projects has seemed to grow in the early nineteen-sixties. West Virginia, in 1962, put some 15,000 men to work at cleaning up roads and shanty towns (at $1 per hour), and the Cook County (Illinois) Public Welfare Department started in the fall of 1961 to have welfare recipients clear slums, neglected yards, etc., under the supervision of the Chicago Sanitation Department.

Public construction repair and maintenance expenditures now run close to $6 billion annually and could be expanded by several billion more, though it is almost impossible to prepare an accurate estimate of the needs and potential from available information. Many communities and states defer needed repairs because the cost, at prevailing construction wages, is prohibitive. Moreover, federal matching funds are available for various types of new construction but not, as a rule, for repairs. State and local governments might deem expansion of repair and maintenance work more attractive if a way were found to bring costs to an acceptable level. Payment of "prevailing" wages, particularly for construction labor, which in 1962 averaged an hourly rate of $3.07, raises the cost of many such projects above their worth. This lessens their chance of being approved.

E. Needed Skills and Common Labor

The image of construction crews as gangs of brawny men with picks and shovels or earth-moving baskets reflects methods still used in China and certain other countries. The image has long been out of date in the United States, where four-fifths of the construction labor force command specialized skills; only 18 per cent are unskilled or common laborers, according to an estimate by former Labor Secretary Arthur Goldberg.

One-fifth of contract construction employment is in engineering construction, where skilled operators and heavy equipment have replaced most of the pick-and-shovel workers.

About half of this employment is on roads, half on dams and similar projects.

Four-fifths of the contract construction force is engaged in building (light) construction. Its work is not highly mechanized and, in fact, it has participated relatively little in technological progress. Building construction is largely in the hands of crafts: two-thirds of the employment is supplied by "special trade contractors"—plumbers, painters, electricians, etc.

Jobs for common labor in construction have been rapidly disappearing. One reason is the insistence of craft unions that only their own members may do such work as unloading pipes, trenching for power lines, stripping concrete forms. A more important reason is that union hourly wage rates have been going up faster for unskilled workers than for skilled. Between July, 1955, and July, 1962, the average hourly rate for building laborers was raised from $2.04 to $3.07, a 50 per cent increase as compared with one of about 32 per cent for craftsmen.[25] At such rates the hiring of unskilled workers becomes increasingly uneconomical and a growing number of laborers are reduced to filling casual jobs with long periods of idleness in between.

A concentration of unemployment at the lowest levels of skill is evident throughout the economy. The unemployment rate of semiskilled workers is half again as high as among craftsmen; among laborers it is more than twice as high. And the lower the level of skill, the greater is the percentage among the jobless who have been out of work for over fourteen weeks or over twenty-six weeks. To make matters worse, the group hit hardest by unemployment, the nonwhites, are even further disadvantaged by the practice of some craft unions of barring them from membership and apprenticeship. Rules prohibiting discrimination on federal construction projects have remained widely unenforced.

Expanded public works programs could add many openings for skilled workers and improve the job market for craftsmen and foremen and reduce unemployment among them. They would offer only modest relief for the unskilled,

25 *Construction Review* (September, 1962), p. 49.

among whom long-term unemployment is heaviest. This would not be a new experience. Even in the nineteen-thirties, when joblessness was quite general, some WPA projects were held up for lack of the necessary skilled labor, although thousands of unskilled workers were available.

That raises the question whether a program intended to alleviate unemployment could be so shaped as to (1) concentrate on creating the type of opening which people with little skill and training can fill and (2) channel practically all funds into wages and as little as possible into site acquisition, equipment, or materials. The usual public works project does not meet these requirements. Construction maintenance and simple repairs could, for the same amount of expenditure, put at least five times as many persons in the hard-core group to work as could new construction.

Changes in the level and type of required skill explain part but not all of the heavy unemployment in construction. Most industries have been upgrading (shifting toward higher skill) jobs, yet hardly any industry has experienced as unfavorable a job trend as has construction, which for some years now has been the industry with the highest—or occasionally second-highest—rate of unemployment. As a rule, the construction unemployment rate has been twice as high as the general rate and even during the main building season seldom less than two-thirds higher. Between 1956 and 1962 all civilian nonagricultural employment increased 8 per cent, but employment in contract construction declined 9 per cent.[*]

This fall in employment was not the result of a shrinkage in demand or a reduction in construction volume. New construction has well

* Editor's Note: Author Freeman wrote at a time when only preliminary data for 1962 were available on employment in contract construction. Final data for 1962 showed a decrease of only 3 per cent from 1956, and preliminary data for 1963 show a slight increase over 1956. Insofar as a constant level of employment in an expanding economy represents a *relative* decline in employment, the author's argument could perhaps be rephrased in these terms. But because the author, who was in Central Asia, could not be reached at the time the manuscript went to press, this editorial note must serve in place of modifications the author might have made in the text.

maintained its share of the national product— about 11 per cent—and exceeded $60 billion for the first time in history in 1962. By how much could the unemployment rate in the construction industry—it has averaged about 12 per cent, seasonally adjusted—be reduced by the addition of a billion dollars in public works funds? At the rate of 100 jobs per $1 million, about 100,000 men could be employed for every billion dollars added. But the *net* reduction in unemployment might be far less, because it appears that the shrinkage in construction jobs may be due to a serious and growing imbalance in the industry's cost structure, which could not be corrected and might be aggravated by public works expansion.

F. Construction Wages and Costs

With mass unemployment seemingly chronic and with public facility needs so large, it has been suggested that public works expansion could be viewed as more than a temporary

offset to downturns in the business cycle.[26] Why not plan for a long-range increase of investment in public works, perhaps from 3.3 per cent of gross national product to 4 per cent or even 5 per cent? That would eliminate the worry about flexibility of the various types of public construction and about having to cut back an economic recovery.

The main consideration against such a policy is its effect on costs. Prices have been rising consistently faster in construction than in the rest of the economy. A deliberate and continued stimulation of demand could lead to an even more serious imbalance. Figure 9–1 illustrates in the form of cost indexes the rise that took place in the prices of construction and of other goods between 1915 (initial year of the Department of Commerce construction cost index) and mid-1962.[27] Percentages of

[26] See, for example, Ewan Clague (p. 179).
[27] Sources: Bureau of Labor Statistics, *Economic Indicators*, December, 1962. Bureau of the Census, *Historical Statistics of the U.S.*, 1960. *Volume and Costs 1915–1956, A Statistical Supplement to*

Figure 9-1

INDEX OF PRICE CHANGES 1915 TO MID-1962

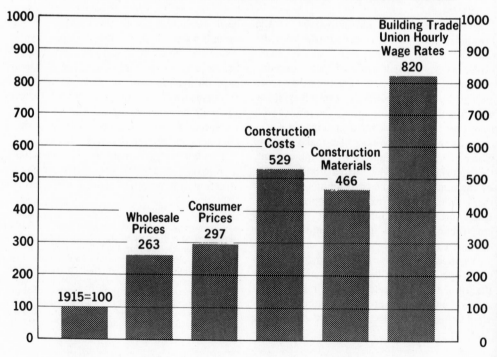

increase over that period were as follows:

Wholesale prices (all commodities)	+163 per cent
Retail prices of goods and services (CPI)	+197 per cent
Construction costs:	
Department of Commerce, composite	+429 per cent
Residences (Boekh)	+434 per cent
Commercial and factory buildings (Boekh)	+458 per cent
Wholesale cost of construction materials	+366 per cent
Union hourly wages in building trades	+720 per cent

Why have construction prices risen twice as rapidly as other prices? Sharper increases in materials prices, particularly lumber, are one reason. Higher wage rates are the other.

It can be questioned whether wage rates increased faster in the building trades than in other industries and to what extent. Since World War II they certainly advanced far more, absolutely and relatively, than in manufacturing. But what counts in terms of cost is not hourly rates but whether productivity advanced in proportion to pay. In construction it evidently did not.

The most authoritative work in this field, John W. Kendrick's *Productivity Trends in the United States* (National Bureau of Economic Research, 1961), shows the average annual increases in output per man-hour 1909 to 1953:

Manufacturing	+2.7%
Mining	+2.8%
Transportation	+3.8%
Construction	+0.3%

Colean and Newcomb, using a different statistical method, concluded that there was virtually no productivity increase in construc-

tion between 1913 and 1951.[28] Clague and Greenberg found an average annual increase in construction output per man-hour during 1953–59 of 0.6 per cent (compared with 2.8 per cent for the total private economy).[29] But building trade wage rates rose 62 per cent between 1951 and mid-1962, and if adjusted for the purchasing power of the dollar, 39 per cent. (Over the same period construction costs increased 27 per cent, retail prices 16 per cent, wholesale commodity prices 4 per cent.) No matter which basis we choose, it appears that over the past half-century when productivity in the total private economy advanced at an annual average of 2.4 per cent per man-hour, construction was almost standing still. There was some advance in recent years in heavy engineering construction, but little if any in building.

The greater rise in construction wages and costs was facilitated by several factors:

1. The big advances took place during the periods after World Wars I and II, when needs and effective demand had accumulated and were impatient to be met. Construction costs in constant dollars—that is, construction prices in relation to wholesale commodity prices—rose most steeply during the nineteen-twenties and after 1947. There was a slight decline in the nineteen-thirties, but construction costs (in constant dollars) stood at the same level in 1947 as in 1931. Facility needs, piled up during World War II, called for a larger construction labor force. Big postwar wage boosts enabled the contract construction industry to expand the number of its workers from 2 million in 1947 (after a low of 1.1 million in 1945) to 3 million by 1956. The subsequent loss of jobs did not halt wage boosts. Table 9–1 shows that job fluctuations have had no apparent effect on changes in wage rates.

2. Two-to-four-year contracts with built-in rate boosts scheduled every six months, which have become frequent in construction, have

Construction Review (September and November, 1962). *Construction Review*, Economic Almanac, 1962, p. 83.

The indexes aim to reflect changes in price for a constant product. The Boekh index includes a correction for changes in labor efficiency. The Department of Commerce index is a composite of indexes for the major classes of construction, properly weighted.

[28] Colean and Newcomb, *Stabilizing Construction* (n. 11), pp. 247–48.

[29] Ewan Clague and Leon Greenberg, "Employment," in *Automation and Technological Change*, The American Assembly (Englewood Cliffs, New Jersey: Prentice-Hall, 1962), p. 120.

TABLE 9–1: ANNUAL INCREASES IN UNION HOURLY WAGE RATES IN BUILDING
TRADES AND CHANGES IN EMPLOYMENT IN CONTRACT CONSTRUCTION, 1955–1962

July 1–July 1	Increase in wage rates				Changes in employment in contract construction	
	All building trades		Building laborers			
	Dollars	Per cent	Dollars	Per cent	Number	Per cent
1955 to 1956	.14	4.6	.14	6.9	+172,000	+6.0
1956 to 1957	.17	5.2	.17	7.8	−101,000	−3.3
1957 to 1958	.15	4.5	.13	5.5	−185,000	−6.3
1958 to 1959	.18	4.9	.14	5.6	+245,000	+8.9
1959 to 1960	.15	4.1	.16	6.1	− 54,000	−1.8
1960 to 1961	.15	3.9	.17	6.1	−142,000	−5.2
1961 to 1962	.13	3.3	.12	4.1	− 27,000	−1.0

SOURCE: *Construction Review*, September and October, 1962; *Monthly Labor Review*, 1961 Statistical Supplement.

insulated wage rates from temporary job declines and pushed rates up regularly year after year.[30] Apparently, only longer-lasting job losses could slow down or halt this trend. To increase demand deliberately by public works acceleration would tend to strengthen the upward trend and make hopes for relatively more stable construction prices illusory.

[30] The typical duration of major union contracts in the construction industry in 1961 was three years. Three-fourths of all contracts for three or more years included deferred wage increases. "Major Union Contracts in the United States, 1961," *Monthly Labor Review* (October, 1962).

3. The Davis-Bacon Act, adopted in 1931 to prop up construction wages and to protect union wage rates from non-union competition, has had more far-reaching effects than was contemplated. It not only raised the cost of governmental construction but pushed up other building prices as well.

Higher construction costs did not go to fatten contractors' profits. In fact, contract construction has become an almost profitless industry as Table 9–2, going back to 1929 (earliest year available), shows.

The sales volume of construction corporations

TABLE 9–2: PROFIT RATE ON SALES IN CORPORATE CONSTRUCTION
AND MANUFACTURING, 1929–1961

Year	Before taxes		After taxes	
	Corporate contract construction (Per cent)	Corporate manufacturing (Per cent)	Corporate contract construction (Per cent)	Corporate manufacturing (Per cent)
1929	4.2	6.9	3.6	6.0
1950	4.7	10.9	2.5	5.8
1955	2.1	8.7	.8	4.3
1956	2.7	8.0	1.3	4.1
1957	2.6	7.2	1.1	3.7
1958	2.2	5.7	.9	2.9
1959	1.6	6.4	.6	3.7
1960	1.2	6.2	.2	3.2
1961	1.1	6.2	.2	3.0

SOURCE: U.S. Department of Commerce, *National Income*, 1954 Edition. U.S. Department of Commerce, *U.S Income and Output*, 1957. *Survey of Current Business*, July, 1962.

multiplied twelve times between 1929 and 1961. But their net profits, meanwhile, declined from $100 million to $74 million. Noncorporate contractors—single and partnership business—who account for a smaller but still substantial share of the contracting volume, particularly among the smaller projects, had somewhat greater profits.[31] But a new set of gross national products accounts, just prepared in the Department of Commerce, shows clearly that during the postwar period in construction as well as in other industries the employees' share increased and the industry's profit share declined.[32]

How do these price trends affect the consumer? He now spends between $6,500 and $7,500 to buy wholesale or retail goods which he could have bought for $2,500 in 1915. But he must pay $13,250 for a house which then cost $2,500.[33] The construction cost of a single-family home which averaged $14,425 in June, 1962, would be only slightly over $7,000 if building costs had risen at the same rate as other prices. The house buyer now gets half the return for the same money in housing as in other goods.

Professor (now Senator) Paul Douglas, who proposed in 1935 "a public works program concentrated upon housing" to combat the depression, qualified his plan: "These expenditures should not, however, be used to bolster up specific 'sticky' prices or to strengthen monopoly control."[34] The trouble is that the price of residential construction has not just been "sticky." It was pushed up faster than other prices through good times and bad. As a result, many potential home buyers have been priced out of the market.

The House committee report on the 1962 public works bill acknowledges the danger that additional demand may drive up prices. But it continues:

> Because this bill is aimed directly at providing jobs for those now unemployed, it cannot be said to be in any sense inflationary. The committee recognizes that if demand were stimulated at a time when the economy is operating at full capacity, it would then increase competition for workers and productive capacity already employed and the result would be to bid up prices. That is not the case today, nor will it be in the immediate future. (Page 19.)

This represents sound economic reasoning. Yet the following took place between 1956 and mid-1962: Construction materials prices declined 0.6 per cent, but construction prices increased 12.1 per cent. The reason? Average hourly earnings in contract construction went up 70 cents, and the union wage rate for building laborers increased 89 cents. Hourly earnings in manufacturing, meanwhile, rose only 44 cents.

In all probability there is a direct connection between this wage behavior and the concomitant employment experience. Construction unemployment rose sharply. Building laborers have been experiencing the heaviest unemployment of all occupations: their unemployment rate averaged 20.3 per cent between 1958 and 1961, which was more than three times the general unemployment rate of 6.1 per cent and twice as high as the rate of the next-highest occupation.

An awareness of these historical facts is necessary to understand the present dilemma: unemployment in construction is high and could be reduced by public works expansion. The letting of several additional billions of dollars in public construction contracts, however, would inevitably reinforce the inflationary trend and unfavorably affect the ability of large groups to buy homes or to shift to better living quarters.

In 1957 I testified before the Joint Economic Committee:

> Consumer resistance has already led to a squeeze on contractors—failures are up one-fourth—and to a slowing up of activities. It

---

[31] *Statistics of Income . . . 1959–60 U.S. Business Tax Returns,* 1962 (Internal Revenue Service, Treasury Department, Washington, D.C.).

[32] "GNP by Major Industries," *Survey of Current Business* (October, 1962).

[33] This is based on the Boekh Price Index which attempts to compensate for changes in the quality and character of buildings.

[34] Paul Douglas, *Controlling Depressions* (Chicago: Norton, 1935), p. 278.

would not be surprising if pockets of unemployment were to appear in some areas—
unless they are absorbed by enlarged public
works. Nor is it unusual that the government is now being asked to help an industry
which has been pricing itself out of the
market.[35]

The New York electricians who struck for a
four-hour day late in 1961 and wound up
getting $198.40 for a thirty-five-hour week
illustrate the current situation.

At the close of 1962, built-in raises contracted
for 1963 were typically 10 to 20 cents an hour in
construction, 6 to 8 cents in other industries.[36]
The injection of substantially increased federal
funds into contract construction at such a time
cannot but add to the upward push. Wider
substitution of Davis-Bacon wage rates, set by
the Secretary of Labor, for the rates now
common in many smaller communities would
intensify the pressure. Continued inflation in
construction costs might drive the cost of homes
beyond the purchasing power of additional
millions of low- and middle-income families
and even deter commercial and industrial
improvements. Thus, a large public works
expansion program, desirable though it appears
from many angles, could conceivably eliminate
more jobs than it adds.

IV. WORK RELIEF—AN ALTERNATIVE TO PUBLIC WORKS ACCELERATION

Work relief, as distinguished from public
works programs, has served during times of
hardship in many countries as a major means of
feeding and occupying able-bodied people who
had no other means of subsistence. This
was particularly true before the establishment
of permanent unemployment insurance and
public assistance programs paying regular cash
benefits. It was widely used in the United

States during the nineteen-thirties, but practically disappeared when the WPA ceased
activities. Few communities employed work
relief during the nineteen-forties and nineteen-
fifties.

Samuel V. Bennett defined the basic difference
between work relief and public works programs:

> The objective of public works programs is the
> construction of needed public improvements.
> The chief objective of work relief programs is
> the provision of aid through employment
> provided to needy persons. From this
> difference of objectives arise the other distinc-
> tions which can be drawn between the two.[37]

Public works projects usually aim at the
building of new structures, mostly medium to
large, which are selected according to the need
for the facility. Workers are selected according
to required skills, projects are let by contract to
private contractors, and the time lag is often
substantial. Work relief projects may involve
new structures but more often consist of repairs
of older ones or types of work outside the field
of construction; they tend to be of medium or
small size, and are selected to fit the occupational capacity of chronically unemployed
persons. The workers are selected among the
able-bodied on the basis of need and the project
is operated by a public agency for public
assistance or for work relief. The time lag is
usually short. Public works projects are
usually let by contract and pay prevailing—
commonly union—wage rates. Work relief is
operated directly by a public agency and tends
to pay either minimum wages or to adjust
benefits to need.

Bennett arrived at the

> . . . conclusion, supported both by logic and
> by the experience of the thirties . . . that work
> relief is promising as a device for getting
> income quickly into the hands of the most
> needy people in the population. Public
> works projects, on the other hand, get income
> to a much smaller number of needy people
> slowly, partially, and by indirect channels.

---

[35] "Public Works—Fond Hopes and Harsh Realities"
and "Federal Expenditure Policy for Economic Growth
and Stability," papers submitted by panelists, Joint
Economic Committee (85th Congress, 1st Session,
1957), p. 1087.

[36] "Wages . . . Strikes . . . Jobs . . . How 1963 Shapes
Up," *U.S. News and World Report* (January 7, 1963).

[37] Samuel V. Bennett, *Unemployment and Relief
from the Local Government Point of View* (Chicago:
A Report of the W. E. Upjohn Institute for Community
Research, Public Administration Service, 1955), pp.
115–16.

Public works programs, therefore, do not appear to be a useful way to make a substantial attack on the problem of unemployed persons.[38]

Work relief does not, as a rule, add to the wage push and the inflationary pressures discussed in the preceding section. It is easy to understand why labor unions favor public works programs and tend to oppose work relief. They also fear that some communities might be tempted to fill certain low-skill jobs by work relief rather than by regular hiring. The crucial argument on the other side is that for every million dollars available, more "hardcore" needy people can be given jobs through work relief than by a public works program.

Recipients of federally aided public assistance programs have generally not been permitted to participate in work relief. The leadership of the social work profession dislikes the idea of requiring persons to work as a condition of receiving public aid and has generally succeeded in discouraging its use.

But the spread of unemployment during the late nineteen-fifties caused a number of communities to resort again to work relief in connection with general assistance, which is not federally aided or controlled. A survey by the Department of Health, Education, and Welfare in the fall of 1961, when 400,000 families (about 1 million persons) were receiving general assistance, found some type of work relief operating in half the states, with about 30,000 persons participating.[39] Seven industrial states accounted for 86 per cent of all persons so employed. In other words, there was little if any work relief in 43 states.

The temporary extension of Aid to Dependent Children to families with unemployed fathers brought suggestions for permitting work relief; and the President so proposed in 1962. The 1962 welfare amendments which extended the program for unemployed fathers for five years allowed the establishment of community work and training programs. The emphasis of the Department of Health, Education, and Welfare is largely on training rather than on common work projects.

There may be serious doubt whether Aid to Dependent Children, which was conceived for a different purpose, is a suitable vehicle for work relief. It probably would be more efficient to operate work relief as a separate program offering unemployed employable persons (including those whose unemployment compensation has run out) opportunity to work in return for subsistence pay. Benefits should be related to the needs of the family. To require the payment of "prevailing wages," particularly in construction, where the hourly rate for common labor now averages over $3, will severely limit the use of work relief and, in many cases, exclude it. It is not desirable to create situations, such as those cited in the previously mentioned Department of Health, Education, and Welfare survey, where supervisors of work relief recipients reported: "They think of this as a permanent career."

Federal matching funds are essential for work relief projects as long as the national government provides up to 82 per cent reimbursement for public assistance expenditures. Otherwise, communities might prefer to qualify needy persons for public assistance rather than for work relief whose total cost they bear locally.

Some work relief projects should be specifically designed for young persons, as were CCC and NYA programs in the nineteen-thirties. Proposals for a Youth Conservation Corps and a Public Service Corps have been considered by Congress, but they encountered difficulty when the sponsors estimated that the cost of the program envisaged by the Youth Employment Opportunities Act would average $4,000 a year per participant.

Work relief is not now widely used because of the strong opposition of labor unions, objections within the social work profession, and the absence of a properly designed program. It could, if authorized, effectively supplement the existing economic security programs and offer a more satisfactory alleviation of long-range unemployment than either an indefinite extension of unemployment benefits or the expansion of a public assistance program such as

[38] *Ibid.*, p. 117.
[39] *Work Relief . . . a Current Look*, Public Assistance Report No. 52 (Department of Health, Education, and Welfare, Washington, D.C., March, 1962).

Aid to Dependent Children or general assistance. It would be especially appropriate in conjunction with a program of maintenance and repairs, such as described above.

V. PROSPECTS

How many additional jobs will the public works acceleration program of 1962 provide? The House Public Works Committee accepted an AFL-CIO estimate of 100 jobs per $1 million expenditure, one-half on-site construction jobs, one-half off-site (in equipment and materials industries). This estimate assumes a somewhat greater job potential than is suggested by the prevailing average construction value of over $15,000 per construction worker (including materials, equipment, and site preparation, excluding site acquisition).

On the basis of the AFL-CIO estimate, $900 million would create 45,000 on-site and 45,000 off-site jobs for one year. The majority of the House Public Works Committee expected state and local governments simultaneously to boost their capital funds by $600 million. The committee projected a combined total of 75,000 on-site and 75,000 off-site jobs, besides the so-called multiplier (jobs in consumer goods industries, etc.).

Part of this increase may be offset by the effect of the program on building wages and costs. It will extend the application of Davis-Bacon wage rates and, in general, tend to strengthen upward trends. The degree of reduction in consumer demand for private residential and other construction is purely conjectural.

As stated at the outset, the 1962 program does not have enough leverage to make a major impact on unemployment or on the national economy. It will help a few hundred of the presently eligible 1,000 or more areas (counties, cities, towns, etc.) to build needed public facilities and to occupy some of their unemployed.

If the program's appropriations were enlarged to several billions of dollars, its effect would, of course, multiply in more than one respect. A large public works expansion program could create several hundred thousand jobs, most of them for skilled operators and craftsmen and

at least half of them in the equipment and materials industries. This would add to effective demand throughout the economy.

It is likely that in a typical public works program (considering on-site and off-site employment) not more than 10 per cent of the job openings would be of the common building labor type which can be filled by low-skilled or unskilled workers. Construction maintenance, repairs, rehabilitation, and clean-up could provide many more jobs than a public works program per million dollars for the type of laborer who constitutes the hard core of long-term unemployment.

The effects of a large public works program would not stop at the directly provided jobs. The record suggests that heavy unemployment in construction is due largely to a serious and growing imbalance in the industry's cost structure. Building trade craftsmen and particularly building laborers have priced construction out of a substantial part of its potential market and many of their fellow union members out of jobs. Billions of additional government contracts would add fuel to the fire and might reduce private demand by an equal amount or more. This could continue as a vicious cycle.

Work relief rather than contract construction may be a more effective way of dealing with protracted unemployment. It is far more flexible in terms of time schedules and of usable skills (and nonskills). It could put to work more idle persons than any other method with whatever amount of public funds becomes available. It could be shaped as a co-operative federal-state-local program if sufficient care were taken to prevent it from degenerating into a boondoggling scheme. Construction repair and maintenance offer many opportunities and are well suited for low-skilled or unskilled workers. Various types of simple manual tasks in public institutions could employ many other men and women through work relief. Although work relief is not so desirable as a regular, well-paid job, it is preferable to indefinitely extended unemployment compensation or public assistance for at least some of the hundreds of thousands who are now without any productive work.

CHAPTER 10

The Public Employment Service

Leonard P. Adams*

I. OBJECTIVES AND ORGANIZATION

THE PURPOSE OF this chapter[1] is to show how the public employment service has developed in the United States, what its objectives have been, and to what extent the objectives have been attained. And since job markets are organized by private agencies as well as by the public service, a brief account of the work done by these agencies is also given. The story of the development of the public employment service properly begins with a summary of the legislation on which it rests.

The employment service system in the United States has evolved from a combination of city, state, and federal legislation over a period of about six decades. Much of this legislation has proved to be ineffectual and impermanent, but the motives which stimulated legislators have continued to live in the minds of students of unemployment and of those who administer the present system of public employment offices. The present objectives are reflected in the five principal federal laws which have provided the general structure and policies for the current public employment service system and in the state laws which have further implemented this general legislation.

* Director of Research and Publications, New York State School of Industrial and Labor Relations, Cornell University.
[1] Much of the information in this chapter is based on a longer manuscript which has been prepared with the financial assistance of the W. E. Upjohn Institute for Employment Research.

A. EARLY LEGISLATIVE BACKGROUND

The first and most important federal legislation was the Wagner-Peyser Act of 1933, which provided for a new bureau, the United States Employment Service (USES), and for a federal-state network of employment offices, financed by federal grants-in-aid and by matching state funds. The second was the Social Security Act of 1935, which provided for the payment of unemployment insurance benefits through local public employment offices. A third federal law in 1939 transferred the USES from the Department of Labor to the Social Security Board and established the Bureau of Employment Security. This bureau was given responsibility for the federal-state public employment service and the federal-state system of unemployment insurance. After World War II the bureau was re-established in the Department of Labor. The fourth law, the Servicemen's Readjustment Act of 1944, expanded the scope of service to veterans to include vocational counseling and testing, established a system of veterans preference in making referrals, and provided for a national veterans placement service with a separate budget. The fifth major piece of legislation, enacted in 1948, transferred the responsibility for farm placement from the Federal Farm Extension Service in the Department of Agriculture to the United States Employment Service in the Department of Labor. These laws, combined with the manpower legislation of the nineteen-sixties referred to below in section V, have determined the

193

structure and general functions of the modern federal-state employment service.

The Wagner-Peyser Act,[2] which in terms of organization, program, and policy is the most important of the federal laws, did not provide for a federal system or for one completely under federal control.   It established a new bureau in the Department of Labor and gave this bureau authority to promote, establish, and maintain a national system of employment offices by means of grants-in-aid to those states which accepted the terms of the law.   By these terms the states must agree to provide a public employment service to assist all workers—including youths, veterans, farm workers, and the handicapped— in finding jobs and assist all employers in finding workers.   Also, the states must agree to adhere to federal standards with respect to the use of funds, to follow regulations issued by the Secretary of Labor, and to make such reports as might be required.   In other respects the states were allowed to establish their own organizations and appoint their own personnel to administer the laws, provided the personnel were selected in accordance with a merit or civil service system.

The basic objectives of the Wagner-Peyser Act sponsors were: (1) to secure a national public employment service by expanding and adding to the systems then existing in many industrial states (there were 120 offices in twenty-three states); (2) to provide uniform policies for major services to be rendered; (3) to provide leadership in program development and to supply technical assistance; and (4) to leave the states a good deal of autonomy, especially in the selection of personnel and the development of programs to meet local needs.

The Wagner-Peyser Act was passed at a time when the number of unemployed in the country had reached an unprecedented level of about 13 million.   Since the states could not implement the law immediately, and since it was necessary to have a national network of offices to register and classify the unemployed, the federal-state system had to be supplemented immediately by creating a system of temporary National Reemployment Service Offices.   The primary

[2] 48 U.S. Statutes 133.

task of both systems for the next several years was to register the unemployed, classify them, and make referrals to public works projects.

The financial inducement of grants-in-aid helped to strengthen the public offices in those twenty-three states which already had such offices when the Wagner-Peyser Act was passed and stimulated a number of other states to open offices.   By 1935, when the Social Security Act became law, thirty-four states had a public employment service system.

The Social Security Act stipulated that unemployment insurance benefits must be paid to claimants only through public employment offices or such other offices as might be approved and that all insurance claimants must register for work at these offices to be eligible for benefits.   The rapid passage of state unemployment insurance legislation created a need for the immediate establishment of employment offices in each state and made the financing of such offices a legitimate charge against the administration of the state insurance system. By 1938 there existed a nationwide network of public employment offices, financed in part by Wagner-Peyser Act grants and matching state appropriations but mainly by funds appropriated for the administration of unemployment insurance.

In 1944 the Servicemen's Readjustment Act strengthened the legislative mandate for supplying services to veterans.   A testing, counseling, and placement service was created for veterans with a special national office and with special placement representatives in all state and local offices.   Preference in referral and placement services was mandated in all public offices for those who had been wounded and disabled and for other qualified veterans before qualified nonveterans.   Veterans constituted a large proportion of the postwar labor supply, and the counseling and testing services which were made available for them were applied also to other workers.

In 1948 responsibility for farm placement work, which had been transferred to the Farm Extension Service during World War II, was returned to the USES and the state and local public offices.   Farm placement work, especially the problem of meeting seasonal labor demands for planting and harvesting crops, has developed into one of the major activities of the public service. To meet these demands, the USES has organized a system capable of placing large numbers of domestic migratory workers, as well as workers imported from Mexico, the British West Indies, and Canada.

Other important legislation that has influenced the course of the public employment service will be mentioned in the next section, which deals with the various concepts of the role of a public employment service in a modern industrial society.

B. EARLY CONCEPTS OF THE ROLE OF THE EMPLOYMENT SERVICE

As the preceding summary of significant legislation implies, the development of the present system of public employment offices in the United States has been an evolutionary process. Its development and present acceptance may be attributed to the emergence in modern society of unemployment of a magnitude great enough to force reconsideration of the existing provisions for the relief of poverty, the concepts of the causes of poverty, and the role that government should play in solving modern problems of employment and unemployment. Specifically, the establishment of public offices in several industrial states around 1900 may be attributed mainly to an attempt either to remove unemployment or to improve the distribution of the nation's human resources. Some of the important aspects of the functions of a national system of public employment offices may be traced to the following developments, both here and abroad, in concepts of unemployment and its causes.

1. With the emergence of unemployment as a serious problem in industrial centers, especially during general business recessions, it became evident that the needy poor were not all shiftless individuals unwilling to work but that many were regular members of the labor force. Hence, it became evident that a system of relief was needed which would differentiate between those able and willing to work and those unable

or unwilling to work. If there were jobs which the able-bodied would take if the whereabouts of the jobs were known, some of the needy could be employed. Thus, the concept of organizing the labor market by providing a center of information and a labor exchange for the use of workers and employers grew out of the analysis of the causes of poverty and the complexities of bringing workers and jobs together in large industrial centers.[3]

2. A complementary concept, expounded by Beveridge,[4] who was influenced by his analysis of British industrial practices and by the German city system of employment offices, was that unemployment grew out of situations in which each plant maintained its own labor force reserve. Workers in the reserve served as substitutes and as a source of extra manpower to meet peak production demands. Beveridge argued that part of this reserve stood idle a good deal of the time and he proposed to eliminate the need for individual labor reserves by creating a central exchange which would register the unemployed, refer them to employers who needed workers, and thus regularize employment.

3. Public employment offices were also regarded by early proponents as a means of curbing the abuses connected with some private employment agencies which created rather than lessened labor turnover. Government-operated offices, it was argued, would either drive the malpracticing private agencies out of business or force them to reform.[5] Undoubtedly, some of the proponents of the public service hoped that it would provide, at no direct cost to the users, service so adequate that private agencies would lose the market. This desired result has never occurred. Private agencies, both the fee-charging and the "free" service type, have

[3] See, for example, Sidney and Beatrice Webb, *The Public Organization of the Labour Market: Part Two of the Minority Report of the Poor Law Commission* (London: Longmans, Green and Co., 1909).

[4] Sir William H. Beveridge, *Unemployment: A Problem of Industry* (London: Longmans, Green and Co., 1909).

[5] Report of Committee on Unemployment, Commission on Employers' Liability and Other Matters, New York State Legislature, Albany, New York, April 26, 1911.

continued to operate and, as will be shown later, play an important part in organizing job markets today.

4. The tendency for immigrants to the United States to stay in the ports of entry while labor shortages existed in the interior of the country, especially on farms, was one of the main reasons that federal legislation was enacted in 1907 to provide a special placement and information service. The objective was to help the farmers and other employers gain access to the incoming flow of workers and to help the latter find suitable jobs.[6]

5. World War I caused manpower shortages in some key industries, such as the railroads, the lumber camps, and some munitions factories. Turnover increased rapidly because of labor pirating and the activities of private agencies. It became necessary, therefore, for the federal government to establish a system of employment offices and to require employers in essential industries to recruit their labor from these offices rather than bid against one another. At the outset of World War II the realization that manpower resources would eventually need to be managed led to the federalization of all state offices, and they became part of the War Manpower Commission for the duration of the war. Thus, the need for a system to manage the recruitment, distribution, and utilization of labor resources in a national emergency has become one of the accepted reasons for maintaining public employment offices.

6. With the coming of unemployment insurance legislation, the normal need for a public employment service to assure that no worker continued to be unemployed if a job existed was accentuated because of the desire to save funds and prevent malingering. It was believed that the principal way to hold abuses in the insurance system to a minimum would be to require that all insurance claimants register at an employment office and indicate regularly their willingness and ability to work.

The central thought behind the first five of these concepts is that a certain amount of unemployment in each local area and among different areas results from limitations in the

6 *Ibid.*

means of communication and the absence of a matching service by which idle workers and vacant jobs can be brought together. The primary function of a public employment office is to supply this service, thus eliminating some unemployment, and to contribute to the optimum use of human resources, especially in periods of national emergency.

These basic concepts of the function of a public employment service system have not only influenced legislation but have also been incorporated in the rules and regulations governing the operation of the service and in the development of a general program and its operating principles.

C. ORGANIZATION AND FUNCTIONS OF THE EMPLOYMENT SERVICE SINCE WORLD WAR II

Toward the end of 1946 the public employment offices, which during the war had been federalized and made the operating arm of the War Manpower Commission, were returned to the states. The offices became once again a part of state employment security programs. In terms of organization this meant, as a rule, re-establishment of former structures, of which there were three patterns. These patterns still characterize present-day local office organization.

One general pattern combines responsibility for the employment service and for unemployment insurance operations under a single administrative head and with a single line of authority from an executive director through a chief of field operations to the field supervisory offices. In many of the largest areas, placement work with people in white-collar occupations and insurance functions at the local office level are now carried on in separate locations and with separate managers. In the smaller areas both operations are, as a rule, carried on at the same location and under the same manager. The employment service organization in New York follows this general pattern.

A second general pattern provides for two separate central office divisions, one for placement and the other for insurance, under a single executive director. Under this arrangement each branch has some staff services of its own and depends for others on a general unit attached to the state headquarters. The regional and local offices are administered by a chief of operations under an executive director. Local placement and insurance operations are managed at one location under a single manager in some areas and in other areas at separate locations, each with its own manager. California provides an example of this general pattern.

A third pattern, found in only a few states, provides for the administration of both functions by a single commission which has established an entirely separate organization for each operation. Under this arrangement insurance and placement operations are administered separately by an executive for each function, with his own organization and staff for training, methods and procedures, research, and publicity. In local offices the two functions are usually carried on at the same location but by separate managers and separate staffs. Arizona provides an example of this pattern.

To assist the federal headquarters office in carrying out its responsibilities under the legislation already described, the states are grouped into regions. Originally thirteen, there are now eleven regions. Each has a director and one or more staff assigned to assist state offices with employment service problems, to review budget and operations, and to make suggestions for improvements in the functioning of the programs.

At the headquarters in Washington, over-all responsibility for the employment service rests with the administrator (formerly the director) of the Bureau of Employment Security.[7] Under him is the director of the United States Employment Service (a title recently re-established), who is assisted by professional staff, including specialists in farm labor, manpower development and utilization, employment service operations, veterans services, and labor-market analysis.

In the postwar period much of the research work on the identification and analysis of new occupations was transferred to selected state

[7] See *Employment Security Review* (April, 1962).

offices. Some research on testing, however, was continued in Washington and in a few selected states. Funds for such research and for revision of operating tools, such as the *Dictionary of Occupational Titles*, were reduced by Congress during the postwar reaction to government spending.

Shortly after the end of the war, the headquarters staff of the employment service began work on the development of a general program for the guidance of state offices. As a result of the review of the basic objectives of the service, its wartime experience, the increased emphasis on counseling and testing for veterans, and the hope that the public service could help attain the national goal of high levels of employment and production as expressed in the Employment Act of 1946, a six-point basic program emerged. It provided for:

1. A placement service [8] for all workers—including youths, the handicapped, farm workers, and veterans—and for all employers.

2. Special services for veterans, as required by the Servicemen's Readjustment Act.

3. Employment counseling and testing for workers, especially youths, with vocational problems.

4. Labor-market information for the use of workers, employers, and community agencies.

5. Industrial services for employers, such as assistance in job analysis and in problems of recruitment, selection, and placement.

6. Information on labor supply and future manpower requirements, which would be of use to schools, industrial development agencies, and many other groups.

This six-point program statement was

[8] The official definition of a placement is: "An acceptance by an employer of a person for a job as a direct result of employment office activities, provided the employment office has completed all of the following four steps: (a) Receipt of an order prior to referral; (b) Selection of the person to be referred without designation by the employer of any particular individual or group of individuals; (c) Referral; (d) Verification from a reliable source, preferably the employer, that a person referred has been hired by the employer and has entered on the job." See Robert Thomas, "Major Aspects of the Public Employment Service, 1947–1957," an unpublished report prepared by the present Assistant Director for Employment Service Administration, Appendix III, p. 1.

incorporated in Part II of the Employment Security Manual of policies and procedures, which has become the general guide for all state services. It was more or less understood that placement services would get major attention, and that the other points were of secondary importance. The testing and counseling services developed slowly, because very few local office staffs were qualified to render these services at the end of the war. Competence in performing other services for employers and communities also developed slowly. Robert L. Thomas, a member of the headquarters employment service staff, estimated that in 1957 staff time spent on employment service work was distributed roughly as follows: 75 per cent on placement work (taking of applications and orders, selection, referral, and verification of placements), 6 per cent on counseling, 5 per cent on labor-market information, 4 per cent on testing, and 10 per cent on all other services.[9]

Until recently the budget formula used by the federal headquarters to distribute funds to the states took account of this time distribution. Allocations, within the limits of the general appropriation to the bureau, were made principally on the basis of the volume of four types of activities: applications taken, placements made, the number of counseling interviews given, and the number of tests administered. The expected volume of each of these activities was multiplied by a time factor in minutes, and the adjusted figure indicated the number of man-years of time required to accomplish the expected results.

Within the general framework of the six-point program, therefore, there could be, and there was, considerable variation in actual accomplishments of the state services. The Wagner-Peyser Act had specified that in order to qualify for a grant each state must submit a plan of action to the Secretary of Labor. This requirement has been interpreted to mean that the state should submit an initial statement covering organization, staff, and a general plan for

carrying on an employment service and then keep headquarters informed of any changes. These plans, therefore, were really organization blueprints rather than blueprints for action designed to carry out the six-point program. Later, the regional offices were given primary responsibility for reviewing and evaluating accomplishments of the states.

A management manual was prepared by headquarters and sent to the states in 1948 to show how standards of performance might be established and how local office performance might be evaluated. Since the use of this management manual was not compulsory, the actual development of standards was left mostly to the discretion of state administrators, with some assistance and encouragement provided by regional office staff. The results of each state's assuming this administrative responsibility will be seen in the next section, where the accomplishments of the state offices are reviewed.

Before passing to a discussion of results, something further should be said about the general frame of reference within which the public employment service has had to operate. From the early days of the USES the Secretary of Labor, as authorized by the act, had issued general regulations which the affiliated states were bound to observe. There had also developed some consensus among administrators on the right way to get things done. From these regulations and agreements on procedure emerged certain "principles" for the conduct of a public employment service in the context of the American social system. The more important of these principles were:[10]

1. The recognition of the need for a separate employment service program.

2. The principal goal: The elimination of unnecessary unemployment. Placement, counseling, testing, etc., are the means to this goal.

---

[9] *Ibid.*, p. 1. Recently the local offices have been spending a good deal of time identifying the job vacancies for which workers might be trained, selecting the trainees, helping arrange for the training program, and placing the graduates of the training courses.

[10] These principles have been adapted by the writer from "Regulations for Co-operation of the United States Employment Service and the States in Establishing a National System of Public Employment Offices," *Federal Register* (October 3, 1946), and from other sources such as a special issue of *The Annals*, American Academy of Political and Social Science, Vol. LIX (May, 1915).

3. Voluntarism: The public offices should rely principally on "selling" their services to employers and workers.

4. Impartiality: The service should not become either a strikebreaking agency or a means to enforce union demands.

5. Best man for the job: The goal of the placement process should be to find the best worker for each vacancy.

6. Business-like methods: Since the service must compete with many alternative ways of filling jobs, its operations should be conducted as efficiently and effectively as possible.

7. Programs based on local needs: Each local office should develop its own program to meet local manpower problems, which vary over time and between areas.

8. Experimentation and research: These are essential to the improvement of a public employment office program, just as in the case of other organizations which must meet severe competition.

9. Not a police organization: Although the employment service must operate with due regard for social policy, as an agency that relies on persuasion for its existence, it cannot be required to police legislation.

10. A center of information: The public service has a responsibility to keep informed about labor-market developments and to supply such information to the public.

These ten principles, it should be understood, constitute a body of theory of operation, which in some instances is given more lip service than actual observance. Not all offices are run as though they were in a highly competitive business. The real test of the effectiveness of the six-point program, the budget system, the principles of operation, and administration at federal, state, and local levels can be found in the record of work done in relation to the available staff and opportunities for service. This record provides a means of testing the adequacy of the general program and the effectiveness of state administrators, supervisors, and local office managers who have been responsible for carrying it out. It is a record of services performed under a system of uniform general policies with decentralized administration.

II. THE NATIONAL RECORD, 1947–1962

A. PLACEMENTS, APPLICATIONS TAKEN, COUNSELING, AND TESTING

Tables 10–1 through 10–4 show the volume of activities of the federal-state system during the nineteen-fifties and during 1947, the first year after the war in which the employment picture was not seriously affected by strikes or postwar readjustments in the labor force. The record of the public employment service during this time, from 1947 through the nineteen-fifties, has been criticized by some people on the ground that it shows lack of initiative and a failure to take advantage of opportunities for service. This accusation will be examined after a review of the record.

The data in Table 10–1 show that the total volume of nonfarm placements increased between 1947 and 1957 by about 8 per cent and between 1947 and 1959 by about 15 per cent, but that these increases were smaller than the rise in either employment or total population. When placements in domestic jobs are eliminated, the remainder of nonfarm placements from 1947 through 1957 show a small loss and only a 7 per cent gain from 1947 through 1959. If all short-time jobs (those lasting less than 4 days, including most domestic placements) are eliminated from the placement data, the record shows a loss for both periods, 1947–57 and 1947–59. It is obvious that the service, so far as nonfarm placements in regular jobs (those lasting 4 or more days) are concerned, was not filling as many openings at the end, as at the beginning, of these periods. The increase in total volume was achieved because more short-time and domestic jobs were filled.

Between 1959 and 1962, the changes in organization and the increase in funds for the service in fiscal years 1961 and 1962, plus an expanding market for jobs, helped the public service to improve considerably its postwar placement record. The percentage increase in total nonfarm placements between 1947 and 1962 was about the same as the increase in nonfarm employment and nearly as large as the increase in population. A large part of the

TABLE 10-1: NATIONAL TOTALS OF NONFARM PLACEMENTS, EMPLOYMENT, AND TOTAL POPULATION, 1947, 1957, 1959, AND 1962

National totals	1947	1957	1959	1962	Per cent difference 1947–57	Per cent difference 1947–59	Per cent difference 1947–62
Total nonfarm placements	5,278,000	5,724,000	6,098,000	6,718,000	+ 8.4	+14.8	+26.6
Nonfarm placements (excl. household)	4,533,500	4,506,600	4,858,400	5,331,000	– .6	+ 7.1	+17.6
Nonfarm placements (excl. short-time)	4,390,700	4,009,300	4,254,600	4,629,900	– 8.7	– 3.2	+ 5.4
Employment in nonfarm establishments	43,881,000	52,904,000	53,380,000	55,325,000	+20.6	+21.6	+26.1
Estimated population totals	154,556,000	170,475,000	177,145,000	185,822,000	+10.8	+23.5	+20.5

SOURCES: Placement data: U.S. Department of Labor, Bureau of Employment Security. Data include Alaska, Hawaii, Puerto Rico, Guam, and Virgin Islands. Short-time includes placements on jobs which are expected to last for less than four days.
Employment data: BLS, *Employment and Earnings*, Feb., 1963, Table B, page 14; excludes territories for all years and Alaska and Hawaii before 1959.
Population data: Bureau of Census, Series P–25, No. 250, 7/3/62, Table 2 and Series P–25, No. 263, 3/15/63; total resident population excluding territories in all years, and Alaska and Hawaii before 1959.

TABLE 10-2: UNITED STATES EMPLOYMENT SERVICE ACTIVITIES, 1947–1962   (In thousands)

Activities	1947	1953	1954	1955	1956	1957	1958	1959	1960	1961	1962
New applications	6,867	7,865	9,054	7,983	8,338	9,181	10,414	9,282	10,117	10,502	10,792
Counseling interviews											
Total	1,398	1,273	1,344	1,453	1,457	1,538	1,612	1,766	1,778	1,876	2,092
Initial	745	764	752	863	848	900	939	1,030	1,036	1,093	1,214
Individuals given tests	145	922	929	1,212	1,393	1,412	1,455	1,720	1,757	1,979	2,254
Placements											
Total	6,327	15,582	14,070	14,958	15,157	14,293	14,408	15,855	15,273	14,708	15,184
Nonfarm	5,278	6,295	5,158	6,052	6,085	5,724	5,126	6,097	5,818	5,902	6,718
Farm	1,049	9,287	8,912	8,906	9,072	8,569	9,282	9,758	9,455	9,806	8,466

SOURCE: U.S. Dept. of Labor, Bureau of Employment Security records. Data include Alaska, Hawaii, Puerto Rico, Guam, and Virgin Islands.

TABLE 10-3: NONFARM PLACEMENTS BY INDUSTRY DIVISION AND SHORT-TIME,[a] 1947–1962 (In thousands)

Industry division	1947	1950	1951	1952	1953	1954	1955	1956	1957	1958	1959	1960	1961	1962
All industries	5,278	5,626	6,552	6,500	6,295	5,161	6,053	6,086	5,724	5,126	6,098	5,818	5,903	6,718
Construction	663	613	—	—	571	459	525	501	432	402	476	409	414	463
Manufacturing	1,835	1,723	—	—	1,943	1,371	1,709	1,613	1,432	1,186	1,545	1,330	1,303	1,509
Transp. & utilities	292	277	—	—	311	214	287	305	275	222	256	237	214	233
Trade	935	1,139	—	—	1,282	1,092	1,297	1,340	1,270	1,132	1,335	1,271	1,350	1,581
Services	1,238	1,535	—	—	1,875	1,731	1,907	1,984	1,990	1,866	2,129	2,153	2,216	2,537
Government	182	209	—	—	151	159	170	182	169	182	207	268	257	232
Other	133	130	—	—	162	135	158	161	156	136	150	150	149	163
Short-time	922	1,319	—	—	1,711	1,541	1,739	1,768	1,715	1,611	1,842	1,813	1,830	2,095

SOURCE: U.S. Dept of Labor, Bureau of Employment Security, "Historical Supplement to Key Facts on Employment Security Operations, 1938–1959" and "Statistical Supplement to the Labor Market and Employment Security" and *Statistical Abstract of the United States*, 1948–1951. The total placement figures do not agree in all cases with those in Table 10–2 because of rounding.

a Short-time includes placements on jobs which are expected to last less than four days.

TABLE 10-4: NONFARM PLACEMENTS BY OCCUPATIONAL GROUP, 1947–1962 (In thousands)

Occupation	1947	1950	1951	1952	1953	1954	1955	1956	1957	1958	1959	1960	1961	1962
Total	5,281	5,625	6,552	6,500	6,294	5,158	6,052	6,085	5,723	5,127	6,096	5,819	5,902	6,725
Professional &														
managerial	55	67	88	83	85	93	103	117	132	136	153	172	197	239
Clerical & sales	595	695	763	749	728	677	804	848	817	766	886	916	935	1,090
Service														
Total	1,237	1,513	1,753	1,820	1,828	1,642	1,802	1,876	1,843	1,677	1,911	1,917	1,948	2,139
Dayworkers	—	—	—	—	—	—	629	636	598	536	590	569	579	612
Skilled	386	400	427	370	329	289	330	331	303	298	343	311	351	382
Semiskilled	697	742	837	858	829	645	836	829	774	673	869	761	769	907
Unskilled & others														
Total	2,311	2,208	2,684	2,620	2,495	1,812	2,177	2,084	1,854	1,577	1,934	1,742	1,702	1,968
Casual workers	—	—	—	—	—	—	492	465	429	361	426	438	369	412

SOURCE: U.S. Dept. of Labor, Bureau of Employment Security, "Historical Supplement to Key Facts on Employment Security Operations, 1938–1959," and "Statistical Supplement to the Labor Market and Employment Service." The total placements do not agree with the totals shown in Table 10–2 and Table 10–3 because of rounding and possibly some minor discrepancies in reporting.

increase in placements in the period 1947–62, however, as in the period 1947–59, was attributable to the filling of short-time jobs, such as day work in households and in trade and service industries.

Table 10–2 shows that the volume of all placements more than doubled between 1947 and 1962, but this was chiefly a result of the increase in farm placements. This increase resulted in large part from the transfer of responsibility for this work from the Department of Agriculture Extension Service to the USES in 1948. Some of the increase in farm placements, however, was attributable to a substantial increase in seasonal peak demands for farm labor and to increased recruitment of foreign and domestic workers, that the public service was asked to undertake.

Three other activities of the public service also show substantial gains in the postwar period. The number of applications for work increased substantially after 1953 as a result of the increase in unemployment during the general business recessions of 1954, 1958, and 1960 and the failure of unemployment to recede to pre-recession levels in the years following the recessions. The number of counseling interviews has also risen substantially since 1947. This increase reflects, in part, a greater need felt by displaced workers for assistance in adjusting to changes in job opportunities. It also reflects the greater competence of employment service staff in rendering this type of service than was the case right after the war, before extensive training in counseling techniques had taken place. The third activity, testing, has grown because of the greater use of the general aptitude test battery in counseling and the use of proficiency tests for selection of applicants for referral.

Tables 10–3 and 10–4 show placements according to industrial and occupational groups and thus indicate the kinds of jobs filled. Industrially, the biggest decline in placements after 1953 occurred in manufacturing and in construction. The decline in manufacturing began after the Korean War and continued throughout the period with brief cyclical reversals in 1955, 1959, and 1962. The biggest

gains took place in trade and in service industries.

From an occupational point of view the public service since the end of World War II has achieved a greater gain in placements in the service group than in any other group. In fact, service jobs now constitute the largest single occupational class of placements, whereas in 1947 the unskilled group constituted the greatest number. Not much change has taken place since 1947 in the volume of skilled or semi-skilled jobs filled. Placements in unskilled jobs have declined with the loss of such jobs in manufacturing and other industries. But there have been substantial increases in the number of clerical and sales jobs filled and, also, in the volume of professional, technical, and managerial placements. These changes in placement volume reflect significant changes in job opportunities in the nation and also indicate the response of the service to the growth of jobs in trade, service, finance, insurance, and real estate industries.

B. Special Placement Services

A review of the placement record would be incomplete without at least a mention of the services which the employment offices have extended to special groups of applicants. In addition to those groups specified in the Wagner-Peyser Act, the public service has been required to provide special help to older workers, European refugees, migratory farm workers, rural residents, parolees, and Indians and to expand its services for high-school youth and the handicapped. As a result of the attention given to these special groups of applicants, the service became known in some quarters as a collection of "specialty shops"[11] rather than as a general employment service dealing with all types of applicants. Those who have questioned the growth of special services have done so for two reasons. They argue that the best way to serve all applicants, including the special groups, is to increase the

[11] A. W. Motley, "Is the Employment Service Becoming a Series of Specialty Shops?" *Employment Security Review* (February, 1957).

general penetration of the service. From a larger volume of openings registered with the service it will then be possible to serve all types of applicants, not merely those in special groups. Further, they point out that too much publicity on special services creates a public image which keeps the best employees from registering for work and employers from filing their best openings.

To some extent the increased work required by these special services has been performed by additional staff. The veterans' service has its special national, state, and local office representatives, and there are now specially trained interviewers in all of the larger offices to deal with the handicapped, school-age youth, and older workers. Veteran placements in 1960 constituted about 20 per cent of the total volume, as compared with 30 per cent in 1947, when many of those discharged from the armed services had not yet found work. Placement of the handicapped has remained at about 4.5 per cent of the total volume during the postwar period. Counseling and placement work with youth has been increasing considerably in recent years. In 1960–61 nearly half of the high schools in the nation were co-operating with local office staffs to provide a counseling and placement service for seniors. Placement services for older workers also have increased, and the record in 1960 showed that one of every three placements involved a person forty-five years or over. This observer has the impression that the growth of these special services has absorbed many of the best placement staff workers.

Mention should also be made of the co-operation of the public service in enforcing federal and state policies on discrimination against minority groups. In the states which have legislation prohibiting discrimination in employment, the public employment service, as are private agencies, is required to carry out this policy in selection and referral practices. In New York the service has also been used as part of the policing machinery, since the local offices are required to report to the enforcement agency those employers who refuse to change discriminatory orders and patterns of hiring.

This policy is in sharp contrast to the recent practice in some southern states of maintaining separate offices and separate sections within offices for Negroes. Efforts have been made to change this practice, and all of these segregated operations were expected to have been eliminated by the end of 1963.[12]

By far the largest of the special placement services is the farm placement service,[13] which is budgeted separately. In sheer numbers the volume of farm placements exceeds all others put together. Nearly all the work of this service is directed toward meeting seasonal farm labor needs. The labor supply is a combination of local recruits, domestic migratory workers, and foreign workers, most of them Mexican. Foreign workers are supposed to be used only when the domestic supply is inadequate and to be paid the prevailing wage rates for American workers. Recruitment and routing of these workers, especially in the Southwest, has involved the service in many activities not common to the operation of an employment service. Making the optimum use of domestic workers has required close co-operation with growers to determine their needs and with other state services to plan the movement of workers from one area to another to meet the needs for help with cash crops and, also, to provide the workers with as regular employment as possible. Considerable success has been achieved in both respects. In fact, the Annual Worker Program for migratory farm labor is a good example of what the original proponents of a public service expected such a service could do to regularize employment.

C. OTHER SERVICES

Space does not permit an extensive review of the other aspects of the general six-point

[12] Letter to the writer from the Director of the USES, September 21, 1962. Also, see responses of Mr. Goodwin and Mr. Levine to questions by Senator Javits, *Hearings*, Subcommittee on Employment and Manpower of the Committee on Labor and Public Welfare, United States Senate, 88th Congress, Part 3, p. 888.

[13] For a discussion of farm employment see William Mirengoff and Mordecai Baill, "A Decade of Changes in Farm Output and Employment," *Employment Security Review* (March, 1958).

program. Also, there is much less information available about some of these activities than there is about placement. This is particularly true of industrial and community services, since no statistical data on the volume of these activities have been published. From personal observation in a half dozen areas, the writer has the impression that these activities vary a great deal from one area to another, depending partly on needs and partly on the initiative and competence of local office staff.

The record shows considerable activity with respect to labor-market information and the development of manpower tools such as testing services and the *Dictionary of Occupational Titles*. The labor-market information program has continued to provide regular estimates on the current and near-future balance between labor supply and demand by area for all major industrial centers and, less regularly, for many of the small centers. This information has kept the country alert to the problems of depressed areas and has helped to stimulate the federal legislation that has provided financial assistance and training programs for these areas. Local labor-market letters have served to keep businessmen and others aware of local business conditions, and the data on employment and unemployment have been helpful to some larger companies and public utilities in developing their own plans. Although these various labor-market reports are intended to provide a basis for local office planning, this writer has the impression that they have served mainly to meet national office requirements.

One of the chief contributions made by the labor-market reporting program has been to encourage business, the schools, and civic groups to take a forward look at skilled, technical, and professional manpower needs for the future. With the co-operation of local business groups, unions, and schools, the service has undertaken a series of special surveys of current and future needs and an appraisal of where the surpluses or shortages will be found in approximately five years. By the end of 1960, some sixty-six such surveys had been made and forty-five more were under way. The analyses of labor needs have been helpful

to schools and training institutes in planning curriculum and counseling students. They have also been useful both to private employers in planning for future labor needs and to the employment service in counseling.

Mention should be made also of the work done at headquarters and in a dozen state offices on the analysis and description of new jobs and on the revision of old job descriptions. It is expected that the results of this work will be used in the new edition of the *Dictionary of Occupational Titles*, now in process of publication. This is the first revision in more than twelve years of a basic tool which becomes rapidly out of date in a dynamic economy.

Further work has been done also on the application of the general aptitude test battery to new groups such as youths under eighteen and men over sixty. This tool has been well received professionally and has been widely used as an aid in counseling youths just entering the labor market and re-entrants, such as married women. The use of proficiency tests has grown at the local office level as more types of tests have become available through the efforts of the state and federal staff. In fact, some employers have used the local offices as their exclusive source of new recruits for semi-skilled jobs, because they have become convinced that the screening provided by the proficiency tests and the general battery furnishes them with better workers than they could select by other means.

Since the passage of the various acts involving manpower planning, training, and re-training (see section V below), some local offices have been spending considerable time planning for training courses, selecting trainees, paying allowances, and attending to other matters connected with the management of such programs. These activities will grow in importance for at least the next few years while the legislation is being tested.

III. COMPARATIVE POSTWAR RECORDS OF THE STATES

Under the federal-state system the implementation of specific employment service programs to meet community needs has been left mainly in the hands of state and local officials. It is appropriate, therefore, to examine the relative records of the states with respect to services performed. These records are shown in tables 10–5 and 10–6 for the sixteen largest states and in subsequent tables for the middle-size and small states.

A. STANDARDS

Any evaluation of state records of services rendered involves the use of standards of performance or "yardsticks" by which the work done in each state can be fairly compared with that done in other states. These standards, when a comparative analysis of all fifty states is attempted, must take the form of quantitative measures which meet the tests of accuracy, objectivity, relevance to key work load items, and fairness. The analysis presented here uses measures which have been developed by members of the employment service staff, as well as some developed by the writer, with these criteria in mind.

It is recognized by all concerned that quantitative data are not an entirely satisfactory means of measuring the accomplishments of any service organization, because mere numbers of transactions cannot show the extent of the service rendered or its qualitative significance. Furthermore, any numerical reporting scheme is not likely to cover all aspects of the work done. These objections to the use of quantitative measures have some validity, but the fact remains that, if we depend on qualitative appraisals, there are very few published data which can be used for interstate comparisons. Furthermore, the advantages of making some quantitative comparisons of state accomplishments seem, to this observer, to outweigh the disadvantages of having no comparisons made at all or of making them on subjective bases which involve a great deal of opinion and judgment by different individuals.

In the comparative analyses presented here, heavy reliance has been placed on the operating numerical reports covering important services rendered, submitted by the states to the Washington headquarters. It is assumed that these reports are compiled honestly and that they reflect an accurate picture of the volume of services rendered and the work done. Most of these data have been published. Wherever possible, data reflecting the quality of services rendered, as in the case of different types of placements, also have been shown.

The choice of the numerical data to be used has been governed by the criterion of fairness which, in turn, requires a test of validity. Obviously, it would be unfair to compare the states with one another on the basis of absolute numbers of activities. An effort has been made, therefore, to find measures of performance which, on the one hand, relate the potential need for service to the capacity for rendering service (as shown by number of staff) and, on the other hand, relate the potential need for service to the work accomplished. For these purposes several different measures have been used and placed side by side in the following tables, so that the reader can see how a particular state or group of states compares with others—not merely on one standard, but on several such standards for the same periods of time.

A brief explanation of the standards used in the tables below will show why these particular measures have been used and also will indicate some of their strengths and weaknesses so that the reader can use his own judgment about the significance of the tables.

First of all, the states have been ranked by size and divided into three major groups, large, medium, and small. Ranking the states by size facilitates comparisons of numbers of staff and work accomplished.[14] It seems reasonable

[14] Two other systems of classification were considered. One was based on the amount of increase or decrease in nonfarm employment since the end of World War II. This classification brought together large and small states with widely differing records. It showed that the volume of employment services rendered, especially placements, is not directly proportionate to the growth of new jobs or the loss of old ones and that a comparison of states based on these factors would not be helpful in understanding the relative postwar records. The other classification that was considered was based on organization structure. This was abandoned, however, because there were very few states in which the most significant difference, a

to expect the size of the state, as measured by the number of its nonfarm employees, to be a significant indicator of the potential need for services. Further, it might be expected that the number of staff allocated to a state would roughly correspond with the opportunities for service and the need for basic services in the state. Finally, it might be expected that the volume of services rendered would bear a close relationship to the opportunities for service and the relative size of staff. For all of these reasons, heavy reliance has been placed on statistical ranking of the state data as one method of measuring relative performance. It should be emphasized that identical ranking-results, across the board, for any given state should not necessarily be expected. There may be differences—in labor-market conditions, in quality of staff, or actual opportunities for performing different services—which account for differences in ranking-relationships at any given time or over a given period of time. For example, the rank of a state on counseling and testing services may be less than expected, in view of its size, because job opportunities may be greater than in other states, and a larger proportion of job seekers can be referred to openings without counseling and testing than is the case elsewhere.

Second, having ranked the states by number of nonfarm wage and salary workers and having grouped them into three major divisions based on size, the next question was: What specific measurements of opportunities for service and work accomplished are available, and which of these should be used? This question is related to another question: What activities are most significant in terms of the goals of the organization and the manner in which staff spend their time? The primary goal of the service has been to reduce unemployment by providing counseling, testing, placement, and informational and technical services. Since there is no comprehensive measure of the

effectiveness of these services as a means of reducing unemployment, we can only use the data on the numbers of placements, etc., as an indication of the achivments of the service. The numbers and types of placements made should get the lion's share of attention, because these data come the closest of any available to providing a measure of the number of job seekers who actually find jobs with the help of the service, and because about 75 per cent of the staff time is spent on this activity. But numbers of placements do not actually show the number of persons helped, because the same person may be placed several times during the course of a month, quarter, or year. This point, however, merely reflects the fact that the unemployed are an ever-changing group of individuals, some of whom may be in and out of jobs several times during a year because of personal reasons or because of the nature of the work, as in the case of seasonal or short-time jobs. It would be interesting and useful to know how many repeaters are included in placement figures; but such data generally are not available.

A more important weakness of the place-ment data, as a measure of the effectiveness of the service in reducing unemployment, is that no distinction is made in the data between placements of the unemployed versus those already employed. In fact, no data are reported on the employment status of job applicants. It has been assumed that the bulk of applicants are unemployed and that most of the un-employed are claimants of unemployment insurance. This assumption is probably a valid one. At least this was the case in the offices that this observer visited within the past two years. But it is true also that some applicants who were already employed were seeking help in finding more suitable employ-ment. This was the case especially where the service had established separate offices or sections to serve professional, technical, and clerical personnel. The volume of placements made in these occupational categories has been a small fraction of all nonfarm placements, but, as Table 10–4 shows, there has been in the postwar period a steady upward trend of

separation of placement and insurance functions, was actually reflected in the basic statewide organization during the period under review. The only system left to be used, therefore, was one based on size of the state as indicated by nonfarm employment.

placements in these categories. With the reorganization of the service in the larger metropolitan areas and the establishment of separate and more attractive offices for serving white-collar workers, a further increase in this type of placement may be expected. There is, of course, no inference intended that the employment service should not be placing workers who are already employed. It was given a mandate to serve *all* workers and employers who ask for help, with the recognition that there is a useful purpose for the individuals and the nation in helping workers find the jobs for which they are best qualified. But the fact remains that the placement data available do not show the employment status of the job seekers when placed and, therefore, they are not a perfect measure of the effect of the service on unemployment. It is likely, however, that placements of persons who are already employed represent no more than 10 to 15 per cent of the total volume.

Other services rendered to job applicants, such as counseling, testing, and supplying job market information, are often useful in directly supporting the placement operation and may result directly in helping people find jobs. They are also carried on independently of placement. The assumption is made that these services do, either directly or indirectly, help individuals find suitable work and assist employers in recruitment and selection of workers. But there is no way of proving, from the data available, what the precise relationship is between these activities and the reduction of unemployment.

A more recent activity of the employment service, which is absorbing a good deal of staff time in some areas, is connected with the identification of labor shortages, training needs, selection of trainees, and subsequent placement work under federal legislation enacted in 1961 and 1962 (the Area Redevelopment Act and the Manpower Development and Training Act). These programs are still in the formative stage and comprehensive data are not yet available on the volume of these activities.

The comparative analysis presented here places heavy emphasis on the placement activi-ties of the employment service because such a large proportion of its time has been spent in the past on this phase of the program. The data on placement show, for each state, the size of staff, the percentage change in place-ments over time, the type of placement, and the penetration ratios. This last measure requires some comment because it has been accepted as a standard of performance by many people in the service but has been criticized by others.

Penetration ratios are calculated by dividing the number of placements made by the service in a given time period by the number of new hires made by employers for the same period of time. The result shows the extent to which the service has participated *directly* in the hiring of workers not previously on the payrolls of individual employers. Unfortunately, data on new hires are available only for manufactur-ing industries and for only about 70 per cent of the states. Estimates of ratios for other industries have been made in selected areas, and some crude estimates of penetration ratios for all nonfarm industries have been made using data on total payroll accessions. But only those ratios for manufacturing which are based on Bureau of Labor Statistics data on new hires and placements reported to the Bureau of Employment Security are believed to be reasonably accurate for most of the large states and for the nation as a whole.

Even when the data are available, the use of penetration ratios as a measure of performance is open to criticism because the number of placements, per se, does not show the total contribution of the service in filling jobs. Some jobs are undoubtedly obtained by workers who get information and/or advice from the service, although they may not actually be referred by it, so that their placement cannot be counted. This is undoubtedly a valid point and should be kept in mind in interpreting the penetration ratio data presented. A further limitation on the usefulness of this measure is that no precise goal or standard of performance in terms of penetration has been established. There are many different ways in which workers find jobs and the employment service could not, even if it wanted to, monopolize the job market.

But if the service participates directly in a very small fraction of the hiring process, it is a sign that it is not a significant factor in organizing job markets and in reducing unemployment. As a general rule, it may be assumed that the significance of the service as a means of filling jobs increases as penetration ratios rise. A comparison of ratios on a state-by-state basis therefore indirectly throws some additional light on the *relative* contributions being made by the service to the organization of job markets and hence on one of its contributions toward the reduction of unemployment.

In general, the following analysis and commentary assume that: (1) the size of the state is a good indicator of its relative opportunities for service; (2) staff should be allocated roughly in proportion to the opportunities for service; (3) work accomplished should be in proportion to the size of the state and the size of its staff; and (4) the effectiveness of the service to the nation, with respect to nonfarm employment, depends chiefly on its work in the largest metropolitan areas where most of the jobs are located, so that the records in the largest states are most significant. There may be good reasons why the records of some states have deviated from these general standards; but in these cases the data still serve a useful purpose in calling attention to the situations which require further explanation.

B. STATE EXPERIENCE

Table 10–5 includes the sixteen largest states, which had 75 per cent of the total nonfarm employment in 1960. It presents their records of placements per staff member, penetration ratios in manufacturing industries in 1959, and percentage change in placements from 1947 to 1959. Penetration ratios for 1959 were used because this was a year of recovery in general business conditions, whereas 1960 was a year when business began to decline again and there were fewer job openings to be filled. A comparison of the change in placements from 1947 to 1959 also was made with general business conditions in mind. Table 10–6

ranks the same states with respect to size, staff used, and major work-load items. The facts brought out by these two tables show that the records of the largest states have been very unequal.

With respect to the change in the volume of placements between the years 1947 and 1959 regular placements (the total less short-time placements) actually declined in eleven of the sixteen states and remained the same in one state. In four states (New York, Massachusetts, Florida, and North Carolina) there were substantial increases. These four states also had above average penetration ratios in manufacturing industries and a larger number of placements per staff member than other states. One other state (Texas) had a high penetration rate and an above-average number of placements per staff member but showed no gain in placements between 1947 and 1959.

When these sixteen states are ranked by size and records of work done, several interesting facts are evident. The four states which had good placement records ranked about as high as might be expected (or even higher), in view of their size, with respect to applications taken, counseling, testing, and types of placement made. For example, New York, the largest ranked first in total placements, in counseling and in professional, managerial, and skilled placements. It also had the largest staff. For some reason, however, the volume of tests given was much smaller than might have been expected in view of the size of the state. In each of the other three states there were also some discrepancies between rank by size and volume of work. Florida ranked relatively low, both in counseling and testing. Since the relative volume of placements was high in this state, there may have been less need for these other services because a larger proportion of applicants was referred to jobs. In several states, for example New Jersey, Indiana, and Virginia, the work accomplished relative to the size of the state and the size of the staff was in most respects, very much out of line.

Some general observations may be made on the basis of the data in these two tables. The placement records of the states have been

TABLE 10-5: PLACEMENT RECORD OF THE LARGEST STATES[a] IN 1960 AND IN THE PERIOD 1947–1959

State	Rank based on nonfarm employment	(1960 Data)					Penetration rate[c] in mfg. (1959) (per cent)	Per cent change in placements (except short-time) 1947–1959
		Nonfarm employment (000)	Staff members[b]	Nonfarm placements (000)	Nonfarm employment per staff member	Placements per staff member		
(1)	(2)	(3)	(4)	(5)	(6)	(7)	(8)	(9)
New York	1	6,188	1,279	808	4,834	632	46	+29.2
California	2	4,917	954	491	5,131	515	18	−12.1
Pennsylvania	3	3,719	738	252	5,040	341	18*	−15.7
Illinois	4	3,417	467	220	7,317	471	23*	−3.1
Ohio	5	3,120	540	212	5,778	400	17*	−27.6
Texas	6	2,505	752	496	3,380	659	56	−0.9
Michigan	7	2,334	406	148	5,749	365	16*	−20.5
New Jersey	8	2,012	309	134	6,510	433	17*	−5.3
Massachusetts	9	1,914	283	160	6,762	565	26	+37.3
Indiana	10	1,429	193	79	7,404	409	23	−28.0
Missouri	11	1,349	233	90	5,800	386	29	−17.9
Florida	12	1,312	309	205	4,240	662	27	+40.3
North Carolina	13	1,191	230	165	5,134	717	44	+31.0
Wisconsin	14	1,186	225	113	5,271	502	44*	−1.9
Georgia	15	1,041	187	120	5,566	641	27	0.0
Virginia	16	1,015	143	84	7,098	587	22	−10.8

SOURCES: Employment and placement data: *Statistical Abstract of the United States*, 1961, pp. 211 and 282. Number of direct staff used: Letter of Louis Levine (BES) to writer. These figures are rough approximations and, therefore, small differences are not significant. Penetration rates in manufacturing: Calculated from turnover rates in B.L.S., *Employment and Earnings*, Annual Supplement, Nov., 1961, p. 138. New hires data are not available for other industries. Percentage change figures, 1947–1959: Taken from "Report of Committee on Employment Service Programs and Operations, 1960," Appendix B, Interstate Conference of Employment Security Agencies. Ranking data are from a mimeographed report prepared by Arizona State Employment Service.

a States with one million or more nonfarm employees in 1960.

b Estimated number of full-time equivalent positions used during the year on employment service work.

c Penetration rate: placements made by the employment service as a proportion of all new hires. Turnover data for calculating penetration rates are available only for manufacturing industries and for only some of the states.

* Estimated by applying the national average new-hire rate to manufacturing employment in the state.

209

TABLE 10-6: THE LARGEST STATES[a] RANKED HIGHEST TO LOWEST ACCORDING TO SELECTED CHARACTERISTICS, 1960

State	Nonfarm employment		Staff members	New applications taken	Nonfarm placements		Type of placement			Counseling interviews	Tests administered
	Number	Number per staff member[b]			Number	No. per staff member	Prof. & Mgr.	Clerical & Sales	Skilled		
(1)	(2)	(3)	(4)	(5)	(6)	(7)	(8)	(9)	(10)	(11)	(12)
New York	1	29	1	2	1	10	1	2	1	1	5
California	2	32	2	1	3	30	3	1	3	2	1
Pennsylvania	3	31	4	5	4	49	4	4	5	3	6
Illinois	4	48	6	7	5	35	9	7	9	7	7
Ohio	5	38	5	4	6	42	11	5	7	4	3
Texas	6	12	3	3	2	7	5	3	2	5	2
Michigan	7	37	7	6	10	45	21	8	8	6	4
New Jersey	8	43	8	8	11	36	15	14	12	12	26
Massachusetts	9	45	10	13	9	24	2	10	10	8	21
Indiana	10	49	15	9	27	40	30	17	26	21	15
Missouri	11	39	11	12	20	43	34	15	29	10	10
Florida	12	18	9	11	7	6	8	6	4	23	14
North Carolina	13	33	12	10	8	4	17	11	6	9	9
Wisconsin	14	34	13	14	14	31	7	9	22	13	12
Georgia	15	35	17	18	13	9	24	22	14	19	18
Virginia	16	47	27	27	25	19	33	25	24	11	23

SOURCES: The same as in Table 10–5.
[a] States with one million or more nonfarm employees in 1960.
[b] Ranked from lowest to highest.

210

unequal relative to their size and number of staff. The data in Table 10–6 suggest, further, that the placement record is indicative of the relative accomplishments of the states with respect to other aspects of the general employment service program. In general, in about half of the largest states in the nation the public employment service record was relatively weak as measured by the change in volume of placements between 1947 and 1959, penetration rates in manufacturing industries, number of placements per staff member, and the rank of these states in other aspects of the services rendered. The reasons for these relative weaknesses may be traced, in part, to different labor-market conditions among the states and, hence, to different opportunities for placement and other services, to management deficiencies, to the number and quality of staff available, and probably to other factors which would be revealed by a more intensive analysis. Some of these additional factors are pointed out below in section D.

One important difference among the states, which deserves special attention, is the ratio of nonfarm employment to staff. In general, the states with the best records of service had the most favorable staffing patterns as measured by this ratio. The ratio in the states with the best records was about 5,000 to 1, whereas the ratios in the states with poorer records were usually higher—very much higher in Illinois and Indiana. These ratios may be a reflection of a budgeting system based on previous recognition of volume of work done and staff used. The resulting lack of staff may in turn be the cause of the relatively poor showing of these states.

The states with better performances (New York, Texas, Massachusetts, Florida, North Carolina, and Wisconsin) have no one organization pattern common to all, nor has there been in these states a uniformly high rate of growth in population and employment since the war. These variables do not, therefore, account for the showing made by these states as a group.

In the case of New York State, the placement record in New York City, where the service provides a central hiring hall under the terms of several labor-management agreements, accounts for most of the high volume of placements and the high penetration ratio for the state as a whole. The record of this state—and one suspects this is also true in the other five states—is in part a reflection of the efforts of good management.

These data on relative performance by the largest states do not reflect the recent changes in staffing patterns and employment service reorganization in the largest metropolitan areas. A comparative analysis, based on data for fiscal year 1962, shows that the number of employment service staff has grown in nearly all of the sixteen largest states since 1960, and that the ratio of nonfarm employment to staff in the states with the best records has been reduced from about 5,000 to 1 to about 4,000 to 1. Placements have also increased with the rise in numbers of staff; in 1962, nine of the sixteen states showed a gain over the volume in calendar 1947, while in 1959 only four showed a gain. However, no substantial changes have occurred in the differences among the states noted above.

The work records in fifteen middle-sized states (Tables 10–7 and 10–8) lead to much the same conclusions as do the records in the sixteen largest states. Only four states (Connecticut, Kentucky, Kansas, and Colorado) show an increase in nonfarm placements between 1947 and 1959. Of these states, Colorado has an outstanding record; it also has the largest number of staff in proportion to nonfarm employment. Other states, such as Minnesota, Tennessee, and Oklahoma, have relatively high penetration ratios and rank high in 1960 work accomplishments but show substantial declines in placement volume between 1947 and 1959. In several of the states the amount of other work done was not in proportion to their size. For example, the volume of counseling and testing in Connecticut was far smaller than might have been expected; in Minnesota and Tennessee, on the other hand, there was much more testing than might have been expected. If the facts have been accurately reported, these differences raise the question whether there has been too much or too little

TABLE 10-7: PLACEMENT RECORD OF THE MIDDLE-SIZED STATES[a] IN 1960 AND IN THE PERIOD 1947-1959

State	(1960 Data)						Penetration rates in mfg., 1959 (per cent)	Per cent change in placements (except short-time) 1947-1959
	Rank based on nonfarm employment	Nonfarm employment (000)	Staff members	Nonfarm placements (000)	Nonfarm employment per staff member	Placements per staff member		
(1)	(2)	(3)	(4)	(5)	(6)	(7)	(8)	(9)
Minnesota	17	926	184	105	5,032	571	44	−18.7
Tennessee	18	918	197	109	4,660	551	54	−29.2
Connecticut	19	913	191	94	4,777	492	32	+ 6.5
Maryland	20	896	147	61	6,095	415	31	− 8.5
Washington	21	817	186	81	4,392	482	28*	− 5.5
Louisiana	22	788	139	72	5,669	518	25	− 8.0
Alabama	23	772	168	90	4,595	536	39	−49.4
Iowa	24	680	151	87	4,490	576	34	−12.4
Kentucky	25	652	143	52	4,559	363	43	+29.8
Oklahoma	26	581	179	130	3,246	726	46	−30.0
South Carolina	27	580	129	75	4,567	591	28	−18.9
Kansas	28	557	141	89	3,950	631	41	+ 6.2
District of Columbia	29	534	84	52	6,353	619	7	−21.3
Colorado	30	511	168	106	3,041	631	66*	+11.7
Oregon	31	507	124	71	4,090	572	36	−13.5

SOURCES AND OTHER FOOTNOTES: The same as Table 10-5.

[a] States with 500,000 to 1,000,000 nonfarm employees in 1960.

* Estimated by applying the national average new-hire rate to manufacturing employment in the state.

TABLE 10–8: THE MIDDLE-SIZED STATES[a] RANKED HIGHEST TO LOWEST ACCORDING TO SELECTED CHARACTERISTICS, 1960

State	Nonfarm employment		Staff members	New applications taken	Nonfarm placements		Type of placement			Counseling interviews	Tests administered
	Number	Number per staff member[b]			Number	No. per staff member	Prof. & Mgr.	Clerical & Sales	Skilled		
(1)	(2)	(3)	(4)	(5)	(6)	(7)	(8)	(9)	(10)	(11)	(12)
Minnesota	17	30	19	16	17	23	26	16	30	31	11
Tennessee	18	27	14	24	15	25	27	23	15	17	8
Connecticut	19	28	16	15	18	32	22	13	13	36	35
Maryland	20	40	25	20	33	39	35	30	25	18	30
Washington	21	19	18	17	26	33	16	12	21	14	17
Louisiana	22	36	30	22	30	29	39	19	18	32	31
Alabama	23	25	22	28	21	26	23	26	17	35	22
Iowa	24	21	24	32	23	21	19	18	34	25	16
Kentucky	25	23	26	25	35	46	31	32	32	15	13
Oklahoma	26	10	20	30	12	2	41	28	27	28	19
South Carolina	27	24	32	34	29	18	38	34	19	42	28
Kansas	28	15	28	33	22	11	27	27	23	30	34
District of Columbia	29	42	37	36	36	14	6	35	51	20	36
Colorado	30	9	21	29	16	11	10	24	11	27	24
Oregon	31	17	33	23	31	22	25	21	33	24	32

Sources: The same as in Table 10–5.
[a] States with 500,000 to 1,000,000 nonfarm employees in 1960.
[b] Ranked from lowest to highest.

213

TABLE 10-9: PLACEMENT RECORD OF THE SMALL STATES[a] IN 1960 AND IN THE PERIOD 1947–1959

State	Rank based on nonfarm employment	(1960 Data) Nonfarm employment (000)	Staff members	Nonfarm placements (000)	Nonfarm employment per staff member	Placements per staff member	Penetration rates in mfg., 1959 (per cent)	Per cent change in placements (except short-time) 1947–1959
(1)	(2)	(3)	(4)	(5)	(6)	(7)	(8)	(9)
West Virginia	32	458	69	26	6,637	362	25	−42.8
Mississippi	33	397	152	92	2,612	605	36	+ 2.2
Arkansas	34	369	131	76	2,818	580	44	−26.8
Nebraska	35	380	86	63	4,418	732	64*	+33.1
Arizona	36	331	141	85	2,347	602	41	+74.7
Rhode Island	37	290	64	24	4,531	375	26	− 1.3
Maine	38	277	45	24	6,155	533	23	−54.8
Utah	39	264	97	41	2,722	423	66*	+18.9
New Mexico	40	237	65	41	3,646	631	39	−11.4
New Hampshire	41	196	43	18	4,600	419	25	− 0.6
Montana	42	167	71	34	2,348	479	60	+26.5
Idaho	43	155	76	47	2,042	618	71	+12.8
Delaware	44	154	22	8	7,000	363	14	−46.0
South Dakota	45	139	42	27	3,369	643	42	+ 6.7
North Dakota	46	124	52	27	2,400	520	97	+32.5
Vermont	47	107	27	11	4,000	407	26	−13.1
Nevada	48	103	40	29	2,585	725	33	+39.4
Wyoming	49	97	25	17	3,900	680	59*	+10.7
Alaska	50	57						

SOURCES AND OTHER FOOTNOTES: The same as in Table 10–5.

[a] States with less than 500,000 nonfarm employees in 1960.

* Estimated by applying the national average new-hire rate to manufacturing employment in the state.

214

Table 10–10: THE SMALL STATES^a RANKED HIGHEST TO LOWEST ACCORDING TO SELECTED CHARACTERISTICS, 1960

State	Nonfarm employment			New applications taken	Nonfarm placements		Type of placement			Counseling interviews	Tests administered
	Number	Number per staff member^b	Staff members		Number	No. per staff member	Prof. & Mgr.	Clerical & Sales	Skilled		
(1)	(2)	(3)	(4)	(5)	(6)	(7)	(8)	(9)	(10)	(11)	(12)
West Virginia	32	44	40	35	44	48	43	38	41	34	40
Mississippi	33	6	23	26	19	16	13	29	20	16	20
Arkansas	34	8	31	21	28	20	37	31	31	22	25
Nebraska	35	20	36	37	32	1	42	36	39	38	33
Arizona	36	2	29	30	24	17	18	20	16	29	29
Rhode Island	37	22	42	41	46	44	48	41	42	41	45
Maine	38	41	44	43	45	27	50	45	40	37	38
Utah	39	7	35	42	39	37	12	33	36	33	37
New Mexico	40	13	41	38	38	11	44	42	37	44	43
New Hampshire	41	26	45	44	47	38	45	47	43	43	46
Montana	42	3	39	39	40	34	29	39	35	3	39
Idaho	43	1	38	40	37	15	40	37	38	40	42
Delaware	44	46	52	52	52	46	52	52	52	49	50
South Dakota	45	11	46	47	45	8	32	49	47	47	47
North Dakota	46	4	43	48	42	28	14	44	49	46	41
Vermont	47	16	49	50	50	41	51	51	50	52	51
Nevada	48	5	47	45	41	3	20	40	44	48	44
Wyoming	49	14	50	49	48	5	49	50	45	50	52
Alaska	50	—	51	51	51	—	46	48	48	51	48

SOURCES: The same as in Table 10–5.
^a States with less than 500,000 nonfarm employment in 1960. The original ranking data from which these figures were taken also included the District of Columbia, Guam, Hawaii, and the Virgin Islands and Puerto Rico.
^b Ranked from lowest to highest.

215

specialization in providing applicants with appropriate services.

Among the small states (Tables 10–9 and 10–10) there were ten which showed gains in placements in 1959 over 1947. These states had relatively higher penetration rates in manufacturing industries than did those states which showed declines in placements in the period 1947–59. Since these ten states constitute more than half of the small states for which records for the postwar period are available, the proportion of the small states with records of substantial accomplishments in proportion to size, staff, and opportunities is, on the whole, greater than the proportions in the large and middle-sized groups. In some of these small states, such as Arizona, Mississippi, and Utah, the general record of work accomplished is outstanding relative to their size and opportunities for placement, counseling, and testing.

C. General Observations

On the basis of the placement records of states in the postwar period and their recent relative showing on key work-load items, some general observations may be made on staffing patterns, on relative output by the staff in different states, and on policy with respect to administrative review of state operations.

It is obvious that by 1960 there had developed a very unequal allocation of funds for staff among the states in the three groups examined. Among the large states the number of nonfarm employees per staff member in 1960 varied from 3,380 (Texas) to 7,404 (Indiana). In the middle-sized group the range was from 3,041 (Colorado) to 6,353 (District of Columbia). Among the small states the range was from 2,042 (Idaho) to 7,000 (Delaware).

These wide differences in staffing may reflect substantial differences in past accomplishments and in budgeting based on the combination of unit-time factors and volume of work. It is hard to believe, however, that the need for service per 1,000 nonfarm workers is more than twice as great in some states than in others.

The staffing patterns in those states with the best general records in each group suggest that there have been three patterns, rather than one. In the large group the states with the best records had an average ratio of 5,000 nonfarm employees to 1 staff member. In the middle-sized group the ratio was about 4,000 to 1 in the states with the best records. The ratio for the ten best small states was about 2,600 to 1.

A second observation is that the work-load accomplishments of the states are not always in proportion to their size. For example, New York, which ranks first in size and in most of the work items discussed, shows a much lower volume of testing than might be expected; Texas, on the other hand, does much more testing than might be expected on the basis of its size. The same differences appear in the data for the states in the other groups. It is impossible to tell from the available data what the causes of such differences are. The extent of variation suggests, however, that the differences may be worth investigating.

A third observation is that the public service has a major administrative task on its hands if the weaker states are to fill the potential needs for services and be brought up to the level of accomplishment of the stronger states. Under the federal-state system this responsibility rests primarily with the headquarters of the USES, which in the past has relied upon the regional offices to review state performances and assist in strengthening the system. The records indicate that a new look needs to be taken at this arrangement and that a more effective policy should be developed for the future.

D. Comments on the National and State Records

A commentary on the public employment service was made by Secretary of Labor James Mitchell at the 1958 meeting of the Interstate Conference of Employment Security Agencies.[15] He argued that placements had not kept pace

[15] *Proceedings*, 22nd Annual Meeting, Interstate Conference of Employment Security Agencies (October 6–9, 1958), p. 11.

with the growth of population and nonfarm employment; that the quality of the services rendered had deteriorated since the war because the volume of short-time placements had increased while those in professional and skilled occupations had declined or increased slowly; and that some states had done a relatively good job, but others had done poorly.

These criticisms were not, in this writer's opinion, entirely merited. They did serve to focus attention on the employment service aspect of the program and in this way have helped to improve the service. But the Secretary's appraisal needs to be read with the following facts in mind:

1. Employment service staff declined about 23 per cent between 1947 and 1957, and no large increase in staff was made possible until the fiscal year 1962.

2. New-hire rates in manufacturing industries and hence the potential for placements declined 36 per cent between 1952 and 1959. But the proportion of the new hires filled by the service increased from 26 per cent in 1953 to 30 per cent in 1961. With respect to the manufacturing sector, therefore, the service could scarcely be blamed for not increasing the absolute volume of placements.

3. Several other factors in the postwar world made the task of the public service difficult. For one thing, in the trade and service industries where an expansion of jobs occurred, the employing units were then—as now—small and scattered and therefore difficult and costly to "sell" on the use of the service. Also, a good deal of the gain in nonfarm employment occurred in industries such as construction and government, where the jobs are usually filled through unions or through civil service. A third factor was the national policy of concentrating promotion efforts on the largest employers in each local area on the assumption that these establishments would provide the greatest opportunity for placements. This assumption was probably no longer valid for many manufacturing plants after 1953 because of the decline in defense work in aircraft plants and shipyards, the introduction of automated equipment, and changes in the

composition of job openings, such as the increase in technical, professional, and clerical jobs (management has shown a tendency to fill jobs in these categories through private agencies). Finally, in many states there was a substantial diversion of staff from placement work to insurance claims work during periods of rising unemployment. This situation was brought under control, though not entirely eliminated, between 1950 and 1955 by the provision in the national budget for temporary insurance staff to meet peak loads; nevertheless, the diversion had hurt the reputation and morale of the placement operation in some states. All of these changes in the opportunities for placement and in available staff must be taken into account in appraising the record of the service.

In an effort to sustain the volume of placements and, also, because of the increased demands for workers in service and trade occupations, the number of placements in these occupations in households and in other short-time jobs was increased. However, this change in the mixture of placements had unfortunate budget consequences because the short-time jobs could be filled more quickly than those for regular workers and, thus, the amount of staff time required per placement declined. This time factor, when multiplied by the volume, showed a total staff requirement that declined each year until 1955 and thus justified further reductions in budget for the service. Budgeting became a vicious-cycle process, which in itself brought about further declines in the volume and quality of services performed.

The extent to which employers place orders with the service and the type of vacancies they expect the service to fill are indices of the acceptability of the service. The Bureau of Employment Security now compiles a record of employer use of the service on the basis of yearly reports from local offices. The reports for 1960 showed that 31 per cent of the 2.8 million nonfarm establishments in the nation were users of the service and that two-thirds of the 220,000 largest employers were users.[16]

[16] *Minutes*, Interstate Conference Committee on Employment Service Programs and Operations (March, 1961), p. 2.

"Users" in this context means employers who place one or more orders with the service. It does not mean that the service actually filled these jobs or that it had a chance to fill jobs for which applicants were available. Employers often give the service orders which they have not been able to fill in any other way. Consequently, figures showing merely the numbers of users of the service can be misleading.

In fact, a survey[17] of hiring practices published in 1958 showed that the trend among large employers since 1953 had been toward more hiring of workers at the company gates and less hiring through agencies. This trend undoubtedly reflects the growing volume of unemployment in the nation and the fact that employers in some manufacturing industries, such as steel, automobiles, and other durable goods, have been contracting rather than expanding their work forces. The workers they have hired in recent years are more likely to have been "call backs" or people in professional, technical, and clerical occupations who often have been recruited through private agencies.

The general hiring patterns of employers in the nation, as shown by many local studies made since the end of World War II,[18] have favored several methods of recruitment other than the employment service. They have filled some jobs by recruitment of friends and relatives of employees, by hiring at the gate,

by advertising, and by exchanging information on job seekers. Also, in some industries, such as construction, printing, men's clothing, trucking, and warehousing, hiring in many places has been done through unions. Private agencies have been used for the hard-to-fill jobs, especially executive, professional, technical, and secretarial positions, which often can be filled only by recruiting applicants who are already employed. The reasons for the use of these methods rather than the public service are: (1) ease of recruitment, especially when there are many suitable applicants unemployed; (2) a belief on the part of some personnel managers that they can do a better job of selection, since they know best what type of person would fit in their organizations (this has meant in some cases a process of selection adverse to minority groups); (3) dissatisfaction with referrals by the public service, which has been accused of not knowing the kinds of skills required, of not acting speedily on orders, and of doing a poor job of selection; (4) a belief on the part of some personnel managers that the best applicants seek jobs on their own initiative rather than through agencies.

These beliefs and practices, plus the tendency of employers to use several channels of recruitment and not rely exclusively on any one source, have kept the participation of the public service down to a minor share in the total number of new hires. Louis Levine has estimated that the service had a national penetration rate in nonfarm industries in 1947 of about 9 per cent and that the rate was about the same in 1957.[19] This estimate, however, is not based on firm statistics since there are no reliable data on the number of "new hires" for most nonmanufacturing industries. A more recent estimate, given to the U.S. Senate Subcommittee on Labor and Public Welfare in 1963 by the Administration of the Bureau of Employment Security, shows a rate of 16 per cent.[19a] The difference of 7 percentage

---

[17] *Personnel* (November–December, 1958).

[18] Some of these studies are: Lloyd G. Reynolds, *The Structure of Labor Markets* (New York: Harper & Bros., 1951); George B. Baldwin, "Talamusa: A Study of the Place of the Public Employment Service," *Industrial and Labor Relations Review* (July, 1951); Richard A. Lester, *Hiring Practices and Labor Competition* (Industrial Relations Section, Princeton University, Princeton, New Jersey, 1954); Charles A. Myers and George B. Shultz, *The Dynamics of a Labor Market* (New York: Prentice-Hall, 1951); Murray Edelman, *Channels of Employment* (Institute of Labor and Industrial Relations, University of Illinois, Urbana, Illinois, 1952); F. Theodore Malm, "Employers and Mobility" (Institute of Industrial Relations, University of California, Berkeley, California, 1952), (Mimeographed); Leonard P. Adams and Robert L. Aronson, *Displaced Workers* (New York State School of Industrial and Labor Relations, Cornell University, Ithaca, New York, 1957); E. William Noland and E. Wight Bakke, *Workers Wanted* (New York: Harper & Bros., 1949).

[19] Louis Levine, "A Look at the Record," *Employment Security Review* (March, 1959), p. 3.

[19a] Robert C. Goodwin, in a prepared statement submitted to the subcommittee on June 20, 1963. See *Hearings, Nations Manpower Revolution*, Part 3, p. 836.

points reflects, in part, the increased volume of work done since additional staff was added in fiscal 1961 and 1962, but it may also be partly due to different methods of estimating with inadequate basic information. Whatever the true figure may be, it is clear that the service has had limited acceptance and use. It has a long way to go before it can claim to be a major source of hiring, if "major" is defined as an all-employer penetration rate of 50 per cent or more.

The relatively weak showing made by the public offices in many of the large states has provided competitors of the service with numerous opportunities for placement work. This is shown by the record growth of private employment agencies in the postwar period.

IV. PRIVATE EMPLOYMENT AGENCIES

There are many private agencies or organizations that help people find jobs. For present purposes they may be divided into two general types, the fee-charging agencies and those that offer free service to a selected membership—for example, teachers' union members—or to such special groups as the handicapped, the blind, etc. More information is available about the business operations of the fee-charging agencies because the U.S. Census of Business since 1939 has periodically collected statistics on their number, employees, fees collected, and location. There are also a few states that regulate such agencies and publish information about them. Little information is available

about the numerous organizations that provide counseling and placement services without charge.

As pointed out earlier, one of the justifications given for the establishment of public employment offices was that such offices would reduce the number of fee-charging agencies by offering a good service without direct cost to workers and employers. Some enthusiasts expected the public offices to supplant the private agencies entirely. As Table 10–11 shows, these expectations have not been realized. The private fee-charging agency business has thrived.

During the decade 1939–48 the number of such agencies increased by more than 50 per cent, the number of their employees more than doubled, and their receipts increased four-fold. During the next ten years the increase in the number of these agencies and their employees was still greater, although receipts did not increase so rapidly. By 1958 the number of employees in the private agencies exceeded those in the public employment offices by more than 50 per cent.

Three aspects of this growth are worthy of note. First, the number of small, one-person or partnership agencies has been declining, while the larger ones have grown more numerous. The largest percentage gains in numbers and in employment occurred in the group with ten or more employees. This group included 50 per cent of the employees in 1950 and 56 per cent in 1958.

Second, about 75 per cent of the fee-charging agencies in 1958, as in 1948, were concentrated in ten states; these ten include the largest metropolitan areas of the nation and the bulk

TABLE 10–11: GROWTH OF PRIVATE FEE-CHARGING EMPLOYMENT AGENCIES IN THE UNITED STATES, 1939–1958

Year	Number of establishments	Receipts (000)	Payroll for year (000)	Paid employees, week ended Nov. 15
1939	1,424	$7,861	$2,777	1,994
1948	2,231	30,784	10,271	4,580
1954	3,153	62,897	24,157	10,028
1958	3,892	100,513	40,418	16,783

SOURCE: U.S. Census of Business (1948, Vol. VII, Service Trade Area Statistics), p. 0.02 and (1958, Vol. V, Selected Service Summary Statistics).

of the agencies are located in these areas. For example, in California 78 per cent are located in the two largest cities and in New York over 70 per cent are located in New York City. Similar concentrations are found in smaller states such as Wisconsin and Arizona.

Third, the growth of fee-charging agencies has not been seriously handicapped by regulatory legislation. (It is uncertain how well this legislation has been enforced.) By 1960 all but six states (Alabama, Mississippi, New Mexico, North Dakota, South Carolina, and Vermont) had passed statutes regulating these agencies.[20] The states without regulatory laws contained only 1 per cent of all the agencies.

All of the ten states in which the bulk of the fee-charging agencies is located have statutes regulating various aspects of the business and guarding against the more flagrant abuses of which a minority of the agencies had been guilty in the past. All ten states prohibit the furnishing of misleading information and fee-splitting with employers. They require agencies to obtain a license, furnish a bond, and post fee schedules. Six of the ten states prohibit the charging of registration fees. In five states the placement fee is controlled by a maximum limit specified in the law, by a maximum set by the administrator, or by the requirement that agencies submit their schedules for the approval of a state official. Most of the ten states place responsibility for the administration of the laws in a state office. In Ohio, the Bureau of Unemployment Compensation is the enforcement agency. Only Massachusetts leaves enforcement in the hands of local authorities.

Very little information is available as to the number and types of jobs filled by the fee-charging agencies or the fees charged by them, because the regulatory offices in many states either do not collect such information or do not publish it. In New York, for example, no data are available on a statewide basis, since the law does not authorize either the state or the city governments to collect information. Also, the enforcement of the legislation in New York is spotty. For example, in New York City there is an inspection unit in the Department of Licenses, but in one upstate city which the writer visited no inspection was carried on by anyone. Under such circumstances the principal regulating device is the requirement for annual licensing, which gives those who have complaints an opportunity to protest the continuance of any agencies that they feel have wronged them. A more effective regulator, however, is the keen competition, which keeps those who depend on repeat orders from doing anything which would earn them a bad reputation. Also the better-known concerns have high standards and have helped police the industry through the associations of private agencies to which they belong.

In most states it is easy to get into the agency business because license fees are modest, $25 to $100 annually being the prevalent range, and the applicant need only present a few witnesses to testify that he is of a good moral character and offer evidence that he will operate in "suitable" premises. These standards make it possible for most applicants to get licenses, and inevitably a few unprincipled operators get into the business. Consequently, there are still some abuses, most of which work to the disadvantage of the job seeker.

In addition to the thousands of fee-charging agencies, there are other thousands of private organizations which provide some counseling and placement services free, usually for selected groups. No comprehensive information is available on the number of such organizations or the volume of their activities. Some idea of the type of organizations which engage in this work was furnished by a survey made in Illinois in 1950.[21] In Chicago in that year there were at least sixteen union organizations that maintained some type of referral and placement service. Several of them constituted the principal hiring channel for the employers concerned. No information was obtained on the volume of placements, but in several industries, such as the building trades, the clothing industry, building services, trucking and warehousing, and hotels and restaurants,

[20] See *Bulletin 209* (Bureau of Labor Standards, Department of Labor, Washington, D.C.).

[21] See Edelman, *Channels of Employment* (*n.* 18), chaps. 4 and 5.

the volume was substantial. At least nine other organizations, some private and some government, participated in the placement process. Also, each of the four hundred American Legion posts in Chicago had an employment officer, and the city office of the legion actively promoted jobs for veterans. In addition to using these agencies, Chicago employers made use of advertising, recruited new workers from among the friends and relations of their employees, and hired at their gates.

While comprehensive information on the placements made by private fee-charging agencies is not available, the data collected from such agencies in a half dozen states visited by the writer indicate that jobs filled by these agencies were, as might be expected, those for which the supply of workers was short and for which the pay was relatively high. Thus, if one were to say that the private agencies deal with openings which the public service lists as shortage occupations, he would not be far wrong. Such a list would include professional workers, engineers and other technical personnel, stenographers, high-grade clerical help, and skilled mechanics. The private agencies recruit such personnel to a large extent, but not exclusively, from among those already employed. They claim to have the "best" workers available and contend that many of these people will not go to a public agency. In some cases they have worked out arrangements with other private agencies for interarea clearance of applicants and job orders on a fifty-fifty, fee-splitting basis.

Not all of the arguments advanced on behalf of the private agencies will bear close scrutiny, but there is no doubt that they offer a service for which job applicants and employers are willing to pay well. Furthermore, their placement work is concentrated on the hard-to-fill jobs. Although there are still some agencies which engage in shady, if not dishonest, practices,[22] one must conclude that the private fee-charging agencies are an essential part of the job-marketing process in the nation at the present time.

[22] Several instances of such practices are reported in Bureau of Labor Standards, *Bulletin 209* (*n.* 20).

Steps have been taken recently to improve and expand the public employment services in those occupational and industrial fields in which the private agencies have done most of their business. Separate offices to serve white-collar workers have been established in most of the largest metropolitan areas. These have attracted many of the highest quality job seekers, of whom a substantial proportion are employed when they register. The public service also offers, by request, placement services to a half dozen professional societies at their annual meetings. These changes are part of a general program for improving the public offices so that they may become more effective placement agencies and community manpower centers for the future. The next section will describe the changes in the public service which have been made by the Kennedy and Johnson administrations, its new duties under recently enacted federal legislation, and the goals set forth for the new U.S. Employment Service.

V. OUTLOOK FOR THE EMPLOYMENT SERVICE

A. THE "NEW" SERVICE

Since 1961 several changes have taken place in the public service which have given it new responsibilities, additional funds, and greater recognition than it has had since its first years under the Wagner-Peyser Act.[23] There has also been an effort to create a new public image of the local office as a community manpower center. These developments have already resulted in some significant changes in the service.

Mention was made earlier of the present organization of the public service within the Bureau of Employment Security and the revival of the title Director of the United States Employment Service. In addition, there has been an effort at the national level to separate

[23] See Louis Levine, "The Employment Service Charts Its Course," *Employment Security Review* (April, 1962), and "New Pathways to Manpower," *Employment Security Review* (October, 1962).

the operations of the employment service from the operations connected with unemployment insurance, to budget the service as a separate entity, and to encourage the states to review their organizations for the purpose of determining whether the insurance and placement operations can be advantageously separated. These changes have been introduced: (1) to call attention to the employment service as a separate function; (2) to change the public image of the service from the negative image of "unemployment office" to the positive image of a community manpower service center; and (3) to strengthen the service in the larger metropolitan areas.

Some progress has been made toward achieving these objectives (see Table 10–1). Additional funds to be used specifically for the employment service were secured from Congress in fiscal 1961 and more funds were appropriated in fiscal 1962. These funds were used mainly to provide more staff for the largest metropolitan areas in those states which agreed to build up the service along lines prescribed by headquarters and to establish separate placement offices along industrial occupational lines in these areas. Nearly all the states agreed to accept the additional funds, and with the help of headquarters staff new offices have been established in more than half of the fifty-two largest metropolitan areas in the nation. No additional funds for the service were provided in the appropriation for fiscal 1963. The changes already made, however, go far toward overcoming the unequal staffing patterns noted earlier, and should in time also strengthen the service in the areas where it has the greatest opportunities for expansion. For the time being at least, the budgeting of the service in these large areas has been based on the need for a public service rather than on the staffing warranted by past performance, as under the previous budgeting formula.

The administrator of the Bureau of Employment Security and the new director of the USES have suggested a new term to describe the new goals of the service; they speak of "the community manpower center."[24] This term has not yet been explicitly defined, but it clearly implies that the service should assume responsibility for manpower planning and utilization, a responsibility that involves much more than merely operating an employment exchange. Each local office is expected to help achieve the national goals of maintaining the highest possible levels of employment and production as expressed in the Employment Act of 1946. The local employment office, therefore, should become the principal organization to plan, co-ordinate, and promote full employment of manpower resources in each community. This means that each office must do more than take account of current manpower needs and try to match demand with the available supply of skills. It must also anticipate future needs and potential imbalances between demand and supply and, together with other community agencies, take appropriate steps (for example, the initiation of training courses) to prevent future problems.

Responsibilities given to the service as a result of the Area Redevelopment Act of 1961, the Manpower Development and Training Act of 1962, the Trade Expansion Act of 1962, the Public Works Acceleration Act of 1962, and the creation of a Manpower Administration in the Department of Labor have helped to define more explicitly what is expected of the "new" employment service in the future.[25] In brief, its duties as outlined in the instructions of the Secretary of Labor cover not only all the services performed heretofore but also responsibility for working with other federal and state agencies to identify the need for training, to select workers for the new training programs, to place workers in jobs after training has been completed, and to evaluate the results of these training programs. The public employment service, together with the state and local school authorities, has been given the principal operating responsibility for carrying out the terms of much of this new federal legislation.

These additional duties have not been accompanied by additional staff or by relief from other responsibilities. While the volume of

24 Levine, "The Employment Service Charts Its Course" (n. 23).

25 U.S. Department of Labor, Secretary's Order No. 4–63, March 1, 1963.

additional work involved has not been great thus far, it will certainly grow as the training programs expand. The situation resembles that encountered by the local offices throughout the nineteen-fifties; and it forces state administrators to decide what services should be given priority when there is insufficient staff and, in a sense, forces further decentralization of program planning. Thus, the public employment service organization finds itself in the early nineteen-sixties with vital new programs to be developed and carried out before there has been time to remedy some of the weaknesses which developed in the postwar period. The implications of this situation for the future of the service are explored in the next section.

B. PROSPECTS FOR THE "NEW" SERVICE

The public service is once again in a period of transition and change as a result of criticism of its past performance, the growth of unemployment, and the new legislative programs which have been enacted to deal with the problems of depressed areas and "class" unemployment. Federal leaders have made it clear that the employment service must not only improve its performance along traditionally accepted lines but must also take on new responsibilities. These new responsibilities, according to national officials, involve more active participation in community planning for full use of manpower resources, the avoidance of labor-market imbalances, and, in general, the promotion, in co-operation with other agencies, of the objectives of the Employment Act of 1946. These are ambitious goals. Their achievement will require some radical changes in the image of the service as it is seen by its own staff and by employers, workers, and the general public. Can the public service reasonably be expected to achieve these goals? Do the goals reflect a need for expansion in the service, and how can they best be attained? These are some of the questions which must be answered by the Congress and by those in the employment service.

The Record. As the above record shows, at the present time the public employment service does not—with a few exceptions—have community acceptance as the community manpower center envisaged by the federal leadership. For the past fifteen years the service has established a record primarily as an employment exchange dealing chiefly with unskilled, semiskilled, service, and short-time jobs. Undoubtedly, recent improvements in the service will, to some extent, change this image; but they will not bring a radical change in the near future, because employers and workers are not likely soon to change their present hiring and job-finding practices.

Other aspects of the present program of the service will also need to be reviewed in the light of the new concepts of the function of the service. The record indicates that very little time has been spent on community development and industrial services. Though the labor-market information programs and the counseling and testing programs have been given somewhat more attention, they also have occupied only a small part of staff time. These facets of the service have not been widely promoted and their availability has not been generally known. Aid to special groups of applicants, such as older workers, youths, refugees, and the handicapped, has received more publicity than have other aspects of the six-point program, and this aid, in some areas, has been successful in terms of placement and of vocational adjustment.

In addition to determining priorities among present programs, the employment service will have to remedy some current weaknesses if it wishes to attain the status of a manpower center. There are significant differences among the states with respect to services rendered, and these probably reflect some weaknesses in administration and staff competence, as well as differences in labor-market conditions. There are also significant differences among the states in the housing provided for the service. In some local areas there is excellent physical equipment, but in others the very appearance of the offices tells the public that the actual status of the service is out of line with what it professes to be. Last, but most significant, the personnel in the service varies considerably in quality from one office to another, a situation which can be partially remedied by the establishment of uniform high standards for new entrants into the service.

This review of the present status of the employment service has placed more emphasis on the weakness of the system than on its strength, yet there have been some outstanding performances in many phases of employment service work. Part of the task of federal and state administrators in improving the service is to identify these exceptionally good operations and to use them in stimulating improvements elsewhere. Space does not permit further elaboration of this point, but the comparative records presented earlier point to some of the states which have done relatively well in the postwar period.

Efforts by federal administrators and staff to provide constructive leadership in improving the service have, in some instances, created feelings on the part of state administrators of excessive federal domination. Under the grant-in-aid system, however, there are distinct limits on the power of federal authorities to require states to adopt new programs or modify old practices. The states can be persuaded to make program changes, but they cannot be forced to do so.[26]

Future Needs for a Public Service. What the public service can do in the nineteen-sixties to improve the organization of labor markets and assist in manpower planning depends in part on which needs for service are recognized and supported by the public. In the writer's opinion there are four important, interrelated needs or opportunities for services which have public support and which the public employment service should make the basis of its general program. These are: (1) a placement operation to provide a competitive service covering all types of workers and jobs, including selection and placement services for training programs; (2) an information and analytical service, both local and national, which will keep the public

informed on present and prospective balances in labor supply and demand; (3) a counseling and testing service for all who face problems of vocational adjustment, but especially for new entrants and re-entrants into the job market; and (4) the service offered to unemployment insurance offices by testing claimants' willingness and ability to work. (A strong placement service is likely to provide the best means of making such tests.) A brief commentary on these points—except the last, which is already widely recognized—follows.

It is generally accepted that there is now, and will continue to be, a need for a strong public placement service. There is no other agency, public or private, to serve the peacetime needs of millions of farm and nonfarm workers and employers who have used its services in the past and have come to rely on it. Furthermore, the outlook for employment and unemployment in the nation in the nineteen-sixties and nineteen-seventies is for greater imbalances in labor supply and demand, for continued rapid technological changes, and for uneven economic growth rates.[27] The principal questions concerning the placement function include the types of jobs which the service should try to fill, the extent to which it should be expected to penetrate the various job markets, and the means which such a public service should be permitted to use to recruit workers and solicit job openings.

A public service, if it is to be recognized as a manpower center, must command community acceptance and respect in terms of its primary task, namely, the reduction of unemployment by means of its placement services. Consequently, it cannot rest on a reputation for serving only part of the job market. The Wagner-Peyser Act gave the federal-state service a legislative mandate to serve all who ask for help, not merely selected groups. Furthermore, the service can develop information needed for counseling, testing, and manpower planning by participating generally in the task of matching workers and jobs.

---

[26] See testimony of Robert C. Goodwin before Subcommittee on Appropriations of House of Representatives, 87th Congress, 2nd Session (1962), *Hearings*, p. 256.

[27] See *Manpower Report of the President* and *A Report on Manpower Requirements, Resources, Utilization, and Training* (U.S. Department of Labor, Washington, D.C., 1963).

How far the public service should be expected to become a central exchange for all jobs and workers is a question to which there seems to be no single answer. Some have said it should be a "major source," without defining the term. Others have set a numerical goal such as a penetration rate of 50 per cent or more, a goal which seems beyond attainment in the forseeable future. Another answer, sometimes given, is that no applicant should go without a referral if there is a suitable job opening and no employer order should be canceled if there is a suitable worker who can be referred. This is a perfectionist's answer, which sets a standard of performance difficult to attain with limited staff resources and time.

Some employment service officials have stressed the importance of speed in filling jobs. This can be done by expediting the usual placement process. It can be achieved also by facilitating transfers of workers from job to job, sometimes without the formalities of registration, selection, and referral. This has been done, to some extent, by both public and private agencies when the jobs are similar.

In practice, the goals for each local office must be set in the light of the local needs and how the program can best satisfy these needs. To fulfill its responsibilities it is not necessary for the service to become the exclusive labor-market center or even to achieve any particular penetration rate. As long as there are so many other hiring channels for workers and employers to use, the public service need not and is not likely to monopolize the market. But it can be, and should expect to be, recognized as one of the important sources of manpower and of jobs—one which all employers and workers use as needed. Numerical goals for placements can be helpful in achieving this result if the goal for each area is set at a level that stimulates improvement over past performances and takes into account the achievements of offices with similar labor-market conditions.

It seems to the writer that the public service, in carrying out its placement objectives, should be free to use any and all legal and effective means which are available to private agencies.

This would include advertising, telephone promotion, promotion by news, and the use of personal résumés. Without free access to these media, the individual offices cannot be expected to be competitive and to win customers for their services—as they must, because workers who are not insurance claimants and employers are free to seek employment services through other channels.

With regard to the information services, it can be said that the need for them will increase in the future. There will be greater emphasis on government programs to overcome the problems of long-term unemployment, of depressed areas, and of worker groups which have difficulty finding jobs in private industries. Programs must be planned to meet these specific needs. Meeting future manpower needs for professional, technical and skilled workers will require more careful planning by schools and by business concerns than heretofore; and this means they will need better information on current and prospective manpower shortages and surpluses. Improvements in the placement programs also will depend to a larger degree on the accuracy and adequacy of the basic information collected on job requirements, on training programs, and on changing occupational patterns in industry and government. In fact, the public employment service has a greater opportunity to become the recognized community manpower center with respect to its information function than it has with respect to any of its other services. The need for such an information service is great, the public can be sold on it, and it has virtually no competition from private sources. The present information services, however, need to be reviewed and strengthened, since there is evidence that these are not well known and do not fully meet the needs of important employer and worker groups, the schools, and private placement agencies.

The opportunities for an employment service to do counseling and testing, especially for youths, for older workers, and for those with problems of vocational adjustment, are well established and will continue in the future. An important aspect of this service, however, is the research work needed to improve the tests and to extend this service to workers in other age and occupational groups. Also, as others have pointed out, more follow-up on the results of counseling is needed in order to make sure that, wherever possible, the service leads the individual to a satisfactory job.

Thus, the public employment service, as it improves its primary function of placement, develops its information and labor-market analysis functions, and provides better counseling and testing services, can expect to make a major contribution to the solution of unemployment and other manpower problems. There are, however, two possible dangers: to continue burdening the service with too many special programs, which distract the staff from the main goals; and to assume that congressional support for the service will continue or be increased without some correction of the major weaknesses in the present system.

There are, at present, too many critics of the service and too few strong supporters. But strenuous efforts to improve the program are likely to meet with a sympathetic and encouraging response from the public, since the need for such a service is great. This need will increase in the years ahead for two reasons. First, the problems of finding jobs or suitable training for the unskilled, for poorly educated experienced workers, and for new entrants into the nation's labor markets seem likely to grow more difficult to solve as the numbers of unemployed increase and as more youths reach working age. A well-operated employment service can place some of these people in jobs; it can screen applicants for training programs; and it can provide helpful information and vocational guidance to youthful job seekers. Second, the expected increase in the shortage of professional, technical, and skilled workers can be alleviated as the service encourages better utilization of the existing supply of such people and helps provide the information needed for manpower planning. These problems of manpower surpluses and shortages will provide the service with unusual opportunities, as well as difficulties, in the years ahead.

CHAPTER 11

Training the Unemployed

Gerald G. Somers[*]

I. THE ISSUES INVOLVED

GOVERNMENT-SPONSORED TRAINING for the unemployed has been attracting great and growing attention in the last few years. Its widespread appeal can be seen in the enthusiastic support received from a diversity of interest groups during the hearings on the Area Redevelopment Act of 1961 (ARA) and on the more inclusive Manpower Development and Training Act of 1962 (MDTA). Further, in the months following passage of the MDTA, retraining of the unemployed was soundly endorsed in the Trade Expansion Act and in the proposed youth employment bill even when other provisions of these measures were severely criticized. Another victory for government-sponsored training was scored in the MDTA amendments passed in December, 1963. Recent state legislation and local welfare programs also have featured retraining, contributing further to its snowballing growth among labor-market policies.

It is not hard to find reasons for this widespread support of government-sponsored training programs for the unemployed. Those who place their faith in education as a major vehicle of general well-being and of long-term economic growth view retraining as an important part of the total education structure. The cost of retraining is seen as a long-term investment in human beings; like the general education process, this investment promises great future returns. Others view retraining as an

attractive remedy, which avoids the "pitfalls" of alternative economic policies. Those whose greatest fear is inflation find retraining more palatable than aggregative fiscal-spending programs. Analysts of the labor market consider it as an essential response to the technological and structural changes which leave pockets of unemployed workers in declining industries, occupations, and areas. Since job vacancies may exist in other industries, occupations, and areas, retraining may serve as an encouragement to labor mobility and appears to be an obvious procedure for matching labor supply and demand.

Retraining is accepted as a sound financial investment as well as an aid to the unemployed. Retraining allowances do not necessarily represent an additional expense; they often take the place of unemployment compensation or relief. Also, by furthering the worker's employment capabilities, retraining reduces the likelihood of future dependence on government transfer payments.

But government retraining programs are not without their critics. And the criticisms appear to have increased as a result of early experience under the recent legislation. The principal criticisms range from broad questions of principle to concern over practical operations of the training programs. Some contend that government subsidies in this field are unnecessary. In a full-employment economy private employers can be expected to continue their traditional practice of training workers for job vacancies; in a depressed economy there is little point in training workers for nonexistent

* Professor of Economics, University of Wisconsin.

jobs. As some economists have argued, the pools of unemployment can be expected to evaporate under the bright sunshine of aggregate full employment even in the absence of government intervention in the allocation of specific labor resources.

The early experience under the ARA and the MDTA has been called upon to support these adverse contentions. It has been pointed out that in the selection of trainees the government-sponsored training programs have by-passed most of the hard-core unemployed, that many workers have been trained for jobs which do not exist, and that the workers who benefit most from the training programs are the very ones who could find employment without government aid.

Government-subsidized retraining programs for the unemployed are something of a novelty in the United States. But the history of public aid to training at the local, state, and federal levels is a long one and not unrelated to the recent retraining programs. The discussion in this chapter, therefore, will attempt to place the recent governmental training programs in the perspective of the development of general government-aided training in this country and, by examining some of the results of the early experience under the training legislation,[1] appraise some of the contending views on the value of the recent programs.[2]

[1] Much of the material in this chapter is derived from research conducted under a grant from the Ford Foundation. Support has also been provided by the Social Systems Research Institute and the Graduate School of the University of Wisconsin. See page 231 for a description of the surveys and procedures. The findings reported in this chapter are based on preliminary analyses and are confined primarily to the West Virginia surveys. The author is indebted to Professor Harold Gibbard, Head of the Department of Sociology, West Virginia University, and Dr. Ernst Stromsdorfer and Graeme McKechnie, University of Wisconsin, for their able assistance.

[2] A variety of viewpoints on the value of retraining can be found in *Training of the Unemployed*, Hearings before the Subcommittee on Employment and Manpower, Committee on Labor and Public Welfare, U.S. Senate, 87th Cong., 1st Sess., March 20 and 21 and June 5–7, 1961. See also "Worker Retraining: Answer to Chronic Joblessness?" *Congressional Quarterly Report* (March 9, 1962); William Glazier, "Automation and Joblessness: Is Retraining the Answer?" *The Atlantic* (August, 1962); and "The Hard Realities of Retraining," *Fortune* (July, 1961).

II. THE DEVELOPMENT OF PUBLIC TRAINING PROGRAMS

A. TYPES OF PROGRAMS

General industrial education under public auspices is a part of American tradition. In 1820 a report prepared by a committee in Boston urged that organized trade instruction be introduced into the high schools. In 1880 the St. Louis Manual Training School, connected with Washington University, became a model for early technical and manual-training high schools.[3] Under pressure from the National Society for the Promotion of Industrial Education, formed in 1906, the Smith-Hughes Act was passed in 1917 to further vocational education in agriculture, industry, and home economics. Vocational courses were expanded into the distributive trades, practical nursing, fishing trades, and others under the George-Deen Act of 1936 and the George-Barden Act of 1946. More recently, the National Defense Education Act of 1958 has authorized the training of skilled technicians. Approximately 22 million persons were enrolled in vocational education classes in the United States from 1918 to 1955.[4] In 1961, alone, 3,856,000 young people were included in these classes.[5]

The federal government assists vocational training through programs carried out in the armed services. Enlisted personnel, enrolled in formal school courses and in on-the-job training programs, acquire skills which can be utilized in civilian life. Government-subsidized education and training for war veterans also reached substantial proportions after World War II under what is popularly known as the G.I. bill. By 1961, 2,375,000 veterans had been enrolled. The monthly average of Korean veterans in training during fiscal year 1962 was 96,400.[6]

[3] Perry W. Reeves, *A Digest of the Development of Industrial Education in the United States* (Washington, D.C.: Government Printing Office, 1932), pp. 2–3.
[4] Roy W. Roberts, *Vocational and Practical Arts Education* (New York: Harper and Brothers, 1957), pp. 289–91.
[5] Sar A. Levitan, *Vocational Education and Federal Policy* (Kalamazoo, Michigan: The W. E. Upjohn Institute for Employment Research, May, 1963), p. 5.
[6] Administrator of Veterans Affairs, *General Report* (Washington, D.C.: Government Printing Office, 1961, 1962).

Vocational rehabilitation is closely related to recent efforts to train the hard-core unemployed. For over forty years the U.S. Office of Vocational Rehabilitation has been retraining handicapped workers for productive employment. The vocational rehabilitation program, although it is distinct from general vocational education, has many of the same objectives. Total expenditures for vocational rehabilitation during the period 1921–55 have been estimated at $356 million, of which the federal government contributed almost two-thirds. More than 850,000 persons received training during this period at an average cost of $420 per person.[7]

Instruction on the job or within the industrial establishment also has benefited in the past, and continues to benefit, from governmental assistance. As early as 1915 Wisconsin placed apprenticeship training under the jurisdiction of the State Industrial Commission. The federal Bureau of Apprenticeship and Training (originally the Apprentice-Training Service), since passage of the Fitzgerald Act in 1937, has worked closely with employers, unions, and vocational schools in establishing apprenticeship programs. During World War II the Training-Within-Industry section of the Office of Production Management was established to assist industry in meeting special wartime manpower needs. This section was a government advisory group, whose major function was to press for the dissemination and utilization of known principles of training as an aid to war production. The group emphasized the training of foremen, who were then to communicate their new knowledge to the rank and file.[8]

B. Relation of Training Programs to the Unemployed

Although the foregoing government training programs may make a significant contribution to the re-employment possibilities of unemployed workers and provide a useful background experience for current programs, they are not primarily designed to aid the unemployed. Separate statistical tabulations are seldom maintained for the unemployed workers and for new entrants into the labor market who register for apprenticeship or for vocational education courses. Apprenticeship courses generally are available only to young entrants into the labor force. It has been claimed that thousands of unemployed workers enroll in vocational education courses, but it is likely that they represent only a small minority of vocational students. One unpublished survey of students at a vocational school in La Crosse, Wisconsin, an officially designated redevelopment area in which two large plants had just shut down, disclosed that only 10 per cent of the enrollees were unemployed. Other surveys confirm the view that few unemployed workers have benefited from previous training in the general vocational school system.

The Training-Within-Industry program of World War II undoubtedly benefited many of the 8 million who were still unemployed at the outbreak of the war. The experience under this program may be fruitful in providing guidance for on-the-job training under the MDTA.

The experience under vocational rehabilitation can also be useful for retraining the hard-core unemployed. For some of them, especially functional illiterates, their handicap may exceed that of the customary trainee in vocational rehabilitation centers. But the current rehabilitation program, because it is geared primarily to the needs of the physically handicapped, benefits only a very small proportion of the total unemployed.

III. RECENT LEGISLATION FOR TRAINING THE UNEMPLOYED

A. State and Local Programs

Sporadic efforts to train unemployed workers through state and local agencies date back at least to the depression of the nineteen-thirties.

---

[7] Roberts, *Vocational and Practical Arts Education* (n. 4), pp. 469–70.

[8] *The Training Within Industry Report, 1940–45*, Bureau of Training, War Manpower Commission, pp. 3–21.

In recent years state vocational education or employment security offices have carried on scattered programs in areas of chronic unemployment. Such programs are found in California, Connecticut, Massachusetts, Michigan, Ohio, Pennsylvania, and West Virginia. As has been recounted in the hearings on the Manpower Development and Training Act and in state reports, however, most of the state and local retraining projects have been crash programs for specific groups of displaced workers or for specific jobs in individual establishments; they have been relatively small, and have been hampered by inadequate legislative appropriations.

In other local programs able-bodied relief recipients are encouraged or required to take retraining. Chicago and Milwaukee, for example, have recently made willingness to accept training a condition for continued receipt of payments by employable welfare recipients. An increasing number of states, twenty-one as of March, 1964, authorize the payment of unemployment compensation to unemployed workers who are not available for work because they are enrolled in training courses. California, Connecticut, Massachusetts, Michigan, and New York have led in this development.

Full-fledged state retraining programs supported by legislative appropriations and specifically designed for the unemployed date back only to 1957. In that year Pennsylvania amended its school code to require the State Board of Vocational Education to arrange courses for the unemployed. In 1959–60 about 2,000 unemployed persons were enrolled in the program.

In July, 1960, the West Virginia legislature appropriated under the newly authorized Area Vocational Education Training Program $400,000 for the year to organize and conduct retraining courses for the unemployed. Similar appropriations have been made in subsequent years. As of February 15, 1961, training programs in thirty-one West Virginia counties had a total enrollment of 1,455.

The Ohio legislature authorized a similar program of retraining for the unemployed in July, 1961. As in Pennsylvania and West Virginia, the program is conducted by the division of vocational education and is entirely financed by state funds.

B. FEDERAL LEGISLATION

The Area Redevelopment Act, passed in May, 1961, provided the first wide-scale federal retraining program for the unemployed. In addition to provision of financial aid for instructors and training facilities in eligible redevelopment areas, the act provides a subsistence allowance to qualified trainees for a maximum period of sixteen weeks. The allowance is equal to the average weekly unemployment compensation payment in the state.

A broader attack through retraining was provided by the Manpower Development and Training Act, passed in March, 1962. Under the original provisions of the act $435 million was to be spent within a three-year period to encourage retraining of the unemployed and the underemployed. Subsistence payments to eligible adult trainees under this act are still geared to state unemployment compensation payments, but they are more liberal than ARA allowances in the duration of payment. Under the original MDTA legislation training allowances can be paid for a maximum of fifty-two weeks.

Unlike ARA retraining, MDTA courses may be offered in relatively prosperous areas as well as depressed areas. The provisions of the MDTA, however, are directed almost wholly to unemployed and underemployed workers. Since state allotments are determined partly by the number of unemployed, it is not surprising that almost one-fourth of the training programs under this act are located in depressed areas. The original MDTA funds, except for a small fraction reserved for young people, were to be paid only to unemployed heads of households who had had at least three years of work experience. Training allowances of $20 per week could be paid to youths between the ages of nineteen and twenty-two, but these payments were limited to 5 per cent of the total expenditure on training allowances. The amendments to the MDTA passed in

December, 1963, are of considerable significance because they demonstrate congressional willingness to expand the training legislation and to respond to needs and shortcomings revealed in initial experience under the act.

The amendments include the following provisions:

1. Whereas the original law required state matching of federal funds beginning July 1, 1964, the federal government will now make all payments under the MDTA program until July 1, 1965, and cover two-thirds of total costs during the following year.

2. The amendments permit raising the weekly allowance paid to trainees to a maximum of $10 above the average state unemployment compensation payment. Eligible for the additional allowances are trainees with dependents and long-term trainees.

3. Trainees are permitted to work part time (up to 20 hours per week) without any loss of training allowances.

4. Basic education may be included in vocational training for workers whose levels of education are very low. The training period for these workers may be extended to a maximum of 72 weeks. This is part of a shift of emphasis from immediate employment to increased employability.

5. Youths between the ages of 17 and 19 are now eligible for training allowances. As a result, youths below the age of 22 can now constitute one-fourth of all persons receiving training allowances.

6. Workers' eligibility qualifications for training were reduced to two years' prior work experience; and when the head of a family is unemployed, another member of that family may receive a training allowance.

7. Tangential to the training provisions, the amendments authorize the allocation of $4 million for experiments in the relocation of unemployed workers.

As of April, 1964, the amendments had not yet taken effect. When they become operative their evaluation will supplement earlier appraisals in guiding the future course of government-sponsored training programs. The utilization of training provisions in the 1962 Trade Expansion Act and those provisions proposed in youth employment legislation are likely to be influenced by experience under the MDTA and the ARA.

IV. EVALUATION OF GOVERNMENT RETRAINING

A. RESEARCH BACKGROUND

Since much of the analysis of this chapter is based on special surveys conducted by the writer and covering early retraining experience (see note 1), it would seem advisable to give some account here of the content, method, and procedures of these surveys.

The major research concentration has been in West Virginia. West Virginia was selected for intensive study because of the prevalence of chronic labor-surplus areas within the state, the establishment in 1960 of one of the few formal programs for retraining the unemployed under state legislation, and the early and widespread inception of retraining courses under the Area Redevelopment Act in a number of the state's depressed areas. The areas selected for study were Harrison-Monongalia counties, a coal-mining, industrial, and agricultural area in the northern part of the state; Huntington-Charleston, the major cities, in the western-central section; and McDowell County, a predominantly coal-mining area, in the southern part of the state.

In each of these areas, 500 respondents were selected for interview. They consisted of (1) those who had completed a training course under the Area Redevelopment Act or under the West Virginia State program (approximately 35 per cent); (2) those who were selected for training on the basis of tests and other criteria but either did not begin their training or dropped out before completion of the course (approximately 25 per cent); (3) those who applied for training but because of test results or other reasons were not referred to training by the employment service (approximately 10 per cent); and (4) a probability sample of workers, selected from the active and inactive files of the employment service office in each area, who were unemployed when the training courses were being inaugurated but did not apply for training (approximately 30 per cent).

The selection of these four subsamples permits a comparative analysis of the subsequent employment experience and mobility of those who successfully completed the retraining program and of control groups of workers who were at specific and progressive stages of distance from completion of a retraining course.

The areas and courses selected for study also facilitated a comparison of the results of training in the same occupation in different areas, different occupations in the same area, state and federal programs in the same area, and general training and training geared to the needs of a specific employer.

The respondents in each survey were interviewed by means of a single detailed questionnaire with appropriate sections for the control groups. Each respondent was asked to sign a form which would authorize access to his social security file. Approximately 95 per cent gave this authorization, thereby permitting a follow-up of their employment experience in the future.

Since almost 30 per cent of the trainees selected for interview in each area had migrated from the area, a special questionnaire was mailed to them. Supplementary interviews also were conducted in several areas where the out-migrant trainees had concentrated, such as Norfolk-Newport News, Virginia; Washington, D.C.; Baltimore, Maryland; Columbus, Ohio; and Chicago, Illinois. It was necessary to rely on the mail questionnaire for the more scattered out-migrants.

A follow-up mail questionnaire, which had a response rate of approximately 70 per cent, was distributed to obtain later information on the employment experience of trainees and control groups. Available non-respondents were interviewed.

Questionnaire schedules designed to evoke appraisal of the training courses and directed to employers, instructors, and employment servic officials were also constructed for use in th various areas of the research.

In addition to the major concentration i West Virginia, field surveys of retrainin experience were conducted by investigator associated with this project in several area where the general appraisal of national pro grams suggested that such an investigatio would aid the analysis. All of these additiona case studies provide a useful comparison wit the West Virginia experience or offer a opportunity to study training and mobilit characteristics which were not available in th West Virginia surveys. The comparison c results was further facilitated by use of the sam or similar questionnaire designs and codes i all areas. The area case studies includ Pottsville-Phoenixville, Pennsylvania; Pitts burgh, Pennsylvania; Carbondale-McNai Illinois; Detroit-Lansing, Michigan; Knoxvill Tennessee; Evansville, Indiana; Fall River New Bedford-Lowell, Massachusetts; Bridge port, Ansonia-Norwich, and New Londor Connecticut; and Antigo-Rhinelander an La Crosse, Wisconsin.

Since the West Virginia surveys were con ducted in depressed areas, the characteristics c the trainees and their post-training employmen experience are not fully representative c trainees in the country as a whole. A compari son of the West Virginia data with the data o ARA and MDTA trainees, however, reveal no major differences in personal characteristic Employment ratios are also similar at som points in the West Virginia post-training perioc but since ARA and MDTA reports provide n continuous employment record after trainin a direct comparison cannot be made. In th subsequent discussion considerable emphasis i placed on the West Virginia findings, as supplement to national data, because the permit types of analysis which are not presentl available in other reports on training.

B. Some Questions on Job Placement

It is clear from national statistics, as well a from our own field surveys, that government ubsidized retraining has thus far achieved only minor reductions in unemployment. This lender achievement is due primarily to the limited period of experience with retraining, the state of the economy, and the scale of the programs relative to the number of unemployed. According to national reports on the ARA courses, between November, 1961 (when the first courses began), and January, 1964, a total of 624 ARA training projects for 28,316 trainees had been approved by the Secretary of Labor. These projects provided training in more than 200 different occupations to the residents of 230 redevelopment areas and 16 Indian reservations. By the end of January, 1964, however, less than 22,000 workers had actually enrolled in functioning ARA courses, and only 16,184 workers had completed their ARA training. Of these, almost 75 per cent were reported to have jobs shortly after the completion of their training course.[9] Reports under the Manpower Development and Training Act indicate that 120,000 trainees had been approved for training in authorized projects by the end of 1963, and 8,000 of these had been authorized to take on-the-job training. Courses had been approved in more than 250 occupations, and approximately 27,500 workers had completed MDTA training by the end of 1963. Approximately 70 per cent of those who had completed their training by then were reported to have jobs, a placement ratio slightly lower than that reported under the ARA.[10] In earlier reports the MDTA had indicated slightly higher employment ratios than the ARA.

Notwithstanding the relatively high placement ratios reported under both programs, it is pertinent to inquire to what extent the present government retraining programs have created more employment for the unemployed and how secure the employment position of trainees is in the months following their training. These are obviously basic questions, and they can be

[9] Data provided by U.S. Department of Labor, Bureau of Employment Security, United States Employment Service, February, 1964.

[10] *Report of the Secretary of Labor on Research and Training Activities Under the Manpower Development and Training Act*, U.S. Department of Labor, February, 1963, pp. 31–46, and March, 1964, p. 33.

fully answered only after much more research and a longer period of analysis. Some considerations relative to these questions are suggested here.

C. TRAINING OCCUPATIONS AND JOB VACANCIES

One important consideration concerns the kinds of jobs for which the workers are being trained. The retraining legislation specifies that these jobs be in occupations in which there is "a reasonable expectation of employment," presumably occupations where vacancies exist and are likely to continue to exist. Major shortages are found in professional and technical occupations, but few ARA or MDTA courses are designed to fill these shortages, and few unemployed workers are likely to qualify for such training. Almost 30 per cent of all MDTA courses are for semi-skilled factory occupations, although many of these jobs are likely to disappear under the continued impact of automation.

Many of the training programs are geared to shortages in the service occupations, such as nurses' aides and orderlies, but the long-term impact of these courses on the unemployed in these areas has been slight. The training allowance is an incentive to enrollment and the trainee is under some obligation to take a job for which he has been trained, yet the shortages in these occupations continue; because of the low wages and poor working conditions characteristic of these occupations, many of the trained workers stay on the jobs for only a short time after placement. Traditionally, hospitals have hired nurses' aides and orderlies who have minimal skills and training and have paid wages and provided working conditions on that minimal level. Trainees in these government programs are given more and higher skills, and the major contribution that such programs can make to these service occupations is perhaps to induce employers to offer wages and working conditions commensurate with these higher skills. The West Virginia surveys indicate that as many as 25 per cent of the women trained in these service occupations withdrew from the labor force shortly after their training.

D. Selection and Characteristics of Trainees

Another basic consideration in the placement record of the retraining programs is the set of criteria by which trainees are selected. The crucial questions are whether the retraining programs are currently enrolling the hard-core unemployed and whether current conditions justify a substantial lowering of selection standards. The answer to the first question depends on one's definition of the hard-core unemployed. The answer to the second question depends on one's willingness to accept an immediate placement ratio below the 70–75 per cent experienced under the early ARA and MDTA programs. A lower placement ratio is likely to result from lower selection standards; a reduction of standards may none the less be justified from the standpoints of long-term economic growth and the general welfare of the unemployed.

As indicated in Table 11–1, the ARA trainees include more long-term unemployed (fifteen weeks or more) than are found among the unemployed as a whole. But only 11 per cent of the trainees are forty-five years of age and over, and only 15 per cent had less than a ninth

TABLE 11–1: CHARACTERISTICS OF ARA TRAINEES AND OF ALL UNEMPLOYED, NOVEMBER, 1961–SEPTEMBER 30, 1963

(Percentage distribution)

	ARA trainees	All unemployed
Age		
Total	100.0	100.0
Under 20 years	13.6	23.4
20–34 years	56.2	35.2
35–44 years	19.2	15.5
45 years and over	11.0	25.9
Education		
Total	100.0	100.0
Under 9 grades	15.2	36.2
9–12 grades	78.1	54.5
Over 12 grades	6.7	9.4
Duration of unemployment		
Total	100.0	100.0
Under 5 weeks	19.3	43.3
5–14 weeks	21.0	32.1
15–26 weeks	13.6	11.4
27–52 weeks	14.3	13.2
Over 52 weeks	31.8	

SOURCE: U.S. Department of Labor, Bureau of Employment Security.

grade education. In a comparable period about 25 per cent of all the unemployed were forty-five and over, and 36 per cent had not completed high school.

In the MDTA program a similar contrast in age and education is found between trainees and all the unemployed in the labor force. Unfortunately, the age and education categories used in the tabulation of these data differ from the categories used in ARA courses, and hence no direct ARA-MDTA comparison can be made for all classifications. As seen in Table 11–2, the proportion of MDTA trainees over forty-five years of age is also relatively small (10.8 per cent), and only 10.5 per cent have less than nine years of education.

TABLE 11–2: CHARACTERISTICS OF FIRST 19,000 MDTA TRAINEES, 1963

(Percentage distribution)

Age	
Total	100.0
Under 19 years	4.2
19–21 years	19.1
22–34 years	44.7
35–44 years	21.2
45 years and over	10.8
Education	
Total	100.0
Less than 8 grades	3.0
8 grades	7.5
9–11 grades	29.3
12 grades	51.1
Over 12 grades	9.2
Duration of unemployment	
Total	100.0
Less than 5 weeks	23.8
5–14 weeks	27.8
15–26 weeks	17.2
27–52 weeks	12.2
Over 52 weeks	19.0

SOURCE: U.S. Department of Labor, Office of Manpower, Automation and Training.

Thus, the MDTA has done little better than the ARA in enrolling hard-core, older and uneducated workers. The contrast between the trainees and the very long-term unemployed (six months or more) is even more marked. In 1962, 32 per cent of the very long-term unemployed were forty-five and over.[11]

[11] *Report of the Secretary of Labor*, February, 1963 (*n.* 10), p. 55.

Further light is thrown on the motivation of unemployed workers and on selection procedures through analysis of the characteristics of trainees and nontrainees in our West Virginia surveys of state and ARA courses. The data indicate that older and uneducated unemployed workers are less likely to apply for training and are less likely to be accepted when they do apply (Tables 11–3 and 11–4).

The nonapplicants may have lacked motivation, ambition, or self-assurance. Many undoubtedly feared that they would fail the admission tests or have difficulty in handling the course material. The tables indicate that older, uneducated workers have grounds for their pessimism. Among the applicants for training, the "rejects" (not accepted for training) were significantly older and had less education than those who were accepted for the training courses.

A comparative analysis of MDTA trainees and the total unemployed indicates that workers with a combination of "disadvantages" are the most likely to be by-passed in selection for retraining. Although the long-term unemployed are generally enrolled in MDTA and ARA courses in proportions larger than their representation in the unemployed population as a whole (see Tables 11–1 and 11–2), they are selected from among the younger and better-educated long-term unemployed. Similarly, older workers included in MDTA courses have significantly higher levels of education than workers in the same age category among the total unemployed (see Table 11–5). Analyses have also shown that nonwhite

TABLE 11–3: AGE OF TRAINEES AND OF CONTROL GROUPS, WEST VIRGINIA SURVEYS, SUMMER, 1962

(Percentage distribution)

Training status	Age								
	0–18	19–21	22–34	35–44	45–54	55–64	65+	NA	Total
Completed training	0.4	15.8	43.7	25.3	12.0	1.8	—	0.9	100.0
Dropped out of training	0.9	14.8	45.3	25.1	11.3	2.0	0.5	—	100.0
In training	—	14.6	53.9	21.3	7.9	2.2	—	—	100.0
Did not report after acceptance for training	4.6	21.5	43.1	20.0	9.2	—	—	1.5	100.0
Not accepted for training	1.6	12.6	23.6	25.2	29.1	7.1	0.8	—	100.0
Nontrainee unemployed*	2.6	9.7	29.4	26.7	21.2	8.4	1.8	0.2	100.0

SOURCE: Ford Foundation Retraining Project: West Virginia field survey, 1962.
* A probability sample of workers who were unemployed at the time of the inception of the training courses but who did not apply for training. The sample was drawn from the active and inactive files of the employment service.

TABLE 11–4: EDUCATION OF TRAINEES AND OF CONTROL GROUPS, WEST VIRGINIA SURVEYS, SUMMER, 1962

(Percentage distribution)

Training status	Highest grade completed								
	1–6	7	8	9	10	11	12	13+	Total
Completed training	1.4	2.0	9.5	8.4	7.7	9.3	50.4	10.4	100.0
Dropped out of training	2.5	4.4	11.3	16.2	14.8	9.4	34.5	5.4	100.0
In training	6.7	5.6	11.2	18.0	14.6	6.7	25.8	11.2	100.0
Did not report after acceptance for training	3.1	3.1	23.1	9.2	16.9	7.7	30.8	6.2	100.0
Not accepted for training	7.1	7.9	24.4	12.6	4.7	10.2	22.8	8.7	100.0
Nontrainee unemployed*	17.2	9.3	20.5	9.3	8.8	7.7	18.5	7.9	100.0

SOURCE: Ford Foundation Retraining Project: West Virginia field survey, 1962.
* See Table 11–3.

TABLE 11–5: EDUCATIONAL ATTAINMENT OF OLDER MDTA TRAINEES IN FISCAL YEAR 1963 AND OF UNEMPLOYED PERSONS IN MARCH, 1962

(Percentage distribution)

Highest grade completed	MDTA trainees over 44 years of age, fiscal year 1963	Unemployed persons over 44 years of age, March, 1962[a]
Total	100.0	100.0
Under 8th	6.8	34.6
8th	15.7	23.3
9th–11th	26.9	18.4
12th	39.4	17.2
Over 12th	11.2	6.6

SOURCE: Chester W. Helper et al., Training Disadvantaged Groups Under the MDTA (Office of Manpower, Automation and Training, U.S. Department of Labor, November, 1963).

[a] Based on data from Special Labor Force Report, No. 30 (Bureau of Labor Statistics, U.S. Department of Labor, Washington, D.C.).

trainees are younger and have more schooling than white trainees.[12]

It is found, therefore, that unemployed workers with a combination of age, education, previous unemployment, and race which places them at a disadvantage in the labor market are being by-passed by the regular government retraining programs. These are the truly hard-core unemployed. An examination of the characteristics of "employable" public welfare recipients in such cities as Chicago and Milwaukee indicates that many of those at the very lowest levels of the labor market are further disadvantaged by records of drunkenness and criminality.

MDTA Experimental and Demonstration Projects. A main retraining hope for these disadvantaged workers lies in the experimental and demonstration projects of the MDTA, which are supported by a special branch of the Office of Manpower, Automation and Training. These had been carried on in a limited fashion

[12] Chester W. Helper et al., Training Disadvantaged Groups Under the MDTA (Office of Manpower, Automation and Training, U.S. Department of Labor, Washington, D.C., November, 1963).

under the original 1962 legislation. As of December, 1963, 31,000 trainees had been enrolled. Most of them were young people under nineteen years of age who had been excluded from the payment of training allowances in regular MDTA courses. The 196? amendments to the MDTA provide for a considerable expansion of projects designed for disadvantaged youths and for other workers with low levels of educational attainment.

The experimental projects, designed specifically for workers who are likely to be by-passed in the regular retraining courses, are worker centered rather than job-opportunity centered. In many of the projects, such as those for young people in Chicago, for Negroes in Norfolk, and for older workers in Milwaukee, vocational training is combined with literacy training and intensive counseling designed to change attitudes as well as to improve employment opportunities.

These demonstration projects are too new to permit any evaluation of their effectiveness, but it is already apparent that energy, imagination, and initiative have gone into their formulation. The flexibility of the approach adopted for these projects augurs well for the hard-core unemployed.

E. ATTITUDES OF NONTRAINEES AND DROPOUTS

The term nontrainee is used here to cover "rejects," those unemployed workers who applied for training and were rejected, and "non-reports," those who were accepted but did not report for training.

Attitudes of Rejected Applicants. Further light is cast on the selection process through an analysis of attitudes of unemployed applicants who were not accepted for training. The West Virginia surveys indicate that this group needs closer attention. Their rejection for retraining is another severe blow in a series of misfortunes that most of these people have suffered in recent years. Special efforts must be made to keep them within the active labor force; in order to do so, however, more must be known about the nature of their reaction after rejection.

There appear to be no comprehensive data on .e workers whose applications for training ere rejected, even though those in charge of atistical reporting for the ARA and the MDTA ·training programs keep voluminous statistics 1 the trainees. In the West Virginia surveys e were forced to reach conclusions on the isis of a very small sample, 122 rejects. It as found that 95 per cent of these rejects felt iat they could have done the type of work fered in the course for which they had iplied. Most of the more than 90 per cent ho took the qualifying tests did not pass. ·ven though three-fourths of the rejects felt iat the tests were fair, much of the bitterness f the rejects centered around the explanation, r lack of explanation, of their non-acceptance. ideed, 25 per cent of the rejects were not formed that they were not accepted; another I per cent stated that they were told they had iiled but that they were given no reasons for ieir failure and no discussions were held with iem about it.

Attitudes and Motivation of Non-Reports and ·ropouts. A surprisingly large number of nemployed workers who passed the screening iterviews and the tests for admission to the rogram did not report for training. As in the ise of rejects, little is being done in the way of illow-up. Analysis of the small West Virginia imple of such persons shows that the reason iost of them did not report was that they btained a job between the time of their pplication and the time of the commencement f the courses (Table 11–6). But a substantial ercentage stated that there was a scheduling onflict, that they could not afford to take 'aining, or that they were prevented by ill ealth—their own or that of a family member.

Somewhat more follow-up has been done nd is being done on dropouts. The Office of 1anpower, Automation and Training conducted rather extensive analysis of the reasons for ropout, and local employment offices are now sked to make regular reports on the reasons or which MDTA trainees leave the program.

A major reason for dropping out of the raining courses before completion appears to ie the inadequacy of the training allowances.

TABLE 11–6: REASONS FOR NON-ATTEND-ANCE OF TRAINING COURSE, WEST VIRGINIA SURVEY, 1962

(Percentage distribution)

A. *Reasons for not reporting after acceptance*

1. Got job	36.5
2. Couldn't afford to take training	7.9
3. No class openings	27.0
4. Bad hours, hours conflicted with a job, etc.	4.8
5. Respondent or member of family was ill	7.9
6. Family responsibilities	1.6
7. Other	14.3

B. *Reasons for dropping out of training course*

1. Got job or was recalled to work	32.8
2. Couldn't forgo wages	10.6
3. Became generally dissatisfied	14.6
4. Bad hours or hours conflicted with job	7.5
5. Health reasons	6.5
6. Respondent or member of family was ill	5.0
7. Thought he couldn't learn the work	2.0
8. Dropped out to study for job test	.5
9. Was dropped for cause: excessive absenteeism	.5
10. Was dropped for cause: other	.5
11. Other reasons	7.0
12. Not ascertained	1.0
13. Failed the course	4.5
14. No transportation	7.0

SOURCE: Ford Foundation Retraining Project: West Virginia field survey, 1962.

Thirty-four per cent of MDTA trainees withdrew in order to take a job or look for work or stated that they could not afford to remain in training.[13] In our West Virginia surveys one-third of the respondents said that they did not continue in the training courses either because they got jobs, or because they were recalled to work; and 10 per cent stated that they could not afford to continue with the training course (see Table 11–6).

The 1963 amendments to the MDTA should help to reduce the number who drop out of training courses for economic reasons. The additional training allowance of $10 per week can serve toward this end, and the opportunity of part-time employment now afforded

[13] *Report of the Secretary of Labor*, March, 1964 (n. 10), p. 35.

trainees will enable many to complete their courses without undue hardship.

Although economic factors are important in causing early termination of training, non-economic considerations also are of major significance. Almost one-third of the MDTA trainees withdrew because of "lack of progress and/or insufficient motivation." And at least one-fourth of the dropouts in the West Virginia surveys expressed dissatisfaction with specific aspects of their course or with retraining in general.

The value of counseling in preventing dropouts is startlingly evident in comparative figures for the regular MDTA programs, which are not geared primarily to the hard-core unemployed, and three local demonstration projects aimed specifically at the hard-core unemployed. For MDTA, the dropout rate is approximately 14 per cent. In a Norfolk program for Negroes the dropout rate was kept to a 10 per cent level; in a Milwaukee literacy-training program conducted by means of television, the dropout figure was almost 25 per cent; in a Chicago literacy-training program for welfare clients, only 50 per cent attended the courses regularly. It would be expected that the dropout rate for the hard-core Norfolk program would be higher than the rate for MDTA, and at least as high as the rates for other hard-core projects.

The low Norfolk rate can be explained in terms of extraordinary interest, effort, and intensive counseling. Those in charge of the project took unusual steps to understand the trainees' problems and, wherever possible, to help solve them. In many cases, it was necessary to explain to the trainees' wives the advantages their husbands would gain by further education and training. The counselors intervened to relieve the pressure of creditors on the trainees, to help settle domestic squabbles, and to aid wherever there were legal difficulties, and even tried to ameliorate the lot of families who suffered because of the low training allowances.

From the experience of the programs and projects and the findings of the surveys it is apparent that more information is needed about the attitudes and motivations of non reports and dropouts. The Norfolk project i evidence that an understanding of trainees problems can be the first step in an imaginativ campaign to prevent dropouts and, by extension perhaps to lower the rate of those who ar accepted but fail to report for training.

F. THE RELATION OF TRAINING TO EMPLOYMENT

A justification for the retraining programs i found in the job placement of unemploye workers who have completed their course Even if 25 per cent of the trainees cannot fin employment, the programs must be considere a worthwhile venture on the score of jol creation. The big unanswered question i whether these workers—the cream of th unemployed from the standpoint of age an education—would have obtained jobs just a readily if they had been by-passed for trainin; but were given the same treatment as were th trainees in careful testing, selection, an placement efforts by the employment service.

Surveys among employers in West Virginia Michigan, and Tennessee indicate that th trainees' new skills are important, but th special screening, testing, and selection o the trainees by the employment service is als a major influence on employers' willingness t hire them. Employers are also influenced b; the special efforts of the employment service t place trainees.

Comparisons between trainees and contro groups consisting of dropouts and nontrainee in the West Virginia surveys permit an evalua tion of the relative importance of training as factor in job placement. As seen in Tabl 11–7, those who were not accepted or who di not apply for retraining had a lower employ ment ratio shortly after the end of the cours than had those who dropped out of the cours after initial enrollment or who completed th retraining course. Whereas only 34 per cen of the workers who had not applied for trainin; were employed in 1962 (shortly after the com pletion of the training course), 60 per cent o those who completed training had foun mployment by this time. Workers who did not report for training after they were accepted were less likely to have found employment shortly after the training course ended than were those who were not accepted for training. On the other hand, workers who dropped out of the training course prior to its completion had a placement ratio (56 per cent) only slightly lower than that of workers who completed the training course (60 per cent). This relatively high placement rate for dropouts can be attributed to the fact that many withdrew in order to take jobs.

In the nine months covered by the surveys, after the end of the course, all of the workers had progressively improved their job status. This trend can be attributed in part to a slight improvement in the West Virginia employment levels between 1962 and 1963. The nontrainees (those who were not accepted, did not report, or did not apply) made substantial employment progress, but they continued to have employment rates well below those who had enrolled in the training courses (see Table 11–7). While these findings indicate the comparative effect of training and nontraining on job placement, they also reflect differences in the personal characteristics of trainees and nontrainees.

A relatively large proportion of the workers withdrew from the labor force in the months following training. Of those who completed the training course, 10 per cent had withdrawn from the labor force at the time of the first survey in 1962, and the rate had increased to 12.3 per cent in 1963. Most of these workers were women who had been trained as clerical workers, nurses' aides, and waitresses. Among those who had not applied or had not been accepted for training, the rate of withdrawal from the labor force was even higher. These high rates may be due to a scarcity of employment opportunities in a depressed area; they may also reflect, as has previously been noted, a lack of commitment to the labor market on the part of many of the female workers who are classed as unemployed.

Although employment rates immediately after completion of the training course were noticeably higher for trainees who were younger,

TABLE 11–7: EMPLOYMENT STATUS OF TRAINEES AND OF CONTROL GROUPS, WEST VIRGINIA SURVEYS, SUMMER, 1962, SPRING AND SUMMER, 1963

(Percent distribution)*

Trainees and control groups	Employment status									
	Employed		Unemployed		Not in labor force		Not ascertained		Total	
	1962	1963	1962	1963	1962	1963	1962	1963	1962	1963
Completed training	60.0	71.6	29.9	15.9	10.1	12.3	—	.2	100	100
Dropped out of training	56.1	68.4	37.4	24.6	6.5	6.8	—	1.2	100	100
In training (in 1962)	9.3	73.8	88.4	17.9	2.3	5.9	—	2.4	100	100
Did not report after acceptance for training	36.9	49.1	52.3	38.6	10.8	10.5	—	1.8	100	100
Not accepted for training	41.0	49.6	42.4	33.6	10.6	15.0	—	1.8	100	100
Nontrainee unemployed†	33.8	56.1	61.5	27.7	4.7	15.6	—	.6	100	100
Total	44.6	63.8	48.0	23.4	7.4	12.0	—	.9	100	100

SOURCE: Ford Foundation Retraining Project: West Virginia field surveys.

* N: 1962 = 1342
  1963 = 1168

† A probability sample of workers who were unemployed at the time of the inception of the training courses but who did not apply for training. The sample was drawn from the active and inactive files of the employment service.

TABLE 11–8: LABOR-FORCE STATUS OF WEST VIRGINIA TRAINEES AT SELECTED TIME INTERVALS AFTER COMPLETION OF TRAINING, BY SEX, AGE, EDUCATION, AND PRE-TRAINING EMPLOYMENT STATUS

*Percentage in Labor Force Status, in Selected Months After Completion of Training**

Selected characteristics of trainees	One month after training			Three months after training			Six months after training			Nine months after training		
	Employed	Unemployed	Not in labor force	Employed	Unemployed	Not in labor force	Employed	Unemployed	Not in labor force	Employed	Unemployed	Not in labor force
Sex												
Male	64	30	6	71	22	7	80	13	7	79	12	9
Female	46	28	26	60	21	19	63	23	14	72	16	12
Age												
19–21	48	43	10	59	32	9	70	16	14	69	13	18
22–34	65	28	7	73	18	9	81	13	6	83	10	7
35–44	53	24	22	69	20	12	73	14	14	76	14	10
45+	60	20	20	60	20	20	60	36	4	71	25	4
Education (years)												
0–8	45	25	30	55	15	30	60	15	25	70	15	15
9–11	53	32	15	69	20	11	71	20	9	77	10	13
12	60	33	7	66	26	8	78	16	6	79	15	6
13+	74	15	11	76	14	10	72	14	14	72	12	16
Employment status one month prior to retraining course												
Employed	79	20	1	82	13	4	82	12	5	81	12	7
Unemployed												
6 mos. or less	46	54	0	76	24	0	81	14	5	77	17	6
7–12 mos.	39	61	0	39	61	0	67	33	0	79	21	0
Not in labor force	44	6	50	54	8	38	60	13	27	69	8	24

SOURCE: Ford Foundation Retraining Project: West Virginia field surveys, 1962, 1963.
* N=294. Responses omitted from this tabulation lacked sufficiently precise work-history data to permit a time period analysis.

ere better educated, and had had less un-
mployment prior to training, at the end of
ine months the differentiation was less sharp
nd the placement ratio for the group as a whole
as exceptionally high (Table 11–8). These
ates differ from those indicated in earlier
abulations because the sample used in Table
1–8 comprised a smaller group of trainees for
vhom time-interval data were available.

Findings on the relationship between personal
haracteristics and job placement under the
ARA appear to be different from the findings
nder the MDTA. ARA trainees, in an
nitial small sample, seem to fare well in the
abor market after their training even if they
re older, less educated, and have experienced
onger periods of unemployment. In an initial
tudy on this relationship under MDTA
raining programs, however, there is found to be
ignificant advantage in post-training placement for younger workers, the better educated,
nd those with less previous unemployment.[14]
The West Virginia surveys bear out the MDTA
esearch findings rather than those of the ARA.

G. Retraining as an Inducement to Relocation

If the retraining investment is to bear fruit
n job placement, the relocation of trained
vorkers, particularly in depressed areas, will
requently be necessary. The West Virginia
urveys reveal that the acquisition of new
.kills through retraining programs may induce
vorkers to move to areas where employment
opportunities are less limited or are related
o their skills. In the study of McDowell
County, West Virginia, a depressed coal-
nining area, it was found that almost one-third
of the workers who had completed training
ander a state program for the unemployed had
noved out of the county by the time of the
nterview stage of the survey. A preliminary
abulation of responses indicated that the
lecision of almost 40 per cent of these out-
nigrants had been influenced by their training.
Unfortunately, the employment ratio of the

[14] Helper *et al.*, *Training Disadvantaged Groups* (n.
12), pp. 23–24.

trained migrants was no better than that of
other migrants; and the employment record of
migrant trainees was no better than that of the
trainees who did not migrate. One reason for
the low placement rate of the trained migrants
can be found in the fact that many of them
moved to other depressed communities in the
state.

A lesson to be learned here is that the major
role of relocation allowances, such as those
included in the 1963 MDTA amendments,
could be to induce not simply more out-
migration but rather a more rational out-migration. By making the allowance contingent on
a move to known job opportunities, as is
stressed in the new legislation, much fruitless
movement could be avoided. A second lesson
is related directly to the planning of training
programs in depressed areas. Older workers
are reluctant to relocate, as is seen in the fact
that less than 3 per cent of the out-migrants
were over fifty years of age. Therefore, training courses for unskilled older workers would be
most effective in low-level service occupations
geared to local opportunities. Younger
workers can benefit from training in some of
the expanding occupations (welding, for example) which presupposes their migration to
areas in which industrial growth is taking place.

V. TRAINING UNDER PRIVATE AUSPICES

The recent emphasis on government-subsidized training programs may tend to obscure
the fact that most of the training in this country
is conducted under private auspices. The
number of workers trained under traditional
corporate programs, mostly on-the-job instruction for new employees and the upgrading of
other employees, dwarfs the numbers trained
under government programs. General Motors,
for example, trains 7,200 employees a year;
Ford, 3,000; and I.B.M., 100,000 employees of
its customers. A 1962 Department of Labor
survey of more than 700,000 establishments
disclosed that 2.5 million workers were enrolled
in company training programs. Active train-

ing programs were related to company size. Three-fourths of the establishments with 800 or more employees had active training programs. An earlier study, made in 1959 in New Jersey by the United States Bureau of Apprenticeship, revealed a similar relationship of company size to training programs: of firms with 4–19 employees, 11 per cent had training programs; of firms with 500 or more employees, 82 per cent had training programs.[15] A number of labor unions also conduct training courses for their members, and there has been some increase in union-management agreements that include training provisions.

From the standpoint of this chapter, however, interest centers on private training programs designed for the unemployed and for those facing job displacement. Such programs are not numerous, and careful evaluations of private training programs are even rarer. In the discussion which follows, programs for the unemployed and for potentially displaced workers are examined under the following headings: company programs, union programs, union-management programs, and government-subsidized on-the-job training.

A. COMPANY PROGRAMS[16]

A number of companies for some time have been aware of the need for programs to retrain workers affected by technological change, and a few companies have conducted well-publicized "crash" retraining projects in the wake of major organizational or structural developments. The General Electric Company, for example, has a formal retraining program for employees faced with technological displacement. The courses generally have been on a short-term basis and provide a modification of skills rather than different skills. The R. J.

Reynolds Tobacco Company adapts its customary program—a combination of on-the-job and classroom training—to the needs of workers whose jobs are affected by changes in tools and methods. In recent years the Ford Motor Company has adapted its on-the-job and classroom upgrading program to the changes brought about by technological advance, especially in hydraulics and electrical maintenance. General Motors uses the General Motors Institute as its central agency for retraining to meet the requirements of technological change. The duPont Corporation uses job training, administered separately in each plant, "to cope with the rapidity of change" in production processes. The Allis-Chalmers Manufacturing Company gives its employees the opportunity to keep abreast of technological changes by making it possible for them to take courses, such as electronics and mathematics, in local vocational schools. The Campbell Soup Company, which stresses training for the upgrading of its employees, is giving increasing attention to the skills required by technological change. Bell & Howell Company states that its regular training program "has been extremely successful in meeting personnel problems of automation, in that it has upgraded many ... employees from unskilled to skilled or technical occupations."

Such adaptations of traditional company training programs to meet the special needs of technological change have been accelerated, on occasion, to provide a cushion to job displacement. Between 1956 and 1960, U.S. Steel gradually replaced the old structural mills at its South Chicago works with modern facilities, displacing 1,346 employees in the process. By 1961, after a "substantial" amount of retraining, 71 per cent of these employees were returned to work in the new mill.[17] Displaced workers at Minneapolis-Honeywell Regulator have been relocated in other assembly jobs after a brief company retraining program.[18] Xerox Corporation was faced with a surplus of manpower when it moved to the manufacture

15 "Employee Training in New Jersey," reprinted in *A Report on Manpower Requirements, Resources, Utilization and Training*, U.S. Department of Labor, March, 1963, pp. 29–76.

16 See Marvin T. Levine, *An Evaluation of Training Programs for Unemployed Workers in the United States* (unpublished Ph.D. thesis, University of Wisconsin, 1963), chaps. III and IV. The data are based on a mail survey of companies to determine their retraining practices.

17 "Corporate Classes," *Wall Street Journal* (August 23, 1961), p. 1.
18 *Ibid.*

of dry electrostatic reproduction machines. In order to avoid layoffs as much as possible and to equip at least some workers with the newly required skills, Xerox offered retraining at the Rochester Institute of Technology to potentially displaced employees under age fifty-five with at least ten years seniority. In the two years after its commencement, 68 of the 178 eligible workers had enrolled in the training course, at an average cost of $1,750 to $2,000 per man.[19]

With regard to these programs geared to teach new skills to potentially displaced employees, especially workers whose positions are threatened by automation, two immediate questions must be answered: "Did training result in an efficient performance?" and "Is the new occupation more protected from the displacement effects of technological change than the old?" Unfortunately, there have been few evaluations of company retraining programs. One interesting research report designed to answer some of these questions has recently been published by the Bureau of Labor Statistics.[20] Studies were made in four firms of training programs for older workers whose positions were threatened by technological change. There is special interest in the retraining of older workers because they constitute a large proportion of the long-term unemployed. Their position is especially vulnerable in plant shutdowns, for then their high seniority offers little protection.

The Bureau of Labor Statistics research findings on the trainability of older workers are encouraging. It was found that there was a great variation among individual performances and that this variation was greater than the difference in performance between older workers and younger workers. Younger workers can acquire specific skills more readily in a short course, but an older worker is likely to perform as well or better in a longer course. It was found, further, that the trainee's level of education is a crucial influence on the success of his retraining. The performance of older trainees with low levels of education was inferior to that of older workers with higher levels of education. These findings should be of interest to employers as well as to government officials concerned with the placement prospects and job opportunities for older workers in an age of rapid technological advance.

B. Union Programs

Only a few unions have sponsored unilateral training programs designed to protect their members against layoffs due to technological or organizational change. Two unions which have the longest history of training, as well as active current programs, are the International Typographical Union (ITU) and the International Brotherhood of Electrical Workers (IBEW). The ITU initiated courses for compositors and linotype operators at the turn of the century[21] and has continued to set up courses to keep its members abreast of technological change. A recent course, for example, is concerned with the replacement of hot-metal processes by photographic methods.

In 1944 the IBEW set up an electronics school at Marquette University for journeymen who wished to specialize in electronics. During 1944 and 1945 approximately 8,000 craftsmen received training, and thereby had a profound impact on the electrical industry.[22] Recently, an IBEW manufacturing local established a ten-week course in wiring and assembly methods. The course was held for two hours each week. Eighty workers enrolled in the course and fifty completed it.[23]

Training courses for their members have also been established by the printing pressmen's union and the photo-engravers' union. As early as 1917, the pressmen established a

19 *The New York Times* (January 17, 1960), p. 58.
20 *Industrial Retraining Programs for Technological Change: A Study of the Performance of Older Workers*, Bulletin No. 1368 (Bureau of Labor Statistics, U.S. Department of Labor, Washington, D.C., June, 1963).

21 Spencer Miller, Jr., "Organized Labor Forestalls Displacement," in Norse A. Cartwright, *Unemployment and Adult Education* (New York: American Association for Adult Education, 1931).
22 William F. Patterson and M. H. Hedges, *Educating for Industry* (New York: Prentice-Hall, Inc., 1946), pp. 38–39.
23 *The Electrical Workers' Journal* (June–July, 1957), pp. 30–32.

printing plant in Tennessee for the purpose of retraining in the operation of new presses. The photo-engravers have conducted training courses for their members since 1924, especially in connection with the development of offset lithographing.[24]

On January 5, 1964, the United Auto Workers announced the opening of the first union-sponsored, white-collar training center, in Detroit. Federal funds have been allocated for the project through the MDTA. Workers eligible for these courses must be (1) unemployed, (2) potentially unemployed (their present jobs threatened by automation or other causes), or (3) at present in low-skill occupations.[25] The new program may set a significant precedent, since union-sponsored training projects have traditionally been sponsored by craft, rather than industrial, unions.

C. COLLECTIVE BARGAINING APPROACHES[26]

In recent years unions and management have tended to work together on retraining programs for displaced or potentially displaced workers in unionized plants. In a number of companies, jointly administered apprenticeship programs have been modified to permit high-seniority employees to be trained. In the Ford Motor Company, for example, opportunities which were formerly limited to workers between eighteen and twenty-six years of age are now open to any employee with seniority who can pass the necessary mental and aptitude tests.[27]

A number of contracts guarantee retraining opportunities for eligible permanent employees in the event of major technological change which threatens displacement. Contractual provisions for such retraining have been negotiated by the New York City Publishers Association and the ITU; by R. H. Macy of New York and the Retail, Wholesale and Department Store Union; by Western Union and the commercial telegraphers; by Griscom Russel Co. and the machinists; and by Pleasantville Instrument Corp. and the IBEW.

Very few of the collective bargaining programs, however, are designed to aid those who are already unemployed. In their study of seventeen cases of plant shutdown, Haber, Ferman, and Hudson found little evidence of training programs to benefit the displaced workers.[28]

The Armour Automation Fund arrangement in Oklahoma City was the one notable exception. As Thomas Kennedy notes in his study of seven union-management automation funds, only the Armour fund attempted to retrain unemployed workers as part of the fund operations.[29] The experience in Oklahoma City has been widely publicized and has been generally construed as an unfavorable commentary on union-management efforts to retrain displaced workers. Haber, Ferman, and Hudson report on this experience:

The most detailed information available concerning the effect of retraining on displaced workers is contained in the study of ex-Armour Company workers in Oklahoma City in 1961. Of the 431 former production workers who were invited to be tested and counseled for a retraining program negotiated by the union with the Armour Company, 210 visited the state employment service for testing. Sixty of the tested workers were recommended for retraining, and fifty of them completed their special training by February 1961. Age was not a factor; Negroes and women were the most eager to receive training.

---

[24] Sumner H. Slichter, *Union Policies and Industrial Management* (Washington, D.C.: The Brookings Institution, 1941), pp. 258–59.

[25] UAW news release, January 5, 1964.

[26] See Levine, *An Evaluation of Training Programs* (n. 16), and Charles C. Killingsworth, "Collective Bargaining Approaches to Employee Displacement Problems," *Studies Relating to Collective Bargaining Agreements and Practices Outside the Railroad Industry*, report of The Presidential Railroad Commission, Appendix, Vol. IV (Washington, D.C., February, 1962), pp. 224–25.

[27] *Automation and Major Technological Change*, papers presented at a conference held under the auspices of the Industrial Union Department, AFL–CIO, April 22, 1958, p. 18.

[28] William Haber et al., *The Impact of Technological Change* (Ann Arbor: Institute of Labor and Industrial Relations, University of Michigan-Wayne State University, 1963).

[29] Thomas Kennedy, *Automation Funds and Displaced Workers* (Harvard University Graduate School of Business Administration, Cambridge, Massachusetts, 1962).

In the early spring of 1962, 41 of these retrained workers were interviewed again to determine the effect of retraining. The results were not encouraging. Forty-six per cent of the 41 retrained workers were unemployed at that time, compared with 34 per cent of the 381 displaced workers who had received no retraining or who had not completed the program. The unemployment rate for retrained workers under age 45 was 37 per cent and for those aged 45 or over, 54 per cent. All but one of the men under age 45, however, had had jobs. Among the 22 retrained individuals who were working in the spring of 1962, only 4 of the 12 younger workers and 2 of the 10 older workers had jobs which appeared to be related to their retraining.

On the surface, the results of the retraining program appear to be poor. Lack of education and lack of skill among ex-Armour workers made them poor candidates for retraining. Among those who finished the course, there were a number of hard-to-place Negro and female workers. The training was of relatively short duration, and job opportunities in Oklahoma City were scarce. These factors make it difficult to pass judgment on the program. Actually, we must conclude that since very little is known about the effects of retraining on displaced workers, further research is certainly indicated.[30]

However, a contrasting experience has been reported by the Automation Fund Committee in the case of the shutdown of the Armour plant in Fort Worth, Texas, in March, 1962. Here George Schultz and Arnold Weber report:

Under the retraining program, 165 persons enrolled in courses for a wide range of occupations. To date, 117 have completed training, 30 are still in training, and 18 dropped out for various reasons. Of the 117 persons who completed training, approximately 86.5 per cent of those actively seeking employment, and 77.5 per cent of the total group, have found jobs. This experience compares favorably with a sample of other workers displaced by the plant closing who did not undertake training. In comparing the experience of males particularly, 95.5 per cent of those who took retraining were working while 72 per cent of those who did not take training were employed. In addition, the trainees generally enjoyed higher wages than the nontrainees. Nonetheless, it should be pointed out that the average earnings of the trainees, especially females, was considerably below the wage levels at Armour and could hardly be considered generous.[31]

It is obvious that the Oklahoma City retraining experience occurred under the worst possible set of conditions—conditions which made an unfavorable result almost inevitable. The economic environment of Fort Worth, on the other hand, and the approach to retraining adopted in the Fort Worth shutdown led to a successful adjustment for the workers and can be construed as a favorable commentary on union-management retraining.

D. GOVERNMENT-SUBSIDIZED ON-THE-JOB TRAINING

The on-the-job training provisions of the MDTA provide an interesting area for experiment with co-operative programs of private and public retraining. The act authorizes training allowances for unemployed workers referred to approved on-the-job training courses, and the government may pay other costs of such programs. Training courses are encouraged not only in individual establishments but also under the auspices of labor organizations, trade associations, community groups, and other qualified agencies. Unlike institutional training programs under the MDTA, these projects are usually developed, approved, and supervised by the Bureau of Apprenticeship and Training of the U.S. Department of Labor. The employment service and vocational education authorities assist in these functions, but their role is limited by the fact that job placement as well as training will frequently occur in the on-the-job training establishment.

---

[30] Haber *et al.*, *The Impact of Technological Change* (*n.* 28), pp. 22–23.

[31] George Shultz and Arnold Weber, *Report to the Armour Committee on the Shutdown at Fort Worth, Texas, November, 1963.* (Mimeographed.)

At this writing the on-the-job training program is too new to provide sufficient data for a detailed analysis. Because of delays in establishing the groundwork of standards and procedures, the first contract was not approved until April, 1963. By the end of 1963, 430 on-the-job projects had been approved, involving 6,733 trainees; but only 44 projects with an initial enrollment of 815 trainees had been completed. Almost all of the trainees who completed their training were hired by the training facility or assured of early placement.[32]

Most of the on-the-job training opportunities under the MDTA were offered by business enterprises in manufacturing industries, primarily for job entry training for such semi-skilled and skilled positions as machine operators, draftsmen, and electronic technicians. In a number of manufacturing firms, the projects were designed for skill upgrading to meet the needs of technological change and avoid occupational displacement. There was also a significant number of on-the-job training projects in service occupations like cooking, hotel housekeeping, and building maintenance, which accounted for over 11 per cent of the total number of trainees receiving on-the-job training.

Three notable advantages of on-the-job training relative to institutional training have been stressed by the Office of Manpower, Automation and Training: (1) The average cost per trainee is substantially less because of smaller charges for instruction and facilities; and since the trainees earn wages during the course of their training, the payments of government training allowances are lower. (2) Trainees are better motivated because of their higher income during training and because of a greater assurance of post-training employment. These factors have resulted in a significantly lower dropout rate. (3) A considerably higher proportion of the trainees are placed on jobs after their training is completed—primarily in the facility where training occurred.

These advantages have also been found in ARA retraining programs which, while not

[32] *Report of the Secretary of Labor*, March, 1964 (*n.* 10), pp. 47–52.

conducted on the job, are geared closely to the needs of a specific employer. In addition to the improved motivation and job placement of trainees, it has been found that the subsidy to the employer embodied in government-financed retraining is an attractive inducement to his expansion of employment opportunities when he has some control over the retraining procedures and content. The West Virginia employer surveys indicate that many employers, especially in service occupations like auto repair and nurses' aides, would prefer government-subsidized, on-the-job training to institutional training. Almost 30 per cent of the employers preferred government subsidies for on-the-job training rather than vocational schools, which are now generally used under the ARA and the MDTA. In view of the late start of the MDTA and the continuing shortage of vocational school facilities and instructors, it is not likely that the goal set by the original program—400,000 trainees—can be achieved in three years without widespread use of on-the-job training.

But there are also dangers involved in government-subsidized on-the-job training. Caution must be observed to ensure that much of the training is extended to unemployed workers, and not only to the upgrading of those already employed. The West Virginia surveys indicate that many employers may prefer to use the government-subsidized retraining provisions in ways which benefit the hard-core unemployed only slightly. Analyses of several ARA training programs in West Virginia and in other states where courses have been designed to fill the needs of a specific employer indicate that the job-placement ratios are considerably higher than average but that the selected trainees are younger and better educated than other ARA trainees. In some of these firms, all of the employed trainees are under age forty-five and all have completed a high school education.

Care must be taken also to see that employees are assured some continuity of employment after the completion of their training. Workers trained for a specific job in a specific plant will be placed in a vulnerable position if they are again set adrift among the unemployed. There ave been some unfortunate experiences along his line under ARA programs geared to a pecific employer. Finally, unions are sensitive o any program which might undermine wage standards.

VI. A NOTE ON FOREIGN EXPERIENCE[33]

Large-scale unemployment and programs to retrain the unemployed are not specific to the United States. In fact, the size and comprehensive nature of some of the training and retraining programs outside the United States, particularly in Canada and in Western Europe, dwarf our own training programs. It is not expected that a direct comparison of these programs with United States programs is valid —there are differences in systems of government, economic policies, availability of resources—but some highlights of Canadian and Western European training programs may serve toward a balanced evaluation of training programs in the United States.

Accelerated retraining programs for adults are found in all European countries. Few of these are designed specifically for unemployed or potentially displaced workers, but are being used extensively to retrain such workers. The training programs are generally part of a set of broad governmental policies to provide assistance to jobless workers and others with little skill. This battery of policies, often referred to in Western Europe as "readaptation," includes not only training allowances but unemployment benefits, relocation expenses, and family allowances while workers are separated from

[33] Good general discussions of foreign retraining can be found in Phyllis P. Groom, "Retraining the Unemployed," reprint from *Monthly Labor Review* (August, 1961); Alfred L. Green, "A Study and Appraisal of Manpower Programs as Related to a Policy of Full Employment in France, Great Britain, The Netherlands, Sweden," New York State Department of Labor, September, 1963; European Productivity Agency, Organization for European Economic Co-operation, *Accelerated Vocational Training for Unskilled and Semiskilled Manpower* (Paris, 1960), pp. 47–48; *Adaptation and Training of Rural Workers For Industrial Work*, report by Mr. Guy Barbichon for Organization for Economic Co-operation and Development, 1961. Citations to training programs in specific countries can be found in these references.

their families. In France, Belgium, West Germany, The Netherlands, Switzerland, and the United Kingdom, unemployed workers who refuse training are disqualified from receiving unemployment benefits.

The national programs in Western Europe are supplemented by international programs of training under the auspices of the Organization for Economic Co-operation and Development and the European Coal and Steel Community. These organizations play a major educational role in the training programs through a series of conferences and study reports; but they also serve the operation of the programs by making retraining funds available to the member countries.

In Canada the Technical and Vocational Training Assistance Act was passed by Parliament in 1960. This law authorizes the federal government to pay 75 per cent of the cost of constructing vocational schools, educating vocational instructors, and training unemployed workers and pay 50 per cent of the cost of vocational training.

In Sweden, often held up as a model in the labor-market field, the number of courses held under auspices of the National Board of Vocational Education, mainly at the request of the National Labour Market Board, had increased to 822 in 1963, involving almost 30,000 trainees. It is anticipated that 35,000 workers, or approximately 1 per cent of the labor force, will be retrained each year in the future.

Although few detailed evaluations of European programs are available, there is evidence that there, as in the United States, retraining courses are of primary benefit to younger workers. Comparable data are not available for all European training programs, but the preference for younger trainees is seen in the age specifications indicated for the accelerated vocational training programs. Some of the countries have established an upper age limit of forty-five, others have a preferred age level below this limit.[34]

Because of Western Europe's full employment

[34] European Productivity Agency, *Accelerated Vocational Training*, (n. 33).

in recent years, training and retraining programs have played a role somewhat different from those established under recent American training legislation. More emphasis has been placed on skill upgrading for employed workers in a tight labor market than on equipping unemployed workers with the basic skills needed for job placement. The European experience, therefore, may be especially instructive in the future U.S. economy when, hopefully, higher over-all employment levels may be achieved.

VII. GAINS AND COSTS OF TRAINING

A. ECONOMIC CONSIDERATIONS

A recent emphasis in economics is the analysis of investment in human beings, that is, investment in human capital. There is a growing conviction that this type of investment has long been neglected as a factor in economic growth. We have placed great stress on the contribution that capital investment makes to increased productivity but not nearly enough on the productivity increase stemming from such investments as those in education, training, health, and mobility.

The programs established under the ARA and the MDTA must be considered as substantial government investments in human beings. When viewed in this light, several questions arise: "What is the rate of return on this investment?" "Is it a wise investment?" and "What are the gains and costs?" Although some research has been done along the lines of these questions,[35] there are still grave methodological problems to be solved before valid answers can be given. If we are to avoid oversimplified and misleading assumptions, it is important to have a long period of follow-up in calculating the rate of return. Also, it appears to be crucial to compare the trainees with control groups in order to arrive at sound conclusions on the values of retraining. Even then, theory problems remain.

Most of the statements, studies, and analyses dealing with this question conclude that training and retraining are a sound investment for the trainee and for society. For the U.S. Department of Labor and the Department of Health, Education, and Welfare it is enough that 70–75 per cent of the MDTA trainees obtain jobs, almost all in training-related occupations. If the formerly unemployed trainee obtains employment following his training, and if the job can be attributed to his training, it is seldom hard to prove that the time he invested in training paid off handsomely. One need only make the correct assumptions about the worker's discount rate and the continuance of employment and earnings in the future.

Similarly, it has been pointed out that training of the unemployed is a sound economic investment for society. Many of the trainees would presumably have received unemployment compensation or relief in the absence of a training allowance; hence, for these trainees the allowance constitutes little net cost to society. (The variety of payments received by ARA and state program trainees in the West Virginia surveys is indicated in Table 11–9.) The on-the-job and institutional costs of retraining under the ARA and the MDTA are usually placed within a range of approximately $450 to $1,250 per trainee. A steady job attributable to the retraining can readily offset these costs in foregone transfer payments and income tax receipts in a relatively short period of time. As one study of retrained workers in Massachusetts concludes:

> Although the control group had similar compensation costs in 1959, its cost by 1962 had increased 28 per cent. On this basis the retrainees' unemployment costs would probably have amounted to about $31,000 in 1962 in the absence of retraining. Actually unemployment payments to this group in 1962 were only $8,000. Thus, for that one year, a saving in unemployment compensation of $23,000 can be attributed to the retraining program.[36]

---

[35] See "Investment in Human Beings," *The Journal of Political Economy*, Vol. LXX, Supplement (October, 1962), especially Part 2; and Theodore W. Schultz, *The Economic Value of Education* (New York: Columbia University Press, 1963).

[36] "Retraining the Unemployed: Part III—Retraining, A Good Investment," *New England Business Review* (April, 1963), p. 2.

TABLE 11-9: PAYMENTS RECEIVED BY TRAINEES AND BY DROPOUTS, WEST VIRGINIA SURVEYS, 1962

A. Number of weeks payment received

Type of payment	1–5		6–10		11–15		16–20		21–30		31–40		Over 40		Not ascertained		Total	
	No.	Per cent	No.	Per cent	No.	Per cent	No.	Per cent	No.	Per cent	No.	Per cent	No.	Per cent	No.	Per cent	No.	Per cent
Training allowances	108	50.9	47	22.2	29	13.7	21	9.9	—	—	—	—	1	.5	6	2.8	212	100.0
Unemployment compensation	34	30.6	27	24.4	11	9.9	7	6.3	12	10.8	5	4.5	6	5.4	9	8.1	111	100.0
Aid to dep. children	—	—	2	9.5	2	9.5	2	9.5	—	—	—	—	9	42.9	6	28.6	21	100.0
Travel allowances	34	15.8	38	17.7	28	13.0	23	10.7	14	6.5	5	2.3	29	13.5	44	20.5	215	100.0
Other payments	2	25.0	1	12.5	—	—	—	—	—	—	1	12.5	1	12.5	3	37.5	8	100.0

B. Payments received per week

Type of payment	$1–$5		$6–$10		$11–$15		$16–$20		$21–$30		$31–$40		Over $40		Not ascertained		Total	
	No.	Per cent	No.	Per cent	No.	Per cent	No.	Per cent	No.	Per cent	No.	Per cent	No.	Per cent	No.	Per cent	No.	Per cent
Training allowances	1	.5	—	—	—	—	1	.5	205	96.7	2	.9	—	—	3	1.4	212	100.0
Unemployment compensation	—	—	1	.9	7	6.3	9	8.1	58	52.3	25	22.5	—	—	11	10.0	111	100.0
Aid to dep. children	—	—	1	4.8	1	4.8	1	4.8	3	14.2	5	23.8	5	23.8	5	23.8	21	100.0
Travel allowances	107	49.8	30	13.9	2	.9	1	.5	1	.5	—	—	1	.5	73	33.9	215	100.0
Other payments	—	—	1	12.5	1	12.5	—	—	1	12.5	2	25.0	—	—	3	37.5	8	100.0

SOURCE: Ford Foundation Retraining Project: West Virginia field survey, 1962.

249

Another study, based on actual training costs and estimated earnings for 12,696 MDTA trainees, finds that: "Training under the Act has made only modest inroads toward alleviating unemployment, but already it has demonstrated vividly the economic value of training as an investment in our human resources."[37]

Public welfare officials also make enthusiastic claims concerning the savings in relief payments attributable to training programs for employable welfare recipients.[38] For these hard-core, long-term unemployed, any job resulting from training can provide an explosive rate of return on the public investment.

An analysis of almost 200 trainees (for whom adequate earnings data were available) who completed the West Virginia training courses reveals that approximately 60 per cent gained in earnings (including wages and transfer payments) in the six months after training as compared with the six-month period prior to commencement of their training course. Only 17 per cent had lower earnings, and 23 per cent experienced no significant change. Among the nonapplicants for training, on the other hand, only 34.7 per cent gained in earnings in a comparable period following completion of the training courses. Here, again, as in a number of the national surveys, there is some evidence of the economic benefits of retraining.

In spite of this evidence and the claims for high rates of personal and societal return on the retraining investment—and the author's own predilection to accept such claims—it must be noted, again, that little valid proof has yet been offered of such a rate of return. Even if trainees do much better in the job market than control groups of nontrainees, as most studies indicate, one cannot be certain that the job record is attributable to retraining. As has

been noted, the record may result from the trainees' youth, higher education, etc.; from the counseling rather than the training; or from the employment service's greater efforts at job placement of trainees as compared with nontrainee job applicants. One may accept the economic values of retraining on faith; but it is no simple matter to lend quantitative precision to one's beliefs.

B. NON-ECONOMIC CONSIDERATIONS

Even if we should come to the conclusion that costs of retraining outweigh the immediate gains, it would not follow necessarily that we should abandon ARA and MDTA retraining, or that private company and union-management programs should be set aside. Although there has been little research on this question, there are already some indications that the real payoff in the retraining of unemployed workers may be a very long-range proposition. If we look for immediate gains in the job market and in wages, we may be disappointed; but it is possible that the retraining experience will regenerate members of the hard-core group of unemployed, restore their confidence, and return them to a commitment to a life of work instead of a life of hopeless idleness. There is some evidence that even if an immediate job is not provided, many of these hard-core unemployed workers have benefited in changed attitudes and outlook. It then can be hoped that in a more prosperous time—and we hope to reach higher levels of employment in the future—these rehabilitated workers will find a place in the labor market.

VIII. CONCLUSIONS

With the amendments to the MDTA adopted in December, 1963, there is no longer any doubt about the commitment of the federal government to the principle of retraining the unemployed. There is now a demonstrated willingness to expand the training activities and make them more flexible.

Experience with the federal programs, especially in their integration with private retraining, has been too brief for a full evalua-

[37] Leroy A. Cornelsen, "Economics of Training the Unemployed," Division of Vocational and Technical Education, U.S. Department of Health, Education, and Welfare, January, 1964. (Mimeographed.)

[38] For example, see the claims of this type made by welfare officials in Pennsylvania, New York City, and Cook County, Illinois, cited in Gerald G. Somers, "Automation, Retraining and Public Welfare," Conference on Automation and Public Welfare, Cornell University School of Industrial and Labor Relations, and American Foundation on Automation and Employment, New York City, October 7–8, 1963.

tion, but there is already some evidence of their benefit to trainees and to society. Much more, however, remains to be done.

The present approach to training under the ARA and the MDTA cannot go very far in bringing about substantial reductions in unemployment or improving the over-all allocation of human resources unless the programs are greatly expanded and integrated with other labor-market policies. Advanced technology is creating many shortages of manpower at high-skill and technical levels. The unemployed, concentrated in low-skill, low-education categories, cannot be trained for these positions. Further, many of the growing opportunities may not be found in localities or even in states where there are large numbers of unemployed. A long-range plan should envis-

age a continuous process of retraining in which all levels of workers are being constantly upgraded so that there may be openings at the bottom of the occupational ladder for retrained unemployed workers. Relocation allowances and an improved employment service clearance procedure are also fundamental in an over-all plan. As an adjunct of these programs, an expansion of educational and vocational opportunities for young people, accompanied by improvements in vocational guidance, are essential for the achievement of long-term labor-market goals.

The potential benefits of retraining for the unemployed are substantial, and the potential will be realized when retraining is accorded a central role in an expanded and co-ordinated system of labor-market policies.

CHAPTER 12

Welfare Services
Elizabeth Wickenden*

I. INTRODUCTION

A. THE WELFARE FUNCTION

ONE OF THE programs of aid for individuals and families suffering economic or social deprivation as a result of unemployment is the social program known as "welfare." Welfare is distinguished from the other remedial measures described in earlier chapters by its residual and adaptive functions. Welfare picks up where other measures leave off, and it is able to custom tailor its services to needs which are either too individual to fit a generalized program or are not yet recognized as requiring a general remedy. In this way welfare both supplements other programs and helps point the way to needed changes in social organization.

Since the specific services offered by welfare are necessarily modified by what is available under other auspices, it is difficult to offer a general classification of welfare services. The difficulty is further complicated by a substantial variation throughout the country in the adequacy of actual program provisions covering the welfare function. Typically, however, welfare services for assisting the unemployed and their families include one or more of the following: financial or other assistance to provide substitute or supplementary income sufficient to meet basic needs for which no other provision exists; direct benefits such as medical, child-care, or training provisions; and social work service directed toward

* Technical Consultant on Public Social Policy to National Social Welfare Assembly, Inc.

assisting the individual, family, or group to solve a particular problem of adaptation or to secure a needed service.

The function of welfare and its relationship to other forms of social aid are perhaps best illustrated by examples of the particular circumstances which cause individuals or families to seek the help of welfare. In all the examples joblessness is the central factor and the individual's resources are inadequate for his needs; but the total configuration of need in each example is different and calls for a different remedy or combination of remedies.

1. An unemployed individual who is normally employed and considered employable in the current labor market may seek temporary or extended help because there are no jobs to be had and his other resources have either been exhausted or are insufficient to meet the basic needs of his family. He may lack coverage by unemployment insurance, or may have exhausted his benefit entitlements, or the level of his benefits may be too low to meet his budgeted needs. His need is primarily for a job, but he must have welfare help if his family is not to starve.

2. Another individual may need help because his education, skills, and experience do not equip him to fill such jobs as are available or provide him with earnings which are so inadequate as to require welfare supplementation. This individual has a problem which lies partly within his own particular circumstances and he needs help (over and above financial aid, if he is destitute) to enhance his employability. This help may take such forms as basic educa-

tion, vocational training, work experience, or specialized counseling. Welfare agencies will frequently assist in securing this kind of help—through referral, purchase, or direct provision—for those for whom they have already accepted some responsibility.

3. Still another individual may be unemployed because of a physical, emotional, or psychological handicap which makes him unfit for existing jobs but which could be mitigated by a combination of medical, rehabilitative, and counseling services. Welfare agencies frequently provide such services or help their clients secure them elsewhere.

4. An individual may be unable to work because of temporary or long-term family responsibilities which might be alleviated through such social aids as day care for children, nursing home or other residential care for the aged, or homemaker service. Providing or securing such services for their clients is also a responsibility of welfare agencies.

5. An individual may be unemployed and in need of help because of an ambiguity, either in his own mind or in current public policy, as to whether he should earn his own livelihood or properly should be supported on a social basis. This confusion is particularly applicable today to unwed or deserted mothers who are solely responsible for the care of their children. It is often aggravated by community attitudes which seek to apply stricter standards of employability to mothers receiving public aid who are members of a minority group or whose conduct is not acceptable. The same kind of confusion also can affect others on the margin of employability. For example, the older unemployed worker displaced by technological or other economic change who has not yet reached the social insurance retirement age finds himself in an economic no-man's-land where welfare help may constitute his only refuge. Another kind of difficulty is experienced by the migratory, seasonal farm worker, whose help is eagerly sought for the harvest period but who finds himself without either acceptance or entitlement after it is passed. Welfare agencies, as intermediaries between social values and individual needs, often find

themselves in the storm center of these conflicts. On the one hand, they strive to help the individual accommodate himself to community expectations through services directed toward enhancing his employability; on the other hand, they typically seek to resolve these ambiguities through a better accommodation of social policy to individual problems by means of social action and through the work of community planning councils.

In all of these situations it is the fitting of social remedy to a particular unmet need or combination of needs that constitutes the ideal function of welfare, however imperfectly it may be realized within the program provisions existing in any specific community today. People generally understand that one role of welfare is to serve as a "court of last resort" for desperate individuals whose circumstances of economic stress oblige them to seek aid, however much this dependence on public aid may be resented. But another function of welfare services is not equally well understood; namely, that welfare services also serve an adaptive or pioneer function in the total process of social development. Welfare services, both public and voluntary, operate on the frontier of social progress by reason of the very fact that they exist to meet socially recognized, but otherwise unmet, needs.

This is demonstrated in two ways: first, in their ability to experiment with new types of social services directed to the needs of particular individuals or groups, services which later may be extended on a broader basis to the general population; and second, in the evidence these services provide of the inadequacy of other measures as presently constituted. There is, for example, no clearer evidence of the (necessary) limitations of the unemployment insurance system than a large number of destitute unemployed persons seeking public assistance or other welfare aid. But this adaptive underpinning function requires that welfare services adhere closely to their own proper role: meeting needs only in terms of particular circumstances within the framework of other available resources. Any other course easily could serve to undermine, rather than to strengthen, the total social fabric by putting welfare into competition with other sources of social and economic support, such as the family, productive employment, or broad-based measures like social insurance.

Within its proper role, however, welfare's functions must undergo constant adaptation to the new needs that develop as a result of changes in the over-all social and economic pattern, the scope of other social programs, and the concept of social responsibility. In a society of changing needs and of a changing complex of social provisions to meet them, there is no fixed standard by which to fit existing welfare programs to desirable welfare functions. The place of welfare services in the total pattern of social measures can only be understood in terms of an evolutionary process in which agencies, programs, needs, and goals interact to create a direction of policy growth. This evolution is spelled out more fully in the later sections describing welfare program provisions and development as they affect the unemployed.

B. THE WELFARE STRUCTURE

The welfare function is not assigned in our pluralistic society to any single, all-embracing agency or program but is scattered among many according to patterns which differ from community to community and from state to state. Welfare services are provided both by tax-supported governmental agencies operating within the framework of law and by a wide range of agencies which are voluntary in terms of the direction, financing, scope, and character of services. Public welfare agencies, largely as a result of the availability of federal aid since 1933, now serve every community in the United States. Their programs and administrative patterns are determined in the first instance by state law and hence vary from state to state, although the requirements of federal aid have encouraged the development of a widening core of common program provisions.

Distinction between public and voluntary welfare services cannot be made strictly on the basis of function, since great variations exist and their basic differentiation lies mainly in

the intangibles of emphasis, degree, and motivation. General availability, however, increasingly has become a distinguishing characteristic of public welfare, since government has tended to assume the responsibility for meeting needs—especially those involving financial aid—which are sufficiently widespread and basic to require the assured financing of taxation. Thus public welfare programs typically operate within a legal framework in which benefits are presumed to be equally available to all persons in a similar situation. Voluntary welfare activity, on the other hand, is characterized by its ability to limit its responsibility; and thus its programs are generally more limited in scope, directed toward a particular need, and highly varied. In a few situations voluntary agencies act as the agents of governmental responsibility, but this is not the typical American pattern. For the most part voluntary welfare agencies, whether under religious or secular auspices, prefer to operate independently and to choose their own function, clientele, and method.

Leadership in the direction and development of welfare programs is furnished nationally by the Welfare Administration of the Department of Health, Education, and Welfare, which administers the federally aided welfare programs, and by a wide range of national voluntary organizations, which represent particular groups or common fields of interest. State public welfare departments carry the principal responsibility for the implementation of state law and are the channel through which federal aid is transmitted to local public welfare agencies, increasingly organized on a county basis. The numerous voluntary agencies generally are local in their organization and functioning and commonly draw their support from a federated fund-raising body or a particular group such as a religious denomination. Planning councils, whose role is to foster co-operation among these many welfare agencies and better adapt their activities to changing needs, function on a community and, to a lesser extent, state level.

This pluralistic approach to welfare needs, facilitated at many points by collaborative planning and consultation, seems particularly well suited to the adaptive function of welfare as it has developed in the American pattern of social organization. It not only gives individuals some choice as to where they turn for help but also contributes to the dynamics of social progress.

The developments of the past thirty years clearly demonstrate the evolutionary role of welfare, both public and voluntary, in an adaptive society. Changes in federal and state laws have moved steadily in the direction of a public program which is at once comprehensive, in that it takes an integrated approach to individual need, and residual, in that it adapts to the availability of other services, both governmental and voluntary. Voluntary welfare agencies have in most instances encouraged this broadening scope of public welfare responsibility while they adapted their own programs to more specialized or experimental activity. This trend has been brought into sharp focus by the passage of the Public Welfare Amendments of 1962,[1] in which financial aid, direct benefits, and social service are treated increasingly as aspects of a unified public welfare program. The subsequent creation of the Welfare Administration to parallel the Social Security Administration, now largely limited to social insurance responsibilities, also served to emphasize the distinctive but comprehensive character of the welfare function. A similar movement is evident also in the states as they review their existing policies and seek to adapt their programs and structure to this changing pattern.[2] In order to clarify the impact of this gradually evolving development in welfare services affecting the unemployed, the sections which follow describe programs both in relationship to particular needs and within the framework of an evolutionary process.

[1] Public Law 543, 87th Congress.
[2] Interesting examples of this process can be found in the following state reports: Final Report and Consultant Reports of the Welfare Study Commission of the State of California, January, 1963; Reports of Pennsylvania State and Local Welfare Commission; *Public Welfare in the State of New York*, Moreland Commission report, January, 1963; Report of a Committee for a Comprehensive Family and Child Welfare Program in Illinois, Illinois Commission on Children, October, 1962.

II. PROGRAMS TO MEET FINANCIAL NEED

A. PUBLIC ASSISTANCE

At the present time the principal source of direct aid for the needy unemployed and their families consists of public assistance given by state and local public welfare agencies in the form of cash payments, medical care, or other benefits. Public assistance is characterized by measurement of the specific needs of individuals or families applying for this aid against a standard established by the administering authority as a minimal level of entitlement. This process, commonly known as the "means test," not only establishes the applicant's eligibility for aid but also determines the amount of assistance he will receive.

The means test plays an indispensable role in reconciling three inter-related attributes of public assistance: (1) The particularizing function of welfare demands a method for the individualization of benefits. (2) The character of public welfare responsibility requires that this be achieved within a procedure which assures reasonably equitable treatment to persons in similar circumstances throughout the state or other jurisdiction. (3) The total resources available to public assistance within that state or jurisdiction limit the aid which can be given. The means test is thus a method of adapting benefits to individual need within an equitable standard and according to the total resources available. Moreover, the residual character of the welfare function requires that it should not compete either with the productive economy, on which it depends, or with measures like social insurance which are intended to prevent need. The means test thus takes into account, in determining the need for public assistance or the amount, the availability of income from possible work, social insurance, or others in the family who have legal responsibility for the applicant.

The distaste with which the means test is commonly viewed reflects a healthy rejection of dependency as a way of life; the best answer to this problem can be found in measures like social insurance and public works, which reduce the incidence of dependency to those unusual circumstances in which the need for adequate, dignified, and individualized aid is self-evident. Public assistance is a necessary underpinning for other forms of social protection; but when it becomes the major source of income for large numbers of people over an extended period of time, public uneasiness is inevitably aroused. Thus its purpose is not only to protect individuals against ultimate need but also to put the spotlight on problems requiring a more effective long-term social remedy.

The pattern of public assistance organization for the needy unemployed in the United States must be interpreted historically. Traditionally, under the poor law this responsibility rested with localities; even state participation in that responsibility is relatively recent. As has been seen in Chapter 1, the federal government did not enter the field of public welfare in an operational sense until 1933, when the overwhelming needs of depression unemployment made federal aid an urgent necessity. The Federal Emergency Relief Administration initially provided the states with undifferentiated emergency relief grants for the alleviation of economic need, whatever its cause. Gradually, however, efforts were made to differentiate program provisions in terms of the nature of the need: work relief for the employable, rural rehabilitation for the destitute farmer, and long-term provisions for the aged and others outside the labor market. These efforts culminated in a series of laws enacted in 1935, especially the provisions which permanently instituted the Social Security Act. These, however, must be seen as part of an over-all policy whereby the federal government undertook to withdraw from the emergency relief field and provided a federal works program for the unemployed and a combination of insurance and assistance for the aged.

Three categories of needy persons were recognized by the federal government as being entitled to long-term support because they were properly outside the labor market: the needy aged (Old Age Assistance); needy children deprived of their normal breadwinner by death, disability, or absence from the home (Aid to Dependent Children); and the needy blind (Aid to the Blind). Any of the needy who were not absorbed by the federal work program (WPA) and the federally aided assistance categories became the sole responsibility of the states and localities through the catchall general assistance program. The subsequent addition in 1950 of a fourth federally aided assistance category, Aid to the Permanently and Totally Disabled, reduced the demands on general assistance but did not touch the problem of assistance to the employable unemployed.

Pressure on the general assistance program to meet needs resulting from unemployment would have been much greater if the labor requirements of an economy preparing for and waging war had not reduced unemployment to a minimum. In fact, during this period (1939–45) many people who were formerly considered unemployable or outside the labor market were drawn back into employment, thus reducing the federally aided categorical assistance rolls as well as those of general assistance. A substantial number of those returning to the labor market were married women, including those with young children; but older workers, inexperienced young people, and the handicapped were also affected. During this period the problem of unemployment played a minor role in welfare policy and program.

Three developments of the postwar years have created a renewed interest in the relationship of public assistance to the labor market. In the first place, the economic readjustments of this period have contributed to the creation of geographic and occupational pockets of prolonged unemployment. In the second place, the growing specialization and mechanization of production have reduced the need for unskilled labor. This has created special problems for poorly equipped young people, for the poorly educated, and for members of minority groups, who have traditionally been restricted to unskilled jobs. In the third place, the social changes of the war and postwar years have modified both the pattern of employability and public attitudes concerning which citizens may properly be expected to work. In particular, these modifications have affected the employment of women, but they have also affected public attitudes toward the employment of older people and the physically handicapped. Thus the distinctions made in 1935 between needy persons who are considered to be "in the labor market" and those who are not expected to work have been substantially modified. Increasingly, economic need has come to be considered—in theory—the sole criterion of eligibility for assistance, even though the categorical distinctions of the Social Security Act, in which entitlement was originally reserved to those considered outside the labor market, persist in modified form.

It was inevitable that a growing incidence of need resulting from unemployment should create strong pressures for federal participation in assistance to the unemployed, especially in the light of this broader concept of entitlement based on actual need. This trend was reflected in the work of the United States Senate Special Committee on Unemployment Problems (Senator Eugene McCarthy, Chairman). After a series of hearings held in thirteen different areas of the country, the committee submitted in 1960 a report which included among its recommendations a proposal for federal financial participation in general assistance.[3] A similar recommendation was made in the same year by the Advisory Council on Public Assistance appointed by the Secretary of Health, Education, and Welfare under provisions of the Social Security Amendments of 1958.[4] No action, however, was taken on these recommendations.

Again in 1961, following the election of President Kennedy, a special Task Force on Health and Social Security considered the problem of the needy unemployed and came forward with a different approach, which was endorsed by the President and fared more successfully with the Congress. This approach involved the temporary extension of the category of Aid to Dependent Children, authorized by Title IV of the Social Security Act, to children in need because of unemployment of a parent. Simultaneously, it was recommended that an extensive study be made of the whole public welfare program with a view to more permanent changes. As a result of this study the Public Welfare Amendments of 1962 were adopted (Public Law 543 of the 87th Congress); one provision of this law was a five-year extension of the authority for states to include, within the newly renamed category of Aid to Families with Dependent Children (AFDC), families with children in need because of unemployment. Other changes in the public welfare provisions of the Social Security Act included in these 1962 amendments will be discussed subsequently. The extension of the AFDC category to those needy unemployed families with children has a special relevancy to this discussion because (1) it returned the federal government to the field of welfare aid for the unemployed and (2) it moved public assistance further along in its development as an ultimate guarantee against want, whatever the cause.

Aid to Families with Dependent Children. The availability of federal financial aid for unemployed families through the AFDC program seems clearly destined eventually to give this program the primary role in assistance to the unemployed. However, the temporary nature of the 1961 authority limited its applicability, and only fifteen states[5] chose to take advantage of the authority during this period. By September, 1963, five more states[6] had passed legislation and bills were pending in two others. In fourteen of the states which originally took advantage of the broadened federal authority, 93,547 families received assistance under this program in the period between May, 1961, and

---

[3] *Report of the Special Committee on Unemployment Problems*, Senate Report No. 1206, 86th Congress, March, 1960.

[4] *Report of the Advisory Council on Public Assistance*, Senate Document No. 93, 86th Congress, March, 1960.

[5] Arizona, Connecticut, Delaware, Hawaii, Illinois, Maryland, Massachusetts, New York, North Carolina, Oklahoma, Oregon, Pennsylvania, Rhode Island, Utah, West Virginia.

[6] California, Kansas, Kentucky, Ohio, and Washington. But it should be noted also that Arizona and North Carolina had discontinued their programs.

February, 1962.[7] Of this number 41 per cent received limited temporary aid because the father returned to his former job or found new work. It is interesting to note that almost half (47 per cent) of the fathers in these families were either ineligible for unemployment insurance or had exhausted their benefit rights more than six months before their application for assistance. In November, 1963, 48,316 families out of a total of 956,540 on the AFDC rolls were listed as receiving this form of assistance because of unemployment.

The impact on unemployment of the AFDC program is not, however, limited to families where need is due solely to the unemployment of a father who remains in the home. Frequently, for example, an absent father cannot make support payments for his children because he is unemployed and, in other cases, he may actually have left home in order to seek employment. But even more significant in the total picture has been the change of attitude and practice regarding the employment of mothers. According to a survey[8] conducted by the Department of Health, Education, and Welfare in 1961, 14 per cent of the mothers then receiving AFDC assistance were working, most of them part time, but their earnings were not sufficient to meet their full needs. Another 12 per cent were considered as possibly employable if jobs were available or if their work skills were enhanced. Still others might be considered available for work if substitute care were available for their children. Since almost one-third of all mothers with children under age eighteen and 45 per cent of all mothers with children of school age were reported to be working outside their homes in March, 1961,[9] such employment has increasingly come to be regarded as a possible alternative for mothers who are receiving assistance. This attitude reflects a profound and, to a considerable extent, controversial change in the concept

underlying the category of assistance to dependent children, which originally assumed such mothers to be outside the labor market.

Another evidence of the extent to which labor-market and other economic conditions affect this form of aid is that many families receive AFDC assistance for relatively short periods of time. For example, the same 1961 study of the AFDC program showed that one-third of all families received this form of assistance for 1 year or less and another 16 per cent for under 2 years, the median length of assistance being 2.1 years.[10] This, too, reflects a substantial shift from the original concept of the program, which assumed a relatively unchanging need for assistance on the part of children deprived of parental support for reasons unrelated to employment conditions. The implications for welfare programs of these changing concepts of employability are discussed in a later section.

Under the financing provisions of the Social Security Act the federal government reimburses the states for a proportion of the average of all payments made to families in the program. This reimbursement is based on a formula by which the federal government pays 80 per cent of the lower part of the grant (up to $17 per individual) and an amount ranging from $66\frac{2}{3}$ per cent to 50 per cent of the remainder up to a $30 average per month per individual recipient. In 1962 the formula was changed to permit the inclusion of a second parent in the matching provisions. In order to qualify for federal aid a state program must meet certain minimum requirements: the program must be available to all eligible applicants in all parts of a state on an equitable basis; payments must be made to the parent (or in certain exceptional cases to another interested individual) in the form of cash or medical care; provisions must be made for social services when needed; the recipient must be given the right of appeal; and other similar requirements.

The average payment per family in November, 1963, for the country as a whole was

[7] Press release, May 6, 1962, U.S. Department of Health, Education, and Welfare.

[8] Press release, January 4, 1963, Bureau of Family Services, U.S. Department of Health, Education, and Welfare.

[9] Research and Statistics Note No. 14 (Division of Program Research, Social Security Administration, Department of Health, Education, and Welfare, Washington, D.C., June 20, 1962).

[10] Press release, January 4, 1963, U.S. Department of Health, Education, and Welfare.

$128.37, ranging by states from $38.05 to $194.42. The survey made in 1961 showed that the total income (including income from other sources) of individuals supported by AFDC averaged roughly $408 per year or less than one-fourth of the average for all individuals in the nation.[11] Total public expenditures in 1962 for Aid to Families with Dependent Children amounted to nearly $1.4 billion.[12]

The category of Aid to Families with Dependent Children has come in for more widespread public challenge and attack than any other form of public assistance. This is reflected in a nationwide review of eligibility that was demanded by the Senate Appropriations Committee in June, 1962,[13] and in a number of local situations such as the much publicized effort of Newburgh, New York, to impose restrictive policies. Basic to these controversies is a confusion of public attitude and policy with respect to the circumstances under which families with children should be entitled to public aid.

Other Federally Aided Assistance Categories. Because of the nature of their eligibility requirements, the three other categories of federally aided assistance—Old Age Assistance (including Medical Assistance for the Aged), Aid to the Blind, and Aid to the Permanently and Totally Disabled—cannot be considered as directed toward the problem of unemployment as such.

It is increasingly difficult to give an absolute definition of employability on a categorical basis because of the emphasis on vocational rehabilitation as a potential resource of the disabled and because many persons over sixty-five consider themselves available for work. The situation of older persons is particularly confusing because continued work is seen by many as a desirable goal, even though the number of opportunities open to older workers is on the decline. However, with the increasing coverage of the Old Age, Survivors, and Disability Insurance program, Old Age Assistance has been increasingly limited to meeting the special needs of the very old, the disabled, and others clearly outside the labor market.

In November, 1963, 2,194,173 needy old persons received Old Age Assistance grants in an average monthly amount of $76.57; and another 152,919 received help under Medical Assistance for the Aged. In the same month 477,348 persons received Aid to the Permanently and Totally Disabled, and another 97,839 received Aid to the Blind.

General Assistance. Needy unemployed individuals and families who do not qualify for the federally aided categories of assistance must turn to state or local general assistance for financial help. In most states, however, general assistance cannot be considered an adequate protection against need growing out of unemployment because of its spotty coverage, many exclusions, restrictive policies, and low level of benefits. Typically, states where the need is greatest, either because of a generally low per capita income or because of concentrated economic problems, have the poorest resources with which to meet that need. According to a special study of general assistance made for the U.S. Senate[14] in 1959, seventeen states made virtually no provision for public assistance to the employable unemployed. In eighteen states full financial responsibility for general assistance was left to the local political subdivisions, with resulting inadequacy and unevenness.

The lack of federal financing and statewide responsibility, with their concomitant reporting requirements, make it difficult to secure accurate figures on the number of persons receiving this form of aid, the amount of help given, or the reasons for their need. However, the Department of Health, Education, and

[11] Press release, April 11, 1963, U.S. Department of Health, Education, and Welfare.

[12] A special form of family assistance, wholly financed by federal funds, is that provided on an emergency basis by the Department of Health, Education, and Welfare for Cuban refugees. Since the inception of the program over 150,000 persons have registered at the Cuban Refugee Center, and a majority of these have required aid. Working in co-operation with voluntary agencies, the department has sought resettlement for persons in this group and employment for those who are employable.

[13] See Report of the Senate Committee on Appropriations, Report No. 1672, 87th Congress.

[14] *Characteristics of General Assistance in the United States,* Senate Special Committee on Unemployment Problems, 1959.

Welfare estimates that in November, 1963, 326,000 families comprising 775,000 individuals received general assistance averaging $65.34 per family for the month.[15] A small number of states and metropolitan communities paid benefits which were much higher than this low average. Thus eighteen large cities reported payments averaging $160.67 per month.

General assistance, as the residuary legatee of England's comprehensive poor law enacted in 1601, is so generally inadequate, restrictive, and demeaning as to constitute an anachronism in modern public welfare practice and philosophy. Its inadequacies as an ultimate protection to the needy unemployed were graphically revealed in testimony presented at congressional hearings in 1961 on the proposal to extend AFDC coverage to children of the unemployed.[16] Especially interesting was the testimony gathered by the National Federation of Settlements and Neighborhood Houses from its member houses throughout the country, which describes the hardships resulting from inadequate assistance provisions for the unemployed in terms of bread lines stretching for several blocks, the eviction of needy families from their homes, family desertion, demoralization, and actual crime. For example, a Chicago settlement house reports:

There has been a 30 per cent increase in unemployment since September 1960. This is determined by and large by the number of persons who daily line the streets in front of the district unemployment office and the number of persons that we have observed in the ward political organization seeking employment. Some of this unemployment has come to our attention through referral.

This is creating criminal elements not before known to the community. Some are seeking any form of public assistance, thus overloading the rolls. . . .

A 33-year-old man known to our agency was found hanged in his apartment just 7 hours ago. He was apparently despondent over not being able to find a job, and un-

employment compensation had been exhausted. His wife and four children had left him and had returned to Mississippi where they had immigrated from 7 years ago. The family had been several months in arrears in rent, and there was not proper food and clothing for the family during the harsh Chicago winter months.

The anachronistic character of general assistance will probably lead to the ultimate absorption of its responsibilities into the federally aided assistance categories as their coverage, already broadened by recurrent Social Security Act amendments, becomes more inclusive. Resistance to this process is often expressed by local relief authorities, especially in states where general assistance remains the sole relief responsibility of local welfare agencies that parallel those of the state or county, which administers federally aided assistance. The persistence of general assistance, however, is also sustained by some of the limitations in categorical assistance. Most notable among these is the authority exercised by states to fix the period of residence within the state that is required before eligibility for such assistance is acquired. The federal law permits residence requirements up to one year in Aid to Families with Dependent Children and up to five years in the other categories (with the notable exception of Medical Assistance to the Aged). General assistance is also perpetuated by the absence of any federal provision for persons in need because of temporary disability or for unemployed workers without dependent children. Some states and localities also prefer to carry the full cost of general assistance so that the program is not subject to such federal requirements as the prohibition against relief given in restricted form as with grocery or rent orders. In the long run, however, the increasing availability of federal financial aid and the greater flexibility permitted by the growing social service emphasis in federal policies seem certain to reduce the scope of general assistance.

B. SURPLUS FOOD DISTRIBUTION PROGRAMS

Public aid is also extended to the unemployed, either directly or indirectly, through

---

[15] It should be noted, however, that not all of these were in need because of unemployment.

[16] House of Representatives, Committee on Ways and Means, Hearings on H.R. 3865, to amend Title IV of the Social Security Act, February 15, 16, and 17, 1961.

three programs designed to increase the domestic consumption of surplus agricultural products. These programs, administered by the Department of Agriculture with the co-operation of the Department of Health, Education, and Welfare, are: (1) direct distribution, (2) the stamp plan program, and (3) the school lunch and the special milk programs.

Through the program of direct distribution the Department of Agriculture makes available to the states for distribution to needy persons surplus foods acquired under its price support and other market stabilization programs. During 1962 over 7 million needy persons received surplus food amounting to 2 billion pounds valued at nearly $365 million. The lack of adequate general assistance in many states and localities makes the surplus food program especially significant for many unemployed or underemployed families.

The Department of Agriculture also has been authorized to experiment in a limited number of depressed areas with a stamp plan in place of the program of direct food distribution. Under this program families who are receiving assistance or who are adjudged to be in need on another basis may, by purchasing food stamp coupons, receive free additional stamps proportionate to their need and use these stamps in local food stores. This program was originally tested in eight localities involving 146,079 needy persons. In his message on agriculture submitted to the Congress on January 31, 1963, President Kennedy recommended legislation "to permit the progressive expansion of the food stamp program into all areas of the nation where conditions warrant its establishment."[17] President Johnson recommended that the stamp plan be included in the war on poverty.

Surplus foods are also used in the school lunch program administered by the Department of Agriculture through state and local school systems. Under this program many children in families of the unemployed receive free or low-cost school lunches. A comparable program is the special milk program designed to assist schools and certain other institutions to encourage increased fluid milk consumption by children.

C. Direct Aid by Voluntary Welfare Agencies

Voluntary welfare agencies generally do not have the resources to provide aid in the form of extended direct financial assistance to the needy unemployed. In some instances, however, especially where public assistance for the unemployed is either grossly inadequate or excludes particular groups such as those without legal residence, emergency or supplementary aid may be given. In 1959 the United Community Funds and Councils estimated that chest-supported agencies spent approximately $12 million for such direct relief. Usually such aid is given in conjunction with social services, which are regarded as the central function of the voluntary agency involved. Thus the Travelers' Aid Societies, concerned with services to transient persons, may extend temporary help to nonresidents who cannot qualify for public assistance. The Salvation Army, Volunteers of America, and certain other religiously-motivated welfare agencies like the St. Vincent De Paul Societies also provide aid such as temporary shelter and other assistance to homeless individuals and families, whose need may result from unemployment. Churches frequently maintain small welfare funds through which temporary assistance is extended to those members of their congregation in straitened circumstances owing to unemployment. Voluntary welfare agencies also co-operate with public agencies in the resettlement of needy refugees.

Another important form of voluntary aid is that given in time of disaster by the American Red Cross and other welfare agencies. Such assistance involves not only the meeting of immediate emergency needs but also the restoration of the means of support, such as the replacement of tools and the provision of limited working capital.

[17] House Document No. 85, 88th Congress.

III. EMPLOYMENT AS A GOAL OF WELFARE POLICY

Welfare programs, both public and voluntary, operate within a framework of social values, which determine the limits and the goals of those programs. One such value, deeply rooted in our society, holds that individuals should, whenever possible, earn by their own labor the means of subsistence for themselves and their dependents. In recognition of this value, welfare agencies seek to carry out their function of protecting the unemployed individual from deprivation by methods that do not lessen the incentive to work and that seek directly to enhance the employability of welfare recipients who are able to work. These policy goals become especially important in cases where the cause of unemployment is believed to lie with the unemployed individual himself because of inadequate educational preparation, lack of needed vocational skills, or insufficient adaptive capacity. They are also important when community conditions result in unemployment which might be remedied by more constructive and imaginative effort to adapt available work to available workers.

Services directed toward enhancing employability assume that there exists a common understanding among public policy-makers, supported by public opinion, as to the situations in which persons receiving public aid are considered potentially employable. Three types of situations are discernible: (1) those in which the individual is clearly expected to prepare himself for and accept such work as is available, (2) those in which the individual is clearly expected *not* to work, and (3) those in which the decision depends on individual circumstances and choice or community policy. The situation at each end of this spectrum is easily identified. There is little debate about the social desirability of an adult male head of a family accepting such employment as the community has to offer; welfare policy would regard such work as an available resource and thus consider such an individual ineligible for assistance. There is equally little doubt that an aged, bedridden individual is not expected

to work and should therefore be assisted through financial aid and welfare services to whatever extent community resources permit. Present attitudes are not equally clear, however, with respect to the many kinds of situations that characterize the middle range of the spectrum. It is in this middle area that specialized welfare services are most needed, as perhaps can best be illustrated by a few examples.

The father of a family with a chronically ill wife is employable if other provisions can be made for the care of his children.

The head of a family might be employable in another community if assurance and help could be given him in facing the risks of moving.

A physically, emotionally, or mentally handicapped person may be able to work if he is given special training and provided with noncompetitive, protected conditions of work.

A widowed or deserted mother of school-age children may be able to work if after-school care is provided for her children.

A young person struggling to realize his capabilities and make his place in the working world may be able to find a job if he is first given a period of work experience and guidance under protective auspices.

In each of these and other similar situations the role of welfare service is to meet the particular condition on which employability depends.

In our culture not only is self-support emphasized as a desirable goal for the individual but public welfare services directed to this end are regarded as a good social investment, especially where they are seen as a means of reducing the heavy cost of continued financial support. The emphasis in the Public Welfare Act of 1962 on services for social and economic "rehabilitation" is predicated in considerable measure on the assumption that services directed to this end will ultimately reduce the heavy costs of public assistance. This optimistic assumption must be qualified, however, by a realistic recognition of three limiting factors: (1) that employment depends, in the final analysis, on the availability of sufficient jobs to absorb all those who are available for work;

(2) that a substantial number of the persons now dependent on public assistance are not able to work because their capacity to work is totally impaired by old age and extreme disability; and (3) that although the availability of work is considered a "resource" in determining the needs of families, some of those in the middle range of conditional employability cannot be asked to seek employment without endangering either their own welfare or that of others for whom they are socially responsible—for example, young people not yet educationally equipped for adult employment or mothers solely responsible for the care of young children.

IV. WELFARE POLICY TO ENCOURAGE EMPLOYMENT

When assistance recipients are referred to full-time employment they usually cease to be eligible for assistance, because their employment is expected to provide sufficient income to meet their full budgetary requirements.[18] But part-time or occasional earnings by assistance recipients present a more difficult problem because they do not provide sufficient income to meet the full family budget. Under the standard assistance procedure any such earnings constitute a resource to be applied against the approved family budget, with a corresponding reduction in the amount of the grant. While this is a logical application of assistance principles, it is highly discouraging to the recipient, who sees no advantage to be gained from his work. It is particularly discouraging in the case of the handicapped person seeking to increase his work capacity, to the older children in assistance families, and to persons whose earning power is relatively marginal.

In the past few years a number of modifications of federal law and interpretation have been made in an effort to overcome the adverse effect of this practice.

[18] A few states are willing to supplement full-time earnings in the case of very large families or other cases of unusual need.

A. Exemption of Earnings and Supplementary Aid

The most liberal of these modifications have been made in Aid to the Blind, a program under which states are now required to disregard the first $85 per month of earned income plus half of the monthly earnings above that amount in determining the need of the recipient. Further, under the provisions of the 1962 Public Welfare Amendments (Public Law 87-543) the state agency must for a twelve-month period disregard such additional amounts of other income and resources as are necessary to a rehabilitation plan designed to help the blind individual achieve full support.

In Old Age Assistance, according to the provisions of this same bill, the states may, if they choose, disregard a portion of earned income. Specifically, they may after December 31, 1962, disregard the first $10 a month of earned income and one-half of the next $40 a month, thus making it possible for an Old Age Assistance recipient to earn up to $30 a month without the amount of his assistance being affected.

In Aid to Families with Dependent Children the law has been interpreted by administrative ruling as permitting older children in such families to retain earnings if they are to be applied to future needs such as educational expenditures. A number of states permit recipients whose assistance grants do not cover the full amount of budgeted need to earn an amount sufficient to cover the difference without affecting the assistance grant. The practice, long followed by many states, of including additional expenses related to employment in the budget of an assistance family with a working member as an encouragement to such employment, is now required by the new provisions of the federal law effective July 1, 1963.

B. Work and Training Projects

One of the ways in which welfare agencies seek to enhance employability is through the sponsorship of work opportunities for particular groups. These are discussed under three general headings: work relief, sheltered work activities for the handicapped, and special projects for young people.

Work Relief. Work relief may be defined as "programs under which recipients of public assistance are required to work on projects sponsored by government or private nonprofit agencies to earn all or part of their assistance payments." [19] Since the ending of the large federal work relief program of the Work Projects Administration, in 1943, work relief projects have been limited to programs of assistance financed entirely by the states and localities. In the case of the four federally aided categories of assistance, the requirement that assistance be given only in the form of a money payment or of medical care was interpreted to preclude the employment of recipients on work relief projects. This prohibition derived from the wording of the federal law but was also a natural corollary of the assumption that persons eligible for these programs were in fact outside the labor market.

A survey conducted by the Department of Health, Education, and Welfare in September, 1961, showed that 30,400 persons receiving public assistance were employed in 438 localities in twenty-seven states (including the Virgin Islands); and 86 per cent of these were employed in seven heavily industrial states (California, Illinois, Michigan, Ohio, Pennsylvania, West Virginia, and Wisconsin). Most of them were recipients of general assistance and hence under state or local control; also, states with high AFDC payments were permitted to require work for that part of the assistance grant which exceeded the matchable federal maximum.

It was the welfare amendments of 1962 that first made provision for work relief within the federally aided assistance programs. The new law authorizes states which wish to do so to establish "community work and training programs," under which an adult member of a family receiving assistance may be assigned to public agencies for useful work which will not displace other workers or replace normal activities of that agency or related agencies. Workers must be paid at prevailing hourly rates with the hours of their work adjusted to the amount of their assistance entitlement. A number of provisions are included to protect the rights of the worker and the welfare of his children. Because the program is intended to enhance the employability of unemployed welfare recipients, as well as to maintain the principle of paid employment as the major income resource of employable people, requirements are included for co-operative arrangements with both the public employment offices and with all agencies offering vocational training.

The effectiveness of this new program will depend largely on the degree to which states are willing to invest their resources in its implementation. No federal funds are available for work supervision, equipment, or materials; [20] and experience under the depression work relief programs, as well as more recent evidence from the states developing community work and training programs, indicates that this lack may severely limit the type of work which can be undertaken. Moreover, the relatively low monthly assistance payments in many states limit the number of hours any one worker can be permitted to work, thus restricting the program's training potential and making for a changing work force. In the states reporting under the preliminary study of the department, the greatest number of workers were used on projects involving the maintenance of streets and roads, custodial work in public buildings, and care of park and recreational facilities. Public assistance recipients have also been employed by public welfare departments on projects which either involve the departments' responsibilities, such as distribution of surplus commodities, or are closely

---

[19] *Work Relief, A Current Look*, Public Assistance Report No. 52 (Social Security Administration. Department of Health, Education, and Welfare, Washington, D.C., March, 1962).

[20] On June 19, 1963, President Kennedy in his message on Civil Rights and Job Opportunities urged that the law be amended to make available an additional $50 million annually to meet the costs of equipment, materials, and additional supervisory or training personnel on demonstration work and training projects.

related to the departments' own objectives, for example, the training of recipients as nursing-home attendants. In the city of Chicago, which has undertaken extensive work relief, assistance recipients have been used in clean-up operations in deteriorated neighborhoods of which many of them were residents. The city has also trained over a hundred of its relief clients to be cab drivers.

In the work relief projects on which information is available most of the participants were family men, but women were also employed to a limited extent in about ninety communities. The new public welfare law authorizing community work and training projects requires that appropriate care and protection be assured the children of any women so assigned to work.

Sheltered Work. A long established activity of many voluntary welfare agencies, and more recently of some public welfare agencies, has been the provision of work opportunities for the physically or mentally handicapped who are able to work under protected conditions but are not yet able to compete in the open labor market. Typically, these opportunities are offered by nonprofit organizations, which pay the workers' wages and sell the products in order to help support the organization. Organizations like the Goodwill Industries, Inc., The Salvation Army, Volunteers of America, and groups that assist persons with specific handicaps (such as the blind, the mentally retarded, alcoholics) frequently develop such sheltered work programs within a welfare framework. In those states where public welfare agencies administer the rehabilitation programs for the blind, work programs both in workshops and at home are a part of the program. Recently, some public welfare agencies have begun to develop other types of sheltered employment for assistance recipients of marginal employability, although it is more typical for such handicapped recipients to be referred to the public agency administering rehabilitation programs.

Youth Employment. Young people offer special employment problems, which are of particular concern to welfare agencies, both public and voluntary. The transition from the dependency of childhood and adolescence to responsible adult functioning has always been a major welfare concern. This concern has been expressed in terms of facilitating this transition both for those average young people whose difficulties are simply those typical of the stage of their development and for those with special problems growing out of a particularly disadvantaged situation, emotional or other handicaps, or actual delinquency. Because the capacity for self-support through employment is a major measure of adult functioning in our culture preparation for work and the securing of employment play a basic part in this welfare concern for young people.

In recent years the growing unemployment among young people[21] has caused welfare agencies to increase their interest in this problem. In addition to the responsible public departments, the National Committee on Employment of Youth and the Committee on Youth and Work of the National Social Welfare Assembly have been particularly instrumental in stimulating and co-ordinating this interest. There are, however, factors that complicate and challenge the work of preparing young people for employable adulthood. Among these factors is the demand for workers with special skills and technical competence, with a corresponding lessening of the job opportunities open to the inexperienced and unskilled workers. On the one hand, this change has prolonged the period of dependency for young people seeking advanced education for professional or highly skilled employment. On the other hand, it has greatly increased the difficulties of young people who drop out of school before they have adequately prepared themselves for the current job market. Other complicating factors are the obligation of young men to perform military service, the current pressures on young people of both sexes toward early marriage, and the economic and social handicaps confronting members of minority groups.

Virtually all welfare agencies serving young people consider vocational preparation in its broadest sense as part of their general function

[21] See Chapter 2, p. 31.

of helping to meet the transitional needs and problems of youth. The degree to which this interest is centered on specific vocational goals depends largely on the age and characteristics of the particular groups of young people involved. Among the voluntary agencies engaged in such activities might be included the Girl and Boy Scouts, Boys' and Girls' Clubs, Young Men's and Young Women's Christian (and Hebrew) Associations, the Catholic Youth Organization, settlement and neighborhood houses, and rural youth organizations like the 4-H Clubs and Future Farmers of America. In recent years public agency activity and public funds also have been directed to this goal, as can be seen in the Youth Board program of New York City and the funds made available to similar local projects through the special youth programs sponsored by some states.

For young people in trouble with the law, special training schools operated under both public and voluntary welfare auspices emphasize vocational goals. A major concern of probation officers, who are increasingly drawn from among persons with welfare training, is the vocational adjustment of young people who have been either placed on probation by the courts or released from training schools.

In the light of current figures on unemployment among young people, the activities and services discussed above have proved to be too few and not sufficiently effective to provide proper training for adult employability. Because lack of well-established work habits or motivation and inadequate work experience constitute major handicaps for young people in the job market, welfare agencies have begun to experiment with actual work projects to give them the necessary experience. Some of these projects are operated on a summer vacation basis, while others have been developed on a part-time or full-time basis for young people no longer in school. For example, in Mobilization for Youth, which is a large-scale saturation program for the prevention and control of juvenile delinquency on the lower east side of New York City, a number of voluntary and public agencies are co-operating and have developed a subsidized work experience and training program called the Urban Youth Service Corps. Under this program enrollees enlist for one year, are assigned to both public and private service projects, and are paid $1.00 an hour up to thirty-five hours a week, with slightly higher wages for those promoted to leadership assignments. This program involves a concurrent evaluative research project, which is under the direction of the Columbia University School of Social Work. A similar program, called the Youth Conservation Corps, has been developed in Philadelphia under the sponsorship of the Department of Welfare. Under this program full-time work is provided during the summer months but half-time school attendance is required during the school year.

Concern for the expansion of education and work opportunities for unemployed youth has played a major role in President Johnson's proposal for a "war on poverty," which includes a three-part program for youth employment: a residential job corps for young men and women; a community program of projects for both boys and girls, to be operated in co-operation with public and nonprofit agencies; and a work-study program for college students.[22]

C. Vocational Preparation, Counseling, and Placement

Job training, counseling, and placement for most groups fall within the primary jurisdiction of other agencies, particularly the schools and employment services. Nevertheless, it is not surprising that welfare agencies, both public and private, find themselves supplementing the services of these other agencies for their own clients. In the public assistance program the pressure to provide these services comes partly from the strong financial incentive to reduce the heavy cost of large case loads. Voluntary agencies concerned with the better social adjustment of groups with particular needs, such as young people, the aging, the

[22] *Message from the President of the United States,* House of Representatives Document No. 243, March 16, 1964.

physically handicapped, and persons of marginal employability, likewise develop special services directed toward the participation of these groups in the labor market.

The present major emphasis in public assistance policy on the reduction of dependency and the restoration of assistance recipients to self-support has given a renewed impetus to this type of service. In some cases this effort takes the form of intensive case review and analysis, with a view to ultimate referral to other community agencies for vocational training, adult education, and placement. In other cases special provisions are made to help assistance recipients with the extra costs involved in preparing themselves for employment. In Iowa, for example, selected mothers receiving assistance were recently given additional funds to cover the costs of day care for their children so that they could prepare themselves for available jobs in such fields as practical nursing, beauty culture, and secretarial service.

Other public welfare departments have developed intensive programs which combine such referral and supportive services with actual participation in training and placement activities.[23] When such activities are undertaken under welfare auspices, it is usually in collaboration with the education, rehabilitation, and placement agencies of the community; and their purpose is to supplement resources which are either inadequate for the total need or do not fit the particular requirements of the welfare clientele. In some cases projects have been undertaken in collaboration with voluntary agencies. Experimental projects of this character will undoubtedly be expanded under the demonstration authority of the Public Welfare Amendments of 1962, which permits for purposes of pioneering efforts exceptions to the regular requirements of the law.

Services Related to Illiteracy. Recent studies of a cross-section of assistance recipients in employable age groups demonstrate the high degree to which such persons are handicapped by lack of education and special skills. Many, in fact, are functionally illiterate. In 1962 a spokesman for the Department of Health, Education, and Welfare, in urging upon Congress a program directed toward adult literacy (not yet enacted), stated:

How are educational attainments and income related to public welfare costs? There are $7\frac{1}{4}$ million persons receiving welfare payments today. Total annual Federal, State and local expenditures for this purpose exceed $4.5 billion. Forty-five per cent of all families with less than $2,000 of annual income have a head of the family with less than an eighth grade education. These families, in turn, constitute the source from which the public welfare rolls develop.

Low educational attainment is a prominent characteristic of mothers receiving welfare payments under the aid to dependent children program. In New York, for example, a 1957 study found almost a fifth of ADC mothers had not gone beyond the fifth grade; in Louisiana, in 1954, half the ADC mothers and three-fourths of the fathers in the home had received a fifth grade education or less; Illinois reported in 1960 that a fifth of their ADC mothers never went beyond the sixth grade. More than Federal welfare burdens are involved as well; the New York study further revealed that in nonfederally-aided assistance families—many of which included children—half the family heads completed no more than six years of schooling.[24]

A recent study of the Chicago AFDC program in Cook County showed less than 18 per cent of the recipients had a high school education, 44 per cent had less than eight years of schooling, and slightly less than 3 per cent had no formal education of any kind.[25] Another study in the same county revealed that while 6.6 per cent of the able-bodied assistance recipients had not completed fifth grade (and thus were classified as functionally illiterate) more than 50 per cent were functionally

[23] For example, see the *Annual Report* of Fulton County Department of Public Welfare, Atlanta, Georgia, 1962, for a description of one such project.

[24] Testimony of Assistant Secretary Wilbur Cohen in hearings before General Subcommittee on Labor, House Committee on Education and Labor, February 14, 1962.

[25] *Facts, Fallacies and Future*, a Study of the Aid to Dependent Children Program of Cook County, Illinois (New York: Greenleigh Associates, 1960).

illiterate when tested for present achievement levels.[26]

In trying to cope with this problem the Cook County Department of Public Aid and the Chicago Board of Education have inaugurated what they describe as a "massive attack on illiteracy in Chicago . . . and a citywide network of training and educational programs for Chicagoans who receive public assistance."[27] Under this program assistance recipients are required to attend literacy and vocational courses.

Placement Services. The New York City Department of Welfare, through its Division of Employment and Rehabilitation, has long made a concentrated effort to assist its employable or potentially employable recipients in finding employment. Its services, which include counseling, individual job solicitation, direct retraining, rehabilitation, and referral to other agencies, were responsible for placing 9,675 persons in jobs during 1961.[28]

The Pennyslvania Department of Public Welfare recently announced that vocational retraining programs for unemployed workers receiving public assistance are currently saving the state about $180,000 annually.[29] The Pennsylvania effort emphasizes referral to the vocational training programs offered by the regular school system of the state and those authorized by the federal Area Redevelopment Act. Under these programs training in thirty different occupations has been extended to public assistance recipients, including practical nursing, power sewing, service station work, machine shop operation, shoe production, and welding. Further, the public welfare department exerts its influence both on the instructing agency, to find places for its clients, and on the clients, to accept the occupation or change of occupation such training offers.

The Activities of Voluntary Agencies. The

function of voluntary welfare agencies in the vocational field is generally more specialized, intensive, and limited in scope. In many cases it is related to broader rehabilitation programs intended to help people with particular handicaps, such as the blind, the mentally retarded, persons with histories of mental illness, or persons with chronic illness which limits their range of occupation. Virtually all agencies concerned with young people—whether still in school or prematurely in the labor market—include vocational counseling as a major part of their task, and some have undertaken training programs on an experimental basis. Agencies serving older people also frequently help them find part-time or specialized employment following retirement from their regular jobs. Voluntary welfare agencies, particularly those with a denominational affiliation, have been active in the placement of new immigrants arriving from abroad, especially those fleeing from political persecution as from Hungary or more recently from Cuba. Other voluntary agencies specialize in assisting former prisoners to obtain and keep employment.

Many voluntary agencies are concerned with the problems of minority groups. Notable among these is the National Urban League. This organization seeks to widen the vocational horizons of Negro young people through special counseling programs in schools; the league also works in a variety of ways to open up new areas of job training and opportunity to qualified Negro workers, often seeking out candidates for new fields and jobs for them to fill.

D. CHILD DAY CARE AND OTHER SERVICES FOR WORKING MOTHERS

No other recent development in the labor-market situation has created a clearer challenge to welfare agencies, both public and private, than the great increase in the employment outside the home of mothers with small children. The fact that today in the United States more than one-third of the women of working age are employed or are actively seeking employment affects welfare policy in a variety of ways. Between 1951 and 1961

[26] Press release, September 21, 1962, Cook County Department of Public Aid.

[27] Press release, March 14, 1962, Cook County Department of Public Aid.

[28] *1961 Annual Report*, Department of Welfare of New York City.

[29] Press release, September 9, 1962, Pennsylvania Department of Public Welfare.

the number of working married women with children under eighteen increased by 3,450,000 to a total of 8,000,000. Thus the original assumption of the Aid to Dependent Children program—that needy mothers responsible for the care of young children were to be considered "outside the labor market" and hence entitled to public support without question of their employability—is increasingly placed in question. Not only are married women entering the labor market by their own choice but public policy-makers are more and more insistent that employment be considered as an alternative to public assistance for mothers who have no other source of income. This was most strikingly revealed in a recent study of the Aid to Families with Dependent Children program in the District of Columbia, undertaken at the insistence of the Senate Committee on Appropriations. As a result of this investigation of 236 cases selected on a random basis, 49 were ruled ineligible on the grounds of the mother's assumed employability.[30] While many welfare spokesmen challenge this trend as socially undesirable, its existence as a factor in current welfare policy cannot be ignored.

Many public welfare policies relating to the employment of mothers are predicated on the assumption that suitable provisions can be made for the care of their children. Day care in group facilities or part-time foster family homes constitute one such provision. Day care may provide for pre-school children during the school day. In a few communities limited provision for day care has been made under public agency operation, but the majority of day-care centers are operated by voluntary nonprofit agencies or by private fee-charging owners. Typically, the nonprofit agencies receive some subsidy and the mother pays on a scale proportionate to her income. To insure minimum standards of operation, public licensing is being increasingly required for day-care centers and programs. The provision of day care by the industries employing the women is not common in the United States, although such provision was made to some ex-

tent during the war years, when the labor of women was considered necessary to the war effort.

Current public concern for additional provision of day care is centered more on the unmet needs of children than on the need to encourage women to enter the labor market. In 1962 the then Secretary of Health, Education, and Welfare reported that approximately 400,000 children under 12 years of age had been found to be under no supervision whatsoever during the time their mothers worked, and that total day-care facilities in the United States could provide for only about 185,000 children.[31] Consequently, on recommendation of the department, the child-welfare provisions of the Social Security Act were amended to make funds available for the expansion of day-care facilities in amounts ranging from 5 to 10 million dollars a year. These funds are provided on a formula basis to state public welfare agencies, and the law requires that co-operative arrangements be made with public health and school authorities for the health and educational aspects of the program. The law also requires each state to set up an advisory committee made up of representatives of public and private groups interested in day care; it specifies that all facilities benefiting by the program be licensed, provides for priority to low-income groups and payments based on parental financial capacity, and insists on safeguards to protect the best interests of mothers and children.

Day care for the children of working mothers, whatever its primary purpose, enhances the employability of women with children and hence affects the policies of assistance agencies. But, because the cost of good day care is inevitably high (it is estimated to be between $18 and $22 per child per week), publicly subsidized day care cannot be viewed primarily as an economy measure, especially when a mother has low earning power and several young children. Its value can be seen more clearly in terms of a better supportive environment for some mothers

---

[30] *Congressional Record*, September 28, 1962, pp. 20025 ff.

[31] From the testimony of former Health, Education, and Welfare Secretary, Abraham Ribicoff, at hearings before the Senate Finance Committee on H.R. 10606, May, 1962.

and children rather than as an adjunct to the needs of the labor market.

E. OTHER WELFARE AIDS TO EMPLOYMENT

In some cases it is socially desirable to provide other forms of welfare aid or service to permit the normal family wage earner to continue to work during times when a temporary or extended family crisis would otherwise necessitate his remaining at home. Such aid is especially desirable when the mother is temporarily incapacitated or absent from the home and substitute care for the children will permit the father to continue his normal employment. Many public and voluntary welfare agencies provide homemakers for this purpose, women especially trained to serve as substitute mothers. Homemakers are also available to assist in the care of aged people or the chronically ill who are not able to care for themselves, thus freeing employed members of the household to continue their normal job responsibilities. In other cases the temporary placement of children in institutions or foster family homes may make possible the continued employment of the parent responsible for the family.

Welfare agencies may also contribute to the employment adjustment of persons away from their normal social base. Traditionally the YWCA, the YMCA, and similar organizations have performed this service for young people newly employed away from home. During the war years and subsequently in communities undergoing rapid expansion owing to defense production, special welfare services were provided by the United Community Defense Services and the USO (for military personnel). Many denominational groups also provide similar assimilative services for members of their own faith.

V. APPRAISAL

Welfare services cannot adequately fulfill their function of underpinning and supplementing other measures to aid the unemployed unless three conditions prevail. In the first place, there must be a basic floor of protection against want, whatever its cause. This basic protection is necessarily a function of government and must be available on a reasonable standard in all parts of the country. In the second place, there must be a lively and imaginative variety of experimental services pointing the way to more effective long-range solutions of current social problems. In the American pluralistic system this development seems to proceed most creatively under multiple auspices, both public and voluntary. In the third place, the welfare task must not be overburdened by too long delayed acceptance of the basic social and economic reforms which could prevent or reduce the needs with which it deals.

At the present time none of these conditions is fully met. The crazy-quilt pattern of public assistance, in which the needy unemployed and their families can expect no public aid whatsoever in some states and very inadequate help in others, can be remedied only by a change in both public attitudes and federal law. The extension of assistance through the federally assisted program of Aid to Families with Dependent Children to those in need because of unemployment in the home is an important step in the right direction. But the federally aided welfare program should cover all needy persons, including those without legal residence in the state where they find themselves; and it must receive more adequate financing if it is to fulfill its function. The present provisions of the federal law, under which needy aged and disabled persons may receive assistance for which federal financial reimbursement is two and one-half times greater than that provided for individuals in families with needy children, has no social or economic justification and can be explained only in terms of prejudiced public attitudes.

On the second front, while public welfare seems to be entering a period of renewed experimental vigor in many areas of social service, it is nonetheless handicapped by the accumulated deficiencies of a long period of relative inertia. Financial contributions to voluntary social welfare agencies have not kept pace with either need or national income. Experimental pioneering has been subordinated to the effort to solidify professional "standards" of social organization and practice, with a consequent dampening of public support and the enthusiasm of volunteers. There is need for realistic and experimental social services to assist people in the growing complexity and interdependence of modern life, and all our resources—both public and voluntary, under both professional and lay leadership—will be required if the challenge is to be met.

The most urgent and compelling problem, however, lies in the excessive burdens, demands, and expectations placed upon the welfare sector of the social structure because of failure to make needed changes on other fronts. Public assistance is no substitute for adequate unemployment, retirement, and health insurance systems; and no amount of social service can take the place of a healthy economy with jobs for all who seek work, sufficient training provisions to fit workers for those jobs, and a nondiscriminatory policy in filling them. Much of the restless criticism currently directed at the efforts of public welfare to compensate for these deficiencies with its own inadequate resources reflects a public anxiety arising from the need for basic changes too long deferred. Relieved of some of these excessive burdens, public welfare would be better able to do constructively and adequately its own job of assisting people who have special needs.

One additional major problem of social adaptation emerges with inescapable clarity from a review of current welfare programs related to unemployment. This is the question of the working pattern itself: who should work and who should be entitled to support by means other than his own earnings? The impact of this question on welfare policy is most clearly seen in current controversies over the conditions under which needy children and their mothers should be entitled to support within the family assistance category. With 45 per cent of all mothers of school-age children working, is employment to be considered a resource when such mothers are needy, especially when their need derives from socially unacceptable behavior? But the basic problem extends far beyond this currently exacerbated question and is a complex one for a society which has

resources more than adequate for the support of all but emphasizes individual earning power as a measure of personal worth. Thus, able-bodied older individuals who have fully earned their right to compensated retirement still feel deprived of status by their withdrawal from the mainstream of employment; restless young people are attracted to the labor market before they are fully prepared for its requirements; and married women—in ever-increasing numbers—feel obliged by economic and personal needs to supplement the family income by their own earnings. In all these cases a conflict of goals and values related to the social role of employment is reflected in the problems faced by welfare agencies.

This is also a problem involving a lag in cultural adaptation. Any review of history will show that society has moved constantly to underpin and supplement the economic role of the family and the individual through a developing spectrum of social benefits and services under both governmental and voluntary auspices. There are no laws that can effectively keep a family together, a mother at home, a restless child at the task of learning; nor can any law give an older person a sense of participating in the life of the community. But it is possible to bolster family income and cohesiveness with social benefits and services that mitigate some of its interpersonal pressures. It is possible to offer a mother responsible for small children supplementary care for those children while she works or a reasonable alternative in terms of a decent and dignified source of income from social programs. It is possible to give to both young people and those in their later years not only adequate support outside the labor market but a recognized place in society. At the present time the public pays a heavy cost in welfare services because of the failure of the wage market to absorb all those properly available for work. But it also pays a heavy price in social maladjustment because of failure to recognize the proper role of social services for those groups who are now obliged to depend upon the wage market because there is a lack of acceptable alternatives and supplementary opportunities for them.

PART IV

Policy Guides for Programs of Aid

CHAPTER 13

The Determinants of Policy

Eveline M. Burns[*]

I. INTRODUCTION: TYPES OF UNEMPLOYMENT AID

NUMEROUS POLICIES AND instruments for aiding the unemployed are available to societies. They are to be found in various combinations in different countries at any given time and in any one country at different times. Broadly speaking, they fall into three groups.

There are measures whose primary purpose is income maintenance. Among these are governmental programs; for example, public assistance (either general or in the form of a special category of unemployment assistance), unemployment insurance or compensation (referred to as unemployment insurance in this chapter), and work relief (where the unemployed worker is employed for a period of time and at rates of pay sufficient only to "earn" the relief he is found to need). There are also organized private measures such as mutual aid, charitable aid, or programs developed as part of the wage bargain, such as severance pay or supplementary unemployment benefits.

Secondly, there are measures both public and private whose primary purpose is to facilitate the reabsorption of the unemployed into the labor market. Among these are counseling, labor-market analysis and assistance in placement through employment services, training and retraining programs, and assisted migration (within or outside a country).

A third group of measures have as their primary purpose the expansion or regularization of the demand for labor. Many of these involve efforts to revitalize the economy as a whole through tax policies, monetary controls, and similar measures; in common with other so-called "preventive" measures, these lie outside the scope of this volume. Two such measures are, however, intimately related to programs for aid to the unemployed. These are programs of area redevelopment and expanded public works. The use of unemployment insurance to stimulate and regularize the demand for labor does not fall within the scope of the symposium, but it is mentioned briefly in this chapter as part of the discussion of policy determinants.

II. THREE MAJOR ATTITUDES TOWARD THE UNEMPLOYED

The extent to which some or all of these measures are adopted by a country at any given time and the respective roles of each appear to be determined, in the first instance, by the importance attached by the society to three kinds of concerns: a concern about the worker as a human being for whom the state of unemployment is held to create certain needs; a concern about the worker as a potential contributor to the economic well-being of the society of which he is a part; and a concern about the economic interests of the rest of the population, whose disposable incomes may be reduced as a result of aid given to the unemployed.

[*] Professor, The Columbia University School of Social Work.

275

A. The Unemployed Worker as a Human Being with Needs

Various views prevail and have prevailed concerning the nature of the needs of unemployed workers.

The Need for Alternative Income

It is assumed generally that unemployment creates a need for income. The ways of satisfying this need range from a grudging provision—under deterrent conditions—of the necessities of life, sometimes in the form of kind rather than cash, to policies that imply, as under some severance pay schemes, that the mere loss of a job creates a right to compensation regardless of whether or not the recipient obtains other work.

Even when aid is conditioned on the continuance of unemployment, there is great variation in the principles on which it is given. Some programs are frankly based on the concept of maintenance related, as in public assistance, to the ascertained needs of an individual and his family or, as in flat-rate insurance benefit systems or the income-conditioned pension type of assistance, to some concept of "average need." Others relate the benefit to the previous wages or earnings of the recipient. Still others attempt a compromise between these two principles: benefits are based on wages, but there is also a minimum benefit and additional benefits for dependents.

The measures vary also in the extent to which they do or do not reflect the view that the standard of living of the unemployed should vary with the standard of living of the rest of society. In the systems that base aid on a "maintenance" concept, the determination of an "adequate" minimum of subsistence, which should be assured to all, is essentially arbitrary and over periods of time is influenced by changes in the general standard of living. But the issue arises also in wage-related benefit systems, for the decision as to the appropriate percentage of wages to be paid as benefit and the exact amount of the money maximum, if any, is equally arbitrary.

The Need for Work

Some societies have interpreted more broadly the needs created by unemployment. Over and above a need for income, they have held that as a human being in a society where employment is an integral part of the normal, status-giving behavior pattern, the unemployed worker needs work as such. Efforts to meet this psychological need have ranged from public provision of employment (public works, work relief, and similar measures) or programs of area redevelopment, to training and other measures intended to promote the speedy re-employment of the worker. Faced with an inability or unwillingness to provide work for all the unemployed, some societies have treated work as a scarce and valuable commodity to be rationed in favor of those who need it most. They have attempted to remove some categories of workers from the labor market, for example, by lowering the pensionable age in the belief that this will make more jobs available for the young.

B. The Unemployed as Potential Contributors to Economic Output

Concern about this aspect of the unemployed worker may focus upon his role as either a producer or a consumer who, because he is unemployed, is not making his potential contribution to the economic well-being of his society.

The Unemployed as Potential Producers

The Effect of Aid on Initiative. The assumption that most people will not work, or at least not work regularly, if they are assured an acceptable income without working, has left its mark on the programs of unemployment aid in most countries. Concern about the effect of aid on initiative earlier resulted in making aid so meager, and available under conditions so deterrent, that few would find it an acceptable alternative to working for a living. This approach is still to be found in the public assistance programs of some of our states. Lately the concern has taken other forms, as growing sensitivity about the worker as a human being has led to a questioning of the desirability of penalizing all unemployed workers because of the suspected moral weakness of some. This change has been hastened by the spectacle of millions of normally self-supporting workers struggling unsuccessfully to find jobs in depression periods and by an increasing ability to differentiate among the unemployed.

The newer expression of the concern about initiative takes the form of efforts to restrict aid to the "involuntarily unemployed" by such devices as limiting aid to those who have had some defined period of employment in the past (thus establishing a presumption that they are normally regularly employed persons) or by requiring the unemployed to report to an employment office at stated intervals and denying them benefits if they refuse work deemed "suitable" or if they are unwilling to undergo designated training programs. Some systems go further and require the unemployed to produce evidence that they are "actively" or "genuinely" seeking work. The policy of maintaining a sizable differential between unemployment aid and what a worker could secure from employment is a very common effort to preserve initiative. The benefit amount is deliberately set at less than 100 per cent of wages (or of take-home pay) in wage-related benefit systems; while in systems based on maintenance, the so-called "wage stop" prevents any payment from exceeding a worker's previous wages, however great his demonstrated needs.

The Effect of Aid on Wages. A more subtle form of the concern about the effect of aid on the worker as producer is the fear that liberal unemployment aid may foster the maintenance of "unduly high" wage rates. It can be admitted at once that the availability of unemployment aid places a floor (albeit a low one) under labor's reservation price. Most unemployment aid systems deny benefits for longer or shorter periods to workers whose unemployment is due to participation in a trade dispute, although they differ in the extent to which workers not directly interested in a dispute but affected by it are also denied aid.

It is by no means clear how vigorously unions are able to press for "unduly high" unemployment-causing wage rates because unemployment aid weakens the resistance of the unemployed members to such a policy. But to the extent that such wage effects are feared, there will be pressures exerted by employers to keep unemployment benefits low.

Effect of Aid on Mobility. Emphasis on the unemployed worker as a productive agent leads also to a concern about the effect of unemployment aid on mobility. On the one hand, certain programs may be favored on the grounds that they prevent undesirable mobility. Thus, it is often held to be an advantage of unemployment insurance that it gives the unemployed worker a breathing spell during which the probability of a revival of demand for his type of skill can be determined and during which he need not take a job at less than his normal skill level. In this way, an economically costly type of mobility may be avoided if, in fact, the decline of demand for his skilled services is merely temporary. Similarly, unemployment insurance has been favored as a device for enabling employers to hold together a labor force which, under the pressure of a need for income, might move elsewhere or to other types of employment and not be available when employers are ready to resume production.

Yet this very feature has given rise to a concern that the availability of aid may discourage desirable mobility. Fears are expressed that it may serve to hold workers in places where prospects for ultimate economic revival are dim, that it may encourage workers to resist a change of occupation or skill, or that, in areas characterized by a preponderance of seasonal employment, it may encourage the perpetuation of a way of life where the worker is content to rely on earnings for only part of the year and on aid for the remainder. Finally, it has been held that employers who should have been forced out of business by normal competitive standards are permitted to continue operations on a partial scale and retain a labor force because unemployment aid plus partial employment provide the workers with an income sufficient to offset pressure to seek jobs elsewhere.

This concern about the discouragement of desirable worker mobility is expressed in policies which limit the duration of the preferred form of unemployment aid (usually unemployment insurance) to some specified period in order to set a time limit to the possible loss of desirable mobility. It also takes the form of the application of special eligibility conditions for seasonal workers or a denial of benefits during the "off season." Where the focus of concern is the effect on employers, policy takes the form of experience rating or similar measures, which aim to assess against the involved employers some or all of the costs of the unemployment benefits drawn by their employees.

Loss of Output Due to Nonutilization of Labor. Emphasis on the unemployed worker as a productive agent also leads to a concern about the loss of national output when unemployment persists. It finds expression in efforts to determine the "why" of unemployment in order to institute remedial measures. The creation of employment services was an early example of this approach. More recent action has included the provision of training and retraining programs, upgrading of the education and skills of unemployed workers, assisted transference, and programs of area redevelopment. The last are especially likely to be favored over transference measures when there is an acute consciousness of the "productive" importance of salvaging society's existing capital investment in a depressed area.

Conversely, societies that are highly sensitive to considerations of national output are likely to regard with disfavor such unemployment aid measures as prematurely retiring the older worker or instituting a general reduction of hours worked. In the extreme case, as in Russia and certain other countries, a concern about national output may explain the absence of any specific unemployment aid program.

Deterioration of Skills and Work Habits. The approach which stresses the unemployed worker as a potential productive agent is also reflected in a concern about the effect of periods of idleness on a worker's existing skills and work habits. It leads to the adoption of measures over and above cash payments, such as public provision of diversified work programs, particularly for certain groups regarded as being especially vulnerable to loss of skills or deterioration of work habits—the long-term unemployed, for example, or young workers who have never had the opportunity to secure a regular labor-market attachment.

The Unemployed as Potential Spenders

The unemployed worker, in addition to being a potential producer, is also a potential spender, and policies have reflected an increasing concern about this aspect of his role. As nonspenders, the unemployed exert a depressive influence on economic activity. In recent years the efforts to secure income for the unemployed made by those motivated primarily by a concern for the worker as a human being have been reinforced by those who regard him as a possible spender and see a measure such as unemployment insurance as a built-in stabilizer —a device for ensuring automatically some minimum level of spending on the part of the unemployed.

This emphasis on the unemployed as potential spenders also has had financial implications. Where the maintenance of spending power is seen as a major objective, efforts are made to ensure that funds are accumulated in advance of anticipated heavy outpayments or that deficit financing is used during such periods so that the economic impact of funds placed in the hands of the unemployed is not entirely nullified by reduced spending on the part of current taxpayers.

C. THE UNEMPLOYED AS THREATS TO THE INCOMES OF OTHERS

As nonproducers who are nonetheless enabled by unemployment aid to continue spending, the unemployed have always been viewed as threats to the freely disposable income of the rest of society. This attitude has influenced policies in various ways. Quite generally, it has operated as a benefit depressant.

It has led, also, to a preference for what are believed to be "cheaper" programs. Those programs restricting aid to cases of demonstrated need, such as public assistance, are preferred to those like social insurance, which, by giving aid on the basis of presumptive need, make payments to many unemployed who would not qualify for benefits under public assistance. Sometimes, especially where the cost impact of aid is extremely visible, as in the case of locally financed aid programs, the tests of need may be very rigorous, and efforts may be made to protect the local taxpayer by application of severe residence requirements.

This view of the unemployed as a threat to other income receivers tends also to work against the use of public works as a form of unemployment aid. For the immediate outlay incurred by such programs (payment of prevailing wages rather than some lower sum, employment of management personnel, use of capital equipment and materials) is greatly in excess of any program that provides merely cash payments. And even though it may be shown that, in fact, the community makes a net gain, since it receives some economic return for its greater expenditure, this argument may not be convincing because of the time lag between the greater outpayment and the enjoyment of the return, the frequent difficulty of attaching a cash value to the product, and because the output may be in a form on which consumers would not normally spend and is therefore undervalued. Some countries have endeavored to minimize the impact of this resistance to spending more on the unemployed by deficit financing of public works. But unless the deficit is regarded as an investment (a view some countries have tried to foster by creating a separate capital budget for such programs), it still may be regarded as a debt which the taxpayers must ultimately repay; and the opposition on the grounds of cost may still remain.

Concern for the interests of current income receivers as against concern for the unemployed also has led to efforts to finance aid by methods which cause the unemployed and their employers to foot the bill. Social insurance systems financed by taxes collected from employers and workers essentially involve a transfer over time of income from employment. But there are limits to the use of this device, set by the levels of wages (i.e., the extent to which an adequate income during employment remains after payment of the taxes) and by the duration of unemployment. Generally, the device is more feasible for the financing of aid for short- rather than long-term unemployment; and it is significant that other sources of revenue have been tapped when social insurance is used as the instrument for providing income during long-period unemployment. Furthermore, as a method of protecting the general income receiver from the costs of maintaining the unemployed, use of the employer payroll tax may be only partially effective because of the possibility of shifting the tax to consumers.

III. THE INEVITABILITY OF COMPROMISE AMONG THESE ATTITUDES

It should be evident from this brief survey of the predominant attitudes toward the unemployed that some of the attitudes are mutually compatible while others are not. The human approach that stresses "adequate" maintenance is consistent with the view that emphasizes the role of the unemployed worker as a potential spender. But it runs counter to the theory which sees him as a potential producer and is concerned about weakening initiative or restricting mobility. The emphasis on a worker's need for work as such is consistent with a concern about society's loss of output when unemployment exists. But it may conflict with the concerns of those who stress the immediate economic interests of current receivers of income. The emphasis on maintenance needs, when constrained by concern about the taxpayer, may lead to policies which restrict aid to those who can demonstrate need or which give relatively greater aid to the primary than to the secondary worker in a family. But to those who stress the role of the unemployed as potential spenders, the relevant fact about all types of workers is that they are income receivers whose purchasing power would be destroyed by unemployment and must be replaced if total demand is to be sustained.

Obviously, difficult choices have to be made, and the types of programs adopted and the roles assigned to each reflect a compromise between these different concerns. Each of the available programs has its own unique characteristics, which bear upon these major social concerns in different ways. The decision to reject or adopt any given program and the determination of its scope are not made, of course, in a vacuum. They are affected by the economic and social institutions and by the value systems of the society in question. In this chapter attention can be directed only to some of the more obvious of these factors and their implications for policy. Each will be treated separately for purposes of exposition, but it must be recalled that the final policy decision will be the result of many factors considered simultaneously. Furthermore, it is also impossible to show the relevance of each factor for each type of aid. The discussion, therefore, will be illustrated mainly by reference to unemployment insurance.

IV. SOME STRATEGIC FACTORS AFFECTING THE NATURE OF THE COMPROMISE

A. THE ECONOMIC CIRCUMSTANCES OF THE SOCIETY

The General Level of Output

Obviously, the richer a society, the higher is the level of living at which it is able to maintain its unemployed, and the greater will be the willingness of current income receivers to do so, since their greater wealth permits them to meet the costs and still retain a sizable, freely disposable income.

But there are complicating factors. All experience has shown that the level of an "acceptable" standard of living fluctuates with the standard of living of the community as a whole. Even in public assistance, many items are now included in the minimum budget that would have been regarded as luxuries at the beginning of the century. On the other hand, the greater the wealth of a community, the more reasonable is it to suppose that workers will have an opportunity to accumulate some savings. Unless allowance is made for the pervasive impact of advertising on spending-savings patterns, the belief that rising wages enable workers to support themselves wholly or in part during short periods of unemployment may weaken the concern about the "adequacy" of unemployment insurance benefits.

The richer the society, also, the more it may be prepared to tolerate some loss of mobility or some degree of voluntary unemployment, and the more willing it may thus be to provide benefits as a right, as under unemployment insurance, for relatively long periods of time with no reference to need and little pressure to accept unaccustomed work.

The Extent and Nature of Unemployment

The sheer magnitude of the volume of unemployment exerts a major influence on policies. Where it is large, there is likely to be growing political pressure for support of the unemployed as they come to form a larger proportion of the electorate. Moreover, the presumption that they can be assisted by the family unit or can utilize their own savings is progressively invalidated by widespread loss of jobs by relatives and friends and by the erosion of savings as unemployment persists. As the costs of supporting the unemployed mount, policy may increasingly reflect the view that aid, at least after some duration of unemployment, should be confined to those meeting a test of need.

At the same time, heavy unemployment is likely to heighten the concern about loss of national output and create a climate more favorable to the provision of public works or other demand-expanding measures; and the objection that public works will bid against private industry for productive resources is weakened as idle men, machinery, and savings accumulate. By the same token, one would expect training programs to be less favored at such times, since the case for further training is not very convincing with millions of trained workers available for work but unable to find it. It might also be expected at such times that there would be a lessened concern about the malingerer. The worth of using administrative resources to ferret out the relatively few malingerers, when there are no jobs available for the much larger number who vigorously seek them, becomes ever more questionable, especially as the easiest of all tests of malingering, namely the offer of work, is least available at such times.

Finally, heavy unemployment is likely to increase pressure for financing by larger units of government, especially the largest, and for two reasons: the greater tax powers and resources of the national government; and, if the society favors deficit financing, its greater borrowing powers.

Regardless of its absolute magnitude, however, the nature of unemployment in itself has policy implications. Especially relevant is the distinction between short-term unemployment (including frictional, short-lived recessional, and seasonal) and long-term unemployment (whether due to long-continued recession, structural changes, or personal characteristics). The specific programs adopted and their scope will reflect the extent to which these different types of unemployment exist at any one time and the degree to which their implications for policy are recognized.

Thus, the nature of unemployment insurance suggests that it is an instrument particularly well fitted to provide for the unemployed during frictional or recessional short-term unemployment. The availability of a specified benefit for a limited period meets the income maintenance objective in a manner believed to be consistent with maintenance of the worker's self-respect and yet sets a limit on possible checks to mobility or initiative. It also serves immediately to channel funds into the economic system at the onset of unemployment, an especially valuable characteristic if the unemployment is recessional.

Unemployment insurance has the further advantage over other methods of injecting purchasing power, such as expanded public works, in that it has an automatic cutoff of expenditures as private employment increases and does not restrict the availability of the worker should there be a revival of demand for his services in his normal type of employment.

Other characteristics of unemployment insurance make it a less satisfactory form of aid for dealing with long-term unemployment of any type. That the benefit typically is half or less of a worker's full-time wages and takes little or no account of his family needs (or, in flat-rate systems, tends to be set at a fairly low level) causes it to be a progressively less effective answer to the need for maintenance as unemployment continues and as borrowing, drawing on savings, or spending only on "nondeferrable" items become less and less feasible courses of action for the worker.

Even if unemployment benefit levels were set in relation to the presumed needs of the long-term unemployed, or if benefit levels were automatically raised after unemployment had persisted for some given time, unemployment insurance would still fail to meet the need, intensified by long-continued unemployment, for work as such. Moreover, as a system that relaxes pressure on workers to change to other kinds of work or to accept lower wages than those to which they were accustomed, unemployment insurance fails to meet the economic adjustment problems of long-term unemployment that is due to structural changes or personal characteristics. Other instruments must be brought into play to deal with unemployment caused by these factors.

Finally, there are financial reasons why unemployment insurance appears to be an unsuitable measure for dealing with long-term unemployment, whatever its nature. It typically is financed partially or, as in the United States, wholly by taxes on employers' payrolls. To justify this method of financing as an effort to promote stabilization action by employers may be plausible when the method is used to finance short-term unemployment aid. But for long-continued recession unemployment, no such justification can be urged, since then the action of individual employers or groups of employers can have little effect on the general level of employment. And to the extent that recourse to employer payroll taxes is defended on the grounds of either social cost allocation or of sheer fiscal expediency (a richly yielding tax that has not been earmarked for any other purpose), its value becomes increasingly questionable when unemployment is heavily concentrated in certain areas or in certain types of industry. In depressed areas or in industries rendered obsolete by technological change, there are no employer payrolls to tax.

The precise duration of unemployment insurance benefits and, therefore, the role of this institution in the total complex of unemployment aid measures will depend on the durational characteristics of frictional and "normal" recession unemployment in individual countries and on certain other factors, such as the willingness of the society to countenance the possibility that some workers may continue to draw unconditional benefits, even though, if pressure were applied, they would take some of the jobs available. But its role also will be determined by the availability of alternative and more appropriate programs. It is perhaps one of the dangers of unemployment insurance that it has seemed to offer an easy answer to the needs created by long- as well as short-term unemployment. It has seemed simpler to extend benefit duration than to grapple with the more difficult problems presented by other measures.

The Prevailing Employment Patterns

The patterns of employment in any given country directly affect the determination of policy. Some unemployed workers are normally full-time workers and seek full-time work. Others normally work less than full time. Among these are married women who may work half time or only at seasonal peaks because of the competing demands of family responsibilities or for other reasons, or students who seek work only during vacation periods. Others may be "target workers," such as the increasing number of social security beneficiaries who work only long enough to earn the

maximum permitted under the retirement test, or the individual with a low level of economic aspiration who works only enough to supply his minimum needs and prefers more leisure to more income if that income must be secured by working. The existence of these different employment patterns presents problems to such a system as unemployment insurance because they affect both the social and the economic significance of "not-working."

Unemployment insurance gives involuntarily unemployed workers rights to payments, and these rights depend on the satisfaction of objective, measurable requirements that are defined with considerable legal specificity, not on judgments as to motivation or on facts about the worker's personal life that are unrelated to his employment status. It is, of course, this nondiscretionary feature of unemployment insurance that accounts for its popularity among workers. As such, it is an instrument perfectly designed to provide aid to the normally full-time worker who seeks full-time work. But it has not proved easy to devise objective, nondiscretionary tests that eliminate other types of workers without penalizing some of the workers who desire full-time employment.

To use the eligibility requirement of a given amount of earnings in some previous, specified period as proof of "regular attachment to the labor market," quite apart from the difficult problem of determining exactly how much work or earnings is evidence of a firm attachment, may be unfair to would-be full-time workers in areas where only one type of seasonal employment is available. It may be unfair also to the normally full-time worker who has suffered spells of unemployment in his base year. It would also penalize the new entrant who may be seeking full-time work but fails to find enough employment to qualify. The offer of suitable work is not an effective test during recessions or in depressed areas or in areas characterized by much seasonal employment. The concept of nonavailability may be effective in eliminating from benefits the student working during vacation, but it is less easy to apply to the married woman without invoking value judgments. Its literal application also may deny benefits to workers for whom benefits would seem appropriate, as when persons undergoing approved training courses are denied benefits on the grounds of "nonavailability." Efforts to disqualify or to demand more rigorous eligibility conditions of certain categories of persons, such as married women, may be unfair to the married woman who genuinely seeks full-time work.

Unemployment aid policy toward such part-time workers reflects two factors: the extent of benefit payments made to them at any given time (in a system dealing with millions, people appear to countenance some small unspecified degree of abuse represented by payments to workers other than those for whom the system was designed); and the extent to which the community is prepared to penalize some would-be full-time workers in order to avoid payment of benefit to those who seek less than full-time work.

B. DEMOGRAPHIC FACTORS

Demographic factors affecting the proportion of workers to nonworkers in a country also affect unemployment aid policies. If, for example, the proportion of the aged and the very young increases greatly, the resulting heavy burden of support for these groups of nonproducers may intensify resistance to more generous aid for the unemployed. Furthermore, an age distribution which results in a large elderly population may foster an influential pressure group that effectively competes with the unemployed for the sympathies and concerns of society (and of politicians in particular), especially in periods when unemployment is mainly of the short-term type and relatively light.

C. SOCIAL INSTITUTIONS AND PRACTICES

Unemployment aid policies reflect, albeit somewhat slowly, the prevailing economic role of the family system, both nuclear and extended. Unemployment insurance appears to assume, in general, a limited role for the extended family. If benefits are payable for relatively long periods, however, some part of the justification for payment of benefits considerably below current wages must involve an assumption that workers have recourse to aid from relatives. Aid given through the public assistance system, in most parts of this country, although not in Great Britain, assigns a larger role to the extended family: relatives' responsibility clauses are common and are often more rigorously enforced with unemployed applicants than with other groups, such as the aged or the blind.

Unemployment insurance policies, on the other hand, reflect ambivalent assumptions concerning the economic role of the nuclear family. If it is assumed that the family is normally supported by the working father, it is difficult to explain benefits that are considerably below full-time earnings and that make no allowance for the number of persons to be supported either through payment of benefits for dependents or, more effectively, through a general system of children's allowances. If it is assumed that part of the family's normal income is supplied by employment of other members of the family, and notably of the wife, it is difficult to explain policies that would differentiate between the benefit status of the presumed "head" and that of other working members of the family group. It seems likely that the increasing tendency of the family standard of living to be dependent also on full-time or part-time earnings of the wife will occasion some serious reconsideration of unemployment aid policies.

The influence of views on the role of the family system is especially evident in the case of families without a male breadwinner, where a choice has to be made between the "family rearing" and the economic functions of the mother. Particularly in the case of the unmarried or deserted mother, the question of her treatment —as an unemployed adult who should accept suitable work if available or as the rearer of children who should receive aid in that capacity —is a major headache in public assistance policy at the present time.

Other social changes affect unemployment aid policies. The increasing extent of home ownership, for example, presents a serious obstacle to policies aiming at geographical transfer of the unemployed and may necessitate more costly measures than normally are found in transfer schemes, especially in depressed areas, where the market for houses is likely to be nonexistent.

D. Importance Attached to Other Values

Given any level of unemployment, any set of employment patterns, and any prevalent role of the family system, social policy toward the unemployed still will reflect other values which are important within the society.

Attitudes toward Individual Dignity and Freedom

With the growth of the economic and political power of labor, it has become increasingly common to avoid policies which restrict the freedom of the worker to decide whether or not to work and to choose among types of work. Moreover, the large body of case law concerned with determinations of suitability of work, availability, and voluntary quitting testify to the desire of society that "unreasonable" pressure should not be put upon the worker. This is so even though the precise line drawn between the interests of society in speedy reabsorption of the worker into production and the worker's desire to hold out for his former kind of work and employment conditions fluctuates with changing economic circumstances. When, for example, maximizing output is vital, as during war, the balance swings against the worker.

It is important to note that opinions as to which measures constitute unacceptable pressure or undue infringement of the self-respect of the worker change from time to time. Much of unemployment aid policy in Great Britain and the United States in recent decades can be explained as an effort to ensure that as few workers as possible have to depend for their support on a system regarded as degrading, namely, public assistance. But what causes degradation? Is it the deliberate imposition of such conditions as loss of civic rights, publication of names of recipients, or payment in kind rather than cash? If so, the liberalization of public assistance, although gradual, may ultimately remove these features and cause public assistance to be regarded as a less degrading form of aid. Is it the requirement to undergo a needs test as such, or is it the particular form of the test of need currently found in American public assistance systems? If it is the latter, a modification in the direction of the income-conditioned pension type of payment, with its legally specified standard allowances and forms and amounts of exempt income, coupled with a restriction of the relatives' responsibility clauses, might make public assistance a more acceptable alternative to unemployment insurance. It is difficult to avoid the belief that policymakers have concentrated too exclusively in recent years on the latter form of aid and have failed to explore the feasibility of rendering alternative programs more acceptable in terms of current values.

Attitudes toward Public and Private Responsibilities

The importance attached at any given time to private versus public responsibility for ensuring aid to the unemployed has also played a role in policy determination. The sheer magnitude of the task in modern industrial societies precludes discussion of the issue in terms of "either-or," because neither industry nor private philanthropy can ensure an adequate and acceptable degree of protection. The question of where the line is to be drawn, however, is still alive in some areas of unemployment aid policy. Workers in strongly organized industries, in a position to secure liberal fringe benefits, still appear somewhat ambivalent concerning the percentage of income that should be secured from private industry rather than from a public program during unemployment. Fears that government may invade realms regarded as the preserve of private industry still serve to limit the types of employment that can be offered through public works. Differences of opinion on public and private responsibility have played a role in inhibiting the expansion of public training and counseling measures. Employers and workers still differ sharply on the policy of utilizing employers in the policing of unemployment insurance applicants.

Attitudes toward Various Levels of Government

Differing opinions on the appropriate roles of the various levels of government have also influenced social policy toward the unemployed. The desire to keep the federal government out of the picture was sufficiently powerful to postpone any federal aid for unemployment relief until the early nineteen-thirties, despite massive evidence of the inability of the localities and the states to finance large-scale relief. The belief that public assistance is a function particularly appropriate for local or, at most, state governments has kept residual relief a state-local responsibility not even subsidized by any federal grant-in-aid, despite recommendations to the contrary by a long series of committees of inquiry over the last twenty-five years.

The preference for administration by one level of government rather than another is partly a matter of principle, of political ideology. In the United States it is probably still true that the prevailing view is that responsibility should be retained in the smaller units and that federal action should be invoked only when it can be shown that the job cannot be done otherwise. But it is probably true also that the preference for action by a given level of government is affected by the extent to which important segments of the community believe their interests to be better represented in, and served by, that level. The strong preference of worker groups for federal action in the area of unemployment aid is connected with labor's belief that state legislatures do not reflect accurately the size and interests of working populations in nonrural areas. Contrariwise, employers appear to believe that their interests are better served by the states than by the federal government.

Attitudes on this issue are also affected by the degree of homogeneity in the economic conditions of a given country. Great differences in wage levels and standards of living point to the undesirability of applying a uniform aid program to the country as a whole. In social insurance systems this problem may be overcome by paying benefits that bear some stated percentage relationship to previous wages and by financing the program with taxes based on wages. But this expedient is not available in public assistance, where the essence of the program is the assurance of some defined standard of living and where the choice of any single basic minimum may well be unduly high in relation to prevailing wage or living standards in some parts of the country and unduly low in others. It is not surprising, therefore, that only one important country, Great Britain, has made public assistance a central government responsibility.

Unemployment frequently strikes unequally in different parts of a country. The very circumstance which increases the need for unemployment aid reduces the ability of the affected areas to finance it. Where the sense of national unity is strong, this situation is likely to lead to an involvement of larger units of government, as was evident in the early nineteen-thirties and again in the measures for federal action to extend unemployment benefit duration in 1958 and 1961. The social invention of the grant-in-aid has served to offset some of the more obvious financial disadvantages of exclusive state or local responsibility for unemployment aid. But at best the dispute about the roles has moved to another sphere. Discussion now turns on the amount and form of federal aid and, above all, on the standards which the federal government may require as a condition for that aid. And attitudes toward the concept of local self-government and the meaning attached to that term will vitally affect the outcome.

A national or federal program usually denotes a single program for the entire country. Where there is wide difference of opinion concerning desirable policies or program objectives, there is likely to be preference for state operation to permit experimentation or to avoid premature commitment to a single policy. It was considerations such as these, coupled with a general preference for state action, that led to the lodging of major responsibility for unemployment insurance with the states in 1935. On the other hand, certain policies, if they are to be applied at all, can function only if operated by the largest unit of government. This would seem to be true of programs of geographical transference or significant measures to revive depressed areas.

Preferences for operation of aid programs by one level of government or another are also probably influenced by the fact that policy consequences are much more visible when applied by the national or federal government. When the fate of the unemployed lies in the hands of hundreds or even thousands of small political subdivisions, it is less easy to know what is being done or what is the level of living at which the unemployed are being supported. National programs project these questions into the limelight, where they can no longer be evaded but must be faced as major issues of national policy.

The Desire for Equality of Treatment

The stronger the belief that persons in similar circumstances should receive similar treatment and the more prevalent the belief in equality as such, the greater will be the pressures toward central rather than local operation of unemployment aid programs. In the United States, for example, organized labor has been concerned about the state-by-state differences in the unemployment insurance rights of workers with similar employment records and, in consequence, has pressed for federal benefit standards. Even labor, however, has been relatively unconcerned about the more glaring differences in the treatment of unemployed persons (and other needy persons) whose support is derived from public assistance. An extensive development of fringe unemployment benefits will accentuate the differential treatment of unemployed workers, as has the recent adoption of a policy of especially generous treatment of workers whose unemployment is traceable to tariff reductions.

It is important to note, too, that the strength or weakness of the desire for equality will influence the extent to which efforts are made to ensure that the standard of living of the unemployed rises or falls with changes in the standard of living of the community as a whole.

E. THE LEVEL OF SOCIAL KNOWLEDGE AND TECHNOLOGY

The state of social knowledge and technology affects unemployment aid policies in various ways, some of which make it easier to handle the problem, while others make it more difficult by revealing new complexities or wider alternatives of choice. The influence of social inventions is obvious. The invention of social insurance has made it possible to provide a form of aid that is acceptable to workers and to the general public and to minimize the role of public assistance. The invention of children's allowances has made it possible to recognize the family responsibilities of the unemployed worker while still maintaining a differential between him and the employed worker. The invention of the cost-of-living index has facilitated a technique, not everywhere utilized, for automatically adjusting money benefits to price changes, thereby maintaining any given desired level of real purchasing power. The invention of the standard budget has provided a tool for identifying certain defined standards of adequacy and measuring program performance in relation to these standards.

Levels of administrative knowledge and skill also affect the range of policies that can be envisaged. The availability of mechanized accounting and computing machinery has permitted the operation of much more complicated benefit, eligibility, and experience-rating systems than otherwise would have been possible. Improved tax-collecting techniques (notably the device of the employer withholding tax) has made feasible a continuously widening coverage of social insurance programs. Improved administrative techniques for testing willingness to work or controlling abuse would clearly affect the role of unemployment insurance by minimizing the adverse effects of applying a single benefit system to workers with varying patterns of employment. The more effective these techniques, the less necessary will be the alternative control of paying benefits that are sizably below normal wages.

Some developments of knowledge, however, complicate the problems of the policymaker by revealing unexpected effects of his policies or the existence of variability where uniformity was assumed. Our growing knowledge of the nature of unemployment and of the employment patterns of workers has already operated in this manner, although our present statistical data are not adequate to provide precise quantification of many of the aspects of the employment market that are relevant to policy determination.

In a much wider area, policy cannot as yet reflect all relevant considerations because of the absence of factual knowledge. The incidence of the payroll tax, the effect of experience rating and, in particular, of different experience-rating formulae, the income redistribution effects of the complex of unemployment aid measures, the extent of abuse—all these are merely illustrations of areas in which the policymaker has to make his choices largely by guesswork. Particularly glaring is the absence of firm knowledge about human psychology: What specifically do people find acceptable or degrading in different forms of aid? How valid is the assumption that if an adequate income is otherwise available people will not work steadily? Is this assumption more valid for some types of workers or societies than for others? Does the validity of the assumption vary with degree of education or family responsibility or income levels or expectations?

Knowledge relevant to policy formulation is continuously growing, nevertheless, and one of the most challenging problems is how to ensure that the new knowledge is brought to the attention of, and utilized by, those who make policy. The administrator is usually immersed in his day-to-day problems; the researchers are preoccupied with the discovery of new facts and relationships within their technical areas; the politicians are subject to organized group pressures, and, in any case, unemployment aid is only one of the many areas of policy with which they deal. Too few people, even in the universities, are concentrating on the effects of new knowledge or newly available data on the formulation of policy.

F. The Ability of the Society to Envisage the Full Implications of Its Stated Policies

It was noted earlier that specific policy decisions involve a balancing or compromise between a large number of frequently conflicting considerations. But it also must be recognized that the programs operative at any given time reflect the extent to which a society envisages the full implications of the policies to which it is formally committed. Indeed, in some instances it may even be questioned whether there is agreement as to the main purpose of the program. The role of unemployment insurance in the United States, as an instrument for assuring income security, has been clearly affected by the fact that its financial provisions reflect two other objectives: stabilization of employment and a specific method of allocating the costs of unemployment. The resulting concentration of the costs on employers, coupled with the potential tax advantages to be secured under experience-rating systems, has assured direct and intensive employer interest in the nature and operation of the program; and this interest appears to have strengthened the forces opposing higher benefits, longer durations, and milder disqualifications.

Lack of clarity concerning the exact purpose to be served by the unemployment insurance benefit has also led to wide differences of opinion about the "adequacy" of benefits and even the definition of the concept of "adequacy."

Even when the general objective is clear, its full implications are not always grasped. Unemployment insurance is held to be dubiously appropriate for workers without a firm attachment to the labor market, but some states have failed to adjust their minimum earnings requirements to rising wage levels, thereby admitting to benefits irregularly employed or short-term workers. Similarly, the trend toward longer benefit duration and, in particular, the adoption by some states of uniform duration logically should have been accompanied by a tightening of eligibility requirements. Yet, except for a few states, this does not appear to have been the case.

One of the avowed objects of experience rating is the reflection in price of the true costs of production (including the costs of unemployment). Yet most states have avoided carrying this policy to extreme lengths and have been reluctant to set maximum tax rates that would reflect the full costs of benefits paid to ex-employees of highly unstable employers. The unwillingness to charge full penalty rates, coupled with policies of noncharging employer accounts with benefits paid to certain types of workers or with the full duration of benefits, has weakened the effectiveness of experience rating as an instrument for allocating the true social costs of unemployment.

The limited scope of unemployment insurance, coupled with the fact that it is today the only permanent program specifically designed to furnish income to the unemployed, implies that assistance for the unemployed not benefitting from unemployment insurance must be furnished either by the residual relief system or by some special measures operated, or at least financed, by the federal government. The financing of residual relief, however, is predominantly a local or local-state responsibility, and the ability of those levels of government to provide adequate funds is least precisely at those times when the residual burden is likely to be heaviest (in depressed areas or during prolonged recessions); also federal aid is not available for the one assistance program, general relief, that is expected to assume the burden of support of the unemployed when all else fails.

There seems to be general agreement that unemployment insurance is the appropriate instrument for providing income to workers during short-period recessions and that, in consequence, it is desirable to arrange for financing over a period longer than a year to avoid the necessity to increase taxes in periods of recession, when outpayments are heaviest, or to cut benefits at a time when they are most needed. The setting of a rate of tax which over a period of years would yield sufficient income to cover costs during that period could result in the accumulation of reserves and their subsequent utilization or in the accumulation of a deficit and its subsequent repayment, depending on employment conditions at the time the policy was instituted. No state, however, is prepared to countenance with equanimity the existence of a temporary deficit in its normal reserve fund.

Unwillingness to accept the full implications of a stated policy was especially evident during the nineteen-thirties, when the federal government accepted responsibility for support of the "employable" unemployed and declared that only work at a "real job" was a suitable form of aid. Yet the unwillingness of the country to meet the heavy outpayments such a policy would have involved led to (1) a rationing of WPA employment by limiting it to needy workers who were given employment for eighteen months only, (2) the payment of less than prevailing wages in many areas, and (3) a considerable limitation of the types of employment the program could offer.

V. CONCLUSIONS

The great variety of forces that exert influence on unemployment aid policy make it impossible to establish any firm guiding principles. The differing values and objectives of societies, the varying social and economic significance of different types of unemployment and of unemployed workers, the changing social and economic environment alike preclude any such effort. At best, some general observations can be made.

First, it is obvious that no single program can provide for all the currently recognized needs of all nonworkers. The realistic problem facing contemporary societies is to determine the appropriate role of each of several forms of aid. This involves clarity in the central objectives of each form and in the features of the program which are crucial to attainment of the aim. It involves, too, a classification of the unemployed (by type or duration of unemployment, normal employment patterns, and certain personal characteristics) to secure the best possible "fit" of program and category of person, and by "fit" is meant, of course, the best available compromise between the interests of the unemployed and of the wider society.

Second, because a variety of simultaneously operating measures must be envisaged, policy must be concerned with all of them. To concentrate attention on one form only (e.g., unemployment insurance) is to invite instability. For so long as the basic needs of any significant number of workers are not met or as long as one system is strongly preferred to others, there will be pressure to extend the scope of the effective or preferred program, with the danger that in so doing some of its essential features will be modified.

Third, despite the many influential forces, the history of unemployment policy here and abroad suggests that the ultimate determinants of policy lie in decisions about the nature of the benefits and the conditions under which they are to be available, rather than in decisions about methods of financing or about appropriate governmental agencies. By and large, it is these last which are modified to permit implementation of society's decisions about benefits and eligibility.

Finally, it will be evident from the preceding discussion of the various forces influencing policy that no one program or set of programs is likely to be permanent. As economic and social conditions change, as there are shifts in social values, so will unemployment aid policy change. The challenging problem is how to identify these changing forces and evaluate their implications for policy so that today's programs reflect today's world rather than the world of yesterday.

CHAPTER 14

Policy Recommendations

Joseph M. Becker, William Haber,* and Sar A. Levitan**

BECAUSE SOME UNEMPLOYMENT is inevitable in an industrialized society characterized by a high degree of freedom and change, programs of aid for the unemployed are a necessity. The recommendations offered in this chapter comprise a reasonably adequate and practical set of programs of aid. These recommendations aim less at long-run, ideal goals than at immediate, interim goals that our society may realistically expect to attain in the near future. But before the recommendations are presented, it will be useful to set out the general principles that guided the thinking of the authors.

I. GENERAL CONSIDERATIONS

A. VARIETY OF PROGRAMS

Any adequate system of protection for the unemployed will necessarily include a variety of programs. Unemployment stems from many different causes and results in many different needs, so that unemployment becomes a family name owned by some very different children. The outstanding impression conveyed by chapters 2 and 3 (as also in pp. 252–53 of Chapter 12) is one of great diversity among the unemployed. Because of this diversity, it is necessary to keep various distinctions in mind while planning programs of aid for the unemployed. Among these distinctions, two are particularly useful as guides to practical policy.

The first useful distinction is between the unemployed who need only income maintenance and the unemployed who need something more—between the unemployed for whom programs of alleviation suffice and the unemployed for whom curative programs are needed.

The first group consists of the regular members of the labor force, whose unemployment is expected to be relatively short and who will find their way back to employment without a major change in themselves or in their environment. This group includes most of the unemployed, and the programs of alleviation are important chiefly because they suffice for the majority of the unemployed.

The other group consists of the unemployed who because of external circumstances or because of their personal characteristics need curative programs. Some live in depressed areas and must leave the areas or have new jobs brought to them through the industrial or commercial development of the areas. Others, even in prosperous areas, experience more than normal unemployment because of personal characteristics. These latter are in the majority and comprise two chief groups: those who are poorly educated, among whom the young and the nonwhites are noteworthy subgroups, and those whose skills have lost their relevance in a changing labor market, among whom the near-old constitute a special problem.

The curative programs are more important than the alleviative programs insofar as the need to which they minister is more intense and

* Dean, College of Literature, Science and Arts, The University of Michigan.
** Research Professor, The George Washington University.

insofar as the good they achieve—when they are successful—is more valuable not only to the individual but to society. On the other hand, the curative programs affect a smaller number of the unemployed, cost more per individual, and are less certain of success. Although curative programs have had relatively little development in America as yet, they are certain to grow in importance and will probably be part of a national manpower policy.

Another distinction useful for practical policy is between the short-term and the long-term unemployed. This fundamental distinction governed the description of the unemployed in chapters 1 and 2. While it is similar to, it is not identical with, the previous distinction between the unemployed for whom an alleviative program suffices and those for whom a curative program is needed.

The definition of "long-term" is necessarily somewhat arbitrary; for the purpose of setting up programs of aid, twenty-six weeks seems the most useful dividing line. When unemployment lasts longer than six months, it represents a situation that demands special action— probably a shift from an alleviative to a curative program. It is not always necessary, however, to wait six months before deciding that an unemployed person could profit from a curative program. Thus, when the Studebaker plant in South Bend, employing more than 7 per cent of the work force in the area, closed suddenly in December, 1963, retraining programs were established almost immediately. But it is difficult to discern the need for curative programs in the early stages of unemployment, and usually the decision will not be made by either the individual or society until unemployment has become "long term."

There will always be the temptation to use the simple, convenient programs of alleviation beyond the point where such programs properly apply. But, as Eveline Burns warns us, the temptation must be resisted. There eventually comes a time when the programs of alleviation should decline further responsibility for the unemployed and yield to curative programs— for the sake of the individual, of society, and of the programs of aid themselves.

B. ORDER OF OBJECTIVES

The second general consideration concerns the relative importance of the objectives which society seeks to attain through the programs of aid. There are two principal objectives: to help the unemployed individual and to help the economy. The effect on the individual and the effect on the economy are the chief norms by which the success of the programs is to be judged.

For all practical purposes the effect on the individual holds the primacy. Our society has a great concern for the dignity of the individual person and is very reluctant to see him "sacrificed" to the social totality. We look upon those who cannot keep up in the competitive race as unfortunates who have some right to the help of the more fortunate. This attitude is so much a part of our social fabric that we would probably be willing to help the unemployed even if we suspected that the programs of aid had some undesirable effects on the general economy. Society owes special consideration to those on whom the burden of changing technology rests with disproportionate weight; for as John Stuart Mill stated in his *Principles of Political Economy*, "There cannot be a more legitimate object of the legislator's care than the interests of those who are ... sacrificed to the gains of their fellow citizens."

But while society bases its decisions primarily on the effects which it expects the programs of aid to have on the individual, it does not ignore the possible effects of those programs on the economy. To the extent that the programs are expected to strengthen the economy, society will be the more inclined to establish and expand such programs. To the extent that the programs are expected to have undesirable effects on the economy, society will be less inclined to adopt them or to favor their further development.

Programs of aid can have desirable effects on the economy; that is, they can strengthen both the demand for and the supply of labor. Income-maintenance programs can help to maintain the desired level of consumer spending as well as the desired degree of labor-force stability. Curative programs by improving the employability of labor can increase the number of employed workers as well as increase their efficiency.

Programs of aid can also have undesirable effects on the economy; that is, they can diminish both the demand for and the supply of labor. Costs connected with the programs, especially those that directly raise the price of labor, can result in a lower demand for labor. The programs of aid can affect the supply of labor by causing the recipients of the aid to decline available jobs as unsuitable or even to withdraw temporarily from the labor force. Any payments to individuals who but for such benefits might find work represent a waste of society's human resources.

In our recommendations we assume that, in the absence of clear evidence to the contrary, the programs of aid, especially the curative programs, have a net favorable effect on the general economy. We prefer to give the benefit of the doubt to the more optimistic expectation because we consider it to be the more probable effect of the programs of aid.

The relationship between programs of aid and the economy has one aspect which is sufficiently important and subtle to warrant further explication. In a free economy, unemployment—more exactly, the threat of unemployment—plays an essential role in the allocation of resources. This holds whether the resource be capital or labor. The allocation of resources in a free economy is unavoidably dependent on the possibility that a resource will be unemployed if the owner of the resource sets too high a price on it or makes some other "bad" economic use of it. If the threat of unemployment should ever become ineffectual, the task of allocating resources would have to be assumed by the coercive power of government—that is, there would no longer be a free economy. The issue involved here is much broader than merely the need to maintain an incentive to work. Since aid to the unemployed can affect all labor costs, including wage rates and conditions of work, and since labor costs are usually the largest part of total costs of production, a major economic issue is involved here.

The need to preserve the regulatory function of unemployment makes it more difficult to devise appropriate programs of aid for the unemployed than for those in other groups— such as the aged, the blind, the ill, the orphaned —who are not competitive members of the labor force. Such persons are behind the battle lines, withdrawn from the fray. But the unemployed are still in the economic battle, still part of the forces that determine the size of the national product and its distribution among the factors of production. Aid for the unemployed inevitably becomes a force that directly influences the competitive struggle. Thus, the need to aid the unemployed so as not to interfere overmuch with the regulatory function of unemployment in a free economy is a limitation that necessarily affects all programs to help the unemployed. Nevertheless, when in doubt as to whether a given program of aid for the individual does interfere "overmuch" with the economy, we shall be acting in accord with our society's dominant values if we give the benefit of the doubt to the need of the individual.

C. ORDER OF MEANS

A third general consideration relates to the choice of means whereby a given program of aid is to be set up and administered: Is it a private or a public responsibility? If public, is it primarily a local, state, or federal responsibility?

The principle of subsidiarity provides a guide for these choices. According to this principle, a higher unit of society should not undertake those tasks which can be performed as well or almost as well by a lower unit. Thus, other things being equal, private action is preferred to public action, and within the public sphere the order of preference is usually local, state, federal.

Some aid to the unemployed is being provided by private agencies, particularly in industry. Private agencies can do much more if they are assisted by government, as in the MDTA program, where the federal government provides grants to employers for on-the-job training. Nevertheless, it remains true that many tasks cannot, or at least will not, be performed by private agencies. It is then necessary to turn to government.

Within government there is a hierarchy. Some tasks can best be performed by local government, some by the state government, and there are still others which, because the local or state governments are unwilling or unable to act, require action by the federal government. Sometimes the best form of action by the federal government is to facilitate action by the state and local governments, for example, through matching grants or tax offsets.

Since the principle of subsidiarity is only one of many principles that must be used in any actual situation, it applies only under the condition "other things being equal." But the "other things" are continually changing in ways that affect the application of the principle of subsidiarity. For the most part they are changing in ways that require more rather than less centralized public action. Because society is growing ever more complex and closely integrated, more planning is necessary; because new tools of management are continually being developed, more planning is possible. The result is a widening of the scope of central government, a trend that necessarily affects the planning of programs of aid for the unemployed.

It is in the light of the above general considerations that the authors offer the following specific recommendations.

II. RECOMMENDATIONS

A. Unemployment Insurance

Unemployment insurance occupies the central place among the programs of aid. It provides more income to more unemployed persons than all the other programs of aid combined. Nevertheless, unemployment insurance has its limitations and cannot do the whole job of aiding the unemployed. It cannot cover all classes of workers, or achieve the nice fitting of benefits to individuals that

can theoretically be attained through relief programs; neither can it pay benefits for an indefinite duration. The following recommendations for unemployment insurance are made with both the importance and the limitations of the program in view.

Coverage. Unemployment insurance ought to be expanded to cover at least three groups. First of all, *coverage should be extended to smaller firms.* Ultimately all sizes of firms should be covered; but if this is not politically feasible within the next few years, a beginning might be made by extending coverage to employers of three or more employees.

Second, *coverage should be extended to most nonprofit institutions.* Although there is a growing recognition that such extension is desirable, only four states currently have such coverage and a few others—California and New York, for example—may act in the near future. The extension of coverage to nonprofit institutions is all the more important because in recent years the nonprofit area of the economy has been accounting for a larger proportion of the total number of jobs.

The history of unemployment insurance indicates that extension of coverage to smaller firms and to nonprofit institutions will probably have to be accomplished by federal action; for during the last decade there has been no amendment to unemployment insurance laws so difficult to get through a state legislature as an extension of coverage. When the nonprofit institutions are covered, the tax provisions should protect these institutions from ever having to subsidize firms in the profit-making sector of the economy.

Third, *coverage should be extended to employees of government.* It is one of the anomalies of unemployment insurance in the United States that government, which compels private employers to provide this protection, has not shown equal concern for its own employees. The federal government finally moved to cover its employees in 1954—nearly twenty years late. A number of the states now cover some of their employees, but about six million government workers still have no protection. The remainder of the job must be done by the state legislatures, since the federal government is prohibited from taxing the sovereign states.

Eligibility. Experience has indicated that in most situations the best test of attachment to the labor market is the number of weeks worked. In recent years, Michigan, Missouri, New Jersey, New York, and Rhode Island have followed Wisconsin's example in requiring that an individual must have worked a specified number of weeks in order to be eligible for benefits. *We recommend that more states include the number of weeks worked as a part of their eligibility requirements.*

Disqualifications. Because in this highly disputable area there is little consensus on principles and little statistical information to guide action, we limit ourselves to one recommendation: *Unemployment insurance beneficiaries who undertake training should not be disqualified from receiving benefits.* We recognize, however, that payments to trainees are not strictly within the scope of any unemployment insurance system, much less of one that seeks to make unemployment benefits a cost of doing business. It is desirable, therefore, that payments to trainees should as far as possible come from programs that are expressly set up to provide training. When unemployment insurance benefits are used to pay trainees, the insurance program should whenever possible be reimbursed by the training program, as is the practice under the Manpower Development and Training Act.

Financing. The high degree of uncertainty that attaches to unemployment makes some form of reinsurance among the states an advisable precaution. *We recommend the adoption of a "catastrophic reinsurance" plan* such as that developed by the Benefit Financing Committee of the Interstate Conference of Employment Security Agencies. Under this plan, a state that experienced a sudden large increase in unemployment could draw on a common fund to meet part of its increased costs. The help would be available only during a period of accelerating unemployment; the continuation of a high level of unemployment would not make a state continuously eligible for such help. This plan spreads the cost of unusual, in the

sense of unpredictable, risks among the states and is merely a logical extension of the insurance principle.

Equalization grants, another proposed plan for spreading the costs of high unemployment among the states, involve a very different issue. These grants are paid to states which have above-average costs, even when the costs are continuing and predictable. Although such subsidies have much to recommend them, they obviously militate against one of the outstanding virtues of the American unemployment insurance system. This system makes unemployment benefits a regular cost of doing business and thus causes the prices of products to reflect their true cost, including the cost of supporting the unemployed. It is not clear, moreover, that equalization grants are necessary and that the high-cost states cannot pay their own way. The difference between unemployment insurance costs in a high-cost state and in an average state represents a very small fraction of total wages or even of total taxes in the high-cost state. Since the high-cost states are typically the industrialized and therefore the wealthier states, they should be able to meet their own business costs.

The unemployment insurance program will need more income in the future than was needed in the past. The additional income can be obtained by either raising the tax rate, or enlarging the tax base, or both. The difference between the impacts of raising the rate and of enlarging the base is not known with any certainty, and without such knowledge it is difficult to choose between the two alternatives. (It is not particularly helpful to recall that the original legislation taxed a larger part of total wages than is currently taxed; for decisions at the beginning of the program were made in the almost complete absence of relevant data.)

An increase in the tax base as against an increase in the tax rate tends to favor firms with low wages and/or much unemployment at the expense of firms with high wages and/or little unemployment, but exactly which firms would be affected is uncertain. Moreover, there is little agreement as to which firms *should* bear the increased tax burden. On the one hand, firms with low wages and/or much unemployment are least able to carry the burden; on the other hand, since such firms are already being subsidized by the taxes of the rest of the firms in the program, the question may be raised whether this subsidy should be increased, especially in a system that aims to make unemployment benefits a regular cost of doing business. In the absence of the needed information and the desirable social consensus, it would seem to be the part of prudence, in accordance with the well-known fiscal principle that an old tax is a good tax, to disturb the existing arrangement as little as possible. An old tax has had time to be assimilated into the economy and to be reflected in the relevant prices and is therefore best left alone. To give proper heed to this venerable principle and yet raise the needed income, *we recommend the sensible compromise of increasing both the tax base and the tax rate.* In this way neither base nor rate will have to be changed as much as would be the case if only one were changed.

Benefit Amount. Perhaps the most important part of unemployment insurance is the adequacy of the benefit structure. Fortunately there is in this important area enough social consensus and enough tested experience to support sound conclusions.

First, there is a general consensus that the unemployment insurance system should pay at least 50 per cent of lost wages, up to some maximum amount. This consensus is broad and deep enough to constitute a significant social force. Second, there is an equally general consensus that if any class of worker should be protected by the system it should be the worker with dependents. Third, it is certain that workers with dependents, who constitute a little over half of all beneficiaries, get relatively less protection than do the workers without dependents. Fourth, it is certain that workers with dependents get less protection largely because their wages are normally higher than the wages of other workers and the maximum benefit is not sufficiently high to allow these primary workers to receive 50 per cent of their lost wages.

It is rare in unemployment insurance that the issues and the relevant facts stand out as clearly as they do in this matter. It is therefore easy to reach the conclusion that the maximum benefit should be high enough to allow at least a majority of primary workers to receive at least 50 per cent of their take-home wage.

It is not entirely clear what maximum benefit will accomplish this. Although the ratio of benefits to wages for actual beneficiaries is the single most important piece of information in the program and the information could be obtained rather easily, it is as a matter of fact almost nonexistent. All that there is to go on are the benefit adequacy studies analyzed in Chapter 5. To the extent that these studies reflect the general situation, they justify a recommendation that *the maximum benefit should be at least 50 per cent of the average covered wage in the state.*

Whether this recommendation should be implemented by state or by federal action is a very disputable point. We are inclined to recommend that it be done by federal action and that Congress require the states to meet this standard in order to be eligible for a tax offset. We recommend federal action for a very simple reason: As of January, 1964, less than one-fourth of all covered workers were in states that met this standard, and there is no indication that a majority of the states are ready to take this obvious step in the near future. However, we consider state action preferable and would welcome any signs of impending state action.

A system of dependents' allowances is of course the most direct and accurate way of assuring that workers with dependents receive adequate benefits. Twelve states now have some such system. Nine of these states use the system of flat benefits, under which the beneficiary with dependents is paid a flat amount for each dependent and hence receives a total benefit which represents a higher percentage of his wage. The remaining three states use the system of variable maximums, under which the same percentage of wages is paid to all beneficiaries but the percentage is carried to a higher maximum benefit in the case of beneficiaries with dependents.

The system of flat benefits is older, simpler, and more adequate. But if a system of dependents' allowances is to be adopted widely, it will probably have to be the system of variable maximums, which is less expensive and more in accord with the insurance character of the program. *We therefore recommend the wider adoption of the system of variable maximums*— always with the understanding that the basic benefit be set sufficiently high to assure that the majority of beneficiaries without dependents also receive at least 50 per cent of their wage.

Duration of Benefits. In this area there is now no pressing duration issue with respect to the program of "regular" benefits, the program which operates at all times and in all places (not merely during recessions or in depressed areas) and pays benefits up to a maximum of 26 weeks. Over the years duration in the regular program has been lengthened, so that by 1964 more than 98 per cent of the covered workers were in states with a maximum duration of 26 weeks and the average worker who actually became unemployed was eligible for about 24 weeks of benefits.

There is a wide and growing consensus that the duration of benefits should be extended during periods of recession. The only real point still at issue is the method to be used in providing the extension. Should the extended program be brought into existence by state or by federal action? If by federal action, should it be financed by means of loans or of grants? Should the required funds be raised by a general tax, a payroll tax, or an employee tax? And what triggering mechanism should turn the program on and shut it off?

However these various questions are answered, it is clearly desirable to provide the answers now rather than to wait until the next recession. The Interstate Conference of Employment Security Agencies has prepared a plan which, while probably satisfying no one's ideal, comes closest to being a compromise acceptable to all. In the ICESA plan the federal government would offer to meet half the costs of any state that set up a recession-triggered program providing up to thirteen additional weeks of benefits. In this plan, the triggering mechanism is based on each state's own employment history. *We recommend the immediate adoption of something like the ICESA plan.*

A few states have begun to pay extended benefits that are available even outside of recessions but only to selected groups of claimants. The future development of this promising experiment will depend partly on the extent to which the curative and the welfare programs can assume responsibility for the long-term unemployed.

B. PROGRAMS OF PRIVATE INDUSTRY

Private plans are marked by the same characteristics which Elizabeth Wickenden noted in her discussion of welfare programs: they are adaptive and pioneering. Private plans achieve a close fit of benefits to individual needs and they pioneer in new directions. *Both functions are worthwhile and it may therefore be hoped that labor and management will continue to develop their own programs of protection for the unemployed.* Three of these programs (in addition to training programs, which are discussed in section F) are particularly promising.

Supplementary Unemployment Benefits. As long as the public unemployment insurance program is limited to paying about 50 per cent of wages for about a half year, there will always be room for private supplementary programs— that is, there will be some workers who will want to take part of their remuneration in the form of added security against unemployment and there will be some employers willing to pay the remuneration in this form.

From the viewpoint of society there is one possible disadvantage to the supplementary unemployment benefit plans: The liberality of the benefits, especially their long duration, may interfere with desirable labor mobility in situations where former jobs are permanently lost. The unemployment benefit plan of the glass industry is free of this possible drag on mobility, as is also the hybrid Extended Layoff Benefit plan of the aerospace industry. However, there is no evidence that this possible disadvantage of SUB has become actual.

Severance Pay. There is probably a growing need—certainly there is a growing appreciation of the need—for severance-pay plans. The constant change that marks the modern economy underlines the need for a program to protect the permanently separated worker. The very fact of change emphasizes also the value of a protective program that does not interfere with desirable labor mobility. For both reasons an increase in severance-pay plans is to be recommended.

Early Pensions. There is an essential similarity between early pensions and severance pay, for both are essentially remuneration for a lost "property right." Most of what was said with regard to severance-pay plans applies to early-pension plans, with the added observation that early-pension plans typically provide more protection than severance-pay plans but for that reason cost more.

In strict theory there is no reason why recipients of severance pay or early pensions should not qualify for unemployment insurance benefits. These plans are not alternatives to the unemployment insurance program, but have their own distinct objectives. It must also be recognized that in the modern economy a worker may "retire" from a particular job, yet not leave the labor market entirely. In practice, the relationship to be established between unemployment insurance and the other programs will depend very much upon the effectiveness of the unemployment insurance test of availability for work. This effectiveness varies with circumstances.

C. Area Redevelopment

Since the Area Redevelopment Act is a long-term program to combat unemployment in depressed areas, it is not surprising that the program got off the ground slowly. Moreover, there were numerous obstacles to the success of an area redevelopment program, not to mention the lack of previous experience with planning for local economic growth. The economic climate during the first three years of ARA operations was not conducive to the success of the program. In an economy of high employment, when the "cup runneth over" for other communities, businesses find it advantageous to locate or expand in depressed areas, where labor is plentiful. But during the first three years of ARA practically all labor markets in the United States experienced various degrees of labor surplus.

The tools that Congress gave to ARA to combat unemployment proved to be of doubtful effectiveness. Under the terms of the act, only businesses which could not get credit at reasonable rates of interest in the open market could qualify for ARA loans. Established enterprises, the major source of economic growth, were in a position to finance expansion from corporate reserves and, in cases where such reserves were not available, could usually obtain loans from conventional lending institutions. The ARA loans have therefore been limited largely to marginal or new enterprises.

The ARA training provisions might have proved effective bait to attract new or expanding industry to depressed areas had Congress not passed within a year after the establishment of ARA the Manpower Development and Training Act, which made available broader training programs in all areas of the country and thus minimized any advantages that ARA training might have given to depressed areas.

The brief experience thus far under ARA makes it difficult to appraise the impact of the program's technical assistance, which could not exceed $4.5 million a year, and the consequent role of ARA in stimulating economic planning for the development of communities. At best, it will be years before these plans bear fruit. As William Miernyk points out, three years of experience is too short a period upon which to make an adequate appraisal of this phase of ARA activities.

The difficulties of ARA have not stemmed exclusively from the overall economic conditions or the limited tools granted to it by Congress. When Senator Douglas originally proposed the depressed area program, he envisioned aid to a few score depressed communities throughout the United States. But as the bill passed through the legislative mill, the criteria for area eligibility were relaxed as a result of pressures from supporters of the bill who desired that their communities qualify for ARA assistance. After the act was passed, the area redevelopment administrators succumbed to further pressures for the designation of still more areas. As a result, the ARA overextended its limited resources. Nearly 1,100 counties (more than a third of the U.S. total), with a population of some 40 million people, were eligible to receive ARA assistance by the end of 1963.

Although ARA could be made more effective by the improvement of the available tools, the overextension of the program makes such an improvement impractical. It can hardly be argued that one-third of the nation's counties are depressed areas. Extending additional help to all these designated areas would create serious inequities and place at a disadvantage the businessmen in the 2,000 nondesignated areas. Moreover, among the designated areas, if the additional help were made equally available to all communities, the economically more viable communities—including the major industrial complexes of Philadelphia, Pittsburgh, Buffalo, and Detroit—would likely benefit most by the federal assistance, while truly depressed areas might get very little or no federal aid.

With the proviso that the number of depressed areas be reduced to manageable proportions and only those communities with a potential for economic development at a reasonable cost be permitted to participate in the program, we offer for consideration the following three-point recommendation to strengthen ARA.

1. Grant accelerated tax amortization to firms locating or expanding in depressed areas. The proposed legislation could follow the provisions of the Defense Production Act of the Korean War.

2. Allow depressed areas larger percentages of federal grants-in-aid than is permitted in more prosperous areas. For example, the ARA defrays 75 per cent of the total cost of urban renewal planning in depressed areas as compared with 67 per cent in other areas. The same principle applied to other federal grant programs—highway and hospital construction, public assistance, education, and others—would increase federal aid to depressed areas.

3. Subsidize mobility of workers from depressed areas. Such a program must be used carefully and flexibly lest it accelerate the mobility of the more educated and skilled workers from depressed areas and thus further deteriorate the human resources in these areas and make them less attractive to new enterprises. However, there are some communities whose economic base has deteriorated so far that they cannot be "saved." In such cases, individuals should be encouraged to migrate to other areas.

Experience under ARA suggests that Congress is not likely to restrict the number of areas eligible to receive assistance and that therefore the proviso to our recommendations is not likely to be fulfilled. On this assumption we offer the alternative recommendation that *the present modest program be continued, with some increase in funds.* We favor the enactment of something like S.1163 (88th Congress), which passed the Senate in June, 1963, but was rejected by the House. This bill would increase to $500 million the present $200 million authorization for commercial and industrial loans and raise the limit on authorized loans for public facilities from $100 million to $150 million. The bill further provides that the grants for public facilities be raised from $75 million to $175 million and that annual authorization for technical assistance be raised from $4.5 million to $10 million. The success of ARA can be measured only by longer-term developments, and the program should therefore be given further opportunity to prove its potential as a tool to aid chronic labor-surplus areas.

D. PUBLIC WORKS

The Accelerated Public Works Act (APWA) of 1962 represents an extension of the philosophy underlying ARA. In both acts Congress recognized that a concentration of unemployment in local communities is a national problem, and both programs are designed to cope with chronic local unemployment, which acts as a drag upon the national economy. The ARA and the APWA differ, however, in that the former is geared to provide long-term economic development and the latter to provide immediate employment. The APWA requires that projects financed under this program be initiated or accelerated within a reasonably short time and that half of the projects be completed within twelve months. The projects financed by the program have to meet "an essential public need" to improve the public facilities in hard-pressed communities in order to make them "better places to live and work."

A program of public works is of dubious effectiveness as a countercyclical device. It has more promise as a method of restoring the economic base of a depressed community or of providing jobs in such a community. The 1962 APWA program seems adapted to achieve the latter objective and to avoid some of the problems that Roger A. Freeman notes with regard to past public-works efforts. At this writing experience under the 1962 act is too brief to be conclusive; but it is noteworthy that the $880 million thus far appropriated under the act have been utilized in areas where high unemployment prevailed.

Construction costs, especially wages, have risen faster than productivity in the construction industry and faster than costs in most other industries. There is no doubt that this disproportion constitutes a limitation on the use of public works to provide jobs. Recent figures, however, seem to indicate that the disproportion has become smaller in the postwar period than it was earlier. Moreover, the conjunction of unmet public needs with unused resources is a consideration that can offset many possible disadvantages in a public-works program.

Experience during the past few years has indicated that a growing number of unskilled and poorly educated workers find it increasingly harder to obtain employment. The problem is particularly severe among young people. In depressed areas the only hope for employment for many of these unskilled workers who have been forced into idleness or who never had an opportunity for gainful employment is to obtain jobs on government-sponsored projects specifi-

cally suited to their meager skills. This suggests to us the need of inaugurating a federally-financed, permanent public-works program, at least in depressed areas.

We recommend that there be a public-works program designed for chronic labor-surplus areas but that it be modified in several ways to make it more effective.

Most of the funds appropriated under the 1962 APWA were expended on projects which required skilled construction workers, and on-site wage rates were determined under the Davis-Bacon Act. As a result, the number of jobs for which unskilled workers could be hired was minimized. *Future federally-assisted public works in labor-surplus areas should put more stress on projects which utilize unskilled unemployed workers.* This would require the allocation of a specific portion of the funds for projects where unskilled labor can be utilized, such as the clearing of streams, construction of fire trails, reforestation, paving of roads, and urban park development. During the Great Depression our society acquired considerable experience with public works of this nature. From such experience we can distill the necessary principles to guide a new program designed for similar local situations.

Future public works should be placed on a more business-like basis. Under the 1962 act the relative economic merits of projects submitted by communities were not decisive; if a project was approvable and funds earmarked for the area had not been exhausted, it was approved without any comparison of its economic merits with the merits of projects in other areas. Future public works should also give greater consideration to the long-run impact of the program. To facilitate the inauguration of long-run projects, it would be desirable to allocate 1 per cent of total appropriations to be distributed to eligible communities in order to assist them in the planning of such projects.

E. THE PUBLIC EMPLOYMENT SERVICE

Among the various functions of the public employment service, the placement function is primary. Nationally, during the past decade, the public employment service has participated in about 10–15 per cent of all new hiring and to this extent has become an established meeting place for the jobless man and the manless job. Although it is an error to make placements the sole measure of the success of the public employment service, placements are, in fact, the service's single most important activity. The success of the employment service in the performance of this central function varies with circumstances. In time of war the public employment service is the principal agent in the placement process and plays a dominant role in the mobilization of the nation's manpower. In peacetime the public employment service makes most of the placements in some of the smaller labor markets and even in the large labor markets supplies some employers with most of their workers; the service also has special programs to cope with mass layoffs and emergency situations such as floods and earthquakes.

The public employment service has at least three other activities, which, unlike the placement function, are unique to the public service. There is no competition for these from the private employment agencies, and, practically speaking, they can be performed only by a public agency. First, the employment service administers a number of special programs for disadvantaged job seekers—the handicapped, minority groups, inexperienced youth, migratory farm workers, veterans, and others. Second, the employment service functions as a source of labor-market information and a center of research in labor-market problems. These two functions properly performed involve much testing and counseling and the organization of community resources.

Finally, the employment service administers the job test to applicants for unemployment benefits. The employment service is both helped and hindered by its relationship to unemployment insurance. The employment service derives practically all its funds from the unemployment insurance taxes; and the requirement that claimants for unemployment benefits register with the public employment service supplies the employment service with most of its clients. On the other hand, employment service personnel are sometimes diverted to unemployment insurance work during times of peak loads in the insurance program; and at all times the close relationship of the employment service with the payment of unemployment benefits obscures the clear image of its own proper function that the employment service would like to project. To minimize the disadvantage of the relationship, the employment service has been gradually separating itself physically from the unemployment insurance program. Though this movement is desirable, its importance must not be exaggerated. The limitations of the employment service in the past have not been due primarily to its relationship with unemployment insurance, and physical separation from the unemployment insurance office will not automatically bring about a significant improvement.

The combination of these basic functions makes the public employment service an indispensable part of the nation's economy, and in recent years the demands made on the service have been increasing. The Area Redevelopment Act of 1961 and the Manpower Development and Training Act of 1962 have placed additional duties on the employment service. In 1964 Congress appropriated the largest sum in our history for vocational training and thus made possible a great expansion of vocational training programs, in many of which the employment service is involved. Still further demands on the employment service would be made by the very recent (1964) Employment Opportunity Act, a part of President Johnson's anti-poverty program. Since the public employment service is destined to play a larger role in the preparation and utilization of the nation's manpower, it needs as never before to be adequate for its task. *Adequacy requires a sound expansion of the scope and an increase in the efficiency of the present federal-state public employment system.* The following recommendations are made with this two-fold end in view.

1. The public employment service must build up close contacts with employers, labor

organizations, the school system, and other community groups. The support of such groups is essential, but it can be won only on the basis of performance and cannot be forced. Any mandatory use of the employment service by either employers or workers is not desirable and in any case is out of the question. The public employment service will need to win acceptance by its works.

2. Since jobs in the commercial and professional fields are expanding, the public employment office must increase its services to employers and job seekers in these fields.

3. The public employment office should continue its special services to disadvantaged workers. This is not only a proper but a necessary function of the public service, for profit-seeking agencies cannot be expected to assume responsibility for such workers. Congress and the Bureau of the Budget must recognize that these special services are unusually costly and must provide adequate funds; otherwise the performance of the special functions will lead to the starvation of the service's regular functions.

4. Because its expanded role has increased the importance of the testing and counseling functions, the public employment service must improve its competence to perform these operations.

5. In the local offices, median and maximum salaries for key positions—the local office manager, the employment interviewer, the labor-market analyst, and the employment counselor—are too low to enable the public service to compete for the necessary personnel. Some states offer starting salaries that are lower than the wages of semiskilled factory workers. Renewed effort should be made to persuade states to raise their salary levels in order to attract personnel equal to the demanding tasks of a modern public employment service. But since the states must continue to perform most of their tasks with current personnel, they should devote increased resources to the improvement of inservice training.

6. Several changes should be made in the formula by which funds are allocated to the states for the administration of the public employment service. To the extent that placement activity is used in the formula, a distinction should be made between easy-to-make and hard-to-make placements. In the past the formula has not adequately reflected the qualitative differences in placements. Moreover, placements should not be given excessive weight. Testing, counseling, and research activities should be given adequate consideration in the formula for allocating funds. We urge that the budget process be reappraised with a view to finding a formula that would encourage local and state offices to concentrate on significant manpower actions.

7. As the scope of the public service broadens to encompass very much more than the job test for unemployment insurance, the propriety of financing the employment service by unemployment insurance taxes inevitably comes into question. Moreover, since a payroll tax is probably the least desirable form of tax from the viewpoint of promoting full employment, it should be used as little as possible. While the use of a payroll tax has offsetting advantages in the case of unemployment insurance, these advantages do not exist in the case of the employment service. It would seem expedient, therefore, to finance the public employment service more from general revenues than from the payroll tax of unemployment insurance.

8. Research in manpower problems is not a new activity for the public employment service, but we believe that even more emphasis should be put on this function in the future. The federal partner in this federal-state system should provide some of the leadership and should invite the co-operation of universities and other organizations to develop a research program designed to increase the capacity of the public employment service at all levels and to deal with the significant developments now taking place in the American economy. One result of this research should be a clarification of the process by which the public employment service can grow out of its original role of a "labor exchange" into its proposed new role of a "manpower center."

9. Additional funds should be made available for the expanded operations of the public employment service. In fiscal 1964 the cost of administering the entire employment security program, which includes unemployment insurance as well as the employment service, was $422 million. In our judgment the employment security program could make excellent use of an additional $100 million, the greater amount of which should be allocated to employment service functions.

F. TRAINING

In recent years the high level of unemployment which has prevailed in the United States has been accompanied by labor shortages in some industries and occupations. The underlying justification for the training provisions in the Area Redevelopment Act and the Manpower Development and Training Act was the assumption that government-supported training programs would equip unemployed workers to fill the existing job vacancies.

Measured by their placement rate, the training programs seem to have been reasonably successful; about 70 per cent of those who completed ARA and MDTA training courses obtained jobs upon "graduation" from the course. However, the impact of these training programs has been rather insignificant in relation to the number of the unemployed. At an average cost of about $1,500 per trainee, federal appropriations for MDTA programs permitted the training of only some 70,000 people in fiscal 1964. Moreover, there is some evidence that the "cream" of the unemployed have been selected for training, and it is possible that most of these would have obtained jobs without the aid of the retraining programs.

When Congress enacted the MDTA, it was anticipated that a significant proportion of the funds appropriated for the program would be utilized for on-the-job training. This anticipation was based to some extent on the major role that employers have traditionally assumed in the training of their employees. Data on the costs of training by private industry are not available, but the total amount must run into billions of dollars each year and attests the important role that private employers play in the training function. It was expected that government assistance under the MDTA would encourage employers to expand their on-the-job training activities by hiring new employees. But only six of every hundred selectees during the first two years of the program were earmarked for on-site training.

The failure to utilize a larger proportion of MDTA funds for on-the-job training has been due to a number of factors. The Labor Department has been excessively cautious in allocating resources to on-the-job training lest government funds be used for training which would otherwise be undertaken by employers. Some unions have opposed training programs in general and on-the-job training programs in particular on the ground that such programs tended to expand the supply of trained labor in their respective jurisdictions and thus to depress wages and reduce union control over jobs, particularly in apprenticeable occupations. Other unions, however, have adopted a more positive attitude toward the retraining programs and have recognized that the programs can be of benefit to those of their members whose jobs become obsolete because of technological change.

There is a need for devising methods to train a larger number of workers on the job. A particularly promising field exists in service occupations, where small employers predominate. Because of the competition for trained workers and the danger of being "raided" by stronger competitors, the smaller employers cannot afford to allocate resources for the training of workers. Arrangements can be made to pool the resources of such small employers and provide training through a combination of existing vocational facilities and on-the-job training paid for by employers. Successful development of such a program would provide some of the additional workers needed in service industries such as television and auto repair. Expansion of government-supported on-the-job training, however, will require the removal of some existing limitations.

Under present regulations federal expenditures for on-the-job training are limited to the cost of instruction and the cost of necessary materials used during training. We recommend a more realistic and effective *on-the-job training program which will permit the use of government funds to pay part of the wages of employees* so that employers will be encouraged to train additional workers and to offer their facilities for such training.

MDTA experience has indicated that traditional vocational education is not adapted to train school dropouts and illiterate older unemployed workers. To reach these groups of the unemployed, the Office of Manpower, Automation, and Training (OMAT) in the Department of Labor has financed special demonstration projects for the development of new training techniques especially suited to these disadvantaged groups. In many cases trainees selected for demonstration projects require schooling in the rudiments of elementary education before they can undertake any training course. Though it is premature at this stage to evaluate this phase of OMAT's work, it is clear that an effective development of these techniques will require more than the limited resources allocated to the retraining program.

A greater incentive should be offered to workers to undertake retraining programs. An average weekly subsistence allowance of $35 is inadequate to support many unemployed, especially heads of families, who would benefit from a retraining program. In recognition of the inadequacy of the original MDTA, Congress amended the act in December, 1963. The 1963 amendments authorized the raising of federal expenditure during 1965 to $407 million, permitted a weekly increase of up to $10 in subsistence payments, and allowed a trainee to work for as much as twenty hours a week without losing any part of his allowance.

Even as amended, MDTA provides scarcely the bare minimum needed for an effective program. We recommend that as additional experience is gained under the program *government financial support be expanded to provide for the annual retraining of about one per cent of the total labor force.*

G. WELFARE PROGRAMS

The various programs of aid thus far considered are like so many protective nets stretched beneath workers who fall out of employment. But all of these protective devices combined are not sufficient protection for some of the unemployed, who fall outside or through all of them. For these unemployed there exists the welfare system, the last life net, which theoretically stretches under all workers and below which our society does not allow—again theoretically—anyone to fall.

Welfare programs are necessary complements to the other programs of aid. Without welfare programs some of the unemployed would lack any kind of aid. Also, without adequate welfare programs other programs are in danger of being twisted to perform functions not proper to them.

Welfare programs differ from other programs of aid in that they do not require the applicant to have a history of work but do require that he be destitute. These programs perform both alleviative and curative functions. The alleviative function is performed chiefly through the program of general assistance, whose theoretical goal is to provide a subsistence income, without limitation of time or place, for every unemployed person who cannot obtain this minimum in any other way. Currently this goal is not being met. In some states no welfare aid of any kind is available to employable persons; as far as public responsibility goes, the unemployed may starve. In other states the welfare aid that is available is not adequate even for subsistence, as that term is generally understood by welfare agencies.

To achieve the welfare goal of providing every unemployed person with at least a subsistence income, federal leadership and support seem to be needed. We recommend therefore that *federal matching grants similar to those provided in the other assistance programs under the social security act be made available for aid to the destitute unemployed.*

The program of Aid to Dependent Children (ADC) was expanded in 1961 to include children in families with an unemployed head. In the absence of an adequate general assistance program, this extension of the ADC program meets a need; it should be retained until a satisfactory development of the general assistance program makes the extension unnecessary.

The unemployed who are eligible for welfare are the most destitute among the unemployed and often need more than mere income maintenance. Frequently they labor under physical, intellectual, or emotional limitations that leave them with only marginal employability. For these unemployed, curative programs are needed.

Although the need of these unemployed for curative programs is greatest, their ability to make use of such programs is least—and for the same reason, namely, that their employability is low. Hence only limited norms of achievement can be set for curative programs intended for welfare recipients. It must be recognized that the chief objective of such programs is not economic but sociological—not to save the taxpayer money, or to increase the national product, but to reduce human misery. If the economic objective can be attained along with the sociological objective, this is a bonus rather than a necessary condition.

We recommend two kinds of curative programs. First, *there should be training programs that prepare welfare recipients to find jobs in the competitive market.* The scope of these programs should include training in the basic skills of reading, writing, and arithmetic. This aid is already available to a limited extent under the MDTA program. Second, since among the unemployed on relief there are some whose employability is so low that even after they have absorbed all the training of which they are capable, they find it impossible, except in periods of extreme labor shortage, to sell their services on the competitive market, *there should be programs that provide jobs outside the competitive market.* For individuals of such limited capacity it is desirable to provide some kind of public, sheltered work. We recommend that experimentation with such work be carried out by the Office of Manpower, Automation, and Training in conjunction with the MDTA program and the recommended program of public works in depressed areas.

Elizabeth Wickenden notes the problem raised by requiring welfare recipients, especially AFDC mothers, to undergo training and accept publicly provided jobs as a condition for receiving welfare aid. This problem, like most of those in the field of welfare, must be solved individually in relation to each welfare recipient's personal situation. We recognize that in some cases the only way to break the chain of poverty and prevent one generation of welfare recipients from breeding another is to restore the head of the family, even if it be the mother, to self-supporting employment. To prevent obvious evils, however, society will need to provide nursery schools for the children of the mothers who are required to work.

III. COSTS AND PRIORITIES

How much does it cost to operate an adequate system of programs of aid for the unemployed, that is, what proportion of society's resources must be set aside for the use of the unemployed?

It would be desirable to give the answer in terms of net costs, for these are the true measure of the burden borne by society in aiding the unemployed. To arrive at net costs there must be subtracted from gross money costs whatever increases in resources result from the programs of aid. For this purpose it is necessary to distinguish those expenditures for direct consumption from expenditures which are properly counted as an investment in the development of human resources. Thus expenditures for training are really a long-range investment in the economic factor of production called labor; if the trainees become productive members of society, the net return on this investment may more than repay the public treasury for the money costs of the training.

Any estimation of net cost must also take into consideration the possibility that an increase in one form of aid may mean a decrease in another. For example, aid supplied by a governmental program partly takes the place of aid that would otherwise have to be provided by the friends and family of the unemployed or by private charitable institutions.

Unfortunately, it is impossible to arrive at

reliable estimates of these net costs, and it is therefore necessary to work in terms of gross costs. Even gross costs can only be approximated because of various gaps and deficiencies in the data. For example, some portion of the aid disbursed by welfare agencies (private and public) goes to unemployed persons, but the available data do not show the proportion. The help given to the unemployed by families and friends is even less measurable. Pensions, especially early pensions, represent to some extent aid to persons who in a real sense are unemployed rather than retired, but this extent is not known. Another gap in the data is private industry's expenditure on severance pay and retraining. The only program of private aid for the unemployed for which data are available is the supplementary unemployment benefit program. From these data we estimate that the annual cost of all supplementary unemployment benefits plans is between $150 and $200 million.

Table 14–1 shows the costs of five public programs of aid for which reasonably accurate figures are available. Fortunately for our purpose, the cost of these programs represents by far the greater proportion of all costs of aid to the unemployed.

The table does not attempt to show probable future costs. Because expenditures for the unemployed in any given period depend largely on the amount of unemployment in the period, and because predictions of future unemployment are notoriously uncertain, the estimates of cost are limited to the current scene. The table shows the cost of the present programs of aid in fiscal 1964, the latest year for which data are available, and includes an estimate of the cost of implementing our proposals for additional aid on the assumption that the proposals had been in effect during this same period.

In fiscal 1964, total funds allocated to the five programs listed in the table amounted to $3.8 billion. If our proposals had been in effect during that year, they would have entailed an additional public expenditure of $1.7 billion, or a total of $5.5 billion. The distribution of these expenditures by program is shown in the table.

TABLE 14–1: ACTUAL AND PROPOSED EXPENDITURES UNDER FIVE PUBLIC PROGRAMS, FISCAL 1964

(Millions)

| | Expenditure | | |
Program	Actual	Proposed Additional	Total
Unemployment Insurance[a]	$2,775	$ 871	$3,646
Extension of coverage		(416)	
Increase in benefit amount		(255)	
Increase in benefit duration		(200)	
Administration of Employment Security	422	100	522
Area Redevelopment Administration	112	93	205
Public Works	365	300	665
Training	139	431	570
All Programs	3,813	1,795	5,608

[a] Calendar 1963.

The total cost of the recommended training programs is divided between MDTA ($411 million), Economic Opportunity Act ($150 million), and ARA ($9 million). These amounts are the same as those recommended by President Johnson's administration. The $300 million in additional funds recommended for public works is intended for various types of community sheltered-work projects.

The total expenditure by society for aid to the unemployed in fiscal 1964 was in excess of the costs shown in the table by the amounts spent by the friends and families of the unemployed, by private welfare agencies, by private industry (especially for supplementary unemployment benefits, severance pay, early pensions, and training), by public (local, state, and federal) welfare agencies, and by some cities and states for training programs and public works. The size of these additional expenditures can only be guessed at, but a not entirely absurd guess would put the total at about $1 billion. Thus society has been allocating to the unemployed about $4.8 billion, or 1.0 per cent of national income, and we are recommending that society increase this amount to about $6.6 billion, or 1.4 per cent of the national income.

The importance to be attached to a given program of aid is automatically indicated by the amount of resources allocated to that program. But this establishes an order of priority only within the programs themselves and leaves unresolved the broader issue of the priority to be assigned to these programs of aid within the framework of total social obligations. Since even in affluent America economics is still the science of scarcity and we do not have enough resources to achieve all our goals immediately, the unemployed must share available aid with many other disadvantaged groups in our society.

It is beyond the scope of this symposium to establish the relative merits of all alternative uses of society's scarce resources. In the considered opinion of the authors, however, the central place of the problem of unemployment in the American economy warrants the allocation of at least 1.4 per cent of the nation's resources for aid to the unemployed.

Ed. Note. At the time of going to press the Economic Opportunity Act of 1964 had just become law. Among other provisions this act authorizes a Job Corps to provide work for young people in residential centers; a Work-Training Program to employ young persons in urban areas; a Work-Study Program whereby young people with low income may earn money to assist them in completing their higher education; a Community Action Program to assist local communities to develop programs for combatting poverty; grants to the states for Adult Basic Education Programs, and special funds to supplement the regular funds available under Title IV of the Social Security Act for community work and training programs.

Index

A

Accelerated Public Works Act. *See* Public Works Acceleration Act

Advisory Council on Public Assistance, 257

Aerospace industry: extended layoff benefit plans in, 113, 116, 146, 296

Age: unemployment rates by, 31–34, 50, 58, 150, 265; and educational level, 34, 243; for early retirement, 151; of trainees, 234–36, 243; and relocation of workers, 241

Agricultural implement industry: SUB in, 116, 119, 120, 121; training, 242

Agricultural workers. *See* Farm workers

Aid to the Blind, 256, 259, 263

Aid to Dependent Children (ADC): extended to children of unemployed, 7, 175, 257, 303; and work relief for recipients of, 191; educational level of recipients of, 267; mentioned, 256

Aid to Families with Dependent Children (AFDC): and work relief for recipients, 191, 264, 304; experience under, 257–59; and earnings of recipients, 263; educational level of recipients, 267; mentioned, 270

Aid to the Permanently and Totally Disabled, 256, 259

Airlines: training for displaced workers, 145; severance pay programs of, 145, 148

Alabama: UI financing in, 76; SUB in, 124; private employment agencies in, 220

Alaska: unemployment in, 38, 40, 56; UI in, 66, 70, 76, 77, 78

Almshouses, 8–9, 14

Aluminum industry: SUB in, 116, 120

American Association for Labor Legislation, 15

American Federation of Labor—Congress of Industrial Organizations, 192. *See also* Unions

American Legion: employment service of, 221

American Motors: and SUB, 119, 130

American Newspaper Guild: and severance pay, 141, 148

American Red Cross, 17, 261

Amount of benefits (in SUB), 118, 120, 124, 127, 130, 146

Amount of benefits (in UI): factors influencing, 79–82; meaning of adequacy of, 79, 82, 90–93, 287; ways of measuring adequacy of, 82–84, 90–93; and studies in adequacy of, 84–93; recommendations concerning, 94, 96, 295–96

Andrews, John B.: quoted, 15

Annual Worker Program for migratory workers, 203

Appalachia: ARA and PARC in, 171

Apprenticeship: government assistance to, 229; under union-management administration, 244. *See also* On-the-Job Training

Area Redevelopment Act (ARA): training allowances under, 75, 166, 230, 237; compared with British program, 162–63, 170–71; legislative history, 163–65, 171–72, 297–98; objectives of, 165, 170, 297; experience under, 167, 233, 297–98; appraisal of, 167–72, 248–51, 297; in Appalachia, 171; and employment service, 207, 222, 300; compared with MDTA, 230, 241, 297; trainees under, 234–36; recommendations concerning, 251, 298, 305; mentioned, 7, 40, 43, 57, 227, 231, 268. *See also* Depressed areas

Arizona: agricultural and seasonal workers, 65; UI duration in, 98; employment service in, 197, 216; private employment agencies, 220; AFDC for unemployed, 257

Armour and Company: severance pay plan of, 143–44, 149, 150n; technological adjustment pay (TAP) plan of, 143, 149; early retirement plan of, 152; retraining for displaced workers of, 244–45; mentioned, 156

Assistance. *See* Relief

Association for Improving the Condition of the Poor (AICP), 9–10, 11, 12, 19

Auto industry: long-term unemployment in, 50, 53; and origin of SUB, 114, 115; SUB provisions in, 116–21, 122, 146; experience with SUB in, 121–22, 128–32; severance pay in, 145, 146, 148; pension rights in, 149; early retirement plans in, 154

Automation. *See* Technological change

IN AID OF THE UNEMPLOYED

edited by JOSEPH M. BECKER, S.J.

designer:	Edward D. King
typesetter:	William Clowes and Sons, Ltd.
typefaces:	Times Roman, Centaur
printer:	Universal Lithographers, Inc.
paper:	Warren's Bookman Offset
binder:	Moore and Company
cover material:	Holliston's Roxite C